D0344976

ON
Politics
AND
Parks

CONSERVATION LEADERSHIP SERIES
Sponsored by the
River Systems Institute at Texas State University
General Editor, Andrew Sansom

ON
Politics
AND
Parks

George Bristol

FOREWORD BY
Andrew Sansom

Texas A&M University Press
College Station

This paper meets the requirements of ANSI/NISO Z39.48-1992
(Permanence of Paper).
Binding materials have been chosen for durability.

Library of Congress Cataloging-in-Publication Data
Bristol, George Lambert.
On politics and parks / George Lambert Bristol ; foreword by Andrew Sansom.—1st ed.
p. cm.—(Conservation leadership series)
Includes index.
ISBN 978-1-60344-762-1 (cloth : alk. paper)—ISBN 978-1-60344-777-5 (ebook)
1. Bristol, George Lambert. 2. Political consultants—Texas—Biography. 3. Conservationists—
Texas—Biography. 4. Democratic Party (Tex.)—Biography. 5. Texas—Politics and
government—1951– 6. United States—Politics and government—1945–1989 7. United
States—Politics and government—1989– 8. Parks—Political aspects—Texas. 9. National parks
and reserves—Political aspects—United States. I. Title. II. Series: Conservation leadership series.
F391.4.B757A3 2012
976.4'063092—dc23
[B]
2012016787

Unless otherwise indicated, all photographs are by the author.

To my kin, who passed on to me their appreciation of literature and the natural world

To my wife Gretchen, **our children** (Jim, Andrea, Adam, Alex, Mark and Jennifer, Jennifer and Thomas), and **our grandchildren** (Evelyn, Sam, Walter, and Henry), who have all inspired me to write my life story so that they might have an appreciation of influences that shaped me and them

To Dick and Joanne Bartlett, who gave of their treasure and property so that others could have a place for grand aloneness to contemplate and write about the natural world

CONTENTS

FOREWORD

I first met George Bristol when I worked for the Texas Nature Con-
servancy in the early 1980s. At the time George served as chairman of The Texas Conservation Foundation and we worked together to add several key parcels to the San Jacinto Battleground, site of the victory which won Texas its independence from Mexico. I
was not aware then of George's long history with the parks movement in America, which
began, as he recounts in this inaugural volume of a new series of books on conservation
leadership, in his youth at Glacier National Park.

Years later, I was given the great privilege of being named Executive Director of
the Texas Parks and Wildlife Department. For nearly twelve years, I worked alongside
the finest group of conservation professionals in the United States and shared with them
the joys and tribulations of managing the fish, wildlife, and park resources of the most
naturally and culturally diverse state in the union. We came to work each day excited
about the challenges we faced. I was proud to serve alongside my colleagues as they accomplished extraordinary things for the rest of us, as well as for future generations, in
spite of the fact that they were chronically and often disgracefully underfunded.

I will never forget the day I was sitting in the state capitol cafeteria in Austin, licking
my wounds from a particularly difficult appropriations hearing, when George Bristol sat
down beside me, announced that he was rotating off the National Parks Foundation to
which he had been appointed by President Clinton, and asked if he could be of any help
to me and to the department. By this time, I had become aware of his substantial political and fundraising skills and I quickly replied "M.O.N.E.Y." Within months, George
founded the Texas Coalition for Conservation and took up the cause.

The first thing I did was introduce him to one of the most successful and socially
conscious businessmen in Texas, David Gochman, who was the owner and chairman
of Academy Sports and Outdoors. Working with George, David breathed life into the
Texas Outdoor Recreation Alliance, an organization of sporting goods industry leaders
that formed a solid base of support for the Coalition. Together, during the first decade
of the new century, these organizations secured more funding for the Texas State Park
System than ever before in its history.

Thus, it is fitting that George's autobiography, *On Politics and Parks*, is made possible by continued support from his generous ally, David Gochman. It is equally fitting that together they launch this exciting new Conservation Leadership Series, a partnership between the River Systems Institute at Texas State University and Texas A&M University Press. Each day, others in our movement, particularly younger conservationists, look to George Bristol as a wise mentor, and these pages are a testament to his many experiences and contributions.

Meanwhile, the Texas Parks and Wildlife Department continues to struggle to find enough funding to do all the things the people of Texas expect of it. I have no doubt that George Bristol will once again be down at the Capitol, walking the halls and working the phones for conservation.

If anyone can do it, he can, and the next generation of conservation leaders will be inspired by his story.

—Andrew Sansom, General Editor

PROLOGUE

Sometime late in the spring of 1961, when I was twenty years old and attending the University of Texas, I learned that a prospective summer job with an oil company would not materialize. That was fine with me, because I really wanted to go to Washington to aid President Kennedy in his work addressing problems at "the edge of a new frontier," as Kennedy put it. But by then all summer internship positions were filled.

Fortunately, I had to go to the Texas capitol and stopped by State Representative Don Kennard's office. Don was from Fort Worth and was a close friend and ally of Congressman Jim Wright. Don and I had campaigned together for Wright in the run-up to the special election held in May to fill Lyndon Johnson's US Senate seat. Wright lost, but we had worked hard, helping him carry a number of Central Texas counties, and he was grateful. Don phoned and told Wright about my situation, and he said that he would look around and find something. What he found was a summer job for me at a national park.

Stewart Udall, President Kennedy's secretary of interior, was a former House member who had served with Wright. National parks were under his jurisdiction and the parks had all sorts of seasonal jobs. A telegram from the National Park Service told me to report to Rocky Mountain National Park. I knew where that was: Colorado. But a second telegram directed me to go to Glacier National Park to work on trails. Mother and I had to find Glacier on a map, and then the challenge was how to get there. As I remember, there was no thought of flying in those days, so that left the bus, car, or train. I didn't have a car, and a bus trip would have taken forever. That left trains: the Rock Island Line to Minneapolis, then the Great Northern's Empire Builder to Glacier. I had to report on June 7, so we made coach reservations, and I expected to arrive at Belton, Montana, on June 6.

I packed as best I could, not knowing what a trail crew worker would need. I borrowed $100 from Granddaddy Donoho, then went to Fort Worth to say goodbye to a girlfriend and catch the train. The Rock Island pulled out in the evening and I began a journey that would last a lifetime.

Throughout the evening and during the next day, I watched the America I had dreamed of unfold: cities and villages, industrial giants and open fields. On the first night I ate from a box lunch that my granddaddy and my step-grandmother, Sue, had brought to the station. There were dining cars, but the meals were expensive, so many passengers, like me, had boxes or sacks of fried chicken, sandwiches, deviled eggs, and apples.

At most stops, I hopped off and ran to the front of the station to look up and down Main Street. In many towns that was the only street. In those days trains stopped more often than they do today, so I got a peek at America—at work and asleep. On and on the Twin Star Rocket rolled northward, into the next day.

In the late afternoon I finally arrived in Minneapolis and got off at its busy, cavernous train station. The depot was huge because of the great number of lines that fed into it. Many, including the Rock Island Line, no longer exist. I was homesick and wondered out loud whether I should head back to Texas. It occurred to me that this was the first journey I was making alone, and it was all the more daunting because it was a journey into the unknown.

Somehow a depressing night passed. Then the announcer called out that the Great Northern would leave on track such and such. When I asked which car would stop at the Glacier Park, I was directed to the last three cars. Still glum, I boarded.

There, before my quickly smiling eyes, were beautiful young women. I am sure there were young men there, but most were girls congregated in those cars, many of them blond Scandinavians from the colleges and universities of Minnesota, recruited to work for the summer at Glacier National Park. Things brightened considerably

In an adjoining car I found a seat—a window seat, fortunately, because I wanted to see as much as possible as we moved toward Glacier. I ate some fruit I had bought in Minneapolis. Then I noticed a number of soldiers playing poker. I asked if I could join, and in a while one dropped out. All the stars aligned and I won several hundred dollars. Having found female coworkers and gotten the right cards, I deemed the Empire Builder my "good luck train."

Sometime the next morning I got luckier. Sitting across from me were a couple—schoolteachers from Libby, Montana. They'd been east to visit kin and were on their way home. I told them of my summer plans. They knew all about the park, it seemed. At lunch, with my winnings tucked in my pocket, I took them to the dining car. By then the terrain outside had begun to change. There were rolling wheat fields and here and there huge boulders planted right in the middle of nowhere. Why? The couple explained that these were the deposits of glaciers—great rivers of ice that once covered the land. As they came and went, they left their reminders across the northern plains. They were also a signal: we were moving closer to Glacier National Park and a mountain range from which some of the boulders were chiseled. Mysterious to me then, fascinating to me today.

By mid-afternoon the Rocky Mountains began to push up over the swells of the plains. They were lovely shades, capped in white, with a background of deep blue sky. Those on the right-hand side of the train were the peaks of mountains in the park. Today, when time permits, I drive out on the plains and then head back toward those mountains and still get a stunning rush of joy and visual comfort.

In the early evening the train stopped at East Glacier. Out the window and up a rise stood East Glacier Lodge, the original showplace hotel of the Great Northern Line. Behind the lodge, and all around, were mountains. As a Texas flatlander, I was awed to my depths. As the train proceeded, we plunged into a canyon, defined by a river then unknown to me; it sparkled, disappeared, and then reemerged in a new twisting setting. We rattled through what I would come to know as snow tunnels. What we did not do was stop at Belton. That station hadn't opened for the season. The couple from Libby told me not to worry, saying they would take me back to the park from Whitefish, Montana, the next stop.

At dusk, which must have been nine o'clock or so—the sun sets late in northwestern Montana in the summer—we arrived. The Great Northern groaned, buckled, and hissed to a stop. Waiting figures rose from platform benches. Smiles were exchanged when passengers and greeters spied one another. After gathering my meager belongings, I stepped off the train onto Montana soil and saw my first mountain sunset. Dusk gave off a fragrance then unknown to me—pines. We piled into the teachers' car and drove toward a darkening canyon—Bad Rock. There I discovered the blue-green sweep of the Flathead River. Early summer peaks flashed by—Tea Kettle—still snow-capped and copper-hued in the fading light. Somewhere a waterfall revealed its slender leg, and then disappeared. A mysterious sign appeared for a Lake Five. A solitary silhouette whipped the air, arcing his line toward an eddy. A trout broke the water's surface—and then dissolved in concentric circles that rippled out across the fire-red flow.

At just dark we arrived. Not knowing where I needed to check in, we stopped at the place with the most activity—the West Glacier Bar. With profound gratitude I thanked the Montana couple—I would never see them again. With my small suitcase and duffel bag, I stood in the parking lot, surveying my surroundings in dim light.

I have often attempted to put into words the feelings I experienced in that moment and what I felt over the next several days and thereafter. I did not know it then, but I was gaining my own sense of place. Texas was and is home, but Glacier National Park would become the home of my heart. Others might share similar feelings, but mine were my own, special and lasting. What I also did not know then, or recognize for the longest time, were the reasons I'd arrived at that entrance to a small bar in the middle of nowhere. Converging influences were merging into a rushing river that would sweep me along in its flow, carrying me toward a life purpose. The people and politics of my early years had coalesced to guide me to a park. From here I would have to run rapids and explore tributaries before arriving at my port of call.

ON
Politics
AND
Parks

PART I

Small Towns
and
Growing Horizons

CHAPTER 1
Early Memories and Influences

I became aware of politics during the latter years of World War II
to the chorusing of cicadas and by the light of fireflies at the Texas State College for
Women (TSCW) camp on Lake Dallas in Texas. That's not to say that I had heard
nothing of politics before then. Politics had always been there. My family, on both sides,
was into politics, taking every side of every issue although they were all for Franklin D.
Roosevelt, except for one or two errant Presbyterians on my daddy's side.

But on those days and nights in the heat of summer, while fish fried and ice cream
handles cranked, I listened to people's chatter—much of it about politics—and it started
to sink in. My Granddaddy Donoho's family went to the college lake camp near Denton
to beat the heat, staying close to home because gasoline and tires were rationed. In the
surrounding woods I had my first experience with the wonders of the natural world, and
in the camp I heard talk of elections. Little did I know that family, politics, and conservation would become the chief paths of my life.

I suspect that the first elections that registered on me were the primaries of 1944
when I was four. In those days, Texas primary elections were held in the summer, and
that is when the real political fireworks took place, since the Democratic victors were
assured of election in November. Maybe that summer my mother and dad, my Aunt
Donnie and Uncle Brooks, and my grandfather, W. S. Donoho, were speculating about
whether or not FDR would run for a fourth term. Whatever and whoever are long
blurred, but the discussions—heated, yet intelligent and civil—drifted into the screened
cabins where my younger brother, David, my cousins, and I were supposed to be down
for a nap or asleep in the twilight of World War II.

That was on my mother's side of the family, the Donohos. My dad's father, Charlie Bristol, Pappy to us, needed no other people to carry on a conversation with about

politics or anything else. He was a blacksmith and horseman in McKinney. When he came home from smithing, he'd work his stabled horses while I sort of helped clean the stalls or simply stood to one side, listening. He would harangue the horses about whatever had gotten his dander up that day. They knew he wasn't barking at them. They were a respectful audience because he brought fresh hay and refilled water troughs as he carried on. Then he'd go inside the house, soap up in a metal tub, using Lava soap—this was before indoor plumbing—shedding the black dust of coal and fire, don his store-bought glasses, then continue to cuss and discuss the day's news while reading a paper, perched on his back-porch bed. I would lie on the other bed there and hang on every word. It was not a recital of headlines, but a discussion with himself, filtered to me through a lingering aroma of ash and soap.

But it was those times I was allowed to go down to his blacksmith shop that most resonated, not only with the sounds of hammer and anvil, but also with local opinion and politics. I can still hear the voices of Speaker of the House Sam Rayburn and other elected officials who would drop by the shop to visit with Pappy and others who often gathered there. Their conversations were lessons to me about the important issues of the day. No question went unanswered and some were quite probing. Even Speaker Rayburn, particularly he, would answer everyone as if he had all the time in the world. In those less rushed times, he did have all the time in the world. Unlike elected officials whose mindless sound-bites and non-answers fill the airwaves today, politicians then used this sort of small gathering to truly inform their constituents. In doing so they informed and inspired a small boy.

On July 3, 1946, Pappy went to his back porch and wept: my dad, Lambert, had died after a sudden heart attack. I would not learn of his death until the next day, so David and I joined in play with the children brought along by their grieving parents. Granny sat in the long room that ran along the back of the house, cried, knitted, and rocked. Soon things seemed back to normal, although they never were entirely the same.

Sometime later that year I began to read. That essential activity was encouraged at every level of my early relationships with other people. It was the genesis of my political education, as well as my general one. Before he died, my dad had read aloud to my brother and me. I am sure there were children's books, but there was also *The Rubaiyat of Omar Khayyam* and Longfellow's epic *The Song of Hiawatha*. To this day—more than sixty years later—I can still quote bits of *Hiawatha* and believe it has one of the finest lyrical rhythms in all of poetry.

Granddaddy Donoho was an English professor at TSCW (now Texas Woman's University), with particular emphasis on Chaucer, Shakespeare, and Browning. While not comprehending them at the time, their poetry and plays were all filled with politics. Dr. Donoho made sure that we were not only indoctrinated with the Saturday matinees of Roy Rogers and Lash LaRue, but also with the likes of *Henry V* and *Hamlet* that played in the evening at the campus outdoor theater. I loved the cowboy movies, but I retained the politics and poetry of those Shakespearean masterpieces. If you think that this was a nerdy boyhood experience, get the DVD of *Henry V* (either Laurence Olivier's 1944 version or Kenneth Branagh's 1989 version) and watch the quick-firing longbow battle at Agincourt. No western gunfight comes close for action. The intrigue at the French court—and courtship of Princess Katherine—rivals that of any present-day Washington DC cabal.

My principal motivator in matters of literature and politics was my mother, Lottie Donoho Bristol, who taught history and was a librarian. That combination, coupled with her passion for politics, provided a lock on my future direction.

I can't remember a moment that we did not have books and classical music records around the house. They were there for our pleasure, not forced on us. Mom was not only a teacher and librarian; she had been, since early childhood, a classically trained pianist and organist. Had the Depression not caused financial hardship, she may well have gone far with her talents. As it happened, she was, until nearly the end of her life, a fine church organist and a much-in-demand pianist for events or just for fun with family and friends. I can still quote—not sing, except alone—all the lyrics of "Mairzy Doats" and know the opening of Strauss's *Death and Transfiguration* and other musical classics. As with books, Mom presented music to us for the joy of it. But it was the political side of Lottie Bristol that fired my imagination and really set my course.

Unless one was deadened by poverty, ignorance, or accident (and there were many in this category), members of my generation, sometimes called the Silent Generation, were molded by positive relationships, influences, and circumstances that cancel out most negatives. So it was for me. Even my father's death was not instantly painful. Not quite six, nurtured and protected by a wide circle of family and friends, I barely sensed the finality of that tragedy. The morning of my father's funeral, my brother and my cousins, Judd and Don, were busy defending Fort Cardboard Box from an assortment of imaginary attackers. While our cap guns snapped away, he was lowered into the earth. Only later would I feel the enormous hole he left.

What I did feel immediately and thereafter was the loving, guiding strength of my mother. Today much is made of and written about single moms, but in 1946 a widow carried on as best she could with little ballyhoo or appreciation of her difficulties. Lottie Bristol's best work was to enrich my life, my brother's, and those of all with whom she came in contact. And she came in contact with a huge number of lifetime friends.

Among those she reached out to were politicians and people interested in politics. She was a passionate Democrat—a liberal Democrat—and a patriot of the first order. Not one of those chest-pounding, holier-than-thou demagogues that posture and pose today, wrapped in the flag, but a true patriot with deep beliefs in country, family and church—the Baptist Church—in towns wherever we went as she strove to improve her teaching and librarian career to better our lot. Taken together, temperament and towns tell the story of Lottie Bristol and were influences that shaped me as I was growing up.

Although we would live in a number of small towns in Texas before moving to Austin in 1952, Denton was the deep soil of my roots. The Denton of my mother's childhood and young adult years did not change a great deal in terms of population. But other, significant changes came one after another. Electricity, the automobile, the radio, World War I, women's right to vote, the airplane, and the Depression all determined how that small Texas community, approximately thirty miles north of Dallas and Fort Worth, went about its daily life in the early twentieth century.

The College of Industrial Arts (now Texas Woman's University), founded in 1903, was why my mother's family was in Denton. My grandfather received a full-time teaching position there around 1913, and he, my grandmother, and mother moved from Decatur, Texas, where he had begun his teaching career at Decatur Baptist College.

By the time I arrived on August 11, 1940, the nation and Denton were on the brink of war and not out of the grip of the Depression. For several months we went to Wichita Falls where Dad was working. Wichita Falls was the latest stop in a line of places they lived after they married in 1937. The Depression dictated taking whatever job was available, wherever.

There was laughter in my family. This is evident in old black-and-white photographs. Because of these, all my recollections of that time are in black and white. Maybe that is how it should be: that's how small children view most things, before age and experience add coloration, prejudice, and choice.

There were birthday parties, cakes with candles. At Christmas, when rationing and lack of funds precluded much and before the holiday turned into the wretched commercial excess it has become, pictures show my brother and me with the one present we each had received. I remember Russell's Department Store, an aromatic wonder in all seasons but especially at Christmastime, even in the war years. I can't recall buying a single item there, but what was important was the wandering up and down aisles, playing hide-and-seek among the clothes, something that remains a part of me, binding me to a town and a time when death whistled down local streets without me hearing its grim tune. Outside the store the entire town square and the courthouse were decorated to celebrate the season. Most store windows had signs that asked shoppers to remember the troops or buy war bonds. I know my dad did, because many years later when I was desperate for cash in high school, someone remembered that he had left a war bond for me in the amount of $50 or $100. Whatever the amount, it was a godsend, with interest, from the grave.

There were trips to my great-grandmother Donoho's farm. Mamaw had traveled, pregnant, with her husband, Claiborne Dixon Donoho, and other relatives, from Tennessee in 1884 to Hill County, Texas. After moving around North Texas, including time in Denton, her beloved husband died in the 1930s, and she remained alone on the farm they had purchased at some point in the 1920s.

Whatever their circumstances, they made sure that my granddaddy and his siblings got a good education. I can't remember the extent of his brother's and sister's, but Granddaddy went to Baylor, graduating in 1900, and then off to Yale to obtain his master's degree. He left by train for New Haven with $500 in his pocket, a farm boy with an amazing intellect and parents committed to fulfilling his promise. His father wanted him to keep exact records of his expenditures. For one year he did just that. Somewhere, at some time, I saw his record book: $5 for books, $10 for a room, a dime for this and a nickel for that, and a grand trip to Hartford, for $5 or so, where he had a grand meal and took in a show at a theater. After a year at Yale, he returned to the black prairie of Hill County, degree in hand and change to spare. Later, after Mother was born, he went to study for a second master's degree at the University of Chicago.

In the war years and afterward, we would go to the farm near Cleburne, in part to visit, and in part to give Mamaw company. She welcomed the company, but not the implication that she was getting too old to live alone. On one occasion the sheriff stopped by and all but said this explicitly. She took his pistol and drilled a squirrel at some distance. "Come back when I can't do that!"

There was a windmill, but no electricity—only coal-oil lamps. There were chickens with plenty of eggs to be gathered. There were soft beds full of ghost stories and a nearby creek never to be visited by little boys alone. Such was the strict rule, but that was just too much to ask. My favorite photo of the time depicts a very muddy cousin Judd and me, caught in the act, with "oh, my Lord" looks of surprise and guilt on our faces. They had the sheriff talk to us about minding our kin and the possibility of jail time. I am sure we listened attentively, even if we didn't take the lecture to heart.

What the trips to Mamaw's provided, besides visits with that remarkable woman to feast on her fried chicken and fried pies, was relief from the war-caused absences of my daddy and Uncle Brooks, though they also reminded us of the war because there was a huge German POW camp on the road to Cleburne. I often think of what became of those men who surely must have experienced loneliness.

Then there was church: the First Baptist Church of Denton, Texas, taught me scriptures and songs I can recite to this day. But for the most part, those early years of Christian training were a time of we going on Sunday to meet our cousins and friends. Together we would illustrate stories of Jesus with crayons and construction paper. I was not saved by baptism by immersion immediately, because in the Baptist Church being saved comes about only when an individual has knowledge enough to make his or her own personal commitment. That still makes great sense to me, as belief in a god is as personal as marriage, and neither should be determined by others or without full knowledge or at least mature faith and trust.

After church we often made our way to the cafeteria at the college where we would eat with Granddaddy, professors, and staff. One Sunday dinner I learned that Granddaddy, the college's Dean White, and others had fought the Ku Klux Klan in the 1920s. That's all I know, but it stuck with me because the purpose of the confrontation was to thwart the ill treatment of blacks. I'm not sure one could characterize Granddaddy Donoho as a liberal or a civil rights enthusiast. I think he was simply a fair-minded citizen who could not accept any group using fear to trample others. There's no question that he passed along that strong sense of fair play to Mother—and she to me.

For the most part, Sunday conversations were about our families and how the war was progressing. What was not progressing was the relationship between my mother and father. At some point in 1945, they separated, and Mother, David, and I moved to Beeville in Deep South Texas.

For the most part my father has been to me a dim collection of mental images, reinforced—perhaps created—by a few black-and-white photographs from now-aging albums carefully crafted by my mother, and snatches of conversations—some tearful—with my mother, my Bristol and Donoho grandparents, aunts and uncles, and Dad's old friends from his years at Texas A&M. This changed when the billfold Dad had with him when he died was discovered and given to me in 2005. Since then I've many times reread and wrestled with its contents.

Fifty-seven years after my father's death, the billfold was unearthed by my cousin Margaret, who was weeding through my aunt Annie Katherine's vast accumulation of near-trash, a collection that bordered on fire hazard. How Annie Katherine came to possess the wallet or why she kept it, she didn't remember. To the unknowing eye it contained

8

nothing more than ID cards, snapshots, and brief letters, yet for me these were Morse Code messages from before he lost the war with himself in an alcoholic sea of doubt and failure. The bits of paper, yellowed letters, and images represent small chapters of obligation and fraternity, things dear and unknown, binding him to me. In them is evidence to fill gaps from what I had earlier gleaned, first from adult whispers and later from conversations with family. Every item tells a separate story, but taken together they indicate a tragedy waiting to climax.

My father's Texas driver's license gives small, antiseptic characteristics. Born on September 20, 1908, George Lambert Bristol was five foot nine, 175 pounds, with brown eyes and brown hair. At the time the license was issued, he and Mother lived at 1915 Fillmore Street, in Wichita Falls. In addition, something I almost failed to notice, the license had expired three years prior to his death. Was this because rationed tires and gasoline made driving impractical? Or did Daddy's drinking make renewal impossible? Regardless of the expiration date, I know my father drove. He came in a borrowed car to pick up my brother and me in late May 1946 in Beeville. This stands out in my memory because the separation a year earlier had been unbearable for a five-year-old boy and the reunion was overwhelmingly joyous. His coming had nothing to do with seeing Mother and reconciling with her, rather it was the threat of polio that hung over our lives for years. He had come to take us to a safer place, as if polio were confined to South Texas.

On the way back to McKinney where he lived with Granny and Pappy, we picnicked on peanut-butter sandwiches at a roadside park and peed between barbed wire strands, trying not to hit the wire. We stopped at the state capitol in Austin, and we visited his school friends from earlier McKinney days who now owned a funeral home in Waco. From there to home, we laughed about how his friends and their children could sleep with dead people in the back room. Or maybe we just laughed at everything because we were happy to be together again.

This is my only memory of us on a road trip.

During Mom and Dad's separation, I think, I was in the very initial stages of learning to read and write, developing what are today called pre-literacy skills. A scrawled, nonsensical letter in my father's billfold, signed "GEORGE, DAVE AND DADDY," is followed with this sentence in Mom's hand: "I have learned to write." There was also a Valentine card from me in the wallet—one of those inexpensive ones, popular then, that kids took to school to hand out. These items are worn, as are laminated photos of me at age one and two that were taken at our home in Denton, 812 Anna Street, where we lived during the war. Maybe he took them out in the evening on the twilit front porch at 1210 Sherman Street in McKinney, as he sensed his heart and world break apart.

I'm not sure when we went back to Denton, why we went, or if all of us did. Dad's draft classification cards up through September 5, 1945, list his home as Wichita Falls, but we moved to Denton and lived with my Granddaddy Donoho sometime after Grandmother Donoho died in 1941. Most of my early recollections are centered in that small, white-framed house. I remember the neighbors there collectively working in the Victory Garden, FDR talking on the radio about the war, and making applesauce. Why we seemed to always have apples during those times I don't know, but I cherish apples and applesauce to this day, partly because it brings back memories of Mom, Dad, sometimes Granddaddy, and eventually my brother, all together in a small world relatively unaffected by war. I have not a single memory of anger, tears, or drinking. Yet at some point, during a time I remember of cousins, Christmases, laughter, and love, something cracked, and the crack kept growing until my dad shattered.

Perhaps in part the initial crack for my father was the loss of his job as a day foreman for North American Aviation in Dallas. He was hired on May 27, 1942, because he was educated, 2-B, and available. His poor eyesight and a missing big toe precluded him from serving in the military, but the work he did for North American was an important part of the war effort. Through my mother's recollections and one dim memory, I believe he was working on developing one of the first US jet engines or planes. I recall going to see him at work, and the scream of engines is still in my memory bank.

He was a foreman in good stead, according to his card, but this was not enough to shield him from the layoffs that followed cessation of war. By March 13, 1946, up to the week before his death, biweekly visits to the McKinney office of the Texas Unemployment Compensation Commission were part of the story of a college graduate, out of work, living with his parents, and separated from us.

It isn't clear to me why Dad and Mom separated or exactly when, leaving him no choice but to go back to his parent's home to sort things out—or not. I can only guess that the frustration of being without a job and family continued his downward spiral, but this frustration didn't kill his sense of humor or hope. Family members with whom I talked said that up to the very end he was full of wit and playfulness, something passed down from his father—certainly not the humorless Scottish Presbyterians on his mother's side. (Granny did have a twinkle in her eyes that somehow revived after my father's death.) In truth Granny's laughter, kind hands, and heart were given over to her children and grandchildren to help us through the tragedy and thereafter. I know she often thought of her "Bub," but she never let on about her heartbreak around us.

Maybe evidence of my father's hope lies in the Masonic Lodge cards that show, through his monthly dues and meetings, that he was initiated, "passed," and "raised" between March 26 and May 21, 1946. Some may say that by that discipline he could have gotten right with God, friends, family, and himself. Whatever his motive in joining, members of that secret order helped prepare him for burial, laid him to rest, and affixed the sign of Freemasonry upon his small white tombstone less than two months later.

It is clear that he hoped to make things right with Mom, as he continued to write her with tenderness and love.

My most vivid memories of my father are from mid-May 1946 to his death. The house at 1210 North Sherman was not only a refuge from polio, or so it seemed. It was the place my father and I were together most at a time in my life when long-term memories began to form. He worked, I know, for pocket change at a friend's watermelon stand. To my recollection, he was home evenings and Sundays. He wasn't drunk, at least in front of a loving, soon-to-be-six-year-old son. We rode Delight, his father's horse, along the relatively car-free streets of McKinney, and sometimes enjoyed a snow cone to beat the heat. There were just three flavors then: grape, orange, and strawberry.

We held Sunday school in the front yard. David and I took nickels to the collection box—tithing was a big part of our Christian upbringing. We sat on the front porch, telling stories, eating fried chicken, and spitting watermelon seeds. We talked of Mother. As it grew dark on those summer evenings long ago, we netted fireflies and cicadas. Then we went inside, listened to the radio, bathed in a big tub on the back porch, and used an outdoor toilet. Then by lamplight my father read to us. *The Song of Hiawatha* most often comes to mind. To this day, I pull it out and reread those melodic lines. My brother and I laughed, and then we cuddled next to our father and went to sleep.

This kept up every day through June, until that final morning in early July when we ran out in the alley and waved good-bye as Dad walked off.

1946

We watched him go that morning,
down the alley to the watermelon stand
where he worked, while he tried to shake the bottle.
At the end he turned, waved, and faded from view.
In the afternoon they came—southern style,
with crusty pies and chicken, fresh-fried;
women and children, bustling—sheepish,
then the men, home from work, solemn—shaken.
In their ignorant happiness, the children played chase

and hung from the bois d'arc
like late afternoon apples until
darkness broke a woman down
behind faded coal-oil shades.
—*George Bristol, 1994*

One other item was hidden alone in my father's sweat-stained billfold: a poem from two years before his death, dated with his birthday, September 20, 1944. For the longest time after first seeing this, I read it only as a greeting from a fellow worker who knew that my dad loved poetry. He had gotten a master's degree in English at the University of Texas, but the depression of the 1930s kept him from finding any literary work.

On an interoffice memorandum labeled "Avoid Verbal Orders," with a nickel attached, one M. Jowell had penned the following:

I hate myself. I'm wracked with grief.
From this pain, I'll know no relief
By forgetting the symbol of the years you've weathered,
I deserve naught but to be tarred and feathered.

I am glad I was reminded in time to repay
Your many kindnesses on this your birthday.
I hope my little present will come in handy,
And pray someone else will furnish the brandy.

Next year I promise to remember the event
And a lovely gift to you I'll present.
But this time I pray to the good Lord above,
That you'll accept this nickel, my good wishes, and a
Heart full of love.

Love has many levels, turns, and permutations: love of God, country, family, and friends. But the phrase "heart full of love" eventually gave me pause. Perhaps it was nothing more than a birthday note between wartime friends in those times when friends were dearly cherished. I hope so. But another possibility exists. Did my father secretly hold great feelings for someone besides my mother? What is almost certain is that M. Jowell, like my mother, has died. What is entirely certain is that after nearly fifty years of remaining a single widow, always wearing her wedding ring, my mother, who did not speak of Dad often, summoned up enough strength after debilitating strokes to tell me that upon her death she wanted to be buried next to him in McKinney, not in the designated Donoho family plot in Denton.

What lay behind this poem in my dad's wallet is of little consequence to me now. It does nothing to fill the void. All the other contents of the billfold close a few of the gaps in my knowledge, but much that I have wished to know about the man I will never know. Every time I go to the cemetery in McKinney, I realize again what true love is. As Shakespeare wrote in Sonnet 116:

> Love is not love
> Which alters when it alteration finds,
> Or bends with the remover to remove:
> O, no! it is an ever-fixed mark.

For all my dad's flaws, there was—and still is—a love between my mother and dad, eternal love, and it does not matter if more than one woman may broken down behind drawn shades after my father died. That is all I need to know.

On leaving the McKinney cemetery in July 1946, Mother returned to Denton, gathered David and me, and we went back to Beeville, a transitional point in our lives. Thereafter we would live as a family without a father.

We lived in Beeville until around June 1947. Our first year there is a blur to me, but I recall our lifelong friends Jack and Lucille Cates, who got Mother a job as teacher and librarian. They took us in and into their hearts.

David and I went to First Baptist Church in Beeville, where there must have been a form of day care, while Mother worked. I know we didn't have a car, and I have vague memories of various people picking us up for one reason or another. I remember that the town had a number of Catholic churches, because it was heavily populated with Mexicans. Some, perhaps most, white South Texans said "Mexicans" with prejudice. For David and me, it was otherwise: most of our friends were Mexican. My brother, who could barely speak English words, much less sentences, at nearly three years old, took Spanish as his first language.

I remember that it was cold, very cold for South Texas. It was dark. Mother and I were already home, so maybe my brother had been with a babysitter. Suddenly the door of our small house flew open, David ran in, rubbed his hands together, and said,

"Mucho fria—mighty cold!" We all celebrated that David had strung words together meaningfully.

After that, Mother encouraged us to learn simple phrases in Spanish. She did not push or demand. She made it fun. I think that in her own subtle way she was telling us that skin color and language should not be barriers but opportunities. Those gentle instructions would continue for the rest of her life.

It was the second year in Beeville that really began to shape my life and ours. An aging aunt, Lena, on the Frederick side of the family—my mother's mother's side—came to live with us. In those days, family truly mattered, so I assume that Aunt Lena was chosen to come live with us, because she was single, to help us make our mourning transition easier.

We lived in a small two-bedroom apartment above a candy factory. The latter was no large operation, but its smells always improved my days and from time to time there were free samples. The apartment wasn't far from the church and my first public school. It would be years before I fully came to appreciate that genius of America then—public schooling—but I loved it from the get-go. I loved the books, my teachers, and my friends, but most of all simply learning. To those who criticize public education, I say, "Fix it, but don't abandon it." It is the foundation of our future. It is how the George Bristols of the world will become educated enough to play a constructive role in society.

I am not sure what all I learned from the Beeville public school system, but I did learn to read. If my teachers did nothing else, they forever opened that door so I could take advantage of all the books that were placed before me by grandparents, my mother, and the public libraries of Texas. On equal standing with public education and public parks, our libraries have been, and should continue to be, a cornerstone of America. Each of these institutions in their own way is essential to a free and thoughtful citizenry.

Despite my happiness in school, it was a hard year. Mom cried behind closed doors. David and I missed both Denton and McKinney. It was a "mucho fria" winter. At one point it was so icy that the owner of the apartment had to send food up to us via the clothesline.

Daddy came to see David and me one last time, call it what you may. One night Mother and Aunt Lena heard us both yelling something like, "He's here! Daddy's here!" The image is still clear to me. Over in the corner by the closet of our small room a figure stood. It was clearly Daddy. David and I both saw him. Then he disappeared, never to return. From time to time I think about the ramifications of that moment. Had it just been me, it could have been written off as the sad longing of a six-year-old boy. But

David and me? I don't know, but I believe Dad stayed around to watch over us. A good God would allow that. Mother and Aunt Lena were so convinced of our story that they never discounted it as a joint nightmare.

Sometime in the spring (I'm guessing it was Easter), Granddaddy Donoho brought Judd and Don to Beeville. Though cousins, we were like brothers: absences were horrific, reunions were joyous. It may have been for only a day or two, but it broke our sad isolation. The trip and the joy were memorialized in a photograph of us with Granddaddy, a photo he later sent to Yale as his alumnus picture.

The rest of our time in Beeville was made bearable by the fact that we knew we were heading home—back to good, ol' Denton—at the end of the school year. Mother was to work on her master's degree in library science that coming summer and had secured a job at one of the Denton schools for the fall—Denton High School, I think.

As I remember it, my great-uncle Bransford, a South Texas automobile dealer, loaded us all in his car and drove us home, letting Aunt Lena off in Venus. I rarely saw her after that, but I will forever have a place in my heart for her. She saw us through.

I still have other pleasant memories of Beeville. It is not far from two Texas historical sites—the Alamo and Goliad—as well as the beach. Somehow Mom, without a car, got us to those places more than once. We soaked up history and the Gulf Coast sun. For all the trauma of the summer of 1946, we were happy. As Hal Holbrook's Mark Twain said about his boyhood in Hannibal, Missouri, "We were all poor and didn't know it. And we were all happy and did know it."

Our visit to Goliad was a multiple treat. We must have gone there in the spring of 1947. Someone took us in a car, and after we visited the hallowed mission, presidio, and grounds we were going back to the parking lot when there before us was a man in full movie-cowboy regalia—Gene Autry, we thought. We ran up, yelling, "It's Gene Autry! It's Gene Autry!" We threw our arms around his long legs (long to a six-year-old and a three-year-old). He laughed and bent down to one knee. "Boys, I'm not Gene Autry, but he's a good friend of mine. I'm Monte Hale." If you had been to as many Saturday cowboy matinees as we had, it was mighty near the mother lode. So we now started yelling, "It's Monte Hale!" He signed his autograph and then we went back to Beeville where I'm sure we told everybody at school and church. We always watched for Monte Hale films at the Saturday matinees after that.

Years later I had the opportunity to meet Gene Autry. He came to Texas for the state's sesquicentennial celebration in 1986. By then he was old and very rich. He flew into Austin on his private plane, bringing his wife and another couple—the Monte Hales.

That evening, at a party for all the stars who had come to be part of an ABC television salute to Texas, I introduced them, saving Gene Autry till last. During my remarks about this legend, I mentioned the Goliad story. Before I could finish, Monte Hale broke in: "I remember that day! Two little towheads hugging my legs, yelling, 'It's Gene Autry!'" Gene Autry was nodding as if in recognition. When he got up to say a few words, he said, "And George, I remember something else. I think your granddaddy was Charlie Bristol from McKinney. He shod my first horse."

CHAPTER 2
Denton, Texas

Our first home back in Denton was a summer-vacated girls' dormi-
tory near campus. It was perfect. It had a piano in the lobby and a great kitchen and was
just down the hill from the college swimming pool. Because Granddaddy Donoho was
a faculty member, we had pool privileges and it seemed every afternoon we swam there,
even though polio raged across Texas and the country. Mom's position was fatalistic: the
dreaded disease would or wouldn't hit us, regardless of what we did. Many parents kept
their children indoors. Aunt Donnie and Uncle Brooks wouldn't let Don and Judd venture out often, but sometimes they came over and we had a splendid time being together
and swimming.

Restrictions to going out did not apply to churchgoing. I suppose most thought
that God's house was a sanctuary against not only sin, but also disease. There in the
summer of 1947 and for the next two years we continued to learn about Jesus, prayed,
and after church walked or drove with Granddaddy's friends to the cafeteria at the college for lunch.

Many of the college students who waited on us in the food line were foreigners who
I would learn were coming to the United States in great numbers to become educated,
then return to their war-ravaged countries to help in the rebuilding efforts. One became
our babysitter and though I can't recall her name I do remember that she cooked us
delicious foods from her homeland: Greece. To this day, I love dolmades (stuffed grape
leaves), horta (boiled greens), and lamb. I believe she was a nursing student. I hope she
found and gave happiness and comfort upon her return. For all the foreign students,
there were few Mexican Americans and there were no blacks, even though Granddaddy
and his friends had fought the Klan. That was true in the public school system too and
would remain so until my junior year in high school. Because blacks weren't schoolmates

of mine, I thought little of them, except that my mother continually warned us not to use the word "nigger" until it was purged from my vocabulary—for the most part.

On Saturdays or in the evenings we would walk downtown or to the open-air theater on campus to go to "picture shows." Saturday matinees were cowboy features, plus a serial and cartoon. There in the semi-dark Dreamland, Palace, Plaza, and Texas theaters we watched Roy Rogers, Gene Autry, Hopalong Cassidy, Lash LaRue, and Monty Hale do right by western town folks, particularly the heart-throbbing ladies.

Although I loved Lash LaRue and later wrote a long narrative poem about him, most of the hype went to Roy Rogers and Gene Autry. We were awash in comic books, cap guns, vests, and hats featuring Roy and Gene. We sang their favorite songs, "Happy Trails" and "Back in the Saddle Again." I still can.

As macho little boys we were stunned when it was announced that Dale Evans, "Queen of the Cowgirls," would marry Roy Rogers. We didn't mind them smiling at each other on the screen—but marry? Nonetheless, when a rumor spread that the couple would be passing through Denton sometime on such and such a date, small children lined the highway for hours. But we saw nothing. Not a glimpse of our hero. At dusk, total disappointment set in for about thirty minutes. Then we played cowboys all the way home and the crisis passed.

That period of time in Denton is like a pleasant dream to me. We were surrounded by Granddaddy Donoho, Aunt Donnie and Uncle Brooks, and cousins Judd and Don, and in 1948 Judd and Don's sister, Carol Ann Holt, joined the troop. Thirty miles east in McKinney were Granny and Pappy, Annie Katherine and Uncle Furman Watters, and cousins Scotty and Margaret.

We walked everywhere: to school, picture shows, swimming, Granddaddy's, and across town to my aunt and uncle's. Life was lived at a slower pace then. Children simply didn't have to be anywhere at a precise time, except school and church. To those two we tried to be there ahead of time to play and see what was happening in our small world.

Of all my memories of that time, nothing remains clearer than ice cream, which after rationing and the war was still a luxury. Ice cream was made from scratch in a hand-cranked device, a magical device of ingenious design. All the ingredients—milk, eggs, sugar, vanilla extract and maybe fresh peaches or whatever was in season—were stirred together, then poured into a round metal container that was placed into a larger wooden barrel. Between the two was space for ice and rock salt, which had to be loaded with an exact formula of layers. Then the crank was fitted over the top of the apparatus. For the next hour or so, mainly the menfolk would take turns cranking the handle. The passing off of the handle was critical so the machine wouldn't freeze up.

At some point, gained only by sweat equity experience, a cranker would exclaim, "She's done." I was amazed, until I was old and strong enough to crank, how the men of my family could gauge to perfection the ice cream's firmness. It had to be firm enough to continue to freeze in its cocoon of ice, salt, and wrapping towels or old blankets, but soft enough to pull out the dasher. Ah, yes, the wonderful, mysterious dasher that blended the mixture—turn after turn—while at the same time compacted it into fresh ice cream. Its real wonder was that as it was extracted, it held heaps of delight that adhered during the freezing. Gathered around were towheaded boys, spoons at the ready. There was no admonishing of "don't get it on your clothes," because in the early years, in the summer, we usually went around in underwear or bathing suits, nothing more, both because it was hot and because we didn't have all that much to wear. Then, by some pecking order, we would clean the dasher, my brother, my near-brother cousins Judd and Don, and I—with spoons or fingers. To this day I still think that the "dasher cream" is the best.

Apart from our happy existence, there was a larger world outside of Denton, and it was changing without me knowing much about it. I was just eight, but I began to pick up the gist of some things. "Truman loved niggers!," I heard. "The son of a bitch integrated the armed services." I also heard that "the commies" were taking over Eastern Europe, wherever that was. Though the war was over, some things were still rationed. Daddy's Social Security survivors benefit was critical for us. To this day when I am asked why I'm a Democrat, I start with survivors benefits and work from there. The check from the SSA kept the wolves from the door—my mom only made between $75 and $100 a month those days as a teacher and librarian.

I never have understood why we don't pay our teachers more. I suppose it is because they were mostly women initially, and the system could get away with near-slave wages for "schoolmarms." But this is disgraceful, and it is catching up with us. We are losing good teachers out of the system, and young people are not attracted to teach. Yet we do not blink an eye at the compensation given to a great many near-hoodlum athletes or the retirement golden parachutes of executives who never found a drop of oil or who ran their companies into the ground.

What's best for America? Giving the former CEO of Exxon-Mobil a bloated retirement package that he and his family cannot possibly spend, while the company lobbyists argue to the Texas Legislature that paying additional personal or corporate taxes is bad for business? Or making sure that all future CEOs and other potential leaders in business, politics, and the sciences have the best teachers and the best schools possible? The answer is clear to me, but apparently not to those in power who are directed by the here and now.

In 1948 I was incapable of thinking of this. However, I did begin to learn how intense politics could be, particularly in an election year. What a year 1948 was! The debate was fierce in both the presidential race of Truman versus Dewey, with Dixiecrat Strom Thurmond thrown in from the race-baiting right, and in the US Senate contest where a young Congressman, Lyndon Johnson, was squaring off against former governor Coke Stevenson. Whether by the campfire or at the stables, I grasped not only the intensity, but also the inconsistencies.

Pappy Bristol talked admiringly about Strom Thurmond, who was sworn to derail Harry Truman, but turned right around and praised Sam Rayburn's candidate, Lyndon Johnson, because Pappy loved Rayburn, yet Rayburn and Johnson supported Truman and the Fair Deal. Go figure! Truman and Johnson won, and that was well received by most of my family.

During those years I began to read in earnest: everything from Red Randall war stories to the Hardy Boys, from Richard Halliburton's travelogues to poetry. Nothing too complicated, but all contributing to my development and expanding the range of my thinking.

Somewhere in there, cousin Judd and I began to collect travel folders. Many magazines had ads from states and foreign countries, ads aimed at tourists. We would carefully fill out the order forms, then beg or borrow three cents and send them off.

"George, Russia came today. When can you come over?" For hours we would discuss going to far-flung, almost mythical places. By the time we stopped collecting those brochures we had hundreds, and we had a pretty good idea of where all the countries were situated, as well as what was in America beyond our home state. With geography as the subject, we could have gone on a quiz show. Today, over sixty years later, I still look forward to the monthly arrival of *National Geographic*. The magazine continues to allow me to travel the world in my imagination and from time to time moves me to go and see for myself.

Something else was spawned by our hobby. Many of the brochures arrived from national parks. Some were later augmented by View-Master stereoscope shows. That device gave three-dimensional life to the wonders of Glacier, Yellowstone, and Yosemite, so much so that to this day Judd and I have a deep passion for all things national park. At some point we became so expert on the subject (expert by eight- or nine-year-old standards) that we wrote a letter to President Truman, asking him to declare Pilot Knob outside of Denton a national park. In reality it was nothing more than an unassuming knob, but to us it was a commanding peak of national importance. We never heard from the president, but that did not cool our enthusiasm for parks—or Truman.

On November 10, 1948, David and I learned that new cousin Carol Ann had been born. There was temporary disappointment that we had not rounded out our basketball team with another male point guard, but before long Carol became the good-natured cheerleader at all neighborhood sports events, and we worshipped her.

I've often wondered why my memories of these years are so rich, so vivid. It seems I can almost recall every day of the two years we lived in Denton, even accompanying sounds: Granddaddy tapping on iced-over windows, David screaming when his tonsils were removed, Roy Rogers and Gene Autry riding and singing through Hollywood canyons, and four boys talking and laughing under covers, long after we were supposed to be asleep.

It was a glorious time to be growing up in America, polio and all. Then mother went and got a job in Orange and we moved again.

CHAPTER 3
Orange, Texas

Orange, Texas, was a brief one-year stopover for us. The town is located near the Gulf of Mexico in Deep East Texas on the Sabine River. My snapshot memory says our time there was about crawdads, Brooks and Nellie Conover, a near hurricane, Korea, and "the bomb."

I am not sure why we left Denton in August 1949. I think it was because Mother, who was still working on her master's in library science, needed library work to complete her degree, and her dear friends, the Conovers, helped her get a position at Orange High School where Brooks was the head football coach.

We moved into a duplex with the Conovers on St. John Street. For a Texas plains kid, the street was strange: crushed oyster shells with ditches on both sides, brimming after rain (which was often) with crawdads. Being so close to the Gulf, Orange was always wet it seemed. When it wasn't raining, it dripped, or steam rose from the saturated ground.

Early on, Brooks and Nellie took us to see the mothballed fleet at the naval yard on the river. For what seemed like miles, ships of every sort, World War I and World War II vintage, lay at anchor. Hopes that these would never go to war again changed on August 29, 1949, with the explosion of the first Soviet atomic bomb—followed by the takeover of China by communists. Those two events saturated the newspapers and radio broadcasts. People talked at the grocery store and at Friday night football games. Even my fourth-grade classmates talked about these events, perhaps not intelligently but constantly. We had photos of the bomb and worried about the possibility of an attack. We practiced climbing under our school desks as quickly as possible. Anchors were weighed, and the mothballed ships sailed off.

I remember the neighbor who lived behind us. He had a large shortwave radio in his garage, which faced the alley through which David and I walked to school. After school, we'd often stop in and listen to strange languages and reports from faraway places. What he'd listen to most were reports from a place called Korea. The "commies," it was said, were on the move and threatening. The "Iron Curtain" was falling across the globe, casting a pall that was to permeate life and politics in America for generations. The Cold War was upon us, even in hot, humid Orange.

But it was not all-consuming. David and I explored the town in all directions, on foot. When I went back thirty-five years later, I found the house, the school, and other places without missing a beat. It was a time and place when small children could walk far and explore without fear. When we weren't walking, it seems we were catching craw-dads with string and bits of bacon. It's funny how something as seemingly insignificant as crawdads can be a significant memory, even a jewel. So new to me, crawdads made a lasting impression. They were everywhere to find and catch.

The crawdad (or crayfish) looks like a small lobster, usually weighing in at only a few ounces, although in 1934 "Ol' Papa Épicé" topped the scale at ninety pounds, or so it was said. Ours were small and lived in holes in the street ditches and front yards.

There were plenty of pleasant diversions. One was Friday night football. Brooks Conover was the high school coach, so I came to know a good deal about the game I would later play. There was a trip to the Galveston beach, Sunday lunches at a famous fried chicken emporium across the arcing Rainbow Bridge in Bridge City, and a trip to Houston to see the sights and visit Aunt Aggie and Uncle Rob. Aggie was my dad's youngest sister, and over the years she and Rob have been mainstays of my life. Today, in their nineties, they still live in Houston and continue that supportive role for me. We traveled to Denton on the train at Christmas. We enjoyed eating the best ham-salad sandwiches ever at the downtown drugstore before Saturday matinees. Mother's colleagues, John and Mary Wheeler, took us on picnics and fishing outings in the Piney Woods lakes and ponds that abound in the area. And we prepared for a hurricane that never hit but left us with a flooded front yard filled with all sorts of creatures, including an evil-looking water moccasin.

Sometime in late 1948 or early 1949, I discovered a girl. A special one, that is—someone whose mere presence caused me to feel undefined vibrations. I don't remember her name now, but I do recall that there was enough different about her from the other girls that caused me to plot how to win whatever it was a fourth-grader might dream of. It was nearing Valentine's Day and at the time our Valentine cards, those of rich and poor kids, were penny punch-outs—ten to a sheet. When punched, small tabs fringed the card. If you didn't really care about the recipient you simply signed your name. In several of my elementary school classes we dropped the cards in a box, they were drawn, and the recipient's name was called out.

For those who were special to you, you carefully cut or whittled away the tabs on the cards, wrote something extra, like "Good Luck" or "You're the Best," and put them in envelopes, properly addressed. The object of my new interest was more than special and she deserved more than one card, I thought—an entire sheet of cards. So for what seemed like weeks I labored, removing the unsightly tabs and writing meaningful phrases of nine-year-old adoration. On Valentine's Day I got to school early with ten envelopes addressed to her, and put them in the drawing box. Then the hours crept by. I dared not look at her. Party time arrived and names were called. Her name was called more than ten times, but I thought I was still in the running. I did notice that she had a little purse and that she placed her cards in the purse without opening any of them. Then the bell rang and I walked home mystified.

The next day at school she came up to me, smiled, and said "thank you." That was that, but on reflection in later years I am now certain her parents must have laid down the law to stay away from one so brash as me, but not before properly thanking me for the cards, if not the sentiment that lay behind them.

Sometime in the spring of 1950, I learned what mother wasn't—a seamstress. In our grade school there was to be a square dance team as part of the school pageant or some other celebration. My western shirt had to be made to specification. We went to Woolworth's and bought the pattern and materials. On arriving home, Mother laid it all out and began to cuss. I think David and I went over to the neighbor's to listen to the war news. Mom was still stewing, sewing and cussing, when we got home. That went on every night for a week. Something had to give.

Somehow Mother found out that Granny Bristol was in Houston, a blessed hundred miles from Orange, and Granny could sew up a storm. She came on the bus, and peace settled over St. John Street. Within a day or two the light-blue, red-fringed cowboy shirt was finished, modeled, and worn with pride to the dance. Thereafter for several years I would trot out my wonderful shirt to wear, even to church services. I figured God could have cared less.

Then, in the summer of 1950, the Conovers moved to Temple and we went to Weatherford. Orange passed away, as quickly as it had come into our lives. Mostly I remember the crawdads.

CHAPTER 4
Weatherford, Texas

Weatherford, Texas, in 1950, was about one hundred honky-tonks,
body shops, and revival tents west of Fort Worth. Back then I don't think moral standards dictated that honks and the canvas crowds had to be zoned five miles apart. The
bar owners knew there would be backsliders and the bible thumpers knew that dancers
and boozers needed saving—at least once a month, if not every Sunday morning and
Wednesday night.

The town itself was protected by rolling plains and its own set of serious church
congregations. Of course we joined the First Baptist Church. It's where I gave myself to
the Lord and was full-body baptized, totally submerged. If I remember correctly, both
sides of the family, Methodist and Presbyterian included, came from all over to give witness and support for this Baptist equivalent to bar mitzvah.

Not that I knew what a bar mitzvah was. I don't remember meeting a single Jewish
person in those years of my childhood. There may have been a synagogue in Weatherford, but I never saw it. I'm not sure I even knew Jews existed as living people, although
the Bible of the Baptists was chock-full of references to them. Jesus was one. Jesus was
never a Christian, which came as a shock to me thirty years or so later when I began to
revisit religion.

Of all my church-related activities in Weatherford and elsewhere, none was more
rewarding than the work David and I did for the Lottie Moon Christmas Offering. To my
recollection, I thought then that Lottie Moon was a missionary to the unsaved of Africa. I
thought all missionaries went to Africa. I think she did a great deal of work with children.
She was near sainthood in a church that did not recognize earthly saints, or at least they
had to be dead for centuries. Moon was a living symbol of Christian sacrifice, and money
was raised in her name and for her work. What prompted my brother and I to fulfill our

mission to the greater glory of the Lord was she shared Mother's first name. I was also intrigued with Africa, because I had read all of Richard Halliburton's travelogues, and was fascinated with *National Geographic,* having seen the pictures of bare-breasted women who certainly needed saving as soon as possible: not a moment to lose for funding for Lottie Moon. Given all the *Playboys, Penthouses,* and worse on the newsstands today, maybe the Baptists should have brought Lottie Moon home to save us.

We must have had a long lead time because David and I took it upon ourselves to deliver a huge jar filled with pennies, nickels, dimes and quarters. This was no easy task since we certainly would not miss a Saturday cowboy movie or hamburger, and we had also been saving for bikes. But it was the Lord's work and had to be done—one mowed yard, one BB-gun sparrow shoot, and one caddying job at a time. We saved in secret, not even telling Mom. I know this because our arrival and presentation was planned and dramatic.

On the appointed Sunday, we rolled our full jar in a wagon to the church. I'd guess Mom had gone earlier to play the piano or organ. We came in stealth and entered in grandeur. I can't remember where we waited, but at the end of the service a call went out to fulfill the Lottie Moon pledge drive. David and I walked down the center aisle, pulling the wagon with the jar prominently displayed. There was a hush throughout the congregation, then a round of applause, which was only given among Baptists when the situation was entirely unique or the rapture great. Our entrance and gift covered both.

After church, the pastor asked us to stand at the front door and let people shake our hands. Mother beamed. We ate downtown, then walked home to 307 Cleveland Street. As it grew dark, we listened to *The Jack Benny Program* and *Amos 'n' Andy.* We read and studied and then went to bed. Many years later I learned Lottie Moon had done her missionary work in China. No matter. There were plenty of unsaved there too.

Once again we had moved to a new town because Mother had a different job. This time it was as librarian at Weatherford Junior College, five or six blocks from the court-house square on South Main Street. It was one of those small colleges that had sprung up all over the United States. To a large degree American education has succeeded, public schools and great public and private university systems not only educating but fostering culture. It remains to be seen, though, whether publicly funded education, the most democratic idea of democracy, will continue to be honored.

At the time I thought little, if any, about public education. I simply enjoyed it immensely in Weatherford. T. W. Stanley Elementary School was on South Main, and it was there I spent the fifth and sixth grades before graduating to junior high school. I still remember all my teachers and many of my classmates.

It was there that I first played organized football and baseball. It was there that I joined the Boy Scouts. It was on lunch hour there that I often ate at Luke and Blanche Massengale's hamburger shop across the street. It was there that my interest in girls continued—one girl, to be exact: Patty McDermott, who I deemed my first date, because she sat next to me on a school bus trip to the Fort Worth Zoo.

Jack Price and Mr. Davis (I don't know his first name) brought learning alive. By the time I arrived in Weatherford in 1950 I was a serious reader, and those two teachers (and future friends) began to help me connect the dots between history, geography, art, and literature. Between T. W. Stanley's and Mom's libraries, I devoured books, sometimes two or three a week, and what I found out at that time was that I could retain a great deal of what I read if I liked the subject matter. I did not like math.

My life was not all books, sports, and church on Sunday. There were picture shows, haircuts, and hamburgers on Saturday, all for a total of fifty cents, which I made each week with my partner, Michael Parent, mowing lawns, caddying, and shooting sparrows at the local feed mill.

I found out I could not hit the side of a barn with my BB gun, so I got glasses. Most people I know are vain or embarrassed about glasses, but I loved mine. I think subconsciously I had thought I was going blind. Glasses gave me new sight into the natural world. I could shoot sparrows at the mill at the rate of two for a penny, I think, so a hundred on a Saturday nearly covered the price of a Weatherford weekend, leaving my lawn-mowing earning for saving for a bike—and Lottie Moon. Somewhere in my first year there, I got the bike. As I was saving money for it, I shopped at hardware stores and in mail-order catalogs—Montgomery Ward and Sears. I seem to remember that "Monkey Wards" got the nod—I am sure it was the price, but I know that handlebar tassels played a role. David got a bike too, and we were off in all directions. Every spare minute we rode to town and out in the country, to "donkey baseball" (donkeys were used to run the bases) and Mother's library.

Mainly we rode into the countryside to hunt (with BB gun), fish, skinny-dip, and learn about nature. We went onto private farmland with no fear except in the case of one mean son of a bitch who didn't like our trespassing. That's a big difference between then and now. Some fences and private property signs today practically imply instant death, denying youth and average folks access to nature, and this is why public parks and wildlife areas are so vital.

We also rode our bikes in the summer to the public pool where we took lessons and swam practically every day. Mom often came along. She was a beautiful swimmer and did so up to a series of strokes she suffered in her eighty-sixth year. In Weatherford, at some point, Bullet Bristol and Al Mullennix came to sit and watch us through the pool fence. The first was a dog and the second was Mom's beau, and we loved them both.

We'd had a puppy in Orange, but he died of worms early on, so Bullet was our first real pet that I remember. What a dog! He was part collie and part shepherd, smarter than most humans and twice as loyal, and a fierce protector of our little family all his life. He came to us via a neighborhood friend, and Mother didn't know about him for a week or so. We fed Bullet in the dark of night. We took him to school, saying he was sick ("Oh, yes, Mother knows"), but that didn't last. She found out and at first resisted, but Bullet, with his instinct for family, won.

To this day I don't know how Bullet figured out our schedules. He had no formal training, but he learned quickly. Mother, David, and I got through with school at different times. Bullet somehow came to know our schedules, and, starting with David, he escorted us home: David at 3:00 p.m., me at 4:00 p.m. and Mom at 5:00 p.m. It wasn't a particularly tricky route, but he did it several times a day, rain or shine.

He was single-minded in his tasks. Once he got started, he stopped for no one and nothing. Pit bull in the way? Bullet would blow past without a thought, growl, exchange of sniffing, or ego peeing. I never saw him urinate when he was fetching one of us. On our way home he'd relax a little, but he never took his eyes off us.

On Saturdays he would follow us around town through our chores, haircuts, and hamburgers. When it was time for the Saturday matinee, he'd find shade. When we came out, there he'd be, ready to run home, as David and I usually reenacted Roy Rogers's latest exploits, which always meant riding (running) down Outlaw Canyon (Main Street) at full speed. Later Bullet Bristol got so good at gauging time that he would go visiting around the square but then be back in front of the movie house to greet us. I am convinced he could tell time.

Bullet's occasional companion watching us swim, Al Mullennix, was the county judge (Parker County). Looking back, I realize he was a big, rawboned country boy, but to David and me then, he was godlike. He grew to love Mother and she him. He also grew to love us as much as we worshipped him.

Al had grown up in Parker County, attended North Texas State College, and then served in the Pacific during World War II. After the war he completed his undergraduate degree thanks to the GI Bill of Rights—one of the finest laws ever enacted. The Servicemen's Readjustment Act of 1944 was patriotism in its highest form, a national postwar economic blessing that allowed millions of returning soldiers to attend or go back to college instead of immediately flooding a job market that was temporarily shrinking after the war. To those who say that government can't get anything right, I say read up on the history of the GI Bill of Rights. It gave the United States an educated workforce in the 1950s and '60s. It kept the country from being thrown back into the Depression, and it did right by those men and women who served.

After getting his degree, Al went to the University of Texas School of Law, but politics was in his blood. He may have run for one other office while he was in law school, but he was county judge when we moved to Weatherford in 1950. Through mutual friends, June and Richard Barnebey, he met Mom. He not only started coming around, he came in a car and he took us places. I'm sure Mom and Al went off on their own from time to time, while June and Richard kept us, but on many occasions they took David and me along. We were a family again and we loved Al beyond words.

One evening we went to Fort Worth to see a young evangelist, Billy Graham. I think David and I were saved again. Al wasn't a churchgoer, but because church was so much a part of our lives, he took part. Afterward we stopped at a honky-tonk where he and Mom danced while we drank pop and wondered about the women who sat at the bar, bathed in neon and not much else.

Above all else, Al taught me practical politics. As county judge, Al had to make the rounds, stump speaking—fish fries and barbeques, black churches and veterans groups—and David and I went along. Al took time to explain why a person or event was important, who the leaders were, and who was at odds. We passed out his cards and learned to listen to what people were talking about. This was before television, so these events were usually well-attended, and folks spoke their minds. I loved it and would dutifully report back to Al what I'd picked up. I simply had that gene that drew me to politics. I am sure for a ten-year-year old boy my reports were not very sophisticated, but he always seemed appreciative and thanked me for the news. On the way home discussed what we had learned. We talked appreciatively of Al's allies and cussed the sons of bitches. There seemed to be a number of the latter, and one who wasn't was an ally, the mayor of Weatherford, Jim Wright, who would later go to Congress and become Speaker of the House of Representatives.

Al's allies were progressive and loyal national Democrats. Since in those days significant politics in Texas and certainly Parker County was limited to the Democratic Party, and fights were between reactionaries and loyalists to the national party. The battles would grow intense, and I had a front row seat. One was either for the party of Jefferson, Wilson, FDR, and Truman, it seemed to me, or for all the forces of evil, ungrateful for the benefits of the New Deal. The divide broke, for the most part, into returning veterans who had enjoyed the benefits of work programs before going to war and the GI Bill afterward, and those who didn't like government, the New Deal, or "niggers."

The causes of Al Mullennix and Jim Wright centered around those GIs, and their spouses and families, and many were teachers or students at Weatherford Junior College. Lottie Bristol, my mom, was always in the thick of the fight, so much so that she became the first Parker County woman delegate to the Democratic State Convention in San Antonio—that was in the summer of 1952. David and I stayed with June Barnebey then, as Richard was a delegate also. The stakes were high. Governor Allan Shivers and his supporters were threatening to bolt the Democratic Party over states' rights, embodied that year in the "tidelands" issue. I did not know a thing about states' rights or tidelands, except that the discussions were heated and the battle lines drawn.

Many years later Governor Shivers would become my friend and mentor, but in 1952 to a boy soon to be twelve, he was the equivalent of Darth Vader to loyal Democrats. I read the newspapers, listened to the radio and conversation. It was high drama and intrigue, exciting. The loyalists lost and walked out of the convention down to La Villita on the San Antonio River where they elected a rump delegation to Chicago. They weren't seated there, as it turned out, but I was very proud of Mother. She was a fighter then and would be for the rest of her life. I admired her greatly. She rubbed off on me then, and I feel her influence to this day.

We even got to see Mom from afar thanks to a strange new phenomenon—television. Seeing Mom at the convention wasn't the first time we had watched TV, it was just the most exciting. Television in the early 1950s was a hit-or-miss proposition—mostly miss, particularly when you lived out in the sticks. To get reception in Weatherford, which was thirty miles from the nearest signal, one needed a housetop antenna. Regardless of the antenna's height, reception in those days was snowy to nonexistent, but this didn't matter. I would watch snow with voices for hours if Larry Mahan's parents or Rodney Kelly's mom would let me. That applied to most of us kids in the neighborhood, because few had television in their homes. We'd go where there was one, and so things got a little crowded for Mrs. Kelly, but she was a good soul and let us look through the living room window. We didn't get much sound that way, but wrestler Gorgeous George, with blond curls and wearing form-fitting tights, left little to the imagination, so we didn't much care. I wonder what passersby thought who saw as many as ten children at a time peering into Mrs. Kelly's window. We would whoop every time George did a body slam, and every time Buck Rogers fired his ray gun. It was high entertainment, and TV was poised to affect our lives forever. Still, most late afternoon and weekend activities remained centered around neighborhood families and friends. We played together, we swam together, and we had potluck suppers together. It was idyllic, and it did not last.

Late in the summer of 1952, with great tears and fears, we left Weatherford for the big city of Austin. I was heartbroken to leave Al and my friends, but Austin would soon mend my heart. There in Austin in the 1950s my general education and my political education would both intensify.

Leaving Weatherford could have been worse: we almost left Bullet behind. Before moving to Austin Mother had gone back to Denton for a visit, while David and I went to Granny and Pappy's in McKinney. Even though she was completing her master's, she took Bullet with her. One afternoon several weeks into our stay in McKinney, Mother showed up with Aunt Donnie or someone else with a car. With tears in her eyes she stammered that Bullet had been lost. We were crushed and demanded to go with her back to Denton to begin a block-by-block search. Assuring us that everything was being done—posters and ads—she left. An agonizing time passed. Several days later the phone rang. Bullet had been found, safe and healthy. A woman had called Mother, saying that she thought her family had our dog. Mother drove over and, sure enough, there was Bullet, happy as ever to see her. But there was not happiness all around. A small boy sat on the front porch, tears running down his cheeks. In that few days Bullet had become the dog he had always wanted: "I hope this isn't your dog, lady." But he was and he would remain so for seven more loyal years.

Al would stay with us about the same length of time. Even though he lived in Weatherford and then Houston, he would come to Austin often. David and I stayed with him in Weatherford for a couple of weeks each summer during the early 1950s. I am certain he and Mother loved each other, and my brother and I adored him. But he drank. I always thought that Mother had had enough heartache with Dad on that score and just didn't want to run the risk of another alcohol-induced broken heart.

CHAPTER 5
Austin

For a twelve-year-old, Austin seemed to have everything: more than a few movie theaters—maybe a dozen, including drive-ins; public parks all over town, capped by Barton Springs, a spring-fed, cold-water gem in the middle of hot Texas; a great university with a then-not-so-great football team; University Junior High School (UJH) at the edge of the college campus; and Baptist churches. Now we attended the University Baptist Church where the great Dr. Blake Smith held forth on Sundays. I was baptized in Weatherford, but I learned true Christianity listening to that thoughtful giant of a man. Not least, politics was everywhere, because Austin was the state capital. Despite my regrets leaving Weatherford, Austin would come to be my home.

We moved in the heat of August. We still didn't have a car. Our first house was on Seventeenth Street near UJH and Allen Junior High, where Mom was to be the new librarian. As always, Mom made friends quickly and the friends took us places. But Austin in 1952 was a town where you didn't really need a car. It was bike accessible in almost any direction. And we could walk most places: to school, downtown, church, and swimming pools. Barton Springs was a bit farther—a two-bus-ride adventure. But if we were short of change (and we usually were), we could bike there in less than an hour.

One of the first places we had to walk was down the hill on Nineteenth Street (now Martin Luther King Boulevard) for groceries. I recall that it was blistering outside. Because we were recent arrivals, the Safeway manager would not take a check from Mom, even though Mom explained that she was a librarian with the public school system. Even then, big corporations were demonstrating their predilection to turn a deaf ear to locals: cash only, otherwise no sale. I never knowingly shopped at a Safeway again.

Farther down the sun-baked street we trudged, tears in Mom's eyes. Lord, it was hot, and so was I. At the corner of Nineteenth and San Jacinto we took stock. Across the street was a service station—Willie Kocurek's. The apparent owner was outside, gassing up a car and cleaning its windshields. He was smiling. "Service with a smile" personified was Willie Kocurek.

We crossed over and approached the man. "Yes, Ma'am. What can I do for you?" Mother explained our plight. Kocurek never missed a beat. He motioned for someone to take over for him, got us in his car, and drove us up the hill to Sam Slaughter's grocery store. Inside Kocurek was greeted by one and all, and Slaughter came downstairs from his office. Kocurek explained the situation, and then Slaughter smiled and took Mother by the arm. "Mrs. Bristol, this is Mr. Smith, our chief cashier. Mr. Smith will set up an account for you. You pay when you get paid." Not only were these trusting people of the small-town brand, Kocurek was deeply involved in Austin's education policy it turned out, so he spoke with authority.

Kocurek offered to wait and take us home, but Mom said that we could walk. Off went that most remarkable man, who would be a force among Austin's angels for the rest of the century. Decades later, after retiring, Kocurek would earn a law degree in 1980 and start a legal practice in Austin—he had started law school in 1943, but his plans at the time were interrupted by World War II.

We loaded up a cart with groceries. Mom signed the bill and we started out the door. "Wait a minute," said a young woman. "May I give you a ride?" It was hot—mother agreed. "My name is Janey Briscoe. I'm Sam Slaughter's daughter." She drove us home and we were grateful. Years later Dolph Briscoe, a substantial South Texas rancher—and Janey Briscoe's husband—would run for governor. He was quite conservative, but he always got the progressive Bristols' votes.

It is clear to me now that Austin then was still a town, a small community where people cared about and knew one another. Where gas station owners gave service with a smile, and grocery stores (locally owned) gave the same, extending credit, driving new families safely home, and, as it turned out, delivering groceries on rainy days.

It was an auspicious start for us, with much more in store. In September, school started. I can't say that I loved every moment of my schooling experience in Austin, but I am hard-pressed to remember the bad. I met new friends quickly, like Lee Mayfield, Mike Cotten, Terry Gardner, Sarah Parks, Joyce Webb, Bobby Coonrod, and Gretchen Becker. All of us remained friends, and fifty-three years later Gretchen would become a great love of my life. I'll write about this remarkable woman in another chapter.

At UJH I began to play organized sports, football and baseball. I also acted in school plays. I had the lead role in *The Importance of Being Earnest* and was on the way to stage or Hollywood stardom until a classmate, sitting in the front row during a performance, passed gas thunderously. That event sent him running out of the auditorium and me into catatonic state. My budding acting career terminated, a mysterious hand kept me on the road toward politics—which is another form of acting.

Social acceptance came for a number of reasons in those days and owning a television set was at the top of the heap in the early 1950s. We didn't own one at first, but David and I were determined to have one. Our ability to save money proven, we went into action again. In the fall of 1952, living on Seventeenth Street, we were near the university and its Memorial Stadium. On Saturdays we noticed that football fans would drive around looking for parking spaces. Across the street from our house was a vacant lot, its ownership unknown to us. We appropriated it and turned it into a fine parking lot on Saturdays. The season culminated in the Thanksgiving Day game between Texas and Texas A&M. It seemed as if everyone came to this game. And there were the Bristol boys, hawking our lot and packing 'em in. For some reason, we were also able to use our neighbor's front yard, which had no lawn.

We finished parking, went home, and told Mother that we were taking her on the bus to eat Thanksgiving dinner at the Piccadilly Cafeteria and to a movie—*The Merry Widow*, starring Fernando Lamas and Lana Turner. Then we gave her the rest of the money to go toward a television set. So soon we had our very own rabbit-eared, black-and-white, fuzzy-picture wonder. We could invite friends for hamburgers or sleepovers.

Dances were also part of the social scene. I couldn't dance but this was simply a problem to be thought through. Ironically, it was the Baptist Church, which deeply frowned on dancing, that led to the solution. While walking to church one Sunday, I noticed an Arthur Murray Dance Studio right down the street. In the early fifties the magical Murrays heavily advertised on radio, newspapers, and eventually television. They could transform me into Fred Astaire quickly. So the next week I walked over to the studio. But becoming Fred Astaire didn't come cheap. I talked with the manager who told me the price, and then I talked with Mom who had a little set aside but not enough.

I couldn't write my Granddaddy Donoho, a Baptist's Baptist, for help. So I summoned up the courage of a twelve-year-old who desperately wanted to hold budding teenage girls, and I asked the manager if I could pay him what I had and work off the rest. I don't know if he really did need clean-up help on Saturdays or whether he took pity on a newly arrived country bumpkin, but I got the job and the lessons. And for some reason, I took to dancing: foxtrot, waltz, rumba, and finally the new rage—bop. I had a decent sense of rhythm, and I picked up the steps quickly. The instructors were most generous in their lessons.

Then a major crisis reared its head: graduation day was nearing. I had to have a sports jacket, a tie, and a date! The jacket part was easy. I did need to start wearing a coat to church. So I wrote my Granddaddy Donoho, asking him for money to purchase one.

The date was a stumper for two reasons. First, I didn't know many girls. Second, we still didn't have a car, so even if I had a date I couldn't take her to a dance—or anywhere. I not only didn't have a car, I didn't have a license and I couldn't drive. This was a major logistical problem. I have forgotten exactly what Sarah Parks had enough of to cause me to get past my hang-ups and problem, but I called her and told her I wanted to take her to the graduation dance. I told her we didn't have a car. She either talked to her mother on the spot or called me back with the good news: her mother would drive her to Arthur Murray's.

On the appointed Saturday, I walked to the studio. Then Sarah arrived, popped out of the car, smiling and teenage lovely, and I gave her a corsage. We had a grand time, with no awkwardness. I knew steps that were new to her, so I became a teacher of sorts. Too soon it was over. We walked outside and there was Mrs. Parks. I stammered my thank-yous and good-byes, and started home. Sarah rolled down the window to ask if I needed a lift. Major problem! Our family dog, Bullet, had kept up his habit of walking with us in Austin, and he had accompanied me to the dance.

I must have mumbled something about my dog. Mrs. Parks pulled over and said, "Bullet can ride up here with me, and you and Sarah can ride in the back seat." So there we were. I don't remember anything about the ride home, but I worshiped Sarah's mom, Lena May Parks, thereafter.

Dancing and sports opened up my social world. Then, as now, public school teachers drew miserable pay, so we were poor, but knowing how to dance gave me confidence and standing. My partners and I even won several sock hop contests. And what dancing and the family television set and didn't accomplish, sports did. I wasn't particularly good, but I had staying power. Eventually, because I had to work, I dropped baseball, but I was the best left-handed catcher in the local Little League. I was the only one. I couldn't fire to first base worth a damn, but I could blindside pick 'em off at third.

While I would wind up playing football, the Bristols were really a basketball family after we moved to Austin. Mother loved basketball and when the 1953 state high school tournament rolled around in March, she was determined to go and take David and me, even if it meant missing school. Along the way she got the idea of inviting our cousins Don and Judd down from Denton for the games. We were delirious with anticipation.

While my Aunt Donnie was not sure that was the best idea she'd ever heard, she was finally convinced that by riding the train, and with careful instructions to conductors and porters to watch over them, there was a good chance Don and Judd would show up in Austin in one piece, safe and sound.

You can't imagine the hugging and backslapping that went on at the Austin train station. During the war and in the late forties we'd grown up as brothers. Reunions continued to be joyous and departures were soul-searing.

Early the next morning we hiked over to Gregory Gym on the University of Texas campus. For the next three days we watched the best basketball that Texas high school had to offer. There were several divisions, from that of very small towns—Class B, to the large-city AAA. In my memory there were teams from some very small schools that could have taken on any in all classes, and big-city schools that could have whipped some college teams. Because there were no reserved seats, we quickly devised a system to capture the best front-row seats. Mother would fix sandwiches and apples for lunch. As soon as the morning session was over, four boys and Lottie Bristol would walk out the gym entrance doors, turn around and be first in line for the next session. During the next hour or so, as we waited at the head of a growing line, we ate our lunch. When the doors opened for the next session we would rush to the front-row seats, saving one for Mother. After the afternoon session we'd repeat the process, but this time Mother would treat us to hot dogs and Cokes as we pressed up against the door, waiting for the evening games.

Throughout junior high and high school we attended most sessions of the state basketball tourney. Our front-row technique had gained imitators. By senior high there might have been twenty or twenty-five youngsters spread out in the middle of the first row, saving seats for classmates and girlfriends. For us attending the tournament was a family tradition that has not died. Now, over fifty years later, we continue to gather every March. All seats are reserved in the Frank C. Erwin Center, and we can't sit down front, but if you'd search the top sections and look for white-haired and gray-haired men, you might spot four among a host of friends. That would be the Bristol-Holt cousins, their families and friends.

If UJH was fun, Austin High School was a grand adventure. Sports would continue to be a big part of my agenda. Then, as now, football was king and a door to acceptance. In my senior year Austin High went to the state playoffs and the next year the team from Denton High came to town for a game. Don and Judd played for the Denton Broncos. Our seat-garnering tactics were now an art form. David, friends, and I were there to watch the Holt boys, front row and center. Football began with two-a-day practice sessions in late August or early September. Even if we had started practice at midnight it would have been too hot—it was sweltering—but I loved it. Starting in 1955 we began to build a great team. Much of this can be attributed to our collective talents, but due credit must go to Jim Tolbert, our coach. A big man who had played at the University of Texas, he had a commanding voice. He was tough but he also had a soul. As integration loomed after the 1954 Supreme Court decision in *Brown v. Board of Education,* Coach Tolbert simply said to us, "No trouble!" And there wasn't. In our senior year, as we were headed toward the state playoffs, so was the "colored" high school in Austin—Anderson High. We sent a good luck telegram to them and some of us went to their game. Austin was full of folks who said, "No trouble."

By the time I reached high school, Mother was teaching history and government as well as working in the library, and I know that she cared for each of her students. I never had her for a teacher because of the obvious conflict, but Price Daniel Jr. and Joe Reid did. Price was the son of the governor of Texas, and he was a slacker. Mother sent a message to his parents, summoning them to parent-teacher conference. The word came back that Governor Daniel was way too busy to come, but Mother asserted, "The governor will attend"—and he did. Price Daniel Jr. buckled down and came to love my mother for caring about him. Unfortunately, many years later, other character flaws would lead to his being shot by his wife.

Joe Reid was in the first group of black students who transferred to Austin High. He was a good student, but in our senior year he had backslid to the point that Mom called him and his mother to meet with her. Reid got a firm dressing down and was given six weeks to shape up. It was going to be close: he had to pass Mom's course to graduate. Forty years later Joe Reid remembered: "There I was, dressed in cap and gown, lined up outside City Coliseum for commencement, still not knowing if I would graduate. They were pulling students out of line before they entered the building. Then I saw Mrs. Bristol and froze. Neither of us spoke and then . . . she winked. She was a fair teacher who would go the distance for us." That was Lottie Bristol. She would go the distance for her students, but they had to earn it, white governor's son or first-time Austin High black student. I had been certain before about my mother's position on integration and equality, it wasn't until I attended high school that I learned exactly how strong she was. For the children of governors, senators, and others in positions of authority, Austin High was a college prep school, but for black children it was life changing.

For the most part, Austinites dealt with integration like Mom did. We had outstanding and courageous leadership from Lyndon Johnson and city council members to business owners who made it happen quietly and with grace. It was mostly a non-event, though there were a few diehard "nigger" haters. A group of busybody mothers organized the Terpsichore Cotillion so their girls wouldn't have to dance with "those boys," but the cotillion didn't last long. Black and white, young people were going to the City

Coliseum and the Civitan Club to see, hear, and dance to Fats Domino, Little Richard, and Chuck Berry, as well as Johnny Cash and Elvis Presley. We didn't exactly dance with each other, but we all danced together and I'm not sure that anyone there would have cared if a mixed pair had hit the floor. Racism did not die overnight in Austin, though. It just went underground or turned inward, and sometimes it would bubble to the surface.

A case in point was an incident that took place at Home Drug on Guadalupe Street across from the UT campus. Charles Owens had been one of my best buddies since junior high, and when I got a job at Home Drug I recommended him for a position—or maybe it was vice versa. We were soda jerks together there: old-fashioned soda fountain engineers with all kinds of ice cream behind the marble counter, a juke box at one end, and, over the course of the day, hundreds of beautiful coeds who became more flirtatious if we added (at no charge) extra goodies to whatever they were buying. These were not huge gobs of ice cream or ten cherries on top, just a little tangible something to tell them that they were delightfully recognizable. But it had to be done with professional stealth since the owner was always watching, counting every dime, scrutinizing every cone with a scowling countenance—never a smile.

We continued the practice, aided time to time by a black dishwasher, the hardest-working man I'd ever met. We felt a sense of togetherness because the owner was forever urging us to cut corners, and enforcing harsh and often changing rules. He was particularly abusive to the black fellow, though, often publicly and embarrassingly. One afternoon the owner called our friend a "nigger," berated him in front of customers, and then fired him. Charles and I were at the breaking point but held our tongues. After the owner left, we gave away free ice cream and Cokes, danced to "Little Darlin" on the countertop, threw off our aprons, and walked out during the peak of the afternoon crowd. The assistant manager watched all this with horror, knowing she would catch hell. We stopped, told her that the owner was a cheating racist, and then we left—to cheers from the young customers. We never heard a word from him or the law. Bigotry is such a waste of time and energy.

Because integration was such a non-event, we were permitted to go through junior and high school in an idyllic state. Later known as the Silent Generation, my classmates and I weren't silent. We were simply having the time of our lives. Within six years of graduation in 1958 we would experience the depth of the Cold War, the Cuban missile crisis, and the time-warping death of President John F. Kennedy. But we took advantage of growing up in Austin with smiles on our faces, impressive athletic feats, falling in and out of love, and listening to 45s—many that would wear out, sensing (without deep thought) that we were somehow blessed, whether in homeroom (where Gretchen Becker brightened each day for me with her smile), on our morning paper routes (I had one), and at church or school dances—blessed as individuals, as a group, and as a nation.

The truth was, however, that a great deal of world history flew by almost unnoticed. The Korean War raged in the early '50s. *Sputnik* went up. Sam Rayburn was Speaker of the House, and Lyndon Johnson was the Senate Majority Leader. I knew all of this, but I was too busy being a teenager for it to register deeply, except for the un-American antics of Joe McCarthy. McCarthy's slimy presence dominated the front pages and television for a while in 1954.

There was plenty of talk—mainly negative—around the kitchen table and family gatherings about that demagogue. I came to loathe McCarthy's snarling smile and raised eyebrows, brought into our home by television. I sat transfixed, raging when he spoke or when his attorney Roy Cohn, cow-eyed, whispered in his ear, and hooraying when he was taken apart by Joseph Welch. You'd have thought I was watching a major sporting event. And in a sense I was: politics is a contact sport. I didn't understand all that I saw and heard then, but I knew that an angel of darkness was being defeated by better angels of democracy.

Were there communists in the United States? Yes—and some dangerously treasonable. But as McCarthy rolled around the country having his ego fueled by fawning millionaires happy to ply him with liquor, that non–war hero began to believe that he could destroy anyone in his path. He didn't reckon on the courage of Democratic and Republican senators who finally took him to task. He failed to take into account that bullies aren't tolerated in America for long. Censured by the US Senate, he drowned himself in whiskey and died in 1957.

Mainly we had a grand time of it. Speaking of drinking, Heine Pate, LaVerne Lundquist, and I once escorted a drunken Johnny Cash and carried his equipment into the City Coliseum, where much to our amazement Cash somehow went onstage and stayed upright through his entire act. Off the stage he collapsed, so we helped him back to his car. Somehow he made it to the next show too. Later, after years of trying to kill himself with booze and drugs, Cash righted himself and became an American icon. To this day I still listen to the Man in Black.

On Friday nights in the fall, my friends and I played football. We won most of our games. During our senior year we were on our way to the state championship, we thought, but lost to Port Arthur in a driving rainstorm for reasons never recorded in the sports-page accounts. We flew to Port Arthur on a chartered plane through the storm. That plane ride was a first for most of us. We were green at the gills by the time we arrived, and then we were greeted at the Port Arthur stadium by a crowd of rough-looking oil-field-worker fans who glared down from the bleachers, daring us to win. Someone had flooded the field prior to game time, it seemed. We played a hard-fought game, but lost 14–6. Then we flew back to Austin, many getting airsick again.

The 1957–1958 athletes of Austin High had winning seasons in football and basketball, then won a state championship in baseball. But if sports were the great entertainment and social equalizer, our teachers and what we learned were the great emancipators. By high school I thought that I was reading broadly. But I was not reading with deep thought. Great teachers in English, history, and government began to help me connect more of the dots. Mary Gray and Mary Adkins not only opened up the classics and poetry to me, but they also made literature relevant. Antony Macaluso and Roland Johnson connected concepts of democracy and justice with the realities of politics as actually practiced; whatever gaps they failed to cover, I could find with a quick trip to the state capitol to watch debate there. These worthy public servants would remain my role models and friends for the rest of their lives. I am not a weepy sort, but I cried when Mrs. Adkins, Mrs. Gray, and Mr. Mac died.

One other thing broadened my horizon and become a lifelong habit: reading a daily newspaper. For most of high school I had a paper route—an early-morning route, which after the night of a football game seemed painfully early—and I got in the habit of reading my product from cover to cover, all but the want ads. The *Austin American* (back then there were two editions and the *American* was the morning paper) was well rounded, with extended coverage of politics—after all, Austin was the state capital, and Rayburn and Johnson were prominent figures on the national political scene.

I learned something because of my paper route. Once a month I had to collect from my customers. Back then, before computers and direct billing, paperboys (there were no girl carriers then to my knowledge) were responsible for collecting payments on their route. Some would say that this was indentured servitude, since we didn't make a great deal of money. I fared well, though, because I didn't mind asking for payment and would also run errands for customers in need. By the time I quit, I had a sizeable clientele who either paid extra for the favors I did for them or tipped well at the end of the month. Later in life I continued to be able to ask folks for money, for political and philanthropic causes, but I had also learned early on to listen to people's needs and ills. This served me well, and I found it interesting listening to people's life stories.

In May of 1958 I graduated from Austin High School. Because I was so young, I didn't waste time regretting what I was about to leave. Later I would come to realize how much those times meant—those friends and teacher. That summer I would deeply mourn the passing of our dear friend Bullet—run over by a passing vehicle because he just couldn't move as fast as in his younger days.

Decades later, sometime between my fifty-eighth and my sixty-fifth years, I would come to know that Gretchen Becker's homeroom smile had attached itself to my strongest heart-felt memories. For our fortieth class reunion I was asked to write a poem, and I had to struggle with each line, except those dealing with my thoughts about Gretchen. Those simply flowed onto the pages.

To the Class of 1958

At any moment on any given day
I can't say there was anything
tangible I recalled about you
or all the rest who are gathering
to test the passing of forty years.
Yet in that instance
when I cracked the now-yellowing
annual, each black-and-white
image leapt off pages, flickering
with the remembered colors
of September-morning laughter, or
in the heat-wavering mirage
of two-a-day warriors wilting, or
aftershave stifling after-game sweat
blending with the sweet swells
disturbing angora sweaters as
the forty-five DJ spun heart-
beating tunes against the mirrored
glass ball spinning, disguising
pimples, chaperones, and Supreme
Court symbols whom I have
no memories of dancing,
though surely they must have.

But moments molded in idealized days,
before bullets felled a president
caught us by surprise, came easy.

It is the in-between that turns
compelling. What happened?
What went right, wrong, when,
why, if at all? Regardless,
each of us has become our own
history, loosely woven
into the patterns of others
who danced in that fast-
receding light, revolving on
the end of recollections' string, and, yes,
I seem to recall that
Heine Pate and I tried to write
country songs on the broken back porch
of his broken home, and that black
Ben Glover ran
cross-country until we could
catch up and that
Gretchen Becker made home room
more than a place to check in
with a smile that bent light
and that she was
the prom corsage
I never unwrapped.

* * *

It is not the living or dead;
they have been recorded.
Rather it is the missing who
give pause, like an undefined
afterthought in the still-dark
theater while credits scroll.
For one moment it is as if
they might have had some part
suspended in a script
that mysteriously deleted

their existence in the turning,
and, upon turning back,
all that is left is the undeniable
thought that they were there,
but here in the theater
of memory they move
like ghosts, whispering,
but not necessarily to me.

Recently we celebrated our Austin High fiftieth class reunion. Of all the joys, none was greater than the fact that so many are still alive, in relative good health, and satisfied with how our lives have turned out. Almost without exception, classmates of all stations and colors feel lucky and privileged to have grown up in a time and place that bordered on magical.

That certainly is true for me. There was something extra special about growing up in the '40s and '50s in small-town Texas. We had a freedom of movement and opportunity. We had friends who would remain so over the years. We had extended family that knew each other well and cared. We roamed at will along streets and country roads. Our bicycles and dogs were constant companions. Movies cost nine cents; haircuts cost a half-dollar or so. Christmas and birthdays were gentle times of love, not commercialized extravaganzas.

Desegregation came about in Austin with no known incident. If we were the Silent Generation it is because we smiled a great deal—outwardly and inwardly. And we did the entire period on a few snitched beers: no binge drinking and no drugs. I would not even know that drugs existed until much later, when I sampled marijuana, found it totally lacking in whatever it was supposed to do, and decided just to stay high on life.

We were safe and cared for. That was the gift given us. I am not sure we have done a good job of passing it on.

My paternal grandfather, Charles Todd ("Pappy") Bristol, poses with his grandchildren at home in McKinney, Texas, 1946. Counter-clockwise from left: me, David, Margaret, and Scotty Watters.

Me at age six, about the time I entered public school in Beeville, Texas, in 1946.

Christmas with Granddaddy Donoho (W. S. Donoho) with (left to right) me, David Bristol, Judd Holt, and Don Holt, 1946, Denton, Texas.

Judd Holt and I are caught playing in the creek mud at our great-grand-mother Donoho's farm, circa 1944. "Mamaw" is what we called Margaret Eveline Donoho.

The Bristol and Holt boys have fun bathing at Mamaw's, circa 1945.

Mother: Lottie May Donoho, circa 1930.

Me and Daddy (George Lambert Bristol,
known to the family as Lambert), circa 1941.

My father, my maternal grandfather W. S.
Donoho, and Uncle Brooks Holt frying fish at
the Texas Women's University campsite, 1940.

My father with his parents and sisters. Left to right: Lambert, my grandmother Chrystella ("Granny"), Agnes ("Aggie"), my grandfather Charlie ("Pappy"), and Annie Katherine Bristol, circa 1930.

Pappy Bristol home from blacksmithing, with my cousin Scotty, circa 1938.

My maternal grandmother, Lottie Mae Frederick Donoho, circa 1900.

Lottie Bristol at work as librarian at Weatherford Junior College, 1951.

Granddaddy Donoho (W. S. Donoho) with his parents and siblings. Clockwise from top left: W. S., Bransford, Margaret Eveline ("Mamaw"), Bursie, Claiborne ("Baba"), circa 1900.

On a summer outing, brother David and I pose in Eureka Springs, Arkansas, 1949.

The Johnny Cash rescuers fifty years later, at Austin High 2008 reunion. Left to right: H. D. Pate, Verne Lundquist, and me.

PART II

A Freeing of the Mind and Spirit

CHAPTER 6
College

It was ironic that one of the principal reasons Mother moved us to
Austin was to be near a first-class public university, and that I would then go away to college. For most of my early Austin years, I thought I would eventually attend the University of Texas. Starting in the seventh grade I went to University Junior High, which was attached, as a student teaching facility, to UT. I sold cokes and popcorn at UT football games, which got better with each year of Darrell Royal's long and illustrious career, starting in 1956. I came to love the UT colors, orange and white. But there was family pull on my father's side. My father had gone to Texas A&M, as had his uncles and other members of the family. Mother's alma mater was TWU, the sister school of A&M. I also developed the normal desire to go away from home to college.

In my junior year of high school, my great-uncle Jim Forsyth had given me a summer job in Houston with the promise I could work there every summer through college—if that college were to be A&M. Family ties and tuition funding prevailed. I started in the summer of 1958 at the Texas A&M campus in Junction. That fall I enrolled at A&M in College Station. Leaving Austin was mitigated by the fact that my dear friends Lee Mayfield and Amor Forwood, as well as other Austin High classmates, were headed across the Brazos River to Aggieland.

Like all freshmen Aggies, then and now called "fish," we had to say good-bye to home and girlfriends until Thanksgiving. Lee and I settled in as roommates, started classes and military drills. Then an all-male military institution, it was rich in tradition but short on social life until junior and senior years. It was rigorous, particularly since Lee and I had to work at the mess hall to earn our meals. That meant getting up before dawn, serving breakfast, heading back to our room to study, attending classes, serving lunch, drilling, going to more classes, serving dinner, then studying until lights out. We had to do a great deal of silly things in between, like stand at attention if the three-legged mascot dog, Tripod, needed to pee. He would lean against a fish for support and do his duty. I avoided that dog like the plague, often crossing the street if I saw him coming. Nonetheless we had fun, making it up as we went along. A great deal of it centered on bedeviling a sadistic sophomore who did everything possible to run us off. He went over the line to the point that his peers looked the other way when Mayfield and I filled his room with live chickens, heated its door knob, and flooded it. We gave as good as we got—and more.

We also went to football games, but the Aggies of '58 didn't have a good team. Bear Bryant had left after their great 1957 season for Alabama. We had to stand during the entire game as members of the 12th Man Corps. All of that could have been meaningful had we had dates and if the team had been better, because when the Aggies score, members of the 12th Man Corps kiss their dates. But dates were a rare thing and the team didn't score often. Besides, I was going steady with a girl in Austin. As the fall crept by, her absence was a drag. With each passing week my letters to her became more explicit in describing how I foresaw our reunion at Thanksgiving. Her answers turned up the heat.

In the meantime the team played Southern Methodist (SMU) in Dallas. Freshmen could go on road games and have dates come along, particularly with the "Tessies" of TWU. A friend from Denton had gotten me a blind date. I picked her up at her dorm. We went to Dallas and to the game. We drove back to Denton and I dropped her off at the dorm. And that was it. Not even a peck of a kiss at the game or dorm door. Mayfield and I went back to A&M late on Sunday. It was a couple of weeks before Thanksgiving and the thought of going to Austin and seeing my girlfriend had reached fever pitch. But I would see her first in a week—I'd invited her to come to the bonfire rally that always preceded the last game of the season, with archrival University of Texas, the pinnacle of Aggie tradition. For days all students participated in building a massive pyre. On the weekend before Thanksgiving we would burn the thing down, chanting pagan war cries and trying to kiss our girlfriends whenever possible.

The Sunday night after the SMU game (a shutout loss for A&M) I wrote two letters, one to my TWU date and one to my steady in Austin. The first was formal, polite, and appropriate. The other was hot as a firecracker and, for a Baptist, somewhat provocative, though not by today's standards. Then I put the letters in the mail and eagerly looked forward to the next weekend. On Saturday my Austin girlfriend showed up with her mother—not a good sign. I showed them my room, we ate lunch, and then my girlfriend said she wanted to talk. Her mother took a walk—a better sign, I thought.

In the car she immediately pulled out a piece of paper and handed it to me. It was the letter I'd written to the TWU girl. At first I was stunned. Then I started laughing. I knew that my erotic letter was probably being passed around to roommates at TWU. I shouldn't have laughed. My Austin girlfriend and her mom left in a huff—and forever.

My Thanksgiving holiday was spent in Austin with Mother, David, and Aggie friends who couldn't get home. We went to the game on Thanksgiving Day. I didn't have anyone to kiss, but this was all right because not only did the A&M team lose, they didn't score again. Back at the house, the phone rang. "George, you are famous. Your letter is posted on the bulletin board at Fitzgerald Dorm. Girls from all over campus are stopping by to read it. I think girls from NTSU are coming from across town." My friend from Denton had heard the news and gone over to the dorm. Some months later I went to Denton and, sure enough, there was the letter, dripping with more than innuendo about my thoughts for Thanksgiving 1958.

Years later I was on a plane from New York. My seatmate was a woman from Texas, and we talked about our lives. Somehow we figured out that we had both started college in 1958, and she had attended TWU. After I told her that I had gone to A&M, she launched into what to her seemed the joke of the century—about the Aggie who had inadvertently switched letters. I passed the rest of the flight in silence, not telling her that she was sitting next to a living Aggie joke.

By the spring of 1959 I knew that I didn't want to be an engineer of any sort. I wasn't particularly good at math or science, except political science. One of my professors was an economist and suggested that A&M was not the school for me. For a great many reasons that made sense. The University of Texas had a great liberal arts school. There were more liberal arts scholarships available there than at A&M, I could live at home, and there were jobs to be had. And so I transferred.

The University of Texas in my years there was defined by great teachers, great opportunities, and, for the last two years, my summer work at Glacier National Park. When I enrolled, the Austin campus population was roughly twenty thousand—it is now over fifty thousand. The school and state government were—and are—the principal engines of economic and social interaction. Austin was then approaching one hundred thousand in population, but it still had a wonderful small-town feel.

Because of my financial situation, I lived at home and worked after classes and on weekends. For work I took anything that fit my class schedule and paid money. Soda jerk, night-shift food distributor, state agency clerk, a number of jobs at the university, and one for the Texas AFL-CIO: these plus all sorts of small scholarships gave me the opportunity to continue to take part in one of our grand experiments—public higher education. It was affordable: tuition and books then totaled around $1,000 per semester, this for a full schedule of classes.

At that time the state's secondary and higher education institutions received plenty of revenue from the Texas oil and gas industry. State legislators, though mostly conservative, also believed in higher education and were willing to pay for it with measures that afforded an opportunity for students of limited means to get a first-class education. Well-educated graduates were then recruited into various sectors of the economy. This is an indisputable fact, yet today's conservatives, while mouthing support for education and business, have worked tirelessly to lower the percentage of state appropriations for higher education, so they can brag about lowering taxes and trimming state government. What they are really doing is passing the cost onto students, who often come out of college saddled with huge debt. It is sleazy doublespeak at best and counterproductive for the betterment of society at worst—and it is a lie. Tuition increases paid by parents or students represents a virtual tax, and lately that tax has increased tremendously.

Another thing that has gone awry is the dedicated support of the business community for higher education. There are several reasons for this, all of which are terribly shortsighted, since business, large and small, is the direct beneficiary of a well-educated citizenry. When I was in college in the late 1950s and early '60s, most centers of commerce were locally owned and operated. That was true not only of mom-and-pop operations but also of large corporations. There were no out-of-state banks, savings-and-loans, and the like. Today in Texas, however, there are no major locally owned banks, the saving-and-loan industry is dead, and few large corporations are locally owned.

I see two flaws. First, the entrepreneurs who once owned Texas banks, oil and gas companies, and timber mills were permanent residents who had roots in their communities. They had a sense of place and they wanted that place and its people to have good schools, good health-care facilities, and good libraries. They poured their influence and treasure back into the community. Today most executives stay at a given assignment for three or four years, and then move on. No true sense of place develops, no sense of home, and absolutely no commitment develops, real commitment, to bettering that place.

Running parallel with this, because most major institutions have ownership outside the state—or even outside the country—there is little sense of social responsibility, certainly not when it comes to paying taxes. Local company representatives may mouth platitudes about educational excellence and dole out small photo-op checks, but they rarely get down and dirty. They certainly don't commit much (not even a mouse's share) of their treasure. Many do just enough to make a self-serving media splash. As soon as the photo session is complete, they send lobbyists to the legislature to exempt their industry from paying taxes that support education. My beloved *Austin American-Statesman*, now owned by Cox Communication of Atlanta, has such an exemption, yet the paper's editors champion education and rattle on forever about the undue influence of lobbyists. There are so many tax loopholes and exemptions in Texas that it is a giant scam and a scandalous shame. (Some corporations and leaders, like supermarket chain HEB and its chairman, Charles Butt, really put the oar in deep. They are an exception: HEB is locally owned.) Things once were better, even if many students had to work at paid jobs then as now. After classes started in the fall of 1959, I settled into a routine that I would carry throughout my college years: early-morning study, classes, work, sleep, then study again—with a great deal of fun and beer drinking on the weekends. The University of Texas was beginning to have great football teams again. The age of Coach Darrell Royal was in full swing.

I joined a fraternity—Phi Kappa Psi. I did so mainly at the urging of one of my high school friends, Charles Owens. That experience was fortified, in part, because the University of Texas had glorious coeds, and fraternity membership would increase my chances of getting dates. Everywhere I looked were the most beautiful women ever created, it seemed.

Sometime that fall, Bobby Kennedy came to the campus. Like most Texans I was predisposed to Lyndon Johnson, but I liked Senator Jack Kennedy too. So I went to hear Bobby out. I don't remember a word he said, but I still have the Kennedy button he gave me.

The political excitement mounted in the spring of 1960. That spring I was fortunate to land a filing job in the University of Texas main library. Its vast holdings fascinated me. There were days when I read as much as I filed. The job also allowed me time to do political work. I'd usually walk to the AFL-CIO offices to help mail letters, and to take placards to distribute in support of candidates of the liberal, pro-labor persuasion. I also had opportunities to run things over to the legislature and meet staff there—sometimes House and Senate members, although they weren't there often since the legislature only meets every other year, in odd-numbered years.

Much talk and activity centered on the presidential race. Texans of all stripes were for Johnson out of loyalty, gratitude, and in some cases fear, but many were intrigued with Kennedy—particularly young people. I was intrigued so I began to follow Kennedy's campaign as best I could in a state whose news media were dominated by Johnson backers. Enough got through to fire my imagination, and the fire kept burning right through the Democratic Party convention in Los Angeles. I had watched previous conventions on television but this was the first time my attention had been so focused on the screen daily. Then I got the best of both worlds: Kennedy tapped Johnson to be his running mate. I believe that was best for the country too.

The night of the acceptance speeches, I whooped and hollered with friends and drank more than one beer. The reality of a dynamic, young Democratic president backed by a wise and seasoned Senate Majority Leader was more than I had hoped for. The same was true for my mother, family, and friends, although we would come to learn that the ticket did not sit well with a great many people and organizations—particularly near-Republican conservative Democrats and many Baptist and other Protestant preachers and church members.

Then a hard reality set in. I had not been able to find a good summer job in 1960, and I was out of money. After talking it over with Mother, we decided I would have to drop out for a semester and get a full-time job. It was a disappointment, but it opened up an opportunity not only to replenish my coffers, but also to work for the Kennedy-Johnson campaign. There wasn't much available in Austin, so I decided to look around the state. My Uncle Brooks finally found me a good-paying construction job in Denton. Since my cousin Judd was away at college, I could have his bed at my aunt and uncle's. We agreed on a fair price for boarding, and I went to work, building dormitories at the North Texas State campus in late August or early September. It was scalding hot. On the first day I had to work under the building, which was an oven with no ventilation. At the end of the day I struggled to my aunt and uncle's house on Alamo Place and fell onto the floor of the boys' room, fully clothed. Several hours later my aunt and uncle found me there and put me to bed. Every day got a little better, but it was a major adjustment.

I became a member of the hod carriers' union local. I already had a deep abiding faith in unions, and I still believe they play a productive and protective role in society. I had worked for the AFL-CIO in Austin, but I had never been a union member before. Unfortunately, I would soon find out that there was a seedy side to some unions, as in all enterprises. Every payday certain "deducts" were made by the local union rep—a fellow from Fort Worth, as I recall. After so many pay periods, some or all of the deductions were supposed to be fully paid up. At some point, several workers, including a number of black laborers, approached me. They told me that they thought they were paid up, but that the "rep" kept deducting. I looked over their pay books, and it appeared that either the rep was mistaken or an outright thief.

Since my time of "payment in full" was approaching, I asked them to let me witness the situation firsthand. The following Friday was the end of my deduction period. I'd either be a target or not. Sure enough, he asked for another payment. I told him that

I was paid in full, and showed my receipt book. I then told him that a number of people had been overcharged and said I was sure he'd made similar mistakes. He mumbled something about checking into the situation. No restitution was made. I called a friend at AFL-CIO state headquarters in Austin, who said that he'd check it out. A few days later someone new from the local showed up and made restitution in full. I never heard after that what happened to the crooked rep, but I learned a big lesson: that even among the best of organizations there can be crooks and point shavers. Also: it doesn't hurt to stand up and be counted. An awful lot of hardworking men shook my hand and wished me well when I quit to return to college.

I learned other valuable lessons during that period. The first was job-related. As the building was erected, we worked higher and higher, and we hod carriers—helpers—worked right at the top, sliding out on wooden beams to help pour concrete. There were no nets or other safety devices. This was before OSHA and other workplace safety measures were pushed forward by Kennedy and Johnson. It was sometimes frightening, particularly toward the end, in late November and December when ice often covered the ladders and beams. One slip and it might be eight stories down to hard ground littered with all sorts of wood, barrels, and such. A few years later I cheered when occupational safety and health laws were enacted, even though I'd sworn in the twilight of 1960 to go back to college, graduate, and get work indoors. Except for working in the great outdoors of Glacier National Park, I have stuck to that resolution.

The second lesson came about through my work and enthusiasm for the Kennedy-Johnson ticket. I'd gone to Dallas to meet my fraternity brothers for the Texas–Oklahoma game. After the game we went to the house of a wealthy alumnus, Russell Reed. The house was full of brothers and alumni. At some point in the evening, living room talk turned to the election, which was then about a month away. Most of the talk was negative regarding the Democratic ticket. I held my tongue until some liquored-up, know-nothing bloviated for what seemed like thirty minutes. I couldn't take it anymore and took him to task, most particularly regarding his rant about how Democrats were bad for the oil and gas "bidness." He walked right into it because I'd had an economics class where the professor had assigned a book or article on how much the oil and gas industry, particularly the independents, relied on Lyndon Johnson, Sam Rayburn, most of the Texas delegation, Senator Russell Long of Louisiana, and other Democrats to carry their water.

Finally we wore out, or the host called it off our heated debate, and the party resumed. Toward the end, Russell Reed called me into his study. I was thinking, "Oh, no, I am going to be read out of the fraternity." Not so. Reed shut the door, explained that while he was for Nixon, he knew the Democrats were safe on oil and gas, that his friend was a blowhard, and that he wanted to help me through college. In short, he admired my spunk and that I had facts to back my argument. I told him I wasn't in college just then, but planned to return in January, and said that because of my job I thought I'd be all right financially. We parted good friends and remained so for several years, until his death. He would always call when he was in Austin and take me to lunch or dinner. During our friendship he did loan me $250 once and I had just about paid it off when he passed away. I sent the last check after Reed's death, along with a letter to his widow, telling her how much his friendship had meant to me. She and I then kept in touch.

A third learning experience reached into the very core of my world—the Baptist Church. Wherever we moved we latched onto the local church. But above all was the First Baptist Church of Denton, Texas. It was the signpost and the steady rock of my religious experience, so naturally I went to church there while working in Denton. It was wonderful to be back among relatives, particularly the Holts and Granddaddy Donoho. We still ate often at the TWU cafeteria, something that dipped into my memory well.

On the Sunday before Election Day, our pastor, Dr. Armstrong, let loose a diatribe on Kennedy and Catholics. It was embarrassing. Finally the head deacon—I forget his name—got up and said that he was a Republican who had not decided how he was going to vote, but one of the deciding factors wouldn't be anti-Rome rhetoric. He walked out of the church. So did I, and I did not go back to the pure blood of the saved or to the First Baptist Church of Denton for decades.

Later I did talk with Dr. Blake Smith in Austin about this. He assured me that many Baptists had voted for Kennedy and that he was one of them. But the damage had been done. I felt bad about it for years until I joined the Presbyterian Church in the 1970s and was born again.

I find it regrettable that the Catholic Church which Baptists and others railed against in early 1960s is today meddling in all of our lives, interfering with US policy. I find it completely hypocritical for cardinals and bishops to pontificate about abortion and the sanctity of life while committing crimes against young boys and girls who remain scarred for life. My strong feelings are equally scornful of the fact that John Kennedy was branded a robotic tool of the Catholic Church (both he and the Church foreswore that as nonsense) and that today the Church attempts to bully elected officials into compliance with its every dictum. No matter that many of those targeted are at the forefront of programs for civil rights, health care equality, and the elimination of poverty, programs the Church has championed. I think many present-day Baptists and other Christian Right demagogues are equally hypocritical. Too many persons who profess true belief are little better than many extremists of other faiths they rant against.

Regardless of Baptist politicking, the Kennedy-Johnson ticket won—barely. For me this meant an exciting new era was just over the horizon. In December I said good-bye to my fellow workers and the owner of the construction company. Mother and David came to Denton and we celebrated Christmas with the family there. Then I returned to Austin. The year 1961 began like a new day, even while we wrongly thought that the sun wouldn't shine on Nixon's career again.

CHAPTER 7

Moving into My Mountains

I'm sure to some sophisticates the scene, freeze-framed from be-
hind, would have looked like an Edward Hopper or Norman Rockwell painting: a boy
silhouetted in the door frame and an Olympia beer sign blinking in the window, while
lights from the jukebox cast an eerie blue into the night and human forms milled about in
shadows. Perhaps a darting figure would also have been seen within: working behind the
bar was a woman, the manager and soul of the place then and for years to come. Freda
Otsby was the patron saint of the Glacier Park trail crew until her death some forty years
later, even though she would go on to be an outstanding public school teacher.

I spotted her and went up to the bar to get directions to the park headquarters. I
must have said that I was on the trail crew, because she shouted out, "Bruce and Doug,
he's one of yours!" Out of the mass of humanity appeared two young men, Bruce Murphy and Doug Medley, who instantly took me under their wings. After introductions,
they got me a beer. I was too young to buy, by a couple of months—it was June 1961
and I wasn't yet twenty-one—although it didn't seem to matter. In turn they introduced
me to others who would be working on trails, blister rust control, and construction. Little
did I know then that my budding friendship with Bruce and Doug would grow to span
over half a century.

After an hour or so we left for park headquarters and our bunkhouse, but only to
drop off my bags. It was imperative that we drive up the road to Lake McDonald Lodge
to scope out the arriving females who would be working in the park at the hotels, motels,
and other guest facilities. Although I can't recall now exactly where I saw them—in the
lodge or outside at a campfire gathering—it doesn't matter. Young women were there,
seemed hundreds of them, and some of the most beautiful and flirtatious ones said that
they were going to work at the Many Glacier Lodge and Swiftcurrent Motor Lodge. By

then, through Bruce or Doug, I knew that this was where we were headed. After a few get-acquainted beers, we drove back to headquarters and went to sleep.

The next morning I arose at near-dawn and went outside. It was icy, at least by my Texas standards, and clear. Pine boughs and needles were rustling in the breeze, casting off a delicious scent. The night before I had begun to sense something special place about this place, but it was this early-morning moment when I really felt it strongly. The significance to me of my relationship to this place, Glacier Park, would grow with every passing experience there—and continues to grow even to this day.

For the next day or two we had orientation. We learned about trail work and our tools. We discussed rescue and firefighting, but only in classroom abstract. We would learn both by experience later. On our own we carefully studied the bars along what was known as "The Trap-Line." From West Glacier back to the Blue Moon near Whitefish were bars that were only a step or two this side of those in western movies—and most, on any given night, were just as rowdy. They were peopled by lumberjacks, park personnel, truckers, and a scattering of women. The "trap-line challenge" was, if accepted, to have a boilermaker at each bar—a whiskey shot chased with beer. I recall there were seven or eight saloons. The bigger challenge, assuming one made it to the end of the line, was getting home, as most everyone, including drivers, partook. Thank God for icy cold mornings, for hot roast beef sandwiches and coffee at the Highland Café near the entrance to West Glacier, and for watching over us.

After our preliminary training sessions we broke up into groups and pulled out for our assigned work places. I already knew that mine was the Many Glacier area. Exactly where that was situated I could not have said. For the first ten or twelve miles we drove along Lake McDonald, a deep-blue wonder of glacial action and effect. Glacier National Park was named not only for its remaining glaciers, but also for the mountains and lakes they'd carved over the eons. Then we began to move up the Going-to-the-Sun Road, a monumental construction project which was finished in 1932 during the Herbert Hoover administration. Had Hoover appreciated during the Depression how effectively these kinds of public projects could put people to work, he might have expanded his own public works programs. This would have blunted some of the criticism of Franklin Roosevelt who defeated Hoover in the 1932 presidential election, and who assuredly believed in such programs.

For miles we drove along the road, blasted from the face of glacier-carved walls. I could not believe what lay below and above: lush valleys lined by streams, foaming waterfalls, and greenery beyond belief. To the sights, Doug, Bruce and others began to put names for us newcomers, names that I would come to know permanently: McDonald

Creek, Heaven's Peak, Packer's Roost, Birdwoman Falls, the Weeping Wall, and Logan Pass. Located at the pinnacle of the road, Logan Pass was seemingly at the top of the world, certainly at the top of my known world. Looking out in every direction I was awed to the core. From that point I could see peaks, some of such distance that they were in Canada. Others rose and fell along the Continental Divide. All were still snowcapped and dazzling. Here and there glaciers were pointed out. To my untrained eye their outlines were blurred by late snowfall, but I would come to know each and trek across most.

Soon we started down the east side of the divide, continuing on the Sun Road. If the west side of Glacier is verdant, the east side is stark, moderated by the magnificence of St Mary's Lake and flowering meadows on the fingers of false prairie. Again I began to find new vistas, punctuated by new names: Siyeh, Piegan, Wild Goose Island, Sun Point, and Red Eagle. None held meaning for me, yet each seemed to reconfirm that I had arrived at the place of my heart.

At the bottom of the road we pulled into St. Mary village. Bruce, Doug, and others knew the Black family who had opened the lodge and other facilities there shortly after World War II. We shook hands all around, ate lunch, and continued toward Many Glacier. Out of St. Mary's the terrain changed again. Mountains to the west ran to rolling prairie to the east and north, all of it Blackfeet tribal lands. My untrained eye saw land that did not look fertile, except in the rich river bottoms. With no knowledge of the place yet, it occurred to me that the Indians had gotten taken. It all came together in the pitiful prairie village of Babb: a bar, a general store, a few shack-like houses, and a church on a hilltop. That church to this day continues to haunt me. I wrote a poem about its relationship to the Babb Bar and townspeople there.

Babb Bar

Someone died in Babb, Montana,
probably some whiskey-soaked local.
They took him to the tin, windblown church
on the hill across from the Babb Bar.
I watched them pass, red-leathered faces
stone-faced, misplaced race
dressed in Sunday's best or only.
I guess they stayed inside half an hour,
then came out and lowered him away.
Ten minutes they were all over
here, drinking, yelling, and the past closed shut.

Someone was gone—forever to everyone.
But, I noticed as I left, just on the ridge
overlooking the grave,
a mournful, ragtag hound.
He's been there four days now.
Christ, I can't have a decent drink
for following that old sheep dog
and desperately needing one.

All that had gone before—Going-to-the-Sun, St. Mary Lake, the prairies—in no way prepared me for my first full view of the Many Glacier valley. Upon turning off at Babb, heading back west into the park, the road runs along a creek and glacier-produced moraines leading to some rather unspectacular mountains. This goes on for a few miles. Then off to the left is a reservoir—Lake Sherburne (which I would find out was a joint tribal–national park project for irrigation). Again, I saw beauty, but no more so than I would when looking at Texas reservoirs, with a few mountains thrown in. Then I had a glimpse of something greater, a sighting that immediately disappeared, just enough to stir interest. Finally, near a place called Apikuni, the incredibly awesome suddenly leaped into full view. With a visual wrap-around, the mountains rose, glaciers were revealed— Salamander, Grinnell, and Gem, and a lake of sparkling tranquility appeared, Swiftcurrent. From all directions these came together to create a wholeness that would, if viewed by all, I think, bring permanent peace to our tired world.

Our residence for the summer was a doublewide affair that had been used as the press room for the 1960 National Governors Association conference at the Many Glacier Hotel, a temporary building that is still there fifty years later, evidence for the old cliché: there's nothing as permanent in government as a temporary building. In 1961 it was practically new, with showers and bunk beds. These were all we needed. Our meals were prepared by the Many Glacier Hotel staff, and the hot breakfasts, sack lunches, and hot dinners seemed all the more plentiful as we began to flirt with the kitchen staff—those Minnesota beauties I'd seen on the train.

For a day or two we had more orientation with the district ranger, Larry Dale, and his staff. During one of those sessions, the question arose as to whether any of us had ever used dynamite. I had—a small experience one summer on a family friend's farm. That was good enough: I became the lead's assistant. We practiced our dynamiting out on the prairie near Duck Lake, just east of Babb. After a day or so we were deemed fit, and we began to work the trails. I'm glad I learned dynamiting. For a number of days, as we worked the Grinnell Trail, this allowed me to work outside the direct control of Rich Nelson. For reasons unknown to me, our Many Glacier trail leader was about as sour a fellow as I've ever met. The only thing outside of a general disposition problem that made sense was that he was the son of a park superintendent and he resented those of us who were political appointees of a sort, which made no sense since he'd gotten his position through his father's position and influence. After hours and on weekends the trail crew stayed away from him or ignored him. The problem was that he was always lying in wait, ready to stick it to us.

Most of our work relied on shovel and pulaski, the latter an axe and hoe combined in a single tool, developed by Ed Pulaski, the forest ranger hero of the devastating 1910 fire that consumed so much of the Northwest. The bravery of Pulaski and other rangers legitimized the Forest Service, good for public policy, but also led to unintended consequences later in the century: fire again. For the remainder of the twentieth century, including my time in the park, the Park Service had a no-burn policy, which led to tremendous build-up of dry, fallen trees, all waiting to burn.

Before we could get our trail footing and certainly before we went up into the high country, tragedy struck. Two male workers at Many Glacier Hotel had gone missing, and it was known that they were on Mount Henkel, which rose up in back of the trail crew cabin and the Swiftcurrent Motor Lodge. At dawn the district ranger called us together, explaining the situation. Other trail crews, blister rust crews, construction workers, and park personnel were arriving or on the way. The Swiftcurrent parking lot became a command post.

For the first hour or so we scoured the low areas, just to see if one or both had made it down during the night. This also gave the park service more time to bring in some trained mountain rescue people. I'd never been higher than a street curb it seemed, and sometimes that was even perilous. This applied not only to me but also to most of our crew, none more so than Doug Medley, a Mississippi flatlander of the first order. To those more experienced, Henkel was a cakewalk, sloping up into a bowl, with a few cliffs, but to Doug it was Everest, and he was consumed with fear. "We are going to die!" was his constant outcry. Up we went, fanning out all over the mountain. Spotters guided us with radios so we could cover all areas of the face. It was not a treacherous face, but for inexperienced young men on their first time on a mountain it was daunting. Mostly we were scrambling on rock, not really climbing, not using ropes.

At some point one of the missing young men was spotted. He turned out to be severely injured, but alive. Delirious, he said that his companion was below him, and then we strapped him into a mountain rescue carrier. Crews with lengths of rope would act as brakemen from above, with handlers on both sides and below gingerly lowering him toward the trail. The rest of us turned back and began to look again at the ground we'd covered.

By now the area was a beehive of activity: rescue teams, ambulances below, headquarters personnel and even the park superintendent on hand. Radios cracked with orders and information, and shadows began to cover the peaks as the June afternoon moved toward evening.

We had not found the missing hotel worker below us so we started back up the mountain, well aware that dusk was setting in. As we ascended I saw a couple of buzzard-like birds circling in close, higher up. I grabbed a walkie-talkie and yelled out, "Do you all have any predatory birds in the park?" "Yes," came the reply, "eagles and osprey." "Then I know where he is," I said.

Hurriedly we made for the area where I'd seen the big birds. There, far above where the other young man had lain, was his companion, dead. It was my first encounter with human death up close, and it was not pleasant—the body had been grotesquely bent and injured by the fall, and dull eyes peered out into nothing. We quickly roped him in and began the lowering maneuver again. Below we could see that a crowd had gathered. The word had spread, and gawkers were out in full force. The radio came alive again, and we were instructed to create a diversion, for some of us to take the body farther down the trail toward the Many Glacier Hotel, while the rest lowered a dummy carrier toward the assembled throng. The tactic worked, and then some of the gawkers became outraged by our action, which pissed me off at the time.

In short order the ambulances and trucks began to pull out. Radios silenced. Fellow trail crews and other employees returned to their bases. The ghouls retreated. By dark it appeared as if nothing had happened. But the day was not over. Employees of the Swiftcurrent Motor Lodge had gathered mounds of food prepared for the rescue teams and made it available to our crew. We ate sandwiches and soup, went outside for beer, and washed away the dust and sense of death. Back inside again we danced and sang. And at some point during this exorcism, Ann Hummel of New Haven, Connecticut, fell into my arms for a dance—and we never stopped dancing the entire summer.

Within a day or two, routines were back to normal. Now we were at it full-time, opening the trail to Grinnell Glacier. The glacier and a nearby lake and peak were named after George Bird Grinnell, the stellar American conservationist. Grinnell had not only championed the establishment of Glacier National Park, which finally occurred in 1910 with the help of Louis Hill of the Great Northern Railway, but also founded with Teddy Roosevelt the Boone and Crockett Club, which advocated, among other things, the preservation of the American bison then on the verge of extinction. Later, with Roosevelt's encouragement, he established the Audubon Society. If the gathering of the country's founding fathers was the cornerstone to our ability to thrive as a nation, then men and women who banded together to preserve our remaining untrammeled land at the end of the nineteenth century and beginning of the twentieth century added to the strength of our foundation. These noble souls used, in many instances, their own wealth, influence, and connections to convince members of Congress, often cynical and sometimes bought and paid for, to set aside great and small parcels of our national treasure. In my opinion this championing of "America's Best Idea" has given US citizens a shared sense of pride and civic responsibility. Every opinion poll over the last century has clearly demonstrated that Americans love their parks and are willing to pay for them.

In the summer of 1961 I was coming to love Glacier Park—and getting paid to fall in love. Can you imagine awakening in the middle of paradise, going to breakfast with beautiful women and new friends, hiking through forests and around glacial lakes, climbing mountain trails into the clearest blue sky to work?

Quickly we learned the nature of trails, how to build bridges when necessary, and how to direct drainage and to blast snow off trails, doing so without disturbing the mountains. We plugged dynamite holes to an acceptable level, cranked the handle, and then shoveled the blast-loosened snow down to the trail rock. We didn't disturb the mountain as much as we did tourists who weren't allowed on the trail during blasting, and who were never allowed out on the snow banks, though some made it anyway.

One morning high on Grinnell—four or five miles up—we spied a middle-aged, heavyset woman coming toward us in high heels, pulled by the smallest dog I'd ever seen. How she had made it that far I don't know. Bud Clark was our lead that day and chief of blasting in the St. Mary's district. Bud talked cowboy slow (even though he was from somewhere back east), was married to a Blackfeet woman, and was known to love eating garlic. Approaching the woman he said, "Lady, you're going to have to leave right now." "Well, why?," she huffed. "Because this is grizzly country, and grizzlies hate dogs. Just sure as shootin,' a bear's gonna spot that dog of yours. The dog's gonna turn and run between your legs. The dog will make it, but the bear won't!"

With that image planted in her mind, she stormed back down the trail, dog at the lead, high heels intact. We rolled on the ground for what seemed like an hour.

Most park visitors are sensible, attentive, and law-abiding. A few are careless, reckless, even criminal, and ever so often get seriously injured or die. Posted rules are there in parks for good reason. Park personnel don't blemish the landscape with signage mindlessly. "Danger! Grizzly Country" means exactly that. So does "Trail Closed." It never ceased to amaze me that the most aggrieved and angry park visitors were those who disobeyed signs. That vacant woman in high heels would have been shocked had a bear appeared. She might even have sued.

Sometimes during lunch I'd move down the trail from the other fellows and gaze at the mountains, lakes, and sky, watch the clouds do a dance of fleeing shadows, listen to the rustling trees. Often this was supremely calming, but occasionally, when unseen storms or other changing weather approached, it was magnificently unsettling: frenzied clouds pouring over peaks, boughs whipping and snapping, lakes white-capping. This watching stopped time for me, as if I dwelt in eternity. And it was still just the opening chapter in my education.

When we were working "the Grinnell" we would listen for the tour boat to sound its horn at the far end of Lake Josephine in the late afternoon. The last-trip horn meant that we had thirty to forty minutes to pack our gear, store our tools and dynamite, and then race down the trail to catch the last boat back to our base. It was five miles to the trail head. Though we wore heavy work boots we could run like deer, just as sure-footed, skipping over rocks and jumping streams. It was a sight to see, often to the amazement of tourists. Then we'd ride the boat back toward Swiftcurrent Lake, plowing over the glacier-silt blue of Lake Josephine, one of the loveliest lakes in the land.

Often as not, on the slopes of Grinnell Point, our binoculars would pick up grizzlies rooting for day lilies and berries. Like the bison, this species once roamed the plains and then began to feel the destructive pressure of white settlers. Unlike the bison that stood their ground even as their sisters and brothers were killed, the grizzly retreated into the mountains. There in protective sanctuaries, with help from human conservationists, they have hung on to existence. They are beautiful creatures, and they can be incredibly dangerous if threatened.

The grizzly is a large and powerful subspecies of the brown bear. Its gray-streaked fur and hump above its shoulders are its distinguishing features. For centuries grizzlies covered a wide area of the Northern American plains, but, decimated by ever-encroaching settlers, they were eventually pushed back into the mountains of western Montana and Wyoming. In Montana those mountains became Glacier National Park. Less than one thousand grizzlies remain today in the continental United States.

For the most part grizzlies are loners. They do not seek confrontation with humans, and never have. When confronted, especially if someone comes between mother and cubs, they can be dangerous and swift to attack. A problem in 1961 was that for years the Park Service had allowed these wild creatures to be treated like entertainers, even letting them feed at garbage dumps near park hotels. This allowed tourists to view them in proximity. Over the years this practice allowed the bears to become used to humans. The familiarity would later lead to tragic consequences. The 1967 deaths by grizzly mauling of two young people on the same night—at two separation locations in the park, Granite Park and near Trout Lake—led to major policy changes. Garbage dumps were closed, and practices that lured grizzlies and other wild animals to feed for human enjoyment were ceased, including the practice of feeding by hand.

In 1961 I saw the problem firsthand. One day, the Many Glacier crew was on the way to headquarters for some reason. Somewhere near Lake McDonald we suddenly saw a bear on one side of the road and a little girl on the other side holding out food, with a woman off to her side ready to take a picture. I floorboarded the truck and drove between the bear and the child. That scared the bear off, but not the woman, who berated us for ruining her photo. After listening to her, someone said, "Lady, more than likely the last picture on your roll of film would have been of your daughter's hand or head in that bear's mouth." We drove away with the full knowledge that that woman's actions had been encouraged by misguided park policy. Fortunately for all, that policy would change before long.

In 1961 bears were frequently seen on, above, and below Glacier Park trails. By chance I became the one-man bear patrol. I had brought my handmade slingshot—made of surgical rubber and whittled yoke—which was powerful and, with steel pellets, accurate. If a bear got too close, I'd shoot it in the nose (or at least try to) and it would gallop off. That was the theory, and I only had to test its validity once. It worked, thank God, because a seemingly cumbersome, lumbering bear can cover ground quicker than this Texan could reload a slingshot. They have been clocked at full run at over thirty miles per hour.

For the most part our workday was routine. Bear encounters, rescues, and firefighting were dramatic exceptions. Besides the Mount Henkel search and rescue, we had one more memorable rescue in 1961 and another the next summer. The first started slowly, as one evening a bunch of us were sitting on the front porch of the Swiftcurrent Motor Lodge, drinking beer, making out, conversing, and laughing about this and that. At the time we all felt daring and bold. Suddenly one of us spotted a light moving side to side on the Grinnell Point face. It was as if a light bearer was trapped on a small ledge or section of goat trail. Back and forth went the light. We yelled and blinked lights too. Then someone went for Larry Dale at the ranger station, and he blinked a spotlight, but there was no response. After we informed headquarter authorities of what we'd seen and done, we continued to shoot the breeze, had another beer, and kissed our girlfriends goodnight. Then we went to the trail crew cabin to prepare for a search and rescue and catch a little sleep.

The next morning broke clear. Mist or rain would have made the already challenging cliff face treacherous, even impossible to ascend. Some of us donned numbered football jerseys so that spotters could see where we were on the mountain and know who was where. Then we divided into teams and began our ascent. More experienced climbers, led by Roger Giddings, went around the other side of the mountain, so that they might rappel down into the area where the light had been seen. It was toward the end of the summer, so we were in great shape. We had good boots and by then we knew a bit about roping in and rescue techniques. We would need it all.

The first hour or so was easy climbing. Then we hit the face and things got tough and touchy. Even though it hadn't rained for a while, the face was moist from dew and from being in shade. The wall grew steeper. The good news was that the spotters in the Swiftcurrent parking lot could see us and so help guide us toward likely spots for safe ascent. Again Doug Medley thought his death was imminent. I had no reason to doubt him.

By noon we were about halfway up and the area was abuzz with activity. Headquarters staff members were there in full force. Professional teams search-and-rescue teams were gearing up. An ambulance and doctors arrived below, and a helicopter circled overhead.

Again a crowd gathered, this time watching us scale the dark slate walls. Montana's mountains are made of a more brittle material than the granite of the lower Rockies, and thus much more likely to come off in your hand or crack under foot. Our glacial mountains are not meant to climb. Glacier National Park is a stay-on-the-trails park. Climbing is for experts or those soon to be injured or dead.

Shortly after lunch the radios began to chatter that the rescue was being aborted. The lost climber had been found—in the parking lot. It seems he'd come down at first light, fallen asleep somewhere, and then failed to report in. We could have killed him. I think he was spirited away by headquarters personnel for interrogation to keep him safe from us. We had risked life and limb for a fool, someone who it seemed had no regard for us. A hanging would have been justifiable, I thought at the time, but perhaps that would have been an embarrassment to the Park Service. Our crew's one benefit: another great meal was waiting, prepared by the Swiftcurrent motel employees. Our bunkhouse had been cleaned spick and span. Ann waited. And then we danced into the night.

Another rescue event took place the next summer. We had just come off the Grinnell Glacier Trail. We were met at the trail head by the district ranger, Bob Frauson, who had replaced Larry Dale. By then Frauson was a legend. He had served in World War II in the Tenth Mountain Division—serious skiers and climbers who performed heroic feats—and had joined the Park Service after the war. As far as I can remember he had scaled the tallest peaks in North America and led some of the toughest rescue missions in the parks. We had done some rope training with him, but just enough to get by.

Frauson was ready to go, so we turned right around and headed back up. Again we were in excellent shape (we could work all day and dance all night), and sunset in western Montana comes very late that time of year. We heard that a hotel employee had seen a fellow employee fall and given a fairly precise description of where the fallen person might be. We thought we could hike hard, make the rescue, and head down before dark. We wanted to do so for two very good reasons: bears and girlfriends. We wanted to pluck the fellow off the mountain and get back down for a bit of late-night activity. But that was not to be.

If I learned anything in the mountains, it was that information from someone in shock or near-shock is scrambled at best. One moment you are looking up or down at some of God's greatest handiwork and the next moment your partner has stumbled over a ledge. After trying to reach him or her, you're off in a panicked flash, not stopping to note landmarks. By the time you reach civilization you can only point in a general direction and take a stab at accuracy. That was the case that evening. A hotel employee, it turned out, had burst into the ranger station earlier, babbling that his friend had fallen. After questioning from Frauson, it seemed—which is usually the case—the employees were off the trail, but up or down was a now forgotten blur. It had been determined that the faller had last been seen alive, though, so we thought we could be back in time for cuddling. We would cuddle, it turned out, but not the way we imagined.

As we got to the general area of the fall, we fanned out and yelled, hoping we would be seen or heard. At first this was haphazard, but as night approached we began sectoring each area. Men were searching above, below, and on the trail, while Frauson kept careful notes, all to no avail. Then it began to get dark. Another rule in the park is don't go home in the dark. We had no night gear—no flashlights or torches—and we told Frauson that it was time to go if we were to have a chance to get down safely.

"We stay!," he exclaimed, taking off his backpack and pulling out his sweater and one-man tent. That left the rest of us—six or seven—with nothing but the cold ground and the stars above. I don't think we had a candy bar among us to share for a snack.

I don't know whether Frauson ate after he popped into his little shelter, but we sat around planning his murder until the gathering frosty night air drove us to cuddle. Young men denied the warmth of their bunks or better formed a human pyramid and stayed alive, switching position every thirty minutes or so. We didn't sleep, we simply stayed warm. Bruce Murphy never felt so good—before or since.

Somehow, mercifully, the night passed. Frauson was up and about—happy as only a self-satisfied dictator could be. We coughed, stamped, and cursed under our breaths. Then, to warm up and keep from executing him, we began to fan out. Within thirty minutes we came upon the missing hotel employee, frozen in fear but alive. I went over to him. His feet were in the near freezing water of a small mountain runoff. He didn't move until I reached out and touched him. Then he sprang up, talking a mile a minute. Having gone into deep shock after he had fallen, he had been able to ward off hypothermia, sitting there all night long in a silent trance.

We roped him up and led him off the mountain and down the trail. At the trail head medical and park personnel met us and took him away. I heard later that he had a concussion and minor bruises and cuts.

Bob Frauson praised us for our work. I got the impression that he looked on the whole thing as a testing exercise, as a test of will, and incidentally a rescue. In my darkest moments I thought that he had planted the fellow on the mountainside just to prove to us that we could take whatever was thrown at us. It did prove that we had stamina. After a hot breakfast, we went right back up Grinnell Trail and worked a full day.

Nothing could keep us off that trail. The higher we went, the more beautiful the panorama. Blue sky canopied green forest, lake upon lake, and rock punctured by fast-flowing streams and waterfalls. From time to time a moose with calf, a grizzly sow with cub, or a pair of deer would cut through the brush or ford a stream. Standing at the top, near Grinnell Glacier, one can see four lakes and enough waterfalls to stock a lifetime of memories. I know. I am now in my eighth decade and have experienced fifty years in harmony with Glacier, and I have yet to tire of that scene or others within the park.

But nature has its horrific side: fire. I had heard of some of the killer fires of Glacier over the years, but in 1961 and the early summer of 1962, I saw only single-tree fires and small-area ones after a lightning strike. Without deep knowledge yet about our trail work, we would often saw and hack our way through the product of a misguided policy. Nearly sixty years of "no-burn" windfall had created sections of forest that looked like a giant tumble of pick-up sticks, forest that was impenetrable except by using chain saws and crosscut saws. It was tough, hot, and dangerous work. Tough because all trails were blocked by fallen trees, sometimes ones stacked to above head height. Hot because little breeze could penetrate the forest. Dangerous because sawed logs could cause others to dislodge, trapping crew members in potentially deadly jaws. What we did not know then—and apparently neither did policy makers—was that fire is a natural curative:

it clears out the windfalls, allows fresh plants and grasses to grow on the forest floor. It burns away dried-out logs and creates a slower- and lower-burning ground cover. In our ignorance we rushed to lightning strikes, usually wasting a whole day away from trail maintenance.

Not all fires were small. I'd heard of some of the killer fires of Glacier over the years, though I had never witnessed one. That changed in 1962. By ranger reports and radio we knew the Kintla Lake fire was burning on the other side of the park but that it seemingly was coming under control. On a Friday night we headed to the Babb Bar to drink, dance, and visit with our Blackfeet friends. For some reason, members of the tribe favored the trail crew, even as they were extremely suspicious of other whites—and with good reason, given the screwing the US government had given them over the years. For one thing, we were fellow firefighters. One of the damn few concessions given to various Native American nations is the right to fight fires. I'm sure this started because few others wanted the work. But over the years it became a good-paying privilege and honor. The Zunis, to name just one people, were among the best wildfire fighters in the world.

So there we were on a Friday night, slugging down Olys and dancing the night away. After midnight we started home. How we made it up the road to Many Glacier is a miracle, but somewhere along the road we were flashed to a stop. A ranger yelled that we needed to go to the trail cabin and pack up to fight the Kintla fire, which had roared back to life. At that point we were in no condition to fight marshmallows. For some reason Doug Medley and I shot ahead in his old Cadillac. The others would follow to wherever the crews and rangers were assembling with their tools. And soon Doug began his familiar chant: "We are going to die!" I said that I thought that God had a greater plan for us, although I had grave doubts. Doug said that the way he felt he *wanted* to die, and he was sure that would come true once we reached daylight and the fire. In thoughtful silence we watched the dawn creep up the alpine-glow walls of the Sun Road. It was a long drive to Kintla.

As we drew closer, activity picked up. All sorts of trucks, big and small, were on the move, funneling toward Lower Kintla Lake. Fire-fighting planes flew overhead. Upon arriving we were told where to park. Still awash with beer and sweating profusely, we were dreading the hike and labor of the first day. Then the Bristol luck returned. "Does anyone know how to operate motorboats?" someone yelled. As two southern boys who had grown up on water skis and fishing, Doug and I ran forward. The possibility of survival was at hand.

For the rest of that blessed day we ferried men and equipment across the lake to the trailhead leading to Upper Kintla. While we could not see the fire, it was a constant presence. It hung between earth and sun, turning the sky an eerie red-orange. It smelled of smoke, burning trees, and exploding sap. At the end of the day someone said that park personnel were now available to ferry the boats. However they decided to keep Doug. That was fine with both of us. There he remained for the entirety of the conflagration—with a smile on his face—and he even made the *National Geographic* spread on the fire later. I wanted to meet the fire firsthand.

I met up with a group hiking into the Upper Kintla Lake area and set out. If I remember correctly, I had a solid pair of boots, a couple of T-shirts, extra socks, a pair of workpants and a small toilet kit. After a short walk we arrived at the marshalling camp. It looked like a war zone all around: tents by the score—large mess facilities, equipment caches, a first-aid station, and even a business office. Everyone had to check in. All received some sort of identifying card, so we could go through the meal lines and buy additional clothes and toiletries. Except for new arrivals, everyone was ash- and grime-covered—and exhausted. I easily found the rest of my Many Glacier crew. Then I got a briefing, washed my face in the icy lake, and bedded down. My first impressions were confirmed and expanded at dawn and throughout the next day. Even before dawn hundreds of young men marched off into the darkness to hack and dig lines of defense—fire trenches. A helicopter buzzed overhead. More and more fighters trooped into camp. In mid-morning, smoke jumpers began to drop out of the sky, ready to work against the fire in more isolated areas. And there was the smell of smoke everywhere. We were in a battle against a natural enemy that knew no rules and gave no quarter.

We didn't have to hike far, but we had to go practically straight up. The leading edge of the fire was on the steep slope running down to the lake. We knew exactly what sector to move toward. Once we reached it we began the incredibly arduous work of making fire breaks—trenches about two feet wide—to slow the ground fire. At that point nothing in our area had crowned. Crowning is a firefighter's constant worst fear. Due to wind and windfall trees, the fire climbs to the top of the forest and fans out, jumping from tree to tree at amazing speed. Often as not the fire runs uphill, sucking air and oxygen out of the entire area. Fire is the only beast that can run uphill faster than down. We worked and we listened with a pit-of-the-stomach dread.

By mid-morning, fire-fighting aircraft joined the fray. All these planes were vintage World War II bombers that dropped reddish fire retardant. Because some of the pilots had partaken of the grape on Saturday night, their early runs were mostly inaccurate. One load landed below us, dusting firefighters with pink powder. Another flew straight along the center of the lake, released into the water, and then banked sharply away over the mountains. They got better as hangovers wore off.

I am told that the food was good, but I don't remember that. By the third day breakfast was a trial, lunch was eaten on the run in the fire area, and dinner was a brief way station before throwing myself into my tent and bedroll. I can't adequately describe how dirty we were two or three days into the battle—sweat, ash, and mud seemed to congregate in every pore and in every inch of clothing. We didn't care. We were so exhausted that we collapsed into our tents, not caring if we hit or missed our bedrolls. Without moving an inch during sleep, we would awaken and do it all over again. But it was exciting. It was an endurance contest against a beast that never slept and that had no respect for terrain or young men. The fire was out to burn away a mountain, then move on into the next valley. It only responded to rain and there was none to be had. So we slaved to turn the fiery tide using muscle, numbers, and knowledge, with constant air support.

We fought for a week. Late the following Friday we were told that the fire was under control. The Many Glacier crew packed up and gladly left. We were blackened and tired to the core. A beer joint was at the end of most roads in Montana, if we could just get there, so down the dark, rutted forest road we shot at breakneck speed. Within minutes of our departure, though, the radio squawked and a voice told us to return to base camp. Still we barreled on. Our collective thought was one beer: just one beer and then we'd go back. But it was not to be. We hit a deep rut or a boulder, snapping an axle. Dejectedly we called in and told base to come and get us. Then we learned the news: the fire was crowning!

Returning to the fire was like a revocation of parole, particularly because we knew the fire was crowning. If I remember correctly, we went right to the fire line, then worked all day to slow the monster. Toward the end of the day I witnessed one of the most memorable scenes of my time in Glacier. As we were trooping out of the fire zone, something happened up the lake (a crowning or an out-of-control run), causing men and quadrupeds to run for the shore. Most of the animals were deer, but among them was a huge bull moose. In unison, it seemed, man and beast arrived at a small cliff above the lake and off they dove, not one paying any attention to the other, each concentrating on personal survival. The moose and humans, I recall, swam out from the shore. Then, after getting their bearings, the men began to swim toward a safer shoreline. The moose kept going until it reached the other side of the lake.

And so I learned firsthand about wildfire. And I learned from someone then about the sustainability of the lodgepole pine during fires such as this one. At some point when the temperature of fire reaches a critical degree, pinecones explode. Some of the seeds drop to the ground below, but some are caught in the broiling updrafts and sent, like small gliders on thermals, up and over the fire to safe ground where, after a time, they take root and reappear years later as a new stand. I have thought about that miracle over the years. It reinforces my respect for the process of evolution in nature, while at the same time it renews my belief in a higher being. I believe that in the vastness of time, some superior form gave a helping hand. I know of no better argument for the compatibility of God and his earthly surrogate—nature—working toward the replenishment of their handiwork.

Back at fire camp I got another break. A bookkeeper, of sorts, was needed to work the supply tent. I got the job and for the next four or five days I sold supplies, not taking cash or checks but operating on credit, as in the days of my youth. My associate was a member of the Blackfeet Nation. Many of the purchasers were from the tribe and it made sense to have someone they knew deal with them. Socks, shirts, and pants were carefully entered under proper name and number. It was a land-office business because many workers came ill prepared. Fire fighting can ruin clothing practically on a daily basis, I knew. I got new socks and a shirt myself.

With the exception of one group, I only remember one customer's name, Comes-at-Night. The name stuck with me then and through the years. I asked my coworker and new friend, and he said that it was a family name among the tribe. Sure enough, after work each day other family members stopped by for supplies. My associate and I had a great deal of down time during the day, and in talking with him I learned that the Montana Blackfeet and the Kainai Nation or Blood Tribe members of Alberta together knew one another as the Blackfoot Confederacy or Nitsipai (meaning "original people").

It seems that even these original people couldn't leave well enough alone and live in peace. They were an aggressive and warring people. Over the years they had hunted and warred on foot, but sometime in the early nineteenth century they acquired horses. Then they became accomplished horsemen with massive herds and took on Assiniboine, Cree, Crow, Flathead, and Sioux, holding sway over a vast area of western Canada through Montana to the Rocky Mountains. When they lost their freedom and were reduced to reservation living, maybe they had no one else to go to war with but themselves. I would probably be resentful if I were exiled to a reservation after my people for centuries had roamed at will with the buffalo. No matter if that staple of staples had all but disappeared nearly a century before.

Not all Blackfeet were resentful or downtrodden. Many succeeded as ranchers, educators, and artists. Many were heroic in the twentieth century's world wars. In 1962, I know, many were great firefighters—tireless ones. But there were those within the tribe that never got over the haunting of another time.

Sometime during my second week of firefighting, those long hours we had all worked ran afoul of government regulations: no employee could make more than the superintendent during a pay period. This meant that national park workers, Blackfeet firefighters, and others were now essentially working for free after so many days with overtime pay. This caused uproar, especially among the tribal representatives. My friend was angry, saying that they weren't going to work for nothing. It occurred to me that those rules might only be applicable to park workers like me. I was an official government employee but the temporary workers were not exactly. I told him this and off he went. After much discussion the issue was resolved and the tribe members stayed on. Whether my thought helped, I'll never know. My friend went off on the fire line. In a day or two the fire was contained enough that we were ordered back to Many Glacier. In my time remaining in Glacier that summer of 1962, it seemed that we were better received in Babb and at the bar there than in the past.

As we started toward Many Glacier we called to say that we were on the way. The word spread to employees and girlfriends. When we arrived at the Swiftcurrent store there was a crowd of well-wishers, including the girls with a case or two or three of beer. The scene was memorable. There in the public parking lot of a national park, in the middle of a summer afternoon, ash- and sweat-streaked young men piled out of a van and into the arms of young women and cheering friends. We stripped off our stinking shirts and socks—I think we kept our pants on, then removed the sweat liners from our hard hats and drank beer from them. Some onlookers were aghast. One elderly lady exclaimed, "What are those savage-looking young men doing?" When it was explained that we'd been off fighting fires for two weeks, saving the park, she ordered another case of beer.

After things settled down, we trooped off to the trail crew cabin to shower, shave, and prepare to continue the merrymaking into the night. Arriving, we found the cabin had been cleaned from top to bottom, with fresh sheets and towels, and clean clothes. To this day I marvel at what good shape my crewmates and I were in. We had fought a massive fire for two weeks and yet, after cleaning up, we were ready to go again—and go we did throughout the night.

Who were we? First, all of us were white, middle-class, and firmly molded by the Depression (via our parents' experience), the war, and the 1950s. We had not all grown up in families with white picket fences and two cars, but we were blessed by coming to maturity in a special moment, a relatively gentle time. We also passed through those years absolutely complying with the mores of our parents. They were not rigid Victorians, but much was taboo to them and nothing more so than sex as a topic of conversation. Sex was rarely and barely discussed in the home, church, or school. Much of the little I thought I knew about that forbidden subject was wrong. Out of ignorance or fear or both most of us complied with the set patterns of our parents and grandparents.

But we were on the edge of a new generation and didn't know it. I certainly didn't know it when I arrived at Glacier Park, and I'm positive that this applied to almost all the other arriving young people. What I sensed, though, was newfound freedom, almost from the moment I walked through the door of Freda's bar. I was on my own. This was not the tortured, rebellious generational divorce that lay ahead in the late '60s. This was the peaceful freedom of remoteness.

There were no cell phones or laptops then. Long-distance phone calls were made only in emergencies, birth and death notices, and now and again. The infrequent call was not expected, particularly from a son who wrote home, and Mother was at best several days away by post. She was in Austin, Texas, and I was in faraway Montana. I would have to fend for myself, making my life up as I went about the park. That is not to say that I and my fellow employees were turned loose to run wild. There were park and concessionaire personnel with authority, but they had other things to do than play nursemaid. And many of them were themselves young or had come to the Park Service or the hotels for the sense of freedom here, away from cities and town. Rules, yes. Strict enforcement? Only when certain extremes were broached and certain lines were crossed. We were guided by self-discipline as it applied to work ethic, compliance with park and concession rules, and beer intake, as well as romantic and sexual discovery.

Work ethic and compliance with rules were easy because we did have guidance, real and implied. The mountains could be deadly off the trails, as could grizzly encounters. We knew we had a good thing going, and enthusiasm and joy in the moment that led us to cross barriers was infrequent and never was this barrier crossing done out of malice or mischief. Beer was a friend, but our drinking was tempered by the necessity to get up at dawn every morning, hike five or six miles, shovel snow and rocks, prune bushes and trees, or build something over or under trails and streams, and then hike out and shower and shave. The latter led to romantic and sexual discovery—or so we hoped. Looking back, I see that we fingered the edge of the envelope. And stayed cautiously in bounds.

As mentioned earlier, I really got to know Ann Hummel the night of the June 1961 search-and-rescue mission on Mount Henkel. We had exchanged hellos during the first week and perhaps conversed a bit on the front porch of the Swiftcurrent Campstore or at communal powwows, but it was that night that brought us together. Part of the energy I felt that night in my attraction to Ann was an aftereffect of the enormous tension of that tragic day. It had been my first close encounter with death. I'd been to funerals of elders, but old people were supposed to die. Seeing the lifeless body of a young man on the mountain had hit home, and Ann was there to help me talk it through.

I can't remember whether we kissed that night. That's not important. During the next few days there grew to be an understanding between us that we wanted this special time and place to be ours together. It would be ours with that enormous sense of freedom that allowed us to fall in love in a compatible setting without getting it okayed by parents—or anyone. We became a couple, inseparable when we were not working, in a relationship of companionship and joy. But this was not with complete abandon. We spoke often of the future, and if that was to be fulfilled, then we had to abide by the mores of our past.

Most nights after work we would meet on the front porch, share a beer or two, and talk and laugh until curfew. Sometimes we let the joy take us over the boundaries. For reasons long forgotten, Bruce and Doug decided to raid the girls' dorm after hours. I'd decided the same thing and had climbed in Ann's window. I'd no more gotten inside than here came Bruce and Doug, rattling and snorting down the hall. One girl stepped out in the hall, dancing in her panties and bra. Several others giggled loudly. A housemother awoke. All hell broke loose. Doug and Bruce dove into a room and out the window. Ann and I waited in the dark until the commotion moved to the far end of the hall. Then I laughingly crawled back out the window and headed for the bunkhouse. Home free, or so we thought. Not so: someone spotted me and ratted us out, and we were called on the carpet.

Larry Dale was one of the younger district rangers, not far removed from such frolics, so we weren't fired but simply banished to Poia Lake on a ten day "gypsy." Those work details were necessary, but they were also a disciplinary tool, separating troublemakers—and sometimes the boys from the girls. Off we went into one of the most beautiful and isolated parts of the park, but not before making plans to have the girls come visit us. The edict was that we were forbidden from visiting our girls, but nothing had been said about them visiting us.

Our job was to mend the trail to Poia Lake, then up toward Redgap Pass in the north of Many Glacier and Apikuni Mountain. The primary problems were caused by beavers and flooding. Both had seriously eroded the trail over a long stretch and washed out the bridge over Kennedy Creek. So, like the beavers whose effects we were there to correct, we worked from morning until dark. And working ten to twelve hours a day kept my mind off Annie—to a degree.

Were beavers to be combated or conserved? For most of its existence, the Park

Service has tried mightily to balance the twin charges of the Congressional Organic Act under which it was established: "to promote and regulate the use of the . . . national parks . . . which purpose is to conserve the scenery and the natural and historic objects and the wildlife therein and to provide for the enjoyment of the same in such a manner and by such means as will leave them unimpaired for the enjoyment of future generations." And for the longest time—and rightly so, in my opinion—tourists and their needs, whims, and conveniences came first within defined boundaries. For the most part this was managed splendidly. Stephen Mather, the first director of the Park Service, deeply believed that the parks were dedicated to all Americans and our visitors, and that Americans, once they experienced their parks, would become lifetime devotees and advocate constituents. He was right. Parks are immensely popular today. By huge numbers every public opinion survey demonstrates the popularity of parks and our willingness to support them—even with higher taxes and fees.

But this people-first policy rubbed against its equally important charge: conserving the scenery and wildlife. My trail crew's confrontation with the beavers was a perfect example of the system-wide conflict. On the one hand, tourists needed safe and open trails. On the other, beavers and their dams had been an essential part of the Kennedy Valley ecosystem since at least the last ice age. So our job was to rebuild the trail and bridges with tourist accommodation in mind, while protecting the beavers as much as possible—even as we had to go about the business of dynamiting their lodges. This meant rousting them out and trying to scare them off. We worked diligently to do that. We banged on the lodges and set off dynamite upstream. We patted ourselves on the back when we saw some scurrying off downstream. We were ready to dislodge their abode, repair the trail, and rebuild the bridge. But our girlfriends were on the way, so we stopped, cleaned up as best we could, used bourbon as mouthwash and deodorant, and then hiked to an abandoned ranger cabin. There we partied, necked, and swore eternal love. All too soon they had to get back by curfew (or at least by dawn), and Doug, Bruce, and I headed back to our camp. Little did we know that a beaver was waiting to exact revenge.

Doug Medley didn't fear everything natural. He just had a healthy respect for the unknown, especially the unknown of the pitch dark. And that's where we were: on the trail in the middle of the night with meager flashlights and no moon. Suddenly what may have been the biggest beaver in the park slapped its tail on water nearby—making a crack like a rifle shot. Doug knew he'd been hit or soon would be, and screamed: "Ohmagod, ohmagod! I'm gonna die!" His already huge eyes opened to pie size, and to this day Bruce and I swear that we saw their whites, even in total darkness. We made camp in record time.

Because Ann had promised to come back for a visit on her day off, the last week of our exile was tolerable. We repaired the trail and rebuilt a wondrous bridge that still arched Kennedy Creek in 1997, when I last returned to that heaven- and glacier-sculpted spot. After several days, Ann hiked in with Roger Giddings. By radio I learned that they were coming and the approximate time of arrival. As always, ours was a joyous reunion.

Ann and I were never apart for long that summer. When circumstances intervened to separate us, such as another "gypsy" detail to Ptarmigan Lake, one of us simply hiked after a workday to where the other was. My crew had been banished to Ptarmigan after we'd gotten boisterous one night at the Many Glacier Hotel. I'm not sure that we danced on the tabletops, but know I let go with a resounding cattle call that must have awakened and frightened half the hotel visitors. The hotel manager, Ian Tippet, a proper English gentleman, was high-tea offended. So off we went, and in Ann came to Ptarmigan with Roger again, a special visit since it was my twenty-first birthday. A day or two later I ran out to see her one night—seven miles—and then hiked back to work before dawn. At the drop of a hat we would dance, sometimes until daybreak. While the old traditional steps were sometimes observed, Ann also taught me the latest rage—the twist—and twist we did, night after night.

So it went until the summer began to wound down. We stayed at Glacier as long as possible—till around Labor Day—and then Ann and I drove with her brother and friends to Minneapolis. We made elaborate plans to stay in touch, to see each other at Christmas, and to return to our beloved park in 1962. I did go visit her in Connecticut at Christmas, and we had a wonderful time. She taught me to ski—in a fashion. I took her to New York City, where we went to the Peppermint Lounge and twisted to "The Bristol Stomp," and it was blissful. But the standard bearers of the old mores asserted themselves and intervened. Ann's parents were not favorably impressed or touched by our obvious feelings for one another. They certainly had grave reservations about a return to Glacier for Ann. I suspect that I was too much a Democrat to suit their Republican taste. And they conspired to end our togetherness by setting in motion that traditional deal-breaker, a summer trip to Europe.

I knew none of this at the time. Throughout the spring Ann and I kept in touch, making plans to return to our mountains and valleys. In late May or early June I made arrangements to ride to New Haven from Austin with Mark Tredennick. I had hitched a ride with him and his aunt (a memorable woman) at Christmastime. Mark had a grand family who lived in Meriden, Connecticut, up the road from New Haven, and they had invited me to stay with them.

After settling in with Mark's family, Ann drove to Meriden to fetch me, and we went back to have dinner with her parents. We talked about everything but returning to Montana. Her parents were properly cool. On the return drive to Meriden, Ann broke the news to me. I felt blindsided and crushed, took refuge in a bar, and downed boilermakers to the point of exhaustion and passing out. Somehow I blurted the name "Tredennick" to the bartender, and Mark and his dad came for me, took me to their house where I slept into the next afternoon. Then that wonderful family, from aunt to cousins, hugged me and nursed me back to some semblance of life. I was still crushed and in shock, though. Mark's mother phoned Ann, who drove up immediately. We talked. She told me that she had fought the European trip, but the family pressures were too great. Whatever was said resuscitated me some. Sadly I rode the train to New York City, caught a bus to St. Louis, met Doug Medley at Lambert Field Airport (giving him a loud cattle call), and then headed west and north in his newly purchased, ancient Cadillac.

I would see Ann only one time thereafter, in New York, where we had lunch. Over the years, though, we've kept in contact by phone, now and again, and more recently by e-mail. She has always been a presence in my life because she gave my mountains and valleys an added lift that far transcended the trappings of a stereotypical summer love. She painted those vistas in hues that last to this day, nearly fifty years later. Yet when I go among my mountains I feel no nostalgia or longing. Ann is a presence for me without haunting.

Heading west with Doug, somewhere on those same plains I'd crossed on the train the year before, we began to spot the mountains. My damaged outer layers began to peel away. I was still too wounded to realize the full import of the situation, but later I would come to know that no matter how grim the twists of life might be, I could always escape to Glacier to restore and renew my energy.

We knew where we would be working that summer before we got to the park. I would be with Bruce at Many Glacier again on the trail crew. Doug would be a seasonal ranger at Izaak Walton at the far southern end of the park. We didn't like being separated, but he would come over the pass often to visit us—and the girls. By that year most of the female employees had been moved to former guest cabins that had seen better times. My crew bunked in the same cabin we'd used in 1961. I ached for Annie, but otherwise we took up where we'd left off. I didn't have a steady, didn't want one, but we had "powwows" and hikes. We were rid of the despised Rich Nelson. Bruce was the trail leader. And Larry Zilgit was back from North Dakota. If Bruce, Doug, and I were hellions, Zilgit was our alarm clock and conscience. Every morning we were rudely awakened by his clock radio with the latest farm market report. Larry followed pork bellies like he religiously followed the home run battle of 1961 between Mickey Mantle and Roger Maris—the latter a fellow North Dakotan. He also religiously went to Saturday or Sunday Mass in Babb. He was one of the truly good guys, and I miss him to this day. I hope the pork bellies paid off, that he still keeps score, and that God watches over him. Geoff Feiss from Washington, DC joined us, as did a true mountain man we called "Custer," who had red hair and a flowing mustache, and was our new area leader. While we went off to drink in Babb, Custer read from a box of books he had accumulated. He was killed years later in a logging accident.

As we had the previous summer, we lost crew members who didn't like the work, the mountains, or both, and left. We felt little loss: they were usually slackers, and we couldn't understand why anyone who witnessed our perfect place would want to leave. Because they usually left early in the summer, I can barely remember them now.

We went to work in much the same manner and places as the summer before. We cleared the lower trails, and then blasted Grinnell Trail open quickly. By the Fourth of July we had moved out on trails we had missed in 1961, particularly Swiftcurrent Pass and Iceberg Lake. And now we did so with a higher purpose, we thought. Since late summer of 1961, the construction of the Berlin Wall had created new international tensions. President Kennedy had gone on television about this shortly before we left the park in August 1961. The Cold War was heating up, with confrontation possible at any moment, and we decided to back the president by turning ourselves into a self-trained unit of fast-moving commandos. We started to run everywhere, in full gear, and we were delighted when the new district ranger for rescue training, Bob Frauson, showed us how to belay and rappel. We would need this training to breach the Berlin Wall—or so we pictured.

On one trip to the upper end of the Swiftcurrent valley we had orders to demolish an old CCC camp. This was by then only a few rotting, silent structures, but to us with our vivid imaginations it was a "commie" encampment, so we fanned out in silence as we approached. Then, on signal, I charged the derelict outhouse. Protected by withering support fire, I kicked in the door, only to be confronted and wounded by the largest porcupine I'd ever seen (one of the few I'd seen). When it became apparent what had happened, the other crack commandos rolled on the ground. Because I'd stepped on the critter, I had to pull out a few quills. (Contrary to popular belief they are not able to shoot them at predators—or combat commandos). We removed the two or three remaining structures and then ran all the way back to base camp—some five miles.

To those critics who rant about the inability of government to do anything constructive, I say take a look at the Civilian Conservation Corps. The CCC was one of the most meaningful programs of Franklin Roosevelt's New Deal. To a great degree it was FDR's own idea. The program put several hundred thousand young men to honest, hard work. It gave them a modest paycheck of $30 per month, of which $25 was typically sent home to needy families. It provided the United States with a workforce dedicated to building or rebuilding national, state, and local parks, as well as engaging in other conservation projects. So in turn, it gave citizens splendid places to recreate. Overlying that, the CCC gave most of those boys and their families a sense of hope and pride in their country and themselves. As an unexpected consequence, the program also gave the nation near-ready troops when the United States entered World War II.

In 1962, whatever the trail, whatever the task, the wholeness and holiness of Glacier remained the same for me as the summer before. I never tired of its scenery, the hiking, or the work. It was fulfilling, sometimes sad (in the case of deaths), and sometimes dangerous (as with the 1962 Kintla fire). But in all cases and circumstances it was ultimately exhilarating and healing. Ann Hummel did not fade away for me—she became part of the healing patina, still present somehow. As during the previous summer, those layers of freedom I felt and that sense of wonderful place made it impossible for me not to dance with joy, spiritually and physically. And with both came healing. Spiritually I could get by with a soul-shimmy and a loud "Thank you, Jesus!" But physically, at some point, solitary toe tapping was not enough—dancing required a partner.

I had come to know a young woman named JoAnn Laudon the summer before. She was part of the Minnesota contingency—vivacious, lively, laughing inside and out—and she could dance. She had been hurt too, and Roger Giddings, with whom she'd gone in 1961, was not there. In the summer of 1962 she would work as a hostess in the Swiftcurrent Café. I liked the hot roast beef sandwich and she'd slip me a piece of pie. The beat went on, and one night we started dancing. I'm sure that our first few steps were tentative, but soon enough we both sensed we'd found a source of sensible sensuality. As we grew closer, Ann grew further away. It was working for JoAnn too: by midsummer Roger was a past fancy.

Since Swiftcurrent complex employees had been moved to the older cabins, we didn't have to sneak into an entire dorm and risk disturbing fifty or so young women and several hair-curler-wearing dorm matrons. Now the task was easier. With Doug on the other side of the park, a bored ranger and poker master, we evolved into a team of four that summer—George and JoAnn and Bruce and Nancy. Nancy was another Minnesota beauty. When not confined to the area because of work schedules, we'd all cram into Bruce's small convertible, named Florence, and head to Canada, West Glacier, or to Missoula to visit Bruce's dad who was teaching summer school at the University of Montana. The latter was at least 150 miles south of Many Glacier. How we all fit in that car and avoided permanent back damage is beyond me. I'm guessing that Olympia beer again lubricated the situation.

Sometime in early August, JoAnn's parents came to Glacier on their way to the Seattle World's Fair. They had lived and worked in Seattle during the war and wanted to revisit old friends and haunts. Jim Laudon was as nice a human as I'd met, easygoing, but downtrodden by Harriet who was a towering, hard-nosed, hard-hearted threat to humankind. We welcomed them into our privileged, private world and shared it with them, including a final-night trip to the Babb Bar, where we danced and drank with our Blackfeet friends, who were just back from fighting the Kintla fire.

Back at base we said our good-byes. The Laudons would head off early to Seattle and then see us on their return trip. They went to their trailer and we went to our cabins. Here things get a bit blurry and my recollections differ from those of others. What I recall is that during the night a rainstorm settled over the park, and by morning it was pouring. In one of those quirks of fate, Harriet Laudon commanded Jim to drive by the cabins for one last farewell. In she stormed, only to come eye to eye with Bruce Murphy warmly ensconced on the top bunk. She screamed. He screamed. JoAnn screamed. The couple across the way couldn't believe it. Then I came out from under the bunk, whereupon JoAnn's mother—picture her in gigantic hair rollers—let out a blood-curdling rejoinder that challenged the storm. Confusion and chaos followed. We huddled.

I went outside into the storm. The Laudons were in the car. Mrs. Laudon was crying and Jim was fumbling to light a cigarette. I tried to apologize, but she wouldn't roll the window down. Then Bruce came out of the cabin, in blue jeans but shirtless, and made things worse by exclaiming that he was sure that nothing untoward had taken place that night. That set off another round of caterwauling. Then, mercifully, Jim drove away.

Since the screams had by then drawn a crowd, I told JoAnn that it was better I clear out, so I went back to the bunkhouse. The events of the night and morning weighed heavily. Shortly afterward Bruce and I had to go to West Glacier. There we met up with Doug, drove to Kalispell, saw a movie about the singing von Trapp family—a precursor to *The Sound of Music*, bought an engagement ring, and capped this off with a few bloody beers at Moose's Saloon. Then we drove back to Many Glacier and I proposed to JoAnn. There was dancing in the cabin—and outside it—and this smoothed things considerably when the Laudons returned. As the summer of 1962 came to a close, like in 1961 we stayed as long as possible, till around Labor Day, and then rode the train to Minnesota.

What made such summer adventures possible was getting out of school in late May and not having to return until after Labor Day. That period of more than ninety days not only afforded thousands of young Americans a national park experience that would last a lifetime, it allowed the parks and concessions to be fully staffed during crucial summer vacation months. That has changed for the worse. Today schools go till June and commence again in mid-August, too short a time for employers and employees. Now in many park venues one sees concession employees from foreign countries—particularly eastern Europe—not that this in and of itself is not a bad thing. It establishes the park concept for young people of other countries on stages of our most inspiring landscapes. And not all young adult citizens could take advantage of a national park, even with extended summers. That was not realistic even at the height of hiring during CCC days.

What is practical and realistic is to employ enough young Americans to share the experience and spread the gospel of conservation to their peers and beyond. Most who have worked on trail crews are now living preachers of the benefits and blessings of the natural world. Tourists may be members of the congregation, but those who have worked in the parks will most likely be able to deeply understand the importance of America's natural gifts and so become conservation advocates and leaders. Maybe colleges ought to drop days from Christmas and spring break holidays so that summer vacation can be lengthened. I can think of no better education than time spent experiencing firsthand "our ideal idea," national and state parks.

After leaving Glacier Park in September 1962, I spent a few days getting to know JoAnn's family and friends in Minnesota, and then took the Rock Island back south to Austin. There I got off the train and stepped into the next stage of my life, one that would not allow me to return to Glacier for six years, though it was never far from my thoughts or heart. In June 1963 JoAnn and I were married in Kasson, Minnesota. A part of me has always thought we should have gone back to the park.

Throughout the years, especially in down times and before sleep, the music of Glacier National Park has continued to sing to me, molding a dedicated conservationist and park devotee. The national park is an original concept, noble and democratic: setting aside large and small tracts of treasure land for the enjoyment of citizens and international guests. Over the years those guests have gone home and championed national and regional parks in their countries. "America's Best Idea" is our most enduring export and lasting legacy.

Starting college at the Texas A&M summer school at Junction, Texas, in the broiling heat of 1958 (I am on the left in front).

Family friend Al Mullennix and I stop at a Texas state park, 1961.

My cousin Judd Holt (left) visits me in Glacier National Park in 1961. We hiked to the top of Grinnell Trail in a snowstorm.

A friend visits me at Poia Lake in Glacier National Park, 1961.

Unknown mate (left) and I in Glacier Park, working the Ptarmigan Tunnel Trail in 1961.

Left to right: I take a break from dynamite-clearing Grinnell Trail with Geoffrey Feiss, Bruce Murphy, Larry Zilgitt and unknown mate, Glacier Park, 1962.

"Fire in the hole!"—trail crew blasting on Grinnell Trail, 1962 (I am sitting in the middle, wearing the numbered shirt).

JoAnn Laudon, our friend Nancy, and Doug Medley's old Cadillac, 1962.

PART III

Early
Political Years

CHAPTER 8
Washington, DC

I'd had a longing to go to Washington for years. With the election of
John F. Kennedy and Lyndon B. Johnson, though, this turned to near-obsession. Much
has been written about how President Kennedy attracted the nation's youth to public
service. It was true. I had to go to serve my country—to be a part of the New Frontier. I
had wanted to leave right after the election of 1960, but then I was only a college sophomore with no marketable skills. Had I gone to Washington the next summer I would have
missed Glacier National Park, so it seems that God or fate intervened .

I got my first job at Glacier through the patronage of Jim Wright, and I made it to
Washington through his recommendation to Congressman Homer Thornberry. Wright
had been impressed that his small team of Central Texas volunteers had carried most of
the counties surrounding Austin—Lyndon Johnson's old Tenth District—when he ran
for Johnson's Senate seat in 1961. I had been part of that team.

Thornberry had been elected to the US House of Representatives in 1948, when
Johnson moved to the Senate. In the fall of 1962 it was thought that Thornberry would
have a strong Republican challenge, and Wright recommended me to work the college
crowds and some of the rural counties that I'd worked for him.

The work on campus was easy. There were scores of young people like me who
were enthused by our young president and who wanted to participate in politics. But soon
I discovered that few of them could vote in the Tenth District, if at all. The voting age was
twenty-one in 1962. So I decided to try to organize young professionals in Austin during
the week, and then hit the rural counties on the weekend.

At some point I was asked to go to Bartlett, Texas. My job was to tack up signs and
pass out placards for an upcoming visit by the congressman. Bartlett straddles Williamson
County, which was in Thornberry's district, and Bell County, which wasn't. I didn't know

that then. So I put up signs and posters all over town, which was not an undue burden because in 1962 there wasn't much town to cover.

With a population of probably less than one thousand then, Bartlett was one of those American small towns primarily driven by agriculture. A number of its Main Street buildings were shuttered, as agriculture was fading as regional economic force, but there were good people there and avid supporters. I stopped to visit with people and hand out signs, and I certainly looked up the postmaster. Since the beginning of the republic, the postmaster position has been one of pure political patronage. Members of Congress have recommended appointments, usually after extensive vetting of the wishes of local people, including local political leaders. Some "contests" have been spirited, even pitting friends and families against one another. As some observer once said about the result of the process, a member of Congress invariably wound up with all sorts of disappointed constituents and one ingrate. In fact most postmasters were conscientious public servants, and they were in-touch political resources, particularly in rural communities.

I am sure I spent some time with the Bartlett postmaster. And, as was the case in all the small towns I would come to visit, in a short period I came to know the ebb and flow of local situations, family feuds, views of government policies—favorable and unfavorable, and all sorts of other news and gossip. I would always write up these findings and report them to Thornberry or his staff. Then I kept on moving, out into the countryside. I put up signs along farm-to-market lanes and on leaning rural telephone poles. At the end of the day I went back to Austin.

Several days later a smiling Thornberry came into the office and exclaimed in his booming voice, "George, I think I'll carry a good part of Bell County!" After I allowed that Bell County wasn't in his district, he said, "I know. Bartlett's split down the middle between Bell and Williamson. But when Bob Poage visited the area"—Poage was the congressman whose district included Bell County—"there were Thornberry signs as far as the eye could see!" He laughed, and I joined in, although I was thoroughly embarrassed. Thornberry noticed my chagrin and threw his arm around my shoulder. "As close as this election might be, I may need those extra votes."

I am sure what I and others did helped, but it was the Cuban Missile Crisis that carried the day for Thornberry, as well as other Democrats perceived to be in trouble. As I remember it, Kennedy's bungling of the Bay of Pigs invasion was an issue, but the Cuban Missile Crisis showed how adroit and steely Kennedy could be. It was a tense two weeks. And members of Congress were called back to Washington for briefings. Thornberry left Austin by military jet. Suspense covered the world like black volcanic ash.

I remember several friends gathering at my house to watch Kennedy's speech on the crisis. We held our breath as we listened to the possibility of nuclear confrontation, then nuclear winter.But the Russians backed down, Kennedy's popularity soared, and Thornberry won hands down. Shortly after his election he asked me to go to Washington with him. I was thrilled, but I had reservations. I was going to be married the following June and JoAnn and I had planned to return to our beloved Glacier Park. After that I planned to enter law school in Austin in September. But the urge to serve America, Thornberry, and President Kennedy dominated. JoAnn, her family, my family, and a host of friends agreed, so I made ready to leave after my final exams at the University of Texas. It was mid-January of 1963. JoAnn would join me in June after the wedding.

I flew to Washington, or so I first thought. A dense fog blanketed the city, so we were actually diverted to New Jersey. From there I took a bus to the capital. I was so excited that I couldn't sleep as the bus plunged through the foggy night. We arrived near dawn at the downtown bus station. I gathered up my bags, asked directions to East Capitol Street, where I would stay for a few days, and then began to walk. As I rounded the corner onto Pennsylvania Avenue, the fog broke, sun cracked over the horizon, and there was the Capitol of the United States of America.

In the other direction was the White House. I walked a few blocks, past the Treasury Building. Then I stood at the fence for a good long while, wanting to yell out to President Kennedy that I was in town and reporting for duty. Finally I turned and walked toward the Capitol, watching for important House and Senate members. It was Saturday, though, and I would learn that Congress usually let out on Thursday.

After twenty long blocks, I arrived at the home of Thornberry's chief of staff, Bob Waldron. Even though it was not discussed much, if at all, during those years, I had learned that Bob was homosexual. Because of this I went with some trepidation to stay in his basement apartment for a couple of days. Bob graciously welcomed me, and that kind man helped me throughout my stay in Washington in immeasurable ways. For starters, he helped outfit me. The next evening was the Texas State Society annual Capitol Hill function, and I had a sports jacket but no really good shirt or tie to wear—most of my clothing was being shipped. Bob took me to a store and helped me select the necessary wear, something that would get me through the evening. Late that afternoon we walked to the Longworth Office Building and into Congressman Thornberry's office. Bob took me around and showed me where I'd be working when I was not on duty as a doorman at the House of Representatives.

What exactly a doorman did I could then only guess, but it was a position under the office of doorkeeper. The position of doorkeeper of the US House of Representatives was created in 1789, and the position was chosen by resolution, always along party lines. Over the years many duties besides controlling access to House chambers were added to the position. By the time I got there in 1963, William "Fishbait" Miller had been the doorkeeper for well over a decade and had several hundred employees under his jurisdiction. He oversaw messengers, pages, barbers, and janitors, as well as assistant doorkeepers—doormen like me. These assistants guarded and opened the doors to the House chamber and galleries. To my knowledge all of the positions were governed by patronage. Congress members with seniority could obtain one of these prized positions for one of their constituents. I would not know how prized these were for a time.

Waldron and I then went to the Ways and Means Committee room for the reception. Right off the bat I spied Jim Wright and he introduced me to several members of the Texas delegation and their wives. There was a stir and in walked Vice President Lyndon Johnson and Mrs. Johnson. I made a beeline for them and immediately shook hands with both. In those days security was a great deal looser. Mrs. Johnson warmed up when she found that I was not only a new arrival, but was from Austin and would be working for Thornberry. "Lyndon, George is here to work for Homer." "Come see me soon, George," he said, and turned to greet someone else. I told this to Congressman Thornberry and he replied that Johnson meant it, that I ought to go see him. Johnson had a lifelong habit of getting to know all the young people in Washington from Texas. He was always looking for talent, always encouraging talent. I was beside myself.

I redoubled my efforts and met most of the House members from Texas, as well as my hero, Senator Ralph W. Yarborough, a genuine, old-line, Texas New Dealer. Being from Austin, I knew several of his staff and they welcomed me. I also met Joe McWilliams and his wife, who were old friends of my mother in Texas, and who worked and lived in Washington. They were going to put me up for a week or two, until I found suitable quarters. They were some of the nicest people I would meet in Washington. Throughout my stay they would invite me to their house for dinner, and Joe and I went to several ballgames together.

The next day I went to work at the Capitol. I arrived early to map out my route, but mainly I wanted to familiarize myself with that magnificent structure, inside and out. It was love at first sight, second sight, and thereafter. To this day I never tire of seeing its towering whiteness, turning to pink and gold, rise out of the night or in early-morning light.

For my first several months, I manned a door in the upstairs visitor gallery section. My partner was Gaylord Armstrong of Texas, who was under Congressman Poage's patronage. While State of the Union addresses, foreign dignitary visits, and monumental legislative action drew big crowds, most of the time Gaylord and I would talk politics and sports, or one of us would sit outside to welcome guests and the other could sit inside to watch floor debate. For me this was the best part of the job. For most it might be a dull duty, but it afforded me the opportunity to listen and learn.

Sometimes a parliamentary procedure I didn't understand would come up. I'd make a note of it and when the session was over I'd head for House Parliamentarian Lew Deschler, who had held the job since 1928. Lew knew it all and most of it by heart. He was a big bear of a man, and always had time for inquisitive young House employees. If something tricky or controversial was coming up, Lew would let me know. It was great—Government 101 in action, and I was getting paid for it.

Often the work of Congress is boring, routine, and uneventful, but within a given session huge issues arise in the House and Senate and sometimes fireworks erupt. So locating absent members was an artful necessity and a legal duty of the doorkeeper of the House. I started visiting offices, meeting staffers, and establishing relationships. Not only did I make new acquaintances (some have now been friends for nearly five decades), but I also was able to set up my own little locator network.

Most members of Congress are fine people and hard workers. That was true in 1963. I believe it so today. For the most part in 1963 they had supportive families and friends, were members of churches and civic clubs. They showed up for vote after vote. But some strayed, and it was our job to find them. In thinking of those years I marvel now how fast we could connect—without cell phones or laptops. Phones were all over the place, particularly in the members' cloakrooms. These rooms, off the House chamber, provided space for phone calls, dictation, resting, and horse-trading among the members. As a recognizable insider with proper credentials, I could move in and out of those rooms at will. After using their phones to call members, I visited and listened in on conversations. Members of Congress never seemed to care if I was present. If they needed to talk in private, there were all sorts of small hideaways. Members also came up and would tell me that they were going back to the office or over to the Senate, wherever they needed to be, with the assurance that I'd call them back—or someone would—for the next roll call vote.

It wasn't just Gaylord Armstrong and George Bristol standing at the ready. There were many other doormen—Democratic and Republican. The Speaker's office had staff and there were a series of bells. By the number of bells sounding and lights blinking, a member of Congress could tell when a roll call vote was coming up and when the Congress was in session or out. Most were conscientious and showed up without prodding.

On big-issue days when Congress was in session, I'd read the *Washington Post* thoroughly to glean as much information as possible in order to be informed about the members, particularly the chairmen of committees. That way I'd know who deserved a bit more attention when it came to finding members in a hurry, particularly if a close vote loomed.

I hadn't been working long when one evening the phone rang in Thornberry's office. I answered and a familiar voice said, "Is Homer in?" "No, Mr. Vice President, he's left for the day." "Is this the young man up from Austin?" "Yes, sir." "Well, tell Homer his gala tickets are ready. In fact you could come pick them up tonight." "I will," I probably gushed. "Oh, by the way, George, would you like to go?" "I would, sir, but I can't afford it." He chuckled and said that he'd give me one, and then asked whether I needed two. I said that I was engaged and wouldn't have a date. "Well, come on over and have a good time."

When I got the ticket, it was of the $1,000 variety. One thousand dollars! I called on Bob Waldron's kindness again, and he helped me get an inexpensive but nicely fitting blue suit, which I needed for the doorman's job anyway. On the evening of the event I rode a bus out to the old National Armory. There before me were elected officials and celebrities who I had only dreamed of meeting. I took up a position at the main entrance and greeted as many as would shake hands with me, gawking all the while. Hubert Humphrey, Paul Douglas, giants of the Senate and the House. Movie stars, lobbyists, it didn't matter. I wanted to meet them all. Several Texas congressmen and their wives stopped to say hello. Then the lights flashed and I went in to my seat. It wasn't the first tier of tables, but it was up close to the stage. A band played, a preacher intoned, Frank Sinatra sang, others performed, and then, first in a hush and then to thunderous applause, President and Mrs. Kennedy walked to the stage. I whooped and cheered. Then Vice President Johnson and Mrs. Johnson. I wanted it to last all night—all of that grand red, white, and blue night.

When it was over I took up my place at the main door again, watching my heroes and near-heroes leave. Suddenly a lanky man stopped in front of me—it was Senator Estes Kefauver of Tennessee. I stuck out my hand and said something to the effect that I was George Bristol working for Congressman Homer Thornberry. Then the strangest thing happened. He put his hand on my shoulder and said, "Homer, I hope you can support [such and such] in the Rules Committee next week." Thornberry was a member of the powerful House Rules Committee. I blurted out something, but he was gone.

The next morning I called the Thornberry and told him of my strange encounter. He nearly died laughing and asked where I was. I said that I was in the office—it was probably a Sunday—filing cards. He hung up. A few minutes later the phone rang and it was the congressman with Lyndon Johnson also on the line. I was asked to repeat the story. They both howled and then the vice president said, "George we've wondered when Estes would make his move. You've earned the price of that ticket." They hung up and I pondered the event and the phone call. The next day I asked Thornberry about it. He told me that Kefauver was a heavy drinker and had probably been confused. Six months later Kefauver was dead.

At some point, Gaylord and I were moved downstairs to the main Democratic members' door, right off the floor of the House. We had small books with photos of each member and biographies, and we were strongly encouraged to recognize members by sight and know as much as possible about each. I studied that book like the Bible. In a short period of time, I knew them all—Democrats and Republicans.

When the House of Representatives was in session, a steady stream of visitors appeared, regardless of what legislation was being considered: staffers bringing correspondence to sign and pending committee agendas, as well as constituents and school groups coming to be photographed with their legislators, and lobbyists, although not nearly as many as clog the halls of Congress today. The lobbyists would ask me to call representatives off the floor—and, as often as not, the legislators would not come see them. White House staffers were also there to convey messages to key members, and seemingly every day a disheveled old man who had a bag full of materials about a personal grievance, real or perceived. No one ever came out to see him.

Most session days were fairly short. When Congress was not in session, I would work in Thornberry's office. My job was to keep our constituency file-card system up to date along with a delightful young woman, Caryl Yontz. This was before computers, of course. In the back room were rows of three-by-five file drawers. Each card had as much vital material as possible: birthdates, wedding dates, graduation dates, constituents' service notations, and the like. Caryl and I would scan newspapers for information that we could use to update these files. We would read letters and make notes. It was a learning experience second to none. And because it took time to write or type each new entry, I absorbed it all. By the time Thornberry left Washington I knew a great deal about the people of the Tenth District of Texas. For years this was invaluable knowledge.

Sometime in the first months of 1963 I moved in with a couple of other fellows. We had a nice, though crowded, apartment on New Jersey Avenue—just a short distance from the Capitol. It was great fun, because next door Gaylord Armstrong and some other guys had the upstairs apartment and a great bunch of young women from Texas shared the downstairs one. We all became fast friends and hung out together on weekends. We often went to all sorts of parties and receptions. It seemed that somebody or some organization threw a party every night.

I remember that in the spring the Thornberrys decided to throw a late-afternoon, weekend reception honoring the Johnsons. What I didn't know then was that Vice President Johnson was frustrated in his role, a target of many snide comments by members of Kennedy's inner circle, although not by the president. Because of those slights and being ignored, he was drinking heavier than usual. I'm sure the Thornberrys wanted to boost his spirits and that of Lady Bird.

It was a pleasant evening, with nice weather, and the crowd was enormous. All members of the Texas delegation and their wives and children came, as did key senators and cabinet officials. None was more evident than Senator Everett Dirksen, the Republican Minority Leader from Illinois. Dirksen was a person who quickly captivated a gathering with his oratorical flamboyancy—even in a stage whisper. He was rightly nicknamed The Wizard of Ooze.

Dirksen worked the crowd and praised the Thornberrys for the beauty of their garden, particularly the blooming marigolds (his favorite) that he duly noted with humor had just been planted, he presumed (rightly) in his honor. With a mix of seriousness and humor, Dirksen championed the marigold as the national flower.

At the appointed time, the Johnsons arrived. They flowed out into the crowd, greeting one and all. And one and all included Democrats and Republicans. What was immediately apparent to me—a dyed-in-the-wool Texas Democrat with very little contact with any Republicans—was that they were friends. Members of Congress, families, and cabinet members did more than exchange pleasantries. They truly visited with one another. They liked each other.

I will never forget breaking out of a crowd, and seeing Johnson and Dirksen seated on a bench, in deep exchange over some matter, genuinely enjoying each other's company. I wish that scene could have been taped and replayed in every government class. Here were two highly partisan men (when politics were in order) who knew one another with respect and mutual admiration. Furthermore, their wives and families knew each other. They were friends. That did not mean that they did not fight hard for what they believed in, but they did so with the full understanding that their opponents were just as patriotic. We have lost too much of that camaraderie. Somehow we gave over to the demonizing politics of Lee Atwater and Karl Rove. It is the primary cause of the gridlock that dominates Congress today.

There was no more committed Republican than Everett Dirksen, but he was one who fully understood that patriotism, family values, and honor were not the exclusive possession of his party. He would prove that time and again, particularly in the arena of civil rights. And the issue of civil rights was fomenting through that spring into the summer of 1963.

Washington is a town anchored in rumor and gossip. It is the coin of the realm. The rumor leading up to the March on Washington and the appearance of Dr. Martin Luther King Jr. drove everyone—from senators to lowly staffers—to distraction. The hordes would take over the Capitol. The "niggers" would despoil "our" women. There would be blood in the street! Add to these sentiments a summer heat and mugginess that can be almost insufferable in Washington, and quite a stew was cooking as August 28 approached.

In fact the March for Jobs and Freedom was being planned by less radical members of the civil rights movement. A. Philip Randolph, Bayard Rustin, Roy Wilkins, and Martin Luther King Jr. all believed in nonviolence and peaceful demonstration. That is as American as apple pie, a much-championed concept, but it often falls apart into blind rumor and denunciation, depending on the crowd gathering.

The march took place when Congress was in August recess. At some point I decided to walk down from the Capitol to the Lincoln Memorial. I didn't ask anyone to go with me. I didn't know how my friends felt about civil rights. To call the heat oppressive is inadequate. It was blistering, suffocating. The crowds were peaceful and attentive, though. Somehow the Bristol luck prevailed. I arrived thirty to forty minutes before King's speech and only listened to a couple of other speakers and an entertainer or two first. Some folks had been there all day, and now some stood in the reflecting pool to beat the heat. This was long before bottled water and I doubt whether many had drinking water at hand.

Police were everywhere. Helicopters flew overhead. A crowd estimated at between two hundred thousand and three hundred thousand people milled, stood, and sat in the heat. But the possibility of something sparking an explosion among that crowd evaporated when Martin Luther King began to speak. I had known Dr. King more by his reputation of courageous acts than the sound of his voice, but it did not take much time into his speech that day for me to recognize I was in the presence of greatness and genius. It was apparent that the crowd felt the same. I can't say that one could have heard a pin drop. That would have been impossible with a crowd of that magnitude, but that amplified voice rolled over us like a pronouncement from God. "Inspired" is an overworked word, but Martin Luther King's speech was that. It turned a gathering for jobs and freedom, as important as those were for blacks, into a clarion call for equality. It hit home across America. It awakened and aroused the national conscience. It gave backbone to President Kennedy who had dragged his feet on civil rights. Ultimately, following the tragedy of the Kennedy's assassination a few months later, it gave Lyndon Johnson the cover and the courage to break with his own history and to do right as no president had ever done before for the civil rights cause.

That fall was filled with preparations for Homer Thornberry's departure from Congress. President Kennedy had nominated him to the federal bench and now he spent a great deal of time studying the law and federal procedures. Congress was stalemated on much of Kennedy's domestic legislation. I attended hearings. I watched the comings and goings out of the various committees. We also kept an eye on the special election to take Thornberry's place. There was deep rumbling and dissatisfaction with President Kennedy in Texas. Despite King, the idea of equal civil rights for all was not popular. Many in the Tenth District were not pleased with the treatment Vice President Johnson was getting from Bobby Kennedy and other administration officials. There were even whispers that he would not be asked to be on the ticket in 1964.

At some point wiser heads prevailed and a political damage-control trip to Texas was put in motion. This took place in late November. I don't recall why, but I was at the Department of Labor at the time, running some errand for Congressman Thornberry who was in Texas with President Kennedy. It was November 22, 1963, shortly after noon. When I stepped out of the building, I sensed something was wrong, and then heard the news. In one respect the scene looked like those statues one sees in various urban settings of lifelike people sitting on park benches, playing with children, reading a newspaper. All those before me were frozen, leaning toward cars with open windows, turned to others, while a cab driver in a silent scream that finally exploded told the tale: "President Kennedy's been shot!"

Then they all came to life. People were yelling, car horns blared. I ran for a cab and demanded to be taken to the Capitol. We shot off down Pennsylvania Avenue. The driver turned up the radio. The news was still preliminary. President Kennedy and Governor John Connally had been shot—perhaps others. There was chaos over the airwaves, reporters' voices drowned out by sirens and conflicting voices.

At the Capitol I raced toward Thornberry's office. Everything was becoming a blur. I don't remember stopping or speaking to a single person. I had to get to the office.

This was long before cell phones and handheld computers. I had no news about others in the motorcade. Nothing about the congressman. And what had happened to Lyndon Johnson? On the jammed elevator someone said that he was still alive. Who was still alive?

I had just walked into the office when the news—probably from Walter Cronkite—rang out and slammed into all of us. Bob Waldron began to cry. Then phones were ringing off their cradles. I talked to a county judge in Texas, telling him that I knew only that President John Kennedy was dead. At some point Congressman Thornberry got through, saying that he was heading to the airport and would fly back with soon-to-be-president Johnson and that we should stand by to pick him up.

For the next several hours, darkness—naturally and spiritually—descended. We listened as broadcaster after broadcaster tried to make sense out of the tragedy and fit the pieces together. Sometime in all that misery I remembered to call JoAnn. She had a job downtown by now and was ready to leave work. I told her to come to the Capitol. I didn't know the situation, but I wanted her safely inside and off the streets and in the now heavily guarded Capitol office building. Next I called the doorkeeper's office. They took my name and number, saying that we would be expected to be on duty as part of the funeral ceremonies.

I had often read and heard of a pall spreading over a place, but until that day, until that evening, I had never witnessed one—and I may never again. Everything had changed. All the oxygen of a hopeful era had been sucked out. Thick fog and clouds had rolled in. Thanksgiving Day was forgotten. Televisions were left on for most of the day, and well into the night. From every house the sad blue light of news broadcasts blinked into the November darkness.

Each passing hour led to new revelations. Oswald was arrested and held. Sunday dawned and we joined millions across the nation in memorial church services. Oswald was transferred. In the middle of Psalms 23, Jack Ruby gunned down Oswald. It was all almost too much to bear, but there was much more to witness and bear.

That Sunday the Kennedy funeral procession moved up Pennsylvania Avenue to the Capitol where the president would lie in state. I had to report for duty as the doormen would secure and channel access to the Capitol Rotunda where Kennedy lay. By prearranged protocol, members of Congress and their immediate families were given an entrance to the Rotunda to view the casket. For all of its great symbolism of national sorrow, it was a magnificent setting. Even though hundreds of thousands filed through all evening and into the next day, it was almost silent. Only the clicking of heels and rifle butts sounded as the military guard changed watch. Everything, everyone, was cast in muted shadows. A nation held its breath when Mrs. Kennedy entered along with her family. Bobby Kennedy was zombie-like, Teddy and others not much better. At the height of that sadly beautiful moment, a senator, Vance Hartke of Indiana, tried to sneak, then bully, his way in, with several friends in tow. The rules were clear and at that poignant moment all the more necessary. Others and I turned him away.

Monday, November 26, came none too soon for me. I was tired and drained. I was spiritually exhausted. I knew that we had all had lost someone special: more than a man, more than a president—a tangible personification of common purpose fortified with a deep sense of national pride and public service. In one sense it didn't matter whether President Kennedy had a meaningful legislative scorecard. With his call to public service through the Peace Corps and other programs, he signaled to the world the abiding purpose of the American experience: giving meaning to one's personal and national life by reaching out to lift others up. That image of America, in many different forms, circled the globe and attached to millions. It served us well for a long time.

At some point on Monday the great doors of the Capitol opened. Crowds stood aside as the casket was lowered down the stairs. Then the doors shut. The sky was late-autumn gray. I boarded a congressional bus, sitting, by chance, next to Jim Wright. He told me of the trip to Fort Worth and how well the president and Mrs. Kennedy had been received there. We went ahead of the funeral procession toward Arlington Cemetery. Little would I know how much that spot at the bottom of the Custis Mansion lawn would come to mean to me. I have since, over the years, taken family and friends there, and I have gone alone. My memories are all black and white and gun-metal gray.

Upon arriving I had to stand at the perimeter of the crowd. Again, by protocol design, areas were set aside for family, visiting heads of state and diplomats, members of Congress, and their friends and families—the rest of us. But, as it turned out, my little niche was a perfect observation point. I could see down to the road where the funeral party arrived and by turning I could see the burial site where the eternal flame was already flickering. I watched family and dignitaries take position. Soldiers, sailors, and marines took their assigned posts. Someone prayed. Perhaps a band played. From there it is a blur. Either just before, during, or immediately after the twenty-one gun salute and taps, jets in formation roared overhead in the gray sky. I broke down and cried—finally. It all boiled to the surface. I might have felt some embarrassment at that public display of emotion, but everyone else was weeping, so I just let it all out.

Jim Wright came up and put his arm around my shoulder. We got on the bus and in the gathering twilight rode back to the Capitol. Then I walked home in the dark. It would remain dark for a great while, but a ray of sunlight was on its way in the form of J. J. "Jake" Pickle.

CHAPTER 9

Jake

I never met a person more suited to be a member of Congress than Jake Pickle. I didn't realize that until after his win in a special election on December 21, 1963. I knew about Jake, but because he had such a reputation as being a mainstay of the conservative Democrats I was prepared not to like him.

Under the congressional patronage system that existed at the time, coveted positions were controlled by seniority. Without fanfare those jobs passed within a state delegation to the next-longest-serving member. With Thornberry's move to the federal judgeship, I fell into and then immediately out of Congressman Clark Thompson's jurisdiction. Thompson had served the Galveston area for many years. His wife was the daughter of banker William Lewis Moody Jr.—very wealthy and high on everyone's social calendar. Thompson was sixty-seven then, altogether a loyal but conservative Democrat with no bridges to build or dreams to fulfill. He certainly had no need for a young, full-of-piss-and-vinegar part-time worker. So by arrangement I held the doorman's job under Thompson's patronage, but would work for Jake Pickle because he had plans and he was President Johnson's congressman, which would add prestige but also responsibilities. As a newly elected junior member he would receive minimum allocations for salary, office space, and office location, so a free helping hand was an unexpected bonus for him. For me it would be the break of a lifetime. The problem was that no one mentioned the split arrangement to Jake.

As it turned out, we'd meet sooner than expected. President Johnson's first crucial congressional vote was a Russian wheat deal, which would allow the sale of American wheat to the communist Soviet Union. This was important to grain farmers, but despised by ultra-conservatives. For reasons unimportant here, the deal began to fall apart in the Senate after the House had approved it and all but adjourned for the Christmas holidays of 1963. I had sensed that at that Christmas—more than most—members of Congress and their staffs needed to leave town following the trauma of President Kennedy's assassination. Many of the members had served with Kennedy in the House. Regardless of political persuasion, they were visibly moved and deeply saddened. Like most humans, they longed for the protective arms of home, and at the appropriate moment they fled the capital.

After the Senate changed the bill, the House members needed to be rounded up and brought back. Fortunately someone remembered that Jake Pickle had been duly elected and was eligible to be sworn in as a voting member, and the president needed every vote. So Jake and his wife, Beryl, hurriedly flew to Washington—dropping their Christmas plans in order to support their president.

As a House doorman I was empowered to find and bring House members back to the Capitol, by force if necessary. During that crucial debate on the Russian wheat deal, it almost became necessary. The battle raged back and forth between the House and Senate. At some point, I'm guessing December 22 or 23, it appeared as if a deal had been struck, and representatives again left for the holidays. I had to use congressional privilege to keep canceling and rescheduling a flight to Minnesota, because JoAnn and I were going to her parents' for Christmas. Then the Senate reneged on the deal again.

We had to call airlines and airports to collar members of Congress and ask them to return again. We had to alert state highway patrol offices to be on the lookout for certain cars with certain license plates. One congressman from the South, when stopped, demanded to know by what authority was he being commanded to return to Washington. "By the Commander-in-Chief of the United States of America!," the officer roared. The congressman turned back.

Some members had to be sought in restaurants and bars, and others in places requiring even more discretion. But one was open in his indiscretions. He simply told us he'd be in his car, parked in front of the Capitol, and that I should go out and bang on the trunk. A little later he'd come, vote, and then hurry back out. To my knowledge he never missed a vote.

This particular vote was going to be very close, and that is when Jake Pickle stepped into my life—and he never stepped out until the day he died in 2005. Before returning to Austin he and his wife stopped by the new office to check out his space and help him get his bearings. I was the only one there when Jake came in. I reintroduced myself—I'd met him before—and he asked what I was doing there. "I work for you!" "You do?" he retorted. "How come?" I started to tell him but the phone rang and he had to leave. He put his hand on my shoulder and wished me a merry Christmas. "I look forward to working with you," he said. Jake Pickle had accepted me and forgot to ask, then and later, how I had come to be on his staff.

After the first of the year, January 1, 1964, we got to work—oh, how we worked. Somehow Jake came to trust me right off the bat and my office was behind a partition in his personal office. If something happened to be super-sensitive—a phone call or a visit—he'd ask me to step out, but not often. So from my nearly invisible post, I watched a great congressman bloom.

First, Jake Pickle liked people and absolutely loved being a member of Congress. Just as becoming president allowed Lyndon Johnson to be his own man, becoming a congressman gave Jake Pickle a new lease on life. That first vote was a case in point. Jake was hastily sworn in and he voted. As one of the Democratic doormen, I had a perfect vantage point. There was Jake working the floor, meeting and greeting everyone he could—Democrat and Republican. Every once in a while he'd come over and say, "George, can you point out—?" And he'd name a member of Congress. As doorman I knew where certain legislators generally sat or stood, and I would point them out.

I soon found that Jake was a workhorse. He was assigned to the Interstate and Foreign Commerce Committee, and that winter and spring there was a blizzard of Johnson legislation moving, a great deal of it coming through that committee. So I would write up little briefing papers and go talk to staff of other members. By then I knew a great number of staff and from time to time they would tip me off about this or that. Often I'd have to write my briefings after Congress adjourned for the day, which would sometimes be late. There would be Jake, plowing over the bills, phone calls, and memos.

"George Lambert, did you learn anything today?" We'd chat for a while, partly because he genuinely wanted to know what was going on and partly because he was living alone in a small apartment. Having been recently married, the Pickles had two houses in Austin. That didn't allow much financial leeway for Jake's housing in Washington. So he worked late at the office and we visited often.

In short order Jake became more than a political figure. For me he became a human, a humane being with friends and family, likes and dislikes, a high sense of humor, and a higher sense of duty. I also began to see that he was not a go-along-to-get-along political hack nor was he simply "Lyndon's boy Jake," as he was tagged during the election. He plowed through bill after bill. He discussed and cussed their merits. He sought advice from national experts and Main Street merchants. From the very beginning he brought home the bacon. Today some call it "pork" or "earmarks." But at the time it was an honorable task to fight for projects for one's district among the various appropriations.

Waste? Without doubt, but not as much as denounced today and far less than one defense system lobbied into existence by corporations with their cadre of former (and sometimes present) military officials which after years of cost overruns is often replaced by another "defense" boondoggle. President Dwight Eisenhower's speech warning of the abuses and dangers of the military-industrial complex ought to be publicly read at the beginning of each congressional session. The primary reason for "earmarks" is that neither the sitting administration nor appropriators will cover every project—good, bad, or indifferent in their deliberations. Thus it falls to the individual representative, senator, or sometimes entire state delegations to champion a particular project.

Jake spent hours perfecting his negotiating skills which as a freshman was essential. He was aided by his good nature, willingness to compromise, committee assignment, and the fact that he was the member of Congress representing the president's home district.

Of all the work flowing through of Congress, its committees, and the Johnson White House, nothing was more vexing and monumental than impending civil rights legislation. Some would later say that Jake voted for the civil rights bill because the president expected him to, and that was partly true, but not entirely. Jake Pickle struggled with many sections of the bill. He bounced ideas off constituents. We had a number of Deep South counties in the eastern part of the district. It was tough out there. For the longest time I thought he'd vote against it. The staff was split. There were political opposition rumblings. Jake worked and pondered. But about a month out, I overheard something telling from my little cubbyhole.

A group of businessmen from Alabama who were in the pickle business came into the office. Jake did not ask me to leave, and I concentrated on my task at hand. At some point I began to listen, though, because one of them had mentioned Governor George Wallace. It was not a threat, but a less-than-subtle way of saying that they were connected to Wallace. Then they began to tell Jake that in the bill they were asking him to support all they were looking for was a level playing field and a green light to be able to compete fairly. After several other metaphors, Jake stopped them.

"Boys, if you'll back the civil rights bill and persuade Governor Wallace to do so, I'll back your bill."

There was dead silence, then loud groans. "Congressman, how can you compare the two?"

"Because that is all the Negro is shooting for. A level playing field and a green light. Seems fair to me." The Alabama representatives of the pickle industry beat a civil, but fast retreat. I think they thought their industry's namesake, a potential champion, had lost his mind.

Based on what I'd overheard a good month before the vote, I thought I knew how my congressman would vote. But I wasn't positive. I kept my mouth shut as Jake was still struggling—and working to pass some amendments to make the bill more palatable. What I was learning about Jake Pickle was that he had a deep sense of fair play, that he had fought a war for democracy for all, and that he had a daddy who didn't mind telling him where he stood and where Jake should stand—straight and strong for LBJ. On more than one occasion I heard Jake say, "Yes, Pop. You're right, Pop."

At some point in the spring or early summer of 1964, there was Pop. Jake's father, J. B. Pickle, without much warning, had hitched a ride with the county sheriff or police chief of Big Spring, Texas, and was coming to see his boy, "Jake, you Rascal." At least that's what Jake often told folks was his name for the first five or six years of his life.

J. B. Pickle showed up when Jake had only the small apartment and a boatload of work. Jake rubbed his jowls and thumped his teeth—two memorable ticks. What was he going to do with Pop? At some point I volunteered to take Pop around the Capitol. As a doorman I knew every inch of it, and as a lover of history I knew every painting and sculpture and the story behind each. Little did I know what a remarkable audience I would have. Pop was from Deep West Texas, in his late seventies or early eighties, and had not traveled all that much. I probably thought I could give him a quick tour and then park him in the House Gallery. My mistake.

We stopped at every statue, and he identified and gave me a brief history about each.

At some point we reached the stairs that lead up to the magnificent painting of the Battle of Lake Erie. Pop stopped in front of a crowd of tourists and without hesitation began to recite the poem by Philip Freneau. "To clear the lake of Perry's fleet / And make his flag his winding sheet—" On and on he went, through each stanza to the end. The crowd was transfixed, and then broke into applause. Pop and I went on our way. He laughed to himself.

From time to time we met a senator or House member he recognized. With great courtesy he would introduce himself, saying that he was Jarrell's father. Jarrell is what he called Jake by then. Then he would tell them to support Lyndon Johnson and off we'd go. We had lunch in the House cafeteria and I asked him if he was tired. "Yes," he allowed, but he needed to see Senator Ralph Yarborough. That was fine with me. I was a Yarborough man, but the senator and Jake had not seen eye to eye on matters in Texas. Yarborough was the leader of the liberal wing and Jake had fought him along the way. But if Pop wanted to see the senator, then he would.

As we walked over to the Senate, Pop told me that he knew that Jake and the senator didn't get along, but that they needed to in order to support LBJ. Into Yarborough's office we went. No, we didn't have an appointment, but he was J. B. Pickle of Big Spring, and father of Jake. Eyes were raised. Pretty soon the senator came out and grandly and genuinely welcomed Pop.

Pop got right down to business. "Now, Senator, you've got to get together with Jake. You two are grown men and need to get behind LBJ." The senator readily agreed, citing his support for civil rights legislation. That settled, Pop was off to take a nap back at the apartment.

I told Jake all that had transpired. He lovingly chuckled, "That Pop's a pistol."

A couple of days later, after tours of Washington monuments, Jake and Pop went to see Pop's hero—President Johnson—for lunch. Apparently the president was just as taken with this straight-shooting, un-bashful, and unabashed supporter, to the point that he said that while he had to tend to business, they would visit again. Sure enough, that night the president called and asked Pop if he wanted to fly to New York the next day to open the World's Fair. Pop allowed that he would, but wondered out loud if Jarrell could come along.

The President roared with laughter and assured Pop that that would be fine. J. B. Pickle did not know that one did not unilaterally expand the president's guest list. The next day the Pickles joined the president of the United States. On the trip, Pop absolutely captivated the press corps. One journalist asked his observations. He said (and I paraphrase), "It is something for a clodhopper like me to take my first ride on a plane, and have it be with a president." A follow-up question asked him how did felt now that he had flown. "Well, a fellow could do worse than go down on Air Force One with the president." That afternoon they flew back to Washington. Pop went to take a nap and Jake came to the office. We talked about the day. I saw how pleased and proud Jake was of his beloved father.

Within a day or two Pop left Washington. I only saw him one more time when he came to Austin in the fall to see Jake and campaign for LBJ. Shortly after he got there, Jake came into the office. "George, Pop wants to campaign for the president and he really needs to get a new hat. I think he's had the same hat since the Depression. But Pop is cheap and he won't buy a hat at today's prices. So call Joseph's Men's Wear and tell them to sell Pop whatever hat he wants at his price—probably five dollars. Then tell Mr. Joseph I'll make up the difference."

Off they went. I made the call. Later in the day Jake came back to the office. I asked if they got the hat? "Got the hat? Hell, we got two $100 hats. Pop went in and tried several on, settling on the most expensive one in the store. Just like President Johnson's. Then he asked Phillip Joseph what the cost was. Phillip told him five dollars. Pop thought about it. Took his old beat-up wallet out and said, "In that case I'll take two!"

I often think of that kind, humorous, and well-educated man who had raised, with his wife, children who would all contribute to their country.

After Pop left Washington, I still had a lot to do, not the least of which was to find a place to live in Austin. JoAnn was six months pregnant, due in September. We had decided to go to Austin where I would enter law school and work for Jake in the district office. I went to Jake and said that I needed a week off. Up to that point he still hadn't asked me how I drew my pay. He'd been too busy and it never came up. But take a week off at that busy time? "Oh my, George Lambert, that would be tough. We've got a lot to do." I responded that I appreciated that, but Congressman Thompson and Fishbait Miller had approved. "Why Clark?," Jake asked. "Well, sir, he pays me to work for you." I explained the situation. Jake smiled and said, "Well, then take two weeks!" I told him I only needed a week and would hurry back.

I knew there was a great deal to do and that the final vote on the civil rights bill was being held up by a monumental filibuster in the Senate. Often if things were slow in Jake's office I'd walk over to the Senate to listen to the debate. Great and passionate voices on both sides of the issue would fill the Senate chamber. Nevertheless, there was collegiality and decorum. Opponents on issues often genuinely liked one another. That was because members of Congress in those days stayed in Washington, for the most part, working during the week and visiting one another on the weekend. Not today. They rarely stay in Washington on weekends. So they don't really know one another, much less each other's families. A fellow representative or senator who remains unknown becomes easy to demonize.

The election of 1964 was interesting in a number of respects. First, we thought we'd win, but the civil rights vote was chafing, particularly in the eastern rural counties. Second, the president wanted to carry every county in his old Tenth District, with no exceptions. This was problematic because many of the counties were heavily German, and the German-Americans supported Republicans, certainly at the presidential level, because the Democratic Party, as they saw it, had gone to war against Germany twice. Furthermore, they had been against slavery before, during, and after the Civil War, when most Democrats in Texas and elsewhere in the south were pro-slavery. Finally, the president had pushed all primary opposition to Senator Yarborough aside, and that wasn't sitting well in a number of conservative quarters.

So in order to help in the campaign, I drove back to Texas, pulling a U-Haul, after the August Democratic National Convention. I took the southern route so I could stop off and see Doug Medley who lived in Jackson, Mississippi. We had not seen each other since 1962. The drive was without incident until I got to Mississippi. Not only had the civil rights act finally passed, there had also been tragic murders of three civil rights activist students in Philadelphia, Mississippi, earlier that spring. The tension was palpable and the air was filled with all kinds of hate talk about Johnson, Humphrey, and blacks in general, and "Martin Luther Coon" in particular. At some point, just at the edge of evening, I pulled into a service station to gas up. A salt-and-pepper-haired black gentleman came out to pump the gas and wipe the windows. He came around the trailer and said, "Mister, I seen your Johnson-Humphrey bumper sticker. I took it off. Don't get me wrong. I'm for them, but most of this state is eat alive with fear and hate. So wherever you are going, I'd get there in a hurry." I spent the night with Doug and then drove straight through to Austin.

JoAnn had come earlier, and together we found a nice little upstairs apartment and settled in. On September 15, 1964, James Stanton Bristol made his appearance. We chose the name James because that was JoAnn's father's nickname and it was Jake's given name. Jake agreed to be his godfather. Shortly thereafter we had Jim baptized at the First Methodist Church. His grandparents were there, but Jake made all the arrangements and introduced everybody all around. Until the day he died, Jake took his godfathering seriously. He always asked about Jim and had him over to his house on numerous occasions. But at one point early on, Jake was put to the test. On the night before the 1964 election, Austin had a huge parade for the president. We had worked our butts off to make it right. The night before that, the congressman had given us a final briefing and a thank-you party. There Jake had cautioned my wife that under no circumstances was she to bring the baby downtown the next night—it would be too crowded and dangerous.

As the next day unfolded, election eve, excitement mounted. JoAnn and her friend Kay Shroeder began to talk. They both knew the parade route, and they agreed that they could go down to First Street and see the motorcade, which was supposed to enter around Fourth Street, without going near the crowds. That would have worked, except that unbeknownst to them the route had been changed to bring it up First to Congress. Then the motorcade stopped for a few minutes to allow the bands and such to clear Congress. Suddenly the crowd sensed the presence of the motorcade. They surged toward my wife, who was holding Jimmy. From his car in the procession, Jake saw them and yelled, "My God, it's my boy!" This was a surprise to Lady Bird Johnson who was riding with Jake, who grabbed Jimmy before the cars shot onto Congress—with the president, the First Lady, various dignitaries, and James Stanton Bristol. I knew none of this at the time, as I was at the other end of the avenue, helping guide designated people to a stage.

From my vantage point I could see the approaching motorcade and the crowd, which was all we hoped it would be. My excitement grew as the cars turned toward the Capitol. Then out came President Lyndon Johnson, walking toward me. We shook hands, he moved past, and then out of the blinding television lights came a familiar silhouetted figure, holding someone up. "Here is your boy and he's wet!" Most other elected officials would have chewed me out. But Jake smiled, kissed Jimmy, and went on his way. I hurried home with wet and sleepy Jimmy. It was one of the lasting memories my son and I shared with Jake before his death in 2005. He always loved hearing my story about it—and telling the story himself.

Sometime that fall, Jake sold his house, a house he'd lived in with his first wife before she died in 1952, and where he had raised his daughter, Peggy. It was a clear, crisp day. I went over to help. The movers came and went. The house was bare. Jake's beloved dog, Ike, roamed the front yard, barking and playing. We drank a beer on the front steps. Suddenly Jake said, "George, would you mind if your congressman cried?" Ike ran over. I cried. I liked the man before that but was devoted to him thereafter.

On Election Day we carried the Tenth by huge margins. President Johnson swept the country, the State of Texas and, yes, all the Hill Country German-American counties. Election night was a mob scene of elected officials—every Democrat from the courthouse to the White House won. Worldwide media personalities broadcast live coverage and police protected cars seemingly running in every direction. The streets were jammed with media trucks and paraphernalia. Jake had asked me to drive him, Beryl, and the Thornberrys in the presidential motorcade. He had arranged for a new Lincoln from a local dealer, Roy Butler. Eventually we wound up at the Austin Municipal Auditorium. We drove into the back entrance and ran for the holding room as it was beginning to rain. Inside were the elite of Texas politics: the president and Mrs. Johnson, Governor John Connally and Nellie Connally, members of Congress and other elected officials. President Johnson made and received calls of congratulation. I was listening and watching so intently that I failed to notice a loudspeaker admonition: "Anyone owning a 1965 gray Lincoln, please return to the motorcade area immediately!" I didn't own an old Lincoln, much less a new one, but then it dawned on me, and I raced for the door. There in the pouring rainstorm were six or seven Secret Service agents ready to dump the car on its side. I rushed into the storm, pleading with them to stop. That car was probably priced at two or three times what I made annually. The agents stood down, and one explained that cars in a motorcade needed to be facing out toward the exit with the keys left in them—for instant evacuation. I had done neither. I gave up the keys and went inside looking like a drowned rat.

At some point in the night President Johnson decided that he wanted to go to his ranch, which was approximately fifty miles from Austin. The storm had not let up. Helicopters or planes were out of the question. Cars weren't much better, but when a president wants to go home, the Secret Service finds a way. They decided to narrow the number of cars in the motorcade. The Pickles and Thornberrys went with the president. I gratefully and cautiously drove home to my wife and baby.

For another year I would work for Jake and attend law school. Thereafter, whenever I went to Washington, which was often, I went by his office. At Christmas and other special occasions he always sent me an invitation to join him. He always wanted to know of Jimmy's well-being. To me Jake Pickle was family.

In 1986 I would work for him one last time. In 1984 Ronald Reagan had not only carried Texas, he had even carried "liberal" Travis County, the core of Jake's district. The Republicans were beside themselves, so much so that they ran a poll in 1985, asking, among other things, if interviewees would consider voting for other Republican candidates. Would they consider voting for a Republican congressional candidate? The results were so positive that Carole Keeton Rylander, a longtime Democrat and former Austin mayor, let her ambition get ahead of reality. In the excitement of Reagan's sweep and the results of the poll, Carole changed parties to run against Jake. But the poll had failed to ask if citizens would vote against Jake Pickle. It was a major blunder, but we did not know it at the outset.

As the campaign got underway, we had a great deal to do. I handled campaign finances. Because Jake had rarely had opponents, he had no real list of contributors. He had never taken political action committee (PAC) money. So we had to start from scratch. The hardest job was convincing people that Jake had a race. Who in his or her right mind would run against this beloved icon? Whether or not Carole Rylander had lost her mind, she made much to-do about the vast untold amounts that the Republican Congressional Campaign Committee was going to pump into her campaign. What she and the Republicans had not realized was that they were up against the campaign champ. Not only was Jake a consummate member of Congress, he was a campaign strategist of the first order. Coupled with that, he loved to campaign and loved his constituents. His constituents knew that, and as the campaign progressed they returned that love. At every rally, every forum, every football game, every black church service, people would pour out of the aisle to tell Jake how much he meant to them, how much his help on a matter had meant to a family member. By the end it wasn't a close fight. Even the Republican Congressional Campaign Committee backed off from its much-touted pledge.

The Republican poll had failed to ask if people would vote against Jake. If they had, they could have saved a lot of trouble and money. About three weeks out from Election Day, Ellen Temple and I walked our street for Jake. Ellen was a dear friend and neighbor. While our street was heavily Republican, it came out for Jake—eight or nine to one. Several neighbors commented that Carole Rylander had lost her marbles. She hadn't. It was a temporary mental lapse.

In the closing weeks we ran one of the most positive ads I've witnessed (Jake Pickle never ran a negative ad in his campaigns). It closed with a late-night shot, taken through a lighted window, with Jake working at his desk. "Jake Pickle—Unique—Ours." That said it all, and 71 percent of the voters felt the same way.

Jake would continue to serve with distinction and good humor until 1994. He would help rewrite the social security law to reinvigorate and protect it for years. He would continue to work for his beloved University of Texas. In 1994 he chose not to seek reelection. This was probably great timing as the Republicans took over Congress in 1995. In retirement he remained a positive force of good will and a private citizen extraordinaire, serving on all sorts of civic improvement committees. Jake Pickle was the epitome of the true public servant until his death.

When he passed away in 2005, finally felled by cancer, First Methodist Church in Austin was packed to overflowing. A large group of former colleagues from the House attended, led by Ways and Means Chairman Bill Thomas, a Republican. We met in the aisle before the service. "I had to come, George. We all did." He teared up and then said something telling. "The Speaker and DeLay tried to stop us, but we came anyway!" As it had been a good time to not stand for reelection, maybe it was the right time for Jake Pickle to see his God and his mom and Pop. He would not have understood that sort of petty partisanship.

Sometimes I go out to Jake's graveside. Not to mourn or necessarily to remember, but to simply stand before one of the most solid Americans I've ever known.

CHAPTER 10
In Preparation for Defeat

Although suspect due to its alarming wrapping, of all the gifts Jake Pickle gave me, the most meaningful was his suggestion in 1965 that I go to work for Walter Jenkins.

The year before, in October 1964, Walter Jenkins, who many considered to be the second most powerful man in Washington because of his unrivaled position as President Lyndon Johnson's top aide and confidant, was arrested in the men's room of the YMCA near the White House. He was charged with disorderly conduct for a homosexual act. The scandal exploded across the airwaves and newspapers. Conversation and telephone calls were filled with wild rumors and speculation. People in Austin who knew Walter (and there were many) sat around in stunned silence. Those who didn't know him tittered nose to nose in coffee-shop whispers. The phrases "security risk" and "security breach" cropped up more than once.

Homosexuality was the taboo of taboos. In my protected, Southern Baptist world, it was rarely discussed, thought to be represented by a few very weird people who hung out around bus stations to be preyed upon by town toughs. My only confrontation with it was in 1958, when I worked at my Uncle Jim's company in Houston. As I was saving every nickel I could muster for college, I'd asked him to find the cheapest place possible to rent, which turned out to be the downtown YMCA. Uncle Jim was a straitlaced Presbyterian, so I'm sure he would not have suspected the Young Men's Christian Association to be a hangout for men looking for other men.

Each YMCA room was little more than a monk's cell—a bed and a chest of drawers. There was no air conditioning, just a small fan that only churned the stifling, humid heat. To alleviate the swelter, most occupants slept with their hall doors open, hoping for a bit of a draft.

One night I suddenly awoke to find a man standing in my doorway. He said nothing, but I sensed that he wasn't there to collect the rent. In a bound I swung out of bed and crossed the floor in full lineman-crouching stride, yelling for my friend Miller Zucker as I crashed into the man, trapping him between the door and frame. Miller, who was working in Houston for the summer and living across the hall from me, had been a college football player of size and speed. Into the hall he stumbled and together we manhandled the intruder to the elevator. Reaching the lobby, we demanded that the night manager call the police. He said he would handle the matter. As the man was practically comatose, we retreated to our rooms. Miller told me that he thought the Y might be a home for "queers." With my lack of knowledge I could only imagine what this might mean, but I moved out of the Y—and in with Aunt Aggie, Uncle Rob, and five cousins the next day. Their home was built for three or four, so I slept in a makeshift area in their garage. I soon put the Y incident out of mind.

Jake's suggestion startled me—go to work for Walter Jenkins?—but it shouldn't have. I knew that my friend Bob Waldron was gay, but that had not stopped me from learning from that multitalented man from Arp, Texas, and enjoying his company. He was so open about his sexual orientation that he once announced to a group of male Texas visitors that he'd played running back in college. "Which college?," they asked. "Vassar!," came the reply. It was so outrageous that all laughed and shook their heads nervously. Everything said about "those people" at the time (and "those people" seemed only to be men) was based in ignorance.

After conversations with people I trusted, coupled with my own knowledge of Walter Jenkins's work for LBJ, what I found was a man from Wichita Falls who had served in World War II, was married with six children, and had worked for Johnson during his time as senator, vice president, and then president with honor and devotion, leaving only once to return to Wichita Falls in 1951 to run for Congress. He was crucified in that election, not for being gay but for being a convert to Catholicism. Yes, I found out that he had on another occasion been similarly arrested for disorderly conduct. To me it didn't matter, which was a good, considering that everyone I talked to agreed that working for Jenkins would be a learning experience no government professor could match. But still I was hesitant until I talked with someone who brought it into sharp and deciding focus. One afternoon as I was weighing my decision, the phone rang at home. "George, this is President Johnson and Lady Bird. We very much hope you'll help our friend, Walter. He needs you and you'll learn so much from him. It will mean a great deal to us." I was probably standing at attention by then, trying to figure out if I should salute. I told the president that I valued his opinion and was leaning that way. He said to call him if I had any qualms or questions. Then he thanked me and hung up. The next morning I went to see Walter Jenkins.

What I discovered that day and thereafter was a soft-spoken, gentle man of high intellect and integrity who could talk on a thousand subjects and who seemingly knew everybody in America and a great number of others around the world. For all those years he had worked for Johnson, Walter was the go-to guy and the kind buffer who kept the bombastic Johnson at bay—most of the time. He was a natural mentor and from day one shared much with me, drawing the line at anything that approached confidentiality pertaining to the president. Of particular interest was Walter's proficiency at shorthand. Somewhere in his youth Walter had developed that skill like no other. He kept notes with blinding speed on everything that Johnson said. This was before recordings were used, and certainly before the sophisticated White House taping machines of later years.

Walter told me it helped him keep track of the hundreds of pronouncements, thoughts, and decisions that flowed from Johnson daily. Others would later tell me that those notes were also used by Walter to make Johnson back off after contradictory statements. Apparently Johnson came to appreciate the accuracy of Walter's shorthand.

What I did not find that day or thereafter was any manifestation of Walter's homosexuality. Maybe it was there. Maybe others found it. What I did find was a man struggling to reconnect and recommit to his family who had, starting with his wife, Marjorie, suffered the pain and embarrassment of the incident. The family had been hurt, which might have been deduced from Margie's drinking—which under the circumstances could be understood—and from the edgy and wild behavior of their children. Beth, the oldest daughter, whose love of family and inner strength helped smooth over the rough spots, later in life became her father's bridge partner and they competed internationally. But the dark cloud was always present. The manager of the Austin Club, a popular private watering hole, wrote a letter stating that Walter need not apply for membership, even though he had not contemplated doing so. A comedian at a nightclub spotted him in the audience and shot off a couple of cruel one-liners with Margie and other family present. Time after time some member of the family fell apart. "Dysfunctional" was not in wide usage at the time, but Walter's family was dysfunctional even as its individuals struggled to renew and heal.

Through it all, Walter braved on. Many friends were supportive and encouraging, none more so than Lady Bird Johnson. The president didn't have enough hours in his day to lend support frequently, but Lady Bird seemed to make time to call Walter at the office, and I'm sure she also called the Jenkins home because I know she was equally concerned about Margie and the children. Later she would tell me that she thought Margie was the greatest casualty.

Lady Bird Johnson's personal concern and show of support for the Jenkins family should not be surprising. During the first hours of Walter's tragic misstep, as the president and his wise men, Clark Clifford and Abe Fortas, struggled to gauge the depth of political damage and how best to address the issue, Mrs. Johnson rang up to say that she would be going on national television to express concern and love for Walter. In recently released Johnson presidential tapes, there was much conversation about whether that was the prudent thing to do. After what she thought was sufficient discussion of the matter, she simply reiterated she'd be going on television that evening and said good-bye. Hers was a simple and courageous message. It was well received across the nation, and the incident had no effect on the election of 1964.

Whatever benefit the Republicans might have derived from Walter Jenkins's arrest was thwarted by their own candidate for president, Barry Goldwater. Although some of his staff and other Republicans wanted to make political capital out of the affair, Goldwater made a brief statement of concern and said, in effect, that it would not be an issue. Years later Senator Goldwater and I appeared on the same stage at some national trade group convention. Thrown together in a holding room beforehand, I introduced myself and told him that, even though a passionate Democrat, I held a special place in my heart for him. I told him that I'd worked for Walter and deeply appreciated his remarks on his behalf. Goldwater, the conscience of conservatism, put his hands on my shoulders and said that Walter Jenkins was his friend, had served in his Air Force Reserve unit, had a lovely family, and did not deserve to be kicked when he was down. He would later write in his autobiography, "Winning isn't everything. Some things, like loyalty to friends or lasting principles, are more important." I often think of Goldwater as I watch "Christian" and other leaders publicly revile homosexuality without regard to the personal hurt they cause. I mentally saluted Air Force General Goldwater for stating later that any patriot willing to serve has every right to do so, regardless of sexual orientation.

So finally, with no more trepidation, I went to work with Walter. Our offices were in the Brown Building in Austin—a Johnson property. Walter had a number of consulting clients with whom I began to play a role. Although we discussed the sensitivity of client relationships, I knew instinctively that I could not discuss my work with anyone. I never knew who might try to exploit Walter's close relationship with the Johnsons.

Within a short time I was traveling with him to Washington, New York, and Mexico. It was on-the-job training, and I am sure Walter found little benefit at first. But I studied people and client situations around the clock and at some point someone told

Walter that I was smart and could be trusted. I also soon discovered why Walter needed me. There were many instances where my presence would draw no attention. I could move freely through the halls of Congress and Wall Street without drawing attention from the press or others. Then I would report my findings back to Walter and in the self-imposed isolation of his office or hotel room he'd examine the facts, explain the situation to me, and suggest a solution. From then on, Walter allowed me to deal with matters on my own.

My three years with Walter were filled with varied experiences. I learned of the inner workings of Wall Street, the national politics and governance of Mexico, and the beginnings of an infant industry—cable television. While I played no direct role in the cable business (Walter set up a separate company), I had almost total access to Walter, and I learned through osmosis. Today it is hard to imagine, but in the mid-sixties, great areas of Texas and elsewhere were without a television signal. The towns were too remote and too small to have their own stations. Antennas were the only solution then, but the farther away from the signal, the higher they needed to stick into the sky, seeking (no matter how faint) some signal that would throw an image onto small, black-and-white screens. Driving across flat stretches of Texas you could identify upcoming towns in advance because the antennas would rise above the horizon before the roofs of houses appeared.

Cable systems in those days involved a contract with a sponsoring city, which was usually a thirty-year lease, and a separate contract with either the local telephone or power companies for use of their poles to carry the signal. Usually some agreement would be reached after weeks, perhaps months, of negotiation. In one instance, the fee for pole usage was so onerous that Walter's company decided to install its own poles. Regardless of the problems, it was enlightening to see a new industry grow across Texas.

I thought that Walter and other Texans who saw the need for cable television and acted on it were the beneficiaries of New Deal programs that fostered hydroelectric power and electric co-ops. I know that Lyndon Johnson held up his role in the Lower Colorado River Authority as his grandest achievement. It brought electricity to hundreds of small towns in Texas, in spite of the thwarting efforts by big utility companies that didn't want to shave profits by supplying electricity to rural areas. Big television networks fought the cable concept with the same vigor. They didn't want to supply a signal and they didn't want anyone else to do so either.

Eventually cable pioneers like Walter won out, and television began to come into everyone's life—for good or bad—even in the smallest towns.

As I shared experiences with Walter across the country and in Mexico, the most bizarre and horrifying occurred on August 1, 1966. Early that morning, I had seen JoAnn and Jimmy off. They were walking across the University of Texas campus to a doctor's appointment for Jimmy who was not quite two. At the time, we ran a private boys' dormitory north of campus. The job provided a free apartment and a bit of extra income. After they left I drove downtown to the office. The heat was suffocating, so I hurried inside. Around noon Walter yelled something, and I ran to his office. He had learned that some crazed person was atop the University of Texas Tower and was systematically gunning people down with great accuracy. Former member of Congress Joe Kilgore was in the office and someone suggested we all go on the roof for a look. Since the tower was a mile or so away we thought we'd be safe.

From the roof we watched a young, blond man move this way and that on the tower's top observation deck. Then frequently we saw puffs of gun smoke there. We were so mesmerized by the trauma that we failed to realize that he might be able to hit us, even at that distance. Eventually a police officer came out on the roof and told us to leave immediately, saying that the gunman could easily spot us and hit us with his high-powered, scoped rifle. As we would learn later, Charles Whitman was an expert shot, with full marine training.

On our way down the elevator it finally dawned on me that JoAnn and Jimmy were on Guadalupe Street, right off campus and in the area where the sniper was shooting people. I told Walter that I had to go home, and rushed to my car. Taking a long way home, I headed east away from downtown, then north, avoiding lines of sight to the tower until I arrived at the Wichita Dorm. Panicked, I rushed into the apartment. There was little Jim, eating a snack while his mother listened to the news. JoAnn said, "George, I think some of our boys in the dorm have rifles and are returning fire!" I rushed next door and, sure enough, there on the rooftop were four or five of my charges firing away at the north rim of the tower. And they were doing so with great accuracy. To my knowledge no one was killed from the north side of the tower.

Around 2:00 p.m., Neal Spelce, a newscaster with television station KTBC, announced that two Austin police officers had rushed the tower and gunned down Whitman. As the campus and surrounding area slowly quieted I asked JoAnn where she had been when the massacre began. Fortunately she had passed under the shadow of the Tower on the north side, getting home safely, as Whitman for a long period had fired from the south and west sides. I would later tell my boys that they had probably broken every university rule about possessing and firing guns, but that I was proud of their quick actions and that no reports would be filed. I do not endorse allowing guns on campus. The police have more than enough problems without them, but in this tragic instance it was comforting to know that some of my off-campus tenants from rural Texas had brought their hunting rifles to Austin.

For what seemed like a week, there were daily reminders of the incident: wounded people died or lived, Whitman was found to have had a brain tumor which probably spurred him, Neal Spelce received national recognition for his courageous coverage, and the tower's observation deck was closed to the public for a long time. All of this was fodder for early morning coffee talk with Walter who was most shaken because a friend of his, Paul Bolton of KTBC, had learned of his grandson's death as the list of casualties was being read on air.

At some point life got back to normal, if there can truly be a normal after personally witnessing such a heinous event. And I continued traveling with Walter. Our Washington residence for business was the Madison Hotel. At the time it was the hotel of choice for many business executives, diplomats, and visiting royalty. Its owners, Marshall and Jane Coyne, treated Walter like royalty and me like an accompanying prince. They would often have us and other of Walter's friends over for dinner at their home. Not only was the dinner conversation stimulating, it also broadened my own scope of contacts. But most important were the acts of kindness on the Coyne's part toward Walter. They extended that generosity to me.

On weekends, if I had to stay over to resume business the following Monday, the Coynes would lend me a hotel car. I would take advantage of that by exploring the city and the surrounding area. I roamed from Gettysburg to the Shenandoah Valley to the eastern shore of Maryland. Those day trips heightened not only my interest in American history, but also my desire to learn more about the area by living there again. For the time being I would return to the Madison on Sunday to begin another week of listening and learning. Many times our discussions were held in the bar and restaurant of the Madison. Walter was comfortable there and our table was in a corner, not easily spotted by roving reporters or some ill-willed person. We never had an embarrassing incident.

Of all the movers and shakers I met through Walter, none had more impact on me than Jim Novy of Austin. "Mr. Jim" was in the scrap metal business and very successful. But his consuming passion was Israel and the worldwide situation for Jews. Early on, Walter told me that Jim Novy had been a Johnson supporter since the 1930s. Jim had come to the United States from Russia when he was seventeen, and it was clear to me from our first conversation that he hadn't been in the country long enough to shed a pronounced accent. As I got to know him better, he told me of his early life in America and Austin, and he explained why he was so devoted to Lyndon Johnson. I came to know an extraordinary side of Johnson that few knew.

As the Nazi poison began to leak across Europe in the 1930s, newly elected Congressman Johnson began to pick up frightening stories of the planned elimination of Jews. He got hold of Jim Novy and others to warn them. Through a network of American and European Jews, Johnson made visas and papers appear time after time—often against US policy and even that of FDR. By some accounts over five hundred Jews were secreted out of Europe and brought to Texas, where the Novys and others found them shelter and livelihood. I asked Jim how Johnson did it. He chuckled and shrugged his shoulders, saying only that Lyndon Johnson, even as a congressional freshman, had more contacts in government than the president. "Lyndon just made things happen and American Jews will be forever grateful."

The more I learned from Jim Novy, the more I came to appreciate the duality of Jewish-American allegiance. They were completely loyal to America. Even with its vile pockets and personalities of anti-Semitic bigotry, America was their shelter, their shore of freedom. But at the same time they were people of the Promised Land. For centuries, long before there was a United States, they dreamed of a return to their ancestral home in the deserts of Moses and Abraham.

Over one twenty-four-hour period of my life, that Jewish-American dual devotion was framed in a way that even a twenty-seven-year-old Protestant could understand and appreciate. We had gone to Washington on business and to attend a national benefit of some note. Because Walter could not attend the benefit, I went with Jim and a group of his friends and family. After the event we were to meet Walter back at the hotel. As we got to the lobby, a bellman rushed up and told Jim that an urgent call had come in his absence. I went on to the bar to meet Walter. Later Jim Novy and his son came in. Jim said that war had erupted between Israel and Egypt. It was June 5, 1967, and what was to be known as the Six-Day War had started. Jim said that he needed to go to New York within a day or two and asked if I could go with him. Without hesitation, Walter and I agreed. By June 7 or 8 I was in New York, helping Jim Novy make calls to support a major American fundraiser for the benefit of Israel. On the afternoon of the fundraiser, I had to go to a meeting in the Wall Street district with one of our clients. As I was leaving, Jim stuck an envelope in my pocket and asked me to attend the benefit. Saying that I would, I left without looking in the envelope. After my business meeting, I hurried back to the hotel, freshened up, and headed to the event. Upon arrival at one of New York's largest entertainment halls, I was confronted with a standing-room only crowd. I pulled out my ticket and discovered it was for a reserved seat in front, valued at $10,000. There were the Novys with a large group of Texas friends and their families. Overnight the Jewish-American community had gathered Jewish and non-Jewish supporters and entertainers to raise funds. If my memory serves me correctly, over $10 million had been pledged during the preceding seventy-two hours.

Upon returning home to Austin, I would tell Walter of my experience and what I had learned about America's Jews and President Johnson's support of them. At some point I mentioned all the entertainers who had gathered to perform. When Erich Leinsdorf, the renowned composer and conductor, came up, Walter told me that Leinsdorf was one of the Jews who Congressman Johnson had saved. In later years Leinsdorf would stated that he owed his life and career to Lyndon Johnson. I am sure that Jim Novy was part of that story.

Throughout my time with Walter, Jim Novy would play a role in *my* story. And together they help orchestrate an introduction that was another life-changing gift. In the ebb and flow of my trips to Washington with Jim Novy, he invited me to a reception featuring Vice President Hubert Humphrey. Walter knew of my admiration for Humphrey and got word to him that I'd be attending and hoped to meet him. When we came in, Humphrey was near the door in a receiving line. I introduced myself. The vice president beamed and asked me to wait around a bit. As the greeting line thinned, Humphrey singled me out and pulled me aside. He wanted to know all about Walter and the family. He spoke glowingly of Walter's abilities and humanity. I am certain that he wished Walter were still with President Johnson, particularly as Johnson's mood had darkened as the Vietnam War expansion had not been followed by positive results. Humphrey asked me to stay in touch. Thereafter on several occasions I would seek him out at receptions and events. As 1967 moved toward the election year of 1968, I became convinced that I wanted to work not just for President Johnson's reelection, but also for Vice President Hubert H. Humphrey's. In the increasingly sour times, during America's fracturing debate with itself, Humphrey continued to be a ray of hope for optimism. While he would be criticized for his goodwill and sunny disposition, taken to task by the press and adversaries who had turned sour with the times, I appreciated his attempts to make Americans smile, if not laugh. So I entered the new year of 1968 with the hope that I could play a role in the Johnson-Humphrey reelection campaign.

I talked it over with Walter. Much of my work was on the east coast, so moving to DC made some sense. I also had to tell him that JoAnn and I had separated. I can only speculate now on the reasons why the marriage didn't hold. There are many, but I am convinced that at the core was the fact that we had found each other during a time when both of us had just been disappointed, in a special place—Glacier National Park—where natural beauty and joy seemed to heal our wounds. We were happy, but perhaps that summer was only a bandage and there were no other lasting ties. What if we had returned to the park? Then where would the river have flowed? In January 1968, with Walter's blessing, I returned to DC where, as events unfolded, I would be thrown into a political year marked by shock waves that never seemed to abate.

Over the years I would see Walter from time to time, and often I would think of him. His ultimate gift to me was to come to know the true meaning of stepping into someone's shoes before casting stones. What if Walter had been homosexual? Would it have made a bit of difference? Would I have learned less? Walter Jenkins taught me not only about the levers of power, but also about the courage to press on, even under the darkest of clouds. But my personal benefit came at the expense of the nation. More than one aide and cabinet official of Lyndon Johnson expressed a common belief: Johnson's loss of Walter Jenkins deprived him of his most trusted and effective aide. Attorney General Ramsey Clark went so far as to say that Walter's calm, reasoned counsel might well have changed the course of the Vietnam War and of history.

Charles Dickens began *A Tale of Two Cities* memorably: "It was the best of times, it was the worst of times, it was the age of wisdom, it was the age of foolishness, it was the epoch of belief, it was the epoch of incredulity, it was the season of Light, it was the season of Darkness, it was the spring of hope, it was the winter of despair, we had everything before us, we had nothing before us, we were all going direct to Heaven, we were all going direct the other way." Dickens was referring to the years before and during the French Revolution, but he was prescient. The year 1968 encompassed all of these lines and more. They might have been paraphrased more meaningfully: "It was the worst of times, interlaced with events of mind-numbing horror, with almost imperceptible moments of good news, just enough to keep us—individuals and nation—from going to hell."

For me the year began in one of those downdrafts of blackness. The separation from JoAnn was gut-wrenching because it also meant separating from Jimmy. I can only wish in hindsight that there had been more of those ties that bind. Adding to that dark January was a battle in Vietnam, which the United States won, while in the process losing the war: the Tet Offensive. Tet, the lunar New Year holiday, was—and is—important to all Vietnamese. So much so that the Vietcong and the North Vietnamese Army had observed a Tet truce for a number of years and had signaled they would do so in 1968. Furthermore, there was a renewed hope that General Westmoreland was right to pronounce "light at the end of the tunnel." The Tet Offensive turned off that light. Not only did the Vietcong break the truce, they engaged US soldiers in Saigon, which was considered safe and impregnable. They attacked on many fronts and were defeated at each encounter. Yet Tet was perceived as a major defeat for the United States. The crowning blow was the changed perception of perhaps the most trusted man in America, Walter Cronkite of CBS News. When President Johnson saw Cronkite's support for the war erode, he told aides that the war had been lost. Johnson entered into his own month of darkness and soul searching.

The year before, in Washington frequently, I had volunteered to work for President Johnson's reelection. Through my work with Walter Jenkins I had come to know a number of the major players in the White House, Congress, and the Democratic National Committee (DNC). I went to several meetings and helped on a couple of fundraising projects. I was enough of an insider to be assigned to a team that was supposed to leave for Alaska on April 1 or thereabouts, to secure its delegates. But Alaska had to wait for me. President Johnson announced on the evening of March 31, 1968, that he would not seek the Democratic Party's nomination for president.

At that point Senator Bobby Kennedy and Senator Gene McCarthy were in the race. Although McCarthy hadn't won the New Hampshire primary on March 12, he had done surprisingly well, and some speculated that the close race there drove President Johnson from the arena. I'm not sure. I know that by then he knew he had a weakened heart. I have come to the conclusion over the years that the results in New Hampshire were the final frustration of a man who was heartsick about his health and the war, and from not being able to extend and implement his Great Society programs. By removing himself from the race he hoped that he could find a way to negotiate an honorable end to a war that had deeply divided the country. It was time to return to his beloved Hill Country to seek his own peace and, in what years remained, some sense of joy derived from family, friends, and playing dominoes under the shade trees of the Pedernales River.

Turmoil now reigned within the party. And a few days later national tragedy trumped this turmoil. Dr. Martin Luther King Jr. was murdered in Memphis.

I had gone to a huge political dinner at the Washington Hilton. I was dating Valarie Scott at the time. In the middle of the evening the announcement came. There were shocked gasps, a prayer was said, and then everyone filed out. I think we sensed that this was a tragedy that was a prologue to more. I thought that Valarie ought to come to my apartment until we could determine what would happen. We didn't wait long.

Even though the president, Bobby Kennedy, and others called for calm, peace, and forgiveness in the spirit of Dr. King's creed of nonviolence, large cities coast-to-coast erupted in burning violence, none more so than Washington, and much of its rioting and looting was within blocks of my apartment building. In the morning and throughout the next day, Valarie and I watched television coverage and gazed from the building's rooftop. The nation's capital was burning as it had not since the British invasion in 1812.

Fire engines and police cars raced in every direction. Sirens sounded from every sector. The National Guard was called out. An uneasy peace finally settled in. After two days we finally got a full night's sleep.

The next morning we got one of those surprises that leaven otherwise grim situations. The front desk rang my apartment and I was told that Mr. Mike Scott was in the lobby—it was Valarie's brother. A student at the University of Virginia, he was oblivious to what had been happening. Furthermore, it was spring break or some holiday, and his campus had been practically empty, so he'd had no inkling. Up he drove from the mountains of southern Virginia in an old Volkswagen that had no radio. Yes, he'd noticed a few troops here and there. Yes, there was, come to think of it, the acrid smell of smoke, and yes, the streets appeared to be almost empty. He had tried Valarie's apartment, but neither she nor her roommate were home, so he'd headed to my place in ignorant bliss.

After the usual hugs (and "What in God's name are you doing here?"), Mike reminded us that he had told us sometime back that he was coming. Because the city was in lockdown, we must have played Scrabble or something to pass the time, eaten whatever was in the apartment, watched, and waited. By late Sunday the situation had calmed enough for Mike to head back to Virginia. Later we often laughed about how a college kid in a beat-up Volks, looking like an invading hippie, had crossed Key Bridge in time of full curfew, with the National Guard and police stationed everywhere, into the heart of the riot in the nation's capital, and made it through without being arrested or killed. Sometimes the best thing to do is to keep on coming, looking as if you know exactly what you're doing and where you are going.

By mid-April things returned to quasi-normalcy. Politics were stirring. Vice President Humphrey was edging toward a decision to run for president. As far back as I can remember I had deeply respected Humphrey and his brand of liberalism—forceful conviction without rancor. He truly was the Happy Warrior. He loved politics, progressive policies, and people. He contributed much to the debates over the Peace Corps, agricultural research, Medicare, the Limited Nuclear Test Ban Treaty, civil rights legislation, and more—and to positive outcomes that followed these. It was his clarion call for a meaningful civil rights policy that electrified the 1948 convention. That speech forever established Humphrey as a national figure. It immediately propelled him into the US Senate—the first Democrat from Minnesota ever elected to that body. Part of the reason was the fact that he had begun to forge a lasting merger between the Minnesota Democratic Party and the competing Farmer-Labor Party. United they would become the dominant force within the state, even after his death in 1978. But it was never the same without Humphrey's goodwill and sense of common purpose.

The Democratic-Farmer-Labor Party (DFL) also spawned many other officials of national stature—Orville Freeman (the first DFL governor of Minnesota and secretary of agriculture to Lyndon Johnson), Walter Mondale (US senator and later vice president to Jimmy Carter), and Eugene McCarthy, who would contribute greatly to Humphrey's defeat in 1968. (Someone later said of McCarthy, "He had all the traits of a dog but loyalty.")

By the early 1960s, Humphrey had become a senator's senator, and in 1964 Johnson had tapped him to be his running mate. A northern liberal, Humphrey was also a pragmatist and healer. His kindness, good cheer, and humor won friends on both sides of the aisle. He and Bob Dole worked on all sorts of agricultural and health legislation together, as friends. Humphrey was also a strong Cold War liberal: anticommunist to the core. One can be strong on defense and still uphold liberal principles and beliefs. In Minnesota, Humphrey and his allies fought real communists—the Communist Party was strong for a time in northern Minnesota—and tried to deport some using the Sedition Act. His view of communism as menace put him squarely in the position of most Democratic elected officials, including most liberals. It was the undergirding principle of US commitment in Korea and then Vietnam. So LBJ felt comfortable with Humphrey on both domestic and foreign policy issues. It was not the case, as some old-line liberals and media pundits would have one believe, that Humphrey sold his soul to be on Johnson's ticket. He was and would remain a Cold War liberal, which was also Bobby Kennedy's position for most of his too-short career. Most of the concepts and programs devised to contain communism were the product of Cold War progressives from Harry Truman to Hubert Humphrey and Lyndon Johnson.

The pundits' criticism was badly timed. Hubert Humphrey, early in the Vietnam debate after he had become vice president, had raised serious questions about the wisdom of escalation. Lyndon Johnson committed his most shameful mistake in that mistaken war when he exiled and shunned Humphrey. Without Humphrey's countervailing but loyal wisdom, and lacking Walter Jenkins to patch things up, Johnson waded deeper into the quagmire, with only the "rosy scenarioists" whispering in his ear. That ill treatment continued until Humphrey traveled to Vietnam in 1966 on his own and came back convinced (or wishfully allowed to be convinced) that the US Vietnam policy was on the right track. He was then back in good graces with Johnson, but he was now castigated by growing voices of antiwar protest. "Dump the Hump" became an all-too-familiar protest sign, along with similar ones aimed at LBJ. That change of heart would cost Humphrey dearly, up to and through the 1968 election. It mattered little that in 1967 he went back to Vietnam and that time came away horrified and disillusioned. By then he had become convinced that the US generals were dishonest in their pronouncements. Unfortunately, he was a month or so too early to sway Johnson. Other loyalists, like Clark Clifford, who went from being an unswerving war hawk to being a hawk with serious questions about Johnson's policies, would have to lend their voices of growing concern. I have come to the conclusion that Humphrey's 1967 assessment was the beginning seed of doubt that took hold. We probably will never know the tipping point, although Walter Cronkite's reversal may have been the final straw.

With President Johnson's political withdrawal and announcement that he would devote full time to seeking peace, there would be little political peace for the Democrats, particularly Humphrey. He would have to find a way to set himself apart from Johnson and that would take some time and soul searching. In late April he announced his candidacy, and I went to the first organization meeting. Immediately I volunteered to help wherever needed.

Fortunately, at that juncture, the forces behind Humphrey were what he needed: party regulars, organized labor, hundreds of old-line progressives, African American leaders, and elected officials. He needed to win the caucus states (of which there were many), because he was too late in announcing to file in a number of primary states. These leaders and organizations would give him the instant network and forces necessary to win the nomination. We hit the road running. Bobby Kennedy and Gene McCarthy were in full cry, trying to win over antiwar youth and others who felt disenfranchised. By choice, I was assigned Montana, a state that would hold its precinct caucuses on June 5. After visiting with Jim Rowe, a New Dealer and Johnson insider from Montana who briefed me on the state's politics and made some introductory calls, I flew to Butte to meet a young state legislator, Pat Williams, who was a teacher and recently elected state representative.

An Irishman to the core, Pat became a valuable ally and lifelong friend. After meeting with the mining labor and party leaders of Butte, it was apparent that that part of the state would go heavily for Humphrey, so we headed for the state capital, Helena. I was put up at the Placer Hotel, which housed the already-functioning Humphrey state headquarters. Both Jim Rowe and Pat Williams had laughingly warned me that one of my in-state helpers would be a fellow named Walter Marshall. Although controversial for some of his antics, Marshall was a fixer, essential to any organization, especially an organization thrown together overnight, as was Humphrey's. Need a mailing out overnight? Call Walter! Need signs to appear at precinct meetings? Get hold of Marshall! Need a private plane to barnstorm the small towns on the plains? You got it: Walter. I found him to be all that Rowe and Williams had claimed him to be.

Here I was, in late May 1968, back near Glacier Park country, fighting for Hubert

Humphrey, with solid support from the Democratic Party—and Walter Marshall. Pat Williams and I often chuckle about those days. What we don't laugh about was an event that would unfold throughout the late hours of June 5 into June 6. Bobby Kennedy had been grievously wounded by a gunman after the Democratic primary in California (which he won). By morning he was dead. The same sick hopelessness enveloped me then as during the time of President Kennedy's death and that of Dr. King.

I shut down our headquarters and Robert Kennedy's, which was in the same hotel. His principal representative and I had become good friends. He was a straight-shooting Boston Irishman who loved Humphrey but had to be for Kennedy. We both despised McCarthy and worked together to thwart his Montana efforts. I took Kennedy's rep to the airport, went back to the hotel to learn the caucus results, and then headed for DC. Humphrey carried Montana by a substantial margin, but it was a sad and silent victory.

By the time I landed in Washington, Humphrey had declared a month-long suspension of the campaign out of respect for Kennedy. Valarie and I talked and decided to get married during the moratorium. I knew other states needed organizing. I knew we'd win the nomination, but there would be no break until November. So we got married in June of 1968 and headed back to Montana and Glacier. I had not been back to the park since 1962, except fleetingly during a detour as I had driven between Whitefish and Great Falls with Pat earlier that month. I ached to spend time there. I not only missed its serene beauty, I knew it possessed healing and renewing powers. When the mountains of the park appeared out of the plains, I shed much of my soul-grime that had resulted with my breakup with JoAnn and from King and Kennedy's death. Once inside the protective cocoon of the park, more dark layers peeled away. By the time we moved up the valley road toward the Many Glacier area, I felt healthy enough again to face the rigors of the upcoming convention and campaign.

I had nearly gone back to the park the year before. That year, 1967, was not only the year of the two grizzly bear attacks on the same night, but also the summer that a large section of Glacier was ravaged by fire. Because a great portion of it ran along the Garden Wall, it was difficult to fight and contain. The word went out across the nation for firefighters. I would have gone and considered doing so, but by the time word reached me and I called to inquire, the fire was under control.

Valarie and I spent four or five glorious days in the park, mostly in and around the Many Glacier area. Fortunately the weather was perfect, the sunrises and sunsets inspiring, and the waterfalls and streams in full rush—and the trails engaged Valarie enough so that she too wanted to return. By our final day in Montana the motel phone was ringing or a telegram came, instructing me to report in. It's amazing that people's reliance today on cell phones and the Internet makes real solitude rare. Fortunately the mountains of Glacier still afford that solitude.

It was time to restart the campaign. I contacted Humphrey headquarters and found out that I would next be off to Kentucky. My instructions were simply to get to Louisville and call Mary Helen Byck, the state's national committeewoman, and Wilson Wyatt, Kentucky's national committeeman (in those days each state had one national committeewoman and one national committeeman), and Lieutenant Governor Wendell Ford. So, early in July I flew to Louisville and checked into the Seelbach Hotel—once grand but by then leaning toward seedy. Little did I know that it would take two years to fully check out, because there was no money to pay the bill. I finally got it paid in full.

Through a meeting with former North Carolina governor Terry Sanford and other high-ups in the DNC command, I knew that Kentucky was important. Its caucuses and state convention were late and thus a clear victory would add momentum going into the national convention in Chicago. The University of Kentucky and other colleges and universities had well-organized McCarthy troops—or so we thought. So a solid victory here was imperative to carry Humphrey into Chicago on a high note.

We would need every high note we could muster, because most of the chorus of America was low and coarse. Martin Luther King and Bobby Kennedy were dead, George Wallace was moving into northern states, African Americans were in various stages of anger and despair, antiwar protesters were rallying and their protests intensifying, and Russia was invading Czechoslovakia.

The good news was that party loyalists were rallying. Even those who loved the Kennedys knew that Teddy wasn't ready and McCarthy was no alternative. Humphrey was a known and for the most part a positive known. He had fought hard and played fair. Labor knew this. Blacks knew it. Progressives in general knew it, as did those advocating on behalf of such issues as education, agriculture, and health care. Humphrey had been on the national scene for a long time, doing good things. Now we had to put him over the top in Kentucky.

I quickly settled into the Seelbach Hotel in Louisville, then immediately contacted Byck, Wyatt, and Ford. Shortly thereafter we had a confab on a riverboat near Owensboro, the home area of Doc Beauchamp, the western Kentucky boss, and J. R. Miller, the state chairman. At lunch I sat next to Raymond Bossmeyer of Louisville, an attorney and captivating political figure who seemed to know all aspects of the state and who said that he would be more than willing to share that knowledge with me, whenever I needed it.

Over the course of the day we came up with a game plan. Those leaders would handle those areas where they had control, which was a great deal of central and western

Kentucky. We would use a young team that Terry Sanford was sending from North Carolina to work the university towns. And I was to get together with Ford to map out eastern Kentucky—coal-mining country. I would act as a go-between linking the state leadership and Humphrey headquarters, coordinating surrogate visits, press releases, and the like, and I would also be the chief firefighter to put out disputes that would surely flare up. At the end of the day, Bossmeyer and I made a date for me to come to his house for dinner. Wendell Ford and I settled on a date to meet in Lexington to strategize on the eastern counties.

Bossmeyer was a political heavyweight in Louisville, Jefferson County, and the entire state of Kentucky. Visiting him at home I learned that he was a person of culture and literature. He had one of the finest collections of Gregorian chant manuscripts, and he knew history, particularly that of Kentucky. It was a splendid evening. He would become one of my most trusted sounding boards—an immense help. He would also introduce me to the mysteries and myths of Kentucky bourbon. One night he took me to a famous restaurant, The Old House. The first menu presented listed only bourbons, dating back to the early nineteenth century. I immediately noticed that there were no prices. I questioned that and Bossmeyer told me not to worry. Simply order one—his treat. I am glad he offered that because my early-nineteenth-century Henry Clay shot came and I was told that that small glass cost fifty dollars. Years later I would hear that the restaurant had closed. I wondered at the time if they'd simply run out of all those fine, rare bourbons.

Wendell Ford was the lieutenant governor of Kentucky, a position of little power or influence, save as a stepping-stone to the governor's office or the US Senate. He would serve in both offices in the future, but in 1968 he was down the totem pole of power, except as a party leader and wise counselor. His lack of state constitutional power was mirrored by what I saw on my visit to the lieutenant governor's house. Not a mansion by any stretch of the imagination, the house was in drastic need of repair. It was pouring rain and I spent the first minutes of my first visit with Wendell setting out buckets to catch water leaking from the ceiling. The governor, a Republican, in a political snit had cut off all repair funds for the lieutenant governor. Once we set out the buckets we sat down and went over our statewide plan, and then got to the eastern counties.

I started to say that I probably ought to go over there and meet with folks so they could start reporting in, but I was brought up short: "George, you are not going into any of those counties and they won't be reporting in." For the next hour I would learn about the nuances, sometimes dark ones, of that part of the state. People in the mining area, Wendell said, were prideful, mysterious, and suspicious of the outside world, which included all the rest of the state. "Bloody Harlan" was the epitome of these counties, but there were more like it. A suitable representative would have to be recruited to go in for us. Wendell said that he'd have someone get in touch. When I reported this later to Bossmeyer, he said something like, "George, that's the best, self-preserving advice you'll ever get. Wendell will find the right person."

A couple of nights later there was a knock on my hotel door. I opened the door and there standing in the frame was a huge man in rural garb. "My name is Big Foot Williamson. Wendell sent me."

If I remember correctly, sixteen counties comprised the area in question. I asked Big Foot his strategy. "Well, I'll send my boy out ahead to tell the local leaders to round up the troops. Tell them Big Foot's on the way. Then I come in and say that they are after our great vice president and we need to carry the county for him."

"Who are they, Big Foot?"

"I leave that to their imagination—communists, socialists, hippies, or the IRS. They got their own haunts, enough to stir 'em up."

"What will it cost to do all of that?," I asked.

He took out a small wooden pencil and a little tablet. He asked how many days until the county caucus. Then he figured and announced that he believed that $150 plus liquor would handle it. I told him that the price was right, but—what about the liquor?

"Well, you see, after my boy goes in and I come in, I leave them some booze to mull things over. My boy's already on the way to the next meeting to set things up. Then we do it all over again for the next week or so. I know that sounds like a lot of money, but we have to pay for gas, food, and lodging."

I gave him $200 on the spot, but said that I'd need for him to report in on a regular basis.

"Can't do that."

"Why?," I asked.

"Because I can't afford to stir up any suspicion among my friends, but I'll get word to you when I know. How's that?"

There was something about the man's sincerity and knowledge of the area, plus Wendell's recommendation, that caused me to reach out and shake his hand. We had a drink and I told him that I would get him the necessary cases of booze in the morning. I did—and then off into "the dark and bloody" mystery Big Foot Williamson disappeared.

I related all this to Bossmeyer and asked him why there was so much suspicion. He explained that it was a mountain mentality born out of isolation and exploitation, and he related a story. As a young lawyer Bossmeyer was contacted by an attorney whose client, deceased, had left a sizeable sum to a person in Hazard, Kentucky. Bossmeyer wrote to the county judge or some other official there, asking for help locating the beneficiary. Over the course of the next weeks, Bossmeyer was paid a visit by a man who said that he knew the recipient and would try to find him. Then that man made a series of phone calls that were clearly intended to establish Bossmeyer's credibility and trustworthiness. A month or so later the visitor reappeared, establishing himself as the beneficiary. Even though several thousand dollars were at stake, he'd had to make sure that it wasn't a set-up of some kind.

This story clearly represented a culture that only a Big Foot could deal with, so I wrote a memo to headquarters, stating that I had full faith in Wendell and Big Foot and that we would know the situation when we knew it. Sure enough, as caucus time approached, I received a message that went something like this: "Big Foot's done been here. Courthouse has burned down. Looking for other place to meet. All sixteen counties will be 100 percent for Vice President Humphrey. Thank you."

With the help of Sanford's team of Charlie Smith, Pete Ellington, Ed Graham, and Sapp Funderburk of South Carolina, plus the Kentucky regulars, we carried the entire state by a sizeable margin, including most university and college strongholds, but not without a challenge by the McCarthy forces. In 1968, as in the past, most caucus states were governed by the unit rule. If you carried your precinct, county, or state by 50 percent plus one, all the votes were yours. The McCarthy people were determined to change the rules in mid-game, and institute proportional representation. The concept did have some merit, but only in the future. Party and state laws governed, and in 1968 the unit rule was binding.

I had opened up a line of communication with Joan Bingham, whose family owned the *Louisville Courier-Journal*. She was an ardent McCarthy supporter, but liked Humphrey for his strong progressive bent. We worked it out that they could have their say at the state convention, make several motions with the understanding that they would be voted down, but that we would guarantee that a number of their ranks would be national delegates and alternates. My only requirement was that they be rock-solid Democrats and not simply one-shot firebrands for McCarthy who would not lift a finger to help once the convention was over.

The day of the convention arrived. All was in order, until the eastern counties began to report in—as predicted, 100 percent for Humphrey. That got under the skin of the out-of-state McCarthy coordinator. He rushed across the floor, calling on someone to challenge the sixteen counties. Fortunately I spotted him, and Joan Bingham, Big Foot, and I stopped him before he could reach those counties' delegates seated in the shadows.

"Joan, do you want to tell him or shall I?" That wonderful, cultured, and beautiful woman laid it out: "Of all the counties, those are the most democratic. They had their meetings. Few, if any, of our people showed up. They elected a slate fair and square. So if you insist on challenging their credentials, you are challenging their honor and honesty. I wouldn't go over there if I were you. Get it?"

That was the end of that. Kentucky was safely in the Humphrey column—100 percent. I made sure that Big Foot Williamson was an at-large national delegate or alternate.

This would be my first national convention as a party insider. While I'd made a hurried trip to Atlantic City in 1964, before leaving for Texas, my only role there was as an ardent Lyndon Johnson supporter. Now, in August of 1968, I would go to Chicago as the southern states coordinator. From bystander to a convention floor leader was a big jump. I was appointed to the position because I'd helped win a couple of key states and those wins did not go unnoticed by Jim Rowe and Terry Sanford. They recommended me to Humphrey.

Between the Kentucky state convention and mid-August, I put together my convention team, secured hotel rooms, and visited with and studied the leadership and delegates from each state. My team would be the Terry Sanford warriors from North Carolina, plus a number of coordinators who had worked individual states prior to the national convention. One by one they reported in. While we were confident that the southern delegates would stay loyal, there were grumblings: too little Johnson, too much Wallace, and old turf fights centered mostly on race and local or state politics.

Many of the South's Democratic leaders were Johnson Democrats. They supported a great many of the Great Society programs and represented the populist streak of the South. They supported the Vietnam War—the patriotic streak. They were also edgy about the rising strength of George Wallace who had a solid block of votes in every state, if not a majority, and was heading north with his race-baiting and anti-federal-government call for states' rights.

Not having Lyndon Johnson at the top of the ticket rankled—none more so than in Texas, which was a key state in the convention and would be crucial in November. The key to the state, Lyndon Johnson notwithstanding, was John Connally, who had been discouraged by Johnson's withdrawal, disappointed that he wouldn't be on the ticket with Humphrey, and furious that the unit rule and other party governance rules were being challenged. Connally took it personally. It was a challenge to his authority in Texas.

There is a deep brand of warrior patriotism throughout the South. Part of this involves local pride, part is based on mythology, and certainly part stems from the economic benefit of huge military expenditures in the South: naval bases, arsenals, and other military installations, all obtained by congressional committee chairmen from southern states. Overlying this was the fact that Democrats held practically all state and local offices, and so control of the party apparatus was of paramount importance. It governed elections, patronage, and government expenditures. This situation led to rifts between the all-white, good ol' boy (and not-so-good ol' boy) machines, and southern blacks and their reform-minded allies. Stir it all together and many states had friction enough to lead to floor fights and walkouts.

Adding even further to this stew of democracy was the growing fear and anger over the threats of the Yippies and antiwar organizations that vowed to disrupt both parties' conventions, but that specifically targeted on the Democratic convention. With all this cooking, Valarie and I packed for Chicago. I went ahead, as I had a number of organizational meetings to attend. Valarie and my mother would arrive shortly before the convention started. I had invited Mom because she had always wanted to attend a national convention, and she had a dear friend in Chicago with whom she could to stay.

My southern states command hotel was the old Allerton from which Don McNeill's *Breakfast Club* was broadcast every morning on the radio. Started in the 1930s, the program was still playing in 1968. Lottie Bristol was an honored guest on the show one morning. I had other things to do, principally figuring out how to keep all the southern delegates in Chicago—and in Humphrey's camp.

Every morning our team met to discuss the latest rumors, slights, and fights. We made sure that the vice president, Mrs. Humphrey, and other top officials would visit every state's convention caucus. Through Terry Sanford I requested calls from key Johnson cabinet officers to delegates threatening to walk or boycott. We made sure we had plenty of tickets to spread around. But we needed something more. Because the campaign and the DNC were practically out of funds, I borrowed $10,000 to pay for my team's expenses. We thought about organizing a big party to promote southern unity, but it would have been too expensive to hold. However, I knew that Democrats, assuredly southern Democrats, even southern Baptist Democrats, would enjoy a cocktail or two. I placed a call and got a local distributor to donate enough liquor to keep 'em oiled, happy, and for Humphrey. When the final roll call was taken, all but one-half vote—from Alabama for football coach Bear Bryant—went to Humphrey.

But it was a doomed convention from the outset. Antiwar demonstrators were at full throat, and Mayor Daley and his followers were furious that Chicago and the convention were being torn apart, and that this was being seen on television around the world. The mayor, fueled by bogus reports from the FBI and White House, overreacted, sending out police and the National Guard who violently clashed with demonstrators in the streets. The hurt of Bobby Kennedy's loss still lingered for many, and Senator McCarthy did nothing to heal the wounds—the self-centered rarely do. Of all people, McCarthy was a direct beneficiary of the Democratic-Farmer-Labor party that Humphrey built. Furthermore, he had worked with Humphrey on many issues over the years and knew that he was a committed progressive and decent human being. Behind his professorial antiwar façade, Clean Gene was not a particularly kind man nor was he especially progressive. He left Chicago in a huff after the convention and never got around to truly endorsing his old friend and fellow Minnesotan. He went on to write mediocre poetry.

Apart from the rioting in the streets, those of us immersed in the day-to-day mechanics of convention life and drama were busy from dawn to late at night, and we had no idea of the extent of the damage that Humphrey and the party now faced. Only several days after the convention, as we drove back to Washington, did radio and newspaper reports spell out for us the deep anger, resentment, and disillusionment. With antiwar sentiment and liberal disheartenment, George Wallace's presence, and Lyndon Johnson's absence, there seemed to be no way that the Humphrey-Muskie ticket could eke out a win.

By Labor Day it looked hopeless. The Humphrey organization and the DNC were broke and in debt. Yet a campaign had to be run, if for no other reason than to attempt to reinvigorate the troops enough to protect Senate, House, and state seats.

We had a number of organizational meetings. It became apparent that some wanted to mount a campaign in all fifty states. I thought that was stupid and counterproductive, and I devised a scheme. I had a couple of my people, whom I was paying out of my own pocket, call into each of the southern states, asking for ideas and compiling upcoming events, to come up with signs of activity. I would file these worthless reports practically every evening. In the meantime, I looked for the three or four states where something solid might be stitched together. Texas and Maryland showed real possibility, but had not come together yet.

Nonetheless, a great deal was at stake if Texas went Republican. So the best thing was to keep talking, sending emissaries, and monitoring the situation, which included an equal and even more potent pot that was boiling—President Lyndon Johnson.

When Johnson had taken himself out of the race it had surprised many. Yet he harbored for a time an unrealistic hope—a misguided hope—that he would be able to ride into the convention and save it. Deeper down he surely must have known that this would be a terrible move, and eventually, wisely, he chose not to do that. At the convention, party leaders failed to give him his rightful due, while heaping praise on Bobby Kennedy. A major blunder by the DNC officials, this stuck in the president's craw. So the two mainstays of the Texas Democratic Party, Johnson and Connally, were off licking their own wounded egos.

Then there was Maryland. While not a true southern state, it was under my jurisdiction. Through earlier work I had met a number of the state's young Democratic leaders, including Steny Hoyer, Pete O'Malley, and Speaker Marvin Mandel. The state had a huge black population and a well-oiled Democratic machine. It was also the home of the Republican vice presidential nominee, Spiro Agnew. While popular with most Republicans, in state and out, Agnew had created enemies in Maryland, enough so that in a close race the Democrats might prevail.

Everywhere else in early September was on the near-hopeless list. Florida was a perfect example. Eddie McCormack of Massachusetts was our DNC man in Florida. Former attorney general of the state, with a strong civil rights record, McCormack was the nephew of Speaker of the House John McCormack. For weeks Eddie begged for funds and support. Between the Jewish, black, and loyal Democratic vote he thought there was a chance to carry the state. Finally, to dramatize his plight, he sent me a single, business-size Humphrey-Muskie handout card. In small print he wrote on it, "George, I scraped up enough funds from Joe Robbie (owner of the Miami Dolphins) to print 1,000 of these. I have tacked them all over one telephone pole in northern Florida. Trying to raise funds for another 1,000 for a pole in southern Florida. We are on a roll." This was laughable, but also serious. We were broke—dead broke. I borrowed another $10,000 and sent it out to my field workers in the states with potential.

Kentucky was still in play. The reasoning was that if Humphrey could gain some traction, and Wallace could bleed off enough votes from Nixon, maybe the three-way split would favor Humphrey. So I sent the Kentucky team their per diem and told them to make an assessment. For a week there was silence, though, and finally I called. It seems that the crew had decided to take matters into their own hands. There had been a fall horse race at Churchill Downs, and they had pooled their meager resources and bet on a long shot with the hopes of winning enough to mount a more serious campaign. The horse had died on the first turn. So much for Kentucky.

At some point in mid-September, Terry Sanford came to see me. He was a clear-headed realist, but he had a "Hail Mary" plan. If Humphrey came to the state, specifically to Charlotte, and if we could fill the convention center there (it would hold over fifty thousand people), creating a sense of excitement and legitimacy, maybe, just maybe, we could pull off a miracle. With few options left, I agreed. I pulled most of the field people into North Carolina and went there for a personal review of the situation.

Terry Sanford was a man of tremendous leadership ability and charisma. Clearly at the first meeting which included representatives from South Carolina, his stature among his peers and party regulars was apparent. He carefully explained the situation: the risk of failure if we didn't fill the hall, but the possibility of a winning split if we were successful. All agreed to pitch in. A great Democrat and business leader, C. C. Hope of First Union Bank, found us office space. Terry's team of young warriors was made available. We drew up quotas for every county and organization. I made a call and got a hot rock group—Tommy James and the Shondells—to agree to come. James would campaign for Humphrey right through Election Day. His appearance would guarantee a significant attendance by young people. The plan was beginning to take shape and look achievable.

But my absence from my desk in Washington was drawing some attention and fire. Since I was a volunteer who was paying more than my own way, I told them to fire me. I would continue what I was doing. The more I labored, the more excited I became that maybe we could produce a crowd that would rival those recently drawn by Billy Graham and George Wallace. If so, this would not only be a great local story, it would reverberate nationally: Hubert Humphrey was on the way back.

But a dark cloud trailed Hubert—the war protesters. They disrupted his every speech. They often shouted him down, so that there was no positive nightly news message, only their chanting rant. The polls reflected the continuing sour nightly scene. Something had to give—and we hoped that this would happen before October 2, the date of the Charlotte event. On September 30 we got a break. Humphrey delivered a well-reasoned speech, arguing that a unilateral bombing halt would be an acceptable risk to take to hasten the peace process. While not a complete break with President Johnson, it demonstrated that Humphrey was his own man and could stand up to the president. It was not dramatic, but it was enough. The next day I traveled to Knoxville, where, not by design but by schedule, the vice president was to appear at an evening rally at the University of Tennessee. Because of the prior antiwar demonstrations, there had been discussion about canceling. However, and fortunately, Governor Buford Ellington was insisting on a Tennessee appearance.

Then we almost blew the whole thing. As the band played on and on at the airport, as the autumn sun set, as Governor Ellington and others stewed on the tarmac, frantic calls went out. Where was the vice president? Everyone knew that Hubert always ran late, but not *this* late. About the time that some began to fear the worst, a call came through. The vice presidential plane, because of a scheduling glitch, had landed at Chattanooga, but we were assured it was now on the way to Knoxville.

Upon the plane's landing, we all rushed by motorcade to the university coliseum.

There, row upon row, were people chanting, not with rage but for the vice president: "We want Humphrey! We want Humphrey!" And he gave 'em Humphrey—while giving Nixon hell. It was the brightest spot in campaign to date. And even better than the crowd reaction was that of the traveling press corps: several journalists commented that night that maybe there was a new day dawning.

The next day I flew with the vice president to Florida, briefing him on Charlotte. All through the morning and early afternoon the crowds in Florida grew and cheered wildly. Then we headed for North Carolina. It was late afternoon as we started our descent over the city. There below us, on every road and highway leading into the city and toward the coliseum, were lines of cars and buses. We rushed to the hotel to change. Humphrey had been upbeat all day, but now he was his old exuberant self. For the first time since Chicago I watched this happy fellow begin to relax—and even chortle. In that mood I knew that he would move the crowd and the media.

At the coliseum we went to the underground garage in back, for security reasons, and dashed into a holding room. Terry Sanford and other dignitaries were there. Terry beamed and said that it was good—very good. Hubert could hardly be restrained. At the appointed moment, out we went onto the stage. The crowd went wild, cheering, stomping, and clapping. It was so packed that they had to put viewing screens outside for the thousands who couldn't get in. For one hour or so it was if the war and the divisions of America had dropped away. All participants seemed to remember why they loved Hubert H. Humphrey—the Happy Warrior. The press witnessed this overnight transformation and wrote accordingly.

When Hubert was really excited he would use a favorite expression. After the speech he threw his arms around me and said, "George, man, oh, Manischewitz!" Then we turned and faced the crowd who would have stayed all night, as would have Hubert. But now there was a campaign to wage again, so off to the hotel we roared, only to be faced with another joyful crowd outside and in the lobby. Just maybe—but we were still a long shot.

After the vice president went up to his suite, I met Terry Sanford, his wife, Margaret Rose, and others for a late dinner. I told Terry that I might have to work out of North Carolina, as I was in the doghouse with some in Washington. "No you're not. I've already explained to Hubert that you pulled and held all this together. You're one of the best organizers I ever worked with and that's not just me talking." Had I not been on such a happiness high, I would have cried. Sometime in the early morning I fell asleep, and when I awakened I got ready to fly to Washington on one of the campaign planes.

After Charlotte, with a month to go, we were put in a position of watching and waiting. Even though funds were coming in at an ever-increasing pace, there was still not nearly enough, and it had to be doled out carefully, on a priority basis. I understood that, but it made it difficult to explain to all the organizations and folks who cared about the presidential race and their own local races.

It was decided to show the campaign flag in several states. Senator Robert Byrd and I went to Georgia. Byrd, who at an early age had been a Ku Klux Klan member, gave a rousing speech to a practically all-black audience in Atlanta. First elected to the US Senate from West Virginia in 1958, Byrd had grown in outlook as he had grown in seniority. He had come to be a man who could publicly apologize to this crowd for his earlier KKK membership and the fact that he'd opposed the Civil Rights Act of 1964. There was something extra in the chemistry between the Atlanta crowd and the senator. Maybe it was that they understood how difficult Byrd's journey to that moment had been—not unlike theirs. After the speech, we visited with several key leaders and newspaper journalists, and then flew back to Washington on a small private plane. The weather wasn't particularly bad, but Senator Byrd went white knuckle with every bump. I'd never thought that high political leaders might have the same fears as we mere mortals.

Next I went to Tennessee. Governor Ellington had set up a number of meetings there, starting in Nashville. He brought in all of his top county leaders, urging them to stem the tide, still thinking about the inevitable three-way split in November. Ellington made it personal, saying that he had worked with Humphrey on many agriculture matters when he was Tennessee's agriculture commissioner. He was also a moderate on race and a great friend of President Johnson. He set me up with several black leaders and rainmakers. For different reasons they loved Hubert Humphrey.

Late at night at the Governor's Mansion, I asked Ellington why he liked Humphrey. He gave a very thoughtful and surprising answer that went something like this: Humphrey was what many Democrats wanted to be—a free-spirited progressive with a heart of gold. While Ellington deeply respected Lyndon Johnson (he had served in Johnson's administration and gone to the Johnson ranch on several occasions), he knew that Johnson could be rough and bruising at times, so he and others used to seek out Humphrey, in the Senate and as vice president, to get a message to Johnson. They would also go to Humphrey after a Johnson tongue-lashing to cry on Hubert's shoulder. "Then Hubert would cry on *our* shoulders," Ellington told me. "You just have to love a fellow like that." I grew to like Buford Ellington a great deal. He was a stand-up fellow who didn't cut and run at the first sign of trouble.

Through Ellington I met John Jay Hooker, who had been his opponent in 1966 in the Tennessee Democratic primary for governor. Hooker was a devoted Bobby Kennedy follower and had been devastated by his death. For whatever reasons, John Jay and I hit it off. He looked like a young Andrew Jackson, and he was always on stage—dramatic and humorous. Loud and boisterous, he had great substance and passion. I have never met a more colorful character, and we remain friends to this day.

In 1968 when I met him, John Jay wanted to help Humphrey. As he said, "Crying time is over." John Jay took me to meet another Bobby devotee, John Seigenthaler, whom I would also grow to admire immensely. Sig was running the *Nashville Tennessean*. He too knew that it was time to put aside grief and try to beat Nixon and Wallace.

One of the things I learned about Hubert Humphrey that I witnessed time after time was that very few people held anything against him, and that certainly held for former RFK friends and allies. He was so decent and so rarely carried a grudge himself that it was hard to dislike him, no matter that he'd been a political or legislative opponent.

From Nashville I traveled to Memphis. There was no joy in Memphis in 1968. Garbage haulers' strikes had drained the blood of civil discourse from its citizens, and Dr. King's murder cast a pall so suffocating that one always felt short of political breath. I went through the motions, but saw no hope for any sort of effective coalition. Then, making the whole situation seem surreal to me, Jackie Kennedy married Aristotle Onassis, an aging Greek shipping tycoon.

I don't know why that hit me so hard. I suppose that I thought the Kennedys were above mundane concerns, above money-grubbing, and that Jackie would forever be a solitary, slightly sad keeper of JFK's flame.

In the coffee shop of the old Peabody Hotel, known for its parade of ducks, I stared at a newspaper, drank coffee, and prepared to go to Mississippi via Texas. I went to Texas not only to see my son—Jimmy was by then four—but also to fetch him for the campaign trip to Mississippi. I have no recollection as to why I went to that state. We had decided to make our presence known in all of the states, but most held some hope, no matter how faint, of a three-way split. Mississippi, though, was Wallace country, as was Alabama. There were no friendly state officials there, only a few white liberals and a handful of black leaders, like Aaron Henry, Fannie Lou Hamer, and Charlie Evers, the brother of the slain civil rights leader, Medgar Evers. I called an old friend there who said that things were so bad that he really couldn't come to our press conference or reception, even though he was a good national Democrat. Most of the rest of Jackson felt the same way. The press coverage was minimal and the reception poorly attended. But I'd come, and this would serve me well later—and the rest of the evening was the stuff of small legends.

I think it was Aaron Henry who suggested that I have dinner with leaders of the black community and stay at Charlie Evers's house. I don't think Evers anticipated a four-year-old visitor, but he and his family welcomed Jimmy with open arms. Jimmy was not put off by being with blacks, but he was wide-eyed at those with guns who moved around outside in the yard. Medgar Evers had been killed on June 12, 1963, and vile threats continued to pour in as white officials looked the other way. True evil lurked at the perimeters of light. A four-year-old could not fathom this, but it was apparent that he was nervous as he got out of bed to check the window and go to the bathroom. At some point during the early morning he must have padded off, done his business, and then made a wrong turn into a room where Aaron Henry was sleeping, crawled into bed with Aaron, and went to sleep.

Early the next morning a laughing Aaron Henry came to breakfast, relating how Jimmy had come in and—in the excitement and fright of the night, perhaps—had wet the bed and Aaron Henry. Everyone had a good laugh. I went and changed the bed as Jimmy explained that he was indeed very nervous, watching the shadows and listening to voices pass by his window during the night. Four years old, James Stanton Bristol had ridden in a presidential parade and peed on a civil rights leader. For years afterward Aaron Henry and Charlie Evers would both inquire about their favorite "little pisser."

I remember that night when men and women separated from white society because of the color of their skin welcomed a twenty-eight-year-old white man and his son, and talked about the promise of America, even as guards patrolled outside. For all the demeaning rhetoric thrown at African Americans by race-baiters and other cowards over the decades, and for all the tribulations before that, including the enslavement of their ancestors, most black citizens waited and worked patiently within the law to gain equality.

After Mississippi I took Jimmy to back to Texas and then headed to Washington and the last days of the campaign. Humphrey was on the move and closing. The question remained how much and where. We had to have a couple of small miracles to turn the Electoral College numbers in our favor. There was talk that things might be decided in the House of Representatives and that Wallace might broker a deal. But no deal was made, Humphrey got none of the small miracles, and while the popular vote was nearly a statistical tie between Humphrey and Nixon, the electoral vote broke for Nixon— 290 to 203.

It might have been otherwise. A revelation came very late in the campaign that

President Johnson and his team of peace negotiators were close to a deal with the North and South Vietnamese. So close that the Nixon inner circle were deeply concerned, given the narrowing in the polls, that a peace accord could tip the election to Humphrey. To make sure that did not happen, Richard Nixon and some of his closest advisors committed treason. They convinced (or bribed) South Vietnam President Nguyen Van Thieu to break off negotiations, with a promise of a better deal from a Nixon White House.

From 1969 until the war's end four years later, twenty-five thousand more American youth would die. Several hundred thousand North and South Vietnamese would perish. Richard Nixon would be hounded from office for a later impeachable act and President Thieu would flee the country in disgrace. I would know nothing of the Nixon treason until later. I have never understood why President Johnson didn't publicly call Nixon out.

Right after the election, Valarie and I went to a friend's farm in Virginia to repair, think about the future, and continue plans for a new baby, expected in late January or early February. It was a beautiful spot with enough color remaining in the trees to lift our spirits.

Sometime between then and Thanksgiving I called for an appointment to see the vice president. Even in defeat he was at least outwardly his old self. We discussed the campaign, and we fondly recalled Charlotte. Hubert asked me to consider staying on at the DNC to help rebuild the party. The South would need a lot of attention and revitalization. I desperately wanted to head home to Texas but said that I would give this thought. Then I asked him a question. Why did he talk at such great length, as he was often noted for doing, even if eloquently? He chuckled. "George, my state is full of Scandinavians, Norwegians, Swedes, Finns, and the like. When I first started running for office, I'd give a set little speech on, say, agriculture at this or that town hall meeting. The folks would sit politely silent with their big arms folded across their chests. The women the same, with hands folded in their laps. I'd let 'em have it with both barrels of agriculture. Then I'd quit. No response. No smiles or frowns, just silence." Phlegmatic, quiet Minnesotans—so that was it.

Hubert continued: "Well, by golly, I learned to strike out on national defense, labor, or civil rights or economic policy—one after the other. You see, they knew I'd probably be with them only once. This was their town hall opportunity to hear me out and they wanted it all. So off I'd go on the whole nine yards. And, you know, after an hour or so, someone would clap and say something like, 'You give a mighty good talk, young fellow.' Then they'd file by and shake my hand. I always thought that was the purest and best form of democratic discourse, and I deeply regret we're being relegated to sound bites." I felt the same way and felt that had Nixon chosen to debate Humphrey, the strength of Hubert's deeply held beliefs and well-grounded knowledge would have shone through, perhaps making the difference. We'll never know. Nor will we know whether Hubert Humphrey would have been a good or great president. Johnson, Connally, and others feared he would not. They thought him too weak.

I think that we would have had a good and decent president. We would have had a caring leader. We would have had progressive vision without rancor. Hubert had deep friendships on both sides of the aisle in a time when bipartisanship was joined with respect and honor. All of that may not have made him a great president, but it would have afforded the country a respite from the deep divisions that were unfortunately part of the Johnson legacy. We certainly would not have been visited by a paranoid and treasonous scoundrel who would take the country to the brink of constitutional breakdown.

We will never know for certain, but we do know the rest of the Hubert Humphrey story. After two years, Humphrey ran for the Senate seat vacated by Gene McCarthy, who was anathema in Minnesota after his ill treatment of Hubert. Winning the seat, Humphrey took up in the Senate where he left off. He was much beloved. But even with a new lease on life, it would not last long. After his 1976 reelection to the Senate he was diagnosed with cancer. He carried on in the same warm manner for as long as he could, and his congressional colleagues in the House and Senate honored him with an unprecedented joint session in his honor.

Sometime in the summer of 1977, knowing he was dying, Hubert called me. "Look, George, you may know that I'm dying. I want to raise a substantial fund for what will be the Hubert Humphrey Institute of Public Affairs at the University of Minnesota and I want to do it before I die. I don't want a memorial. I want a bang-up show with my friends. I want you to run the event for me. Can you do it?" I didn't hesitate or look at a calendar. I took down details for a few key contacts, including Helen Reddy and Frank Sinatra.

I spoke with several University of Minnesota officials and shortly flew to Minnesota. We set targets and areas of responsibility. Then I talked with Helen Reddy and her husband/manager, Jeff Wald. They said that they would handle getting stars lined up and that they would produce the entertainment portion of the show. We settled on December 2, 1977. For whatever reason, I was asked to call Sinatra. I did—and surprisingly he returned the call. Sinatra loved Hubert, it seemed. Sinatra said that he had a contractual commitment on that date, but told me to give him a few days and he would work it out. He was a man of his word. Several days later someone called and said to count Frank in, but that he'd need a piano in his suite. No problem.

Within a month it began to come together: commitments, and agreements to cochair the event, by a who's who of performers and American business, academic, civil rights, and political leaders. In fact, the acceptances were so many that we had to create a second program. Many corporations and foundations gave generous gifts, as did individuals and countries. Japan made a magnificent pledge. All the performers agreed to appear for free. But stars, even ones appearing pro bono, have to be instructed not to run up tabs and room service charges. This was an event to fund Hubert Humphrey's dying wish, and every dollar counted—no exceptions without prior approval from me.

We had a marvelous tribute planned from start to finish. The funding and pledges were significant—over $6 million. Hubert, while failing, was in good spirits.

Right after Thanksgiving we traveled to Washington where the event would be held at the Washington Hilton. There I immediately had to put out a fire. Sinatra had requested the piano to rehearse, but the Hilton manager had balked at this. I called one of the event cochairs, Barron Hilton, president of the hotel chain, and the piano went into the suite. This aside, things went smoothly.

The night of the event was all I wished for. The Hilton ballroom was packed—standing room only. The entertainers there poured their hearts out to the great, smiling man who sat front and center with his family and President and Mrs. Carter. There was not a maudlin moment. It was a world-class tribute to a world-class man. Each person there remembered how much he had come to mean to them.

Even the glitch of Lorne Green singing "My Way" before Sinatra's appearance was forgiven. Then Hubert haltingly mounted the stairs to the stage. He told us all how much his life with us had meant to him and how much a life dedicated to service was meaningful and rewarding. It was not the Humphrey of old, verbose. It was the Humphrey of old—kind and caring.

I was near tears. I turned to Sinatra at the next table. Tears were running down his face. I turned to my guests—Lloyd and B. A. Bentsen, Bob and Elizabeth Dole, and Speaker Tip O'Neill and his wife. They were all crying. So I began to bawl like a baby. Most in the audience were crying too, because they knew they were hearing the final words of a man who spent his life trying to marshal the forces of decency. Too soon it was over.

Even in his weakened condition, Hubert H. Humphrey stood on the stage and welcomed well-wishers afterward—one after the other. Out of the corner of my eye I saw Gene McCarthy approaching and blocked his access to the stage. There were hundreds of other more deserving people to shake hands with their friend.

Afterward, by invitation only, a number of us, including the performers, were asked to come to a holding room backstage. There Hubert sat, drained but beaming. One by one he thanked us. I bent over and kissed him on the forehead. He grabbed my hand and softly said, "I knew you could do it. Thank you." I wept again. I went to my room but did not sleep. The adrenalin of sorrow swept over me.

The next morning the phone rang early. "George, I need you down in the lobby right away!" It was Larry Letscher, my event coordinator. I hurriedly dressed and went downstairs. It seemed that some of the stars and hangers-on had thrown an after-hours party, a party that cost $24,000. I was standing there in disbelief when Frank Sinatra walked up to check out. He asked me what the problem was. I told him and he shook his head. "Put it on my tab," he told the cashier. He signed the bill and started to leave. Then he walked back. "Don't ever tell Hubert about this."

I would never see him again, but for all the controversy surrounding him, I have always revered Frank for that moment of generosity, coupled with the insight that it would have taken the magic of the hour away from his friend who had few days left. Nor would I ever see Hubert again. He went downhill rapidly after that. But over the Christmas holiday some friends got him a telephone that he could use at will, and up until his death he found great pleasure in chatting with Senate colleagues, world leaders, family, and friends, including me.

When Humphrey died I tried to make it to his funeral, but bad weather prevented me from leaving Texas. So I watched on television as all those friends and leaders filed by in genuine grief. I spotted Senator Strom Thurmond whom I would learn later had visited his beloved friend in the hospital on several occasions. I have often thought about the unlikely friendship of Hubert and Strom. As Buford Ellington said, "There is something in all of us that wants to be like Hubert." Maybe that was it. Hubert Humphrey loved people, and they in turn loved him.

I wish we could return to that time when causes—just and unjust—were intense but there was a greater sense of respect and love for the men and women across the aisle. I will have to be content with the knowledge that I was a friend of the greatest US legislator of the twentieth century and probably of all time, past and future. As former vice president Walter Mondale put it in remarks to graduates of the University of Minnesota Law School in 2011, a year that marked the hundredth anniversary of Humphrey's birth, "A famous political scientist once said that Hubert Humphrey was a one-person policy incubator who spawned more down-to-earth ideas and accomplishments than practically anyone else in American history." I don't know who that political scientist was, but he or she summarized a life well spent in the arena of politics and public service.

At President John F. Kennedy's funeral, November 25, 1963.

My great high school teacher Anthony Macaluso (back row, holding child) and family visit the US Capitol with Senator Ralph Yarborough (D-TX) (left), Congressman Jake Pickle (right), and me (back center), 1964.

Jake Pickle (D-TX) working the crowd in his 1986 bid for reelection to the US House of Representatives. He won big.

J. P. "Pop" Pickle meets President Lyndon B. Johnson, Spring 1964.

German chancellor Konrad Adenauer visits President Johnson in Texas, 1964.

To George B. [rustol] — with friendship and best wishes
Hubert H Humphrey

I escort Senator Hubert Humphrey at a dinner in Houston honoring Senator Lloyd Bentsen, 1973.

Me (holding phone) as Hubert Humphrey's southern states floor leader at the 1968 Democratic National Convention in Chicago, conferring with Georgia delegates.

PART IV

A Political
Master's Degree

CHAPTER 11

The Democratic National Committee and Bob Strauss

My work for Hubert Humphrey in 1968 and at the Democratic Na-
tional Committee in 1969 brought me in contact with Bob Strauss, but the relationship
was casual. He was the Democratic national committeeman from Texas. Bob's counterpart as committeewoman was the gracious B. A. Bentsen of Houston, whom I will have
more to say about later. Both represented the Johnson-Connally wing of the party, but
because of their tireless efforts on behalf of Humphrey in 1968, I knew they weren't moss-
backs. In fact, Bob Strauss helped engineer a massive last-minute rally at the Houston
Astrodome that was televised statewide. President Johnson and Mrs. Johnson showed up,
John and Nellie Connally attended, and Frank Sinatra entertained. The rally electrified
the troops and Texas fell into the Democratic column. So my first image of Bob was that
of a can-do, national Democrat in a state where those types were getting harder to find.

My experience with Bob and the DNC over the course of 1969 mirrored the party
as a whole. Losing is never easy, particularly to a despised figure like Richard Nixon:
the often brilliant but deeply flawed human was the epitome of the political evil enemy. The party was deep in debt and divided. Meetings were rancorous. Debates were
mean-spirited and accusatory: northern liberals against southern conservatives, with
every variation in between, topped off by fear of, and intimidation by, George Wallace.
Unfortunately, Hubert Humphrey's selection of Senator Fred Harris of Oklahoma to be
chairman of the DNC only added to the problem. But as I observed the meetings and
comings and goings, Bob Strauss was always in there trying to find middle ground with
common sense and high humor.

There were the joyous moments. On January 24, 1969, Mark Lambert Bristol
came into the world. At the time Valarie and I didn't have a car, so when she went into

labor I called our dear friend Jim Shiver. He was one of those good neighbors, romanticized but seldom real. If he could, he would always go the extra mile. I asked him if he could swing by and pick us up. He said that he was walking out the door and would be there shortly. I forgot to tell him that Valarie was in labor. When he got there, she got in the back seat, so Jim still didn't have a clue. "Where to?" "The hospital," I said. "Good Lord!," said he, and off we shot—the wrong way onto Rock Creek Parkway. Fortunately we righted ourselves and made it to the hospital. But heading the wrong way was the least of our problems that day. Our doctor was drunk. I fired him in the hallway and asked an intern and a nurse to fill in. All went well, but the doctor sent a bill. I wrote him a nasty letter and paid him one dollar a month for several years. When we were leaving Washington, I asked Strauss what to do with the remaining debt. He said, "Send the SOB one more dollar. Tell him you're moving to Texas and if he wants to sue you, he'll have to come to Dallas and that the Strauss firm will defend you pro bono with glee." I did what he told me and we never heard another word from the doctor.

Because of my work in the South, I continued to keep in contact with all the party leaders: governors, senators, House members and others. What I found were many fine people who deeply cared about the nation and the party. I had come to know some in 1968, but during 1969 I came to know them well. A great deal of that knowledge stemmed from the fact that there was little to do but discuss the current situation, and for me mostly to listen. Early on, most southern Democratic leaders came to disagree with Senator Harris. It was apparent to them that he was tied to the liberal wing of the party and had his own presidential agenda. Fred Harris could be brilliant and funny, but he could also be preachy. That did not sit well with governors and other elected officials who were trying desperately to hold the party together in their states. Most were also loyal national Democrats who held strong beliefs on the role of government, national and state. Former governor Terry Sanford of North Carolina was known as "the education governor." Senator Fritz Hollings and Governor Bob McNair did much to improve South Carolina's state government efficiency and effectiveness. Governor John Connally was a tireless champion of higher education. Not only that, he called on the business community to support tax increases to pay for education and other programs. During his terms as governor, Connally passed four or five tax increases and left office more popular than when he arrived in 1963. Why? Because, for all his conservatism, as defined in those days, he believed that government had a role to play and sold that role as a positive force. Contrast that leadership to that of today: demagogues who rant about lowering taxes, then let college tuition and other fees be raised to make up the difference.

There were still the overarching problems of race relations and civil rights. Most of the elected officials who governed the South in those days were not supportive of George Wallace (most loathed him), but they were not vocal champions of civil rights. The difference between them and Wallace, for the most part, was that they were civil and wanted to get on with the business of laying the foundation for opportunity for all citizens. But they had to move cautiously. They deeply appreciated Lyndon Johnson's courageous stand on civil rights. It took the burden off their backs, giving them the federal law to proceed to right age-old wrongs.

Equally important, most were World War II veterans and well-educated patriots who believed that they had been fighting for democracy for all and who wanted nothing more than to fashion good government. Racism was for them a waste of time, anathema to what they'd fought for. But their positions often fell on deaf ears in Washington among leaders like Fred Harris who saw too many things in simple black and white. Harris and others who sat on the Kerner Commission (a national commission to study the depth and cause of racism in America) found that racism was national in scope and permeated society everywhere. It was not just a Southern problem. But George Wallace and all the old southern demagogues and bullying race-baiters of the past had poisoned the well. It was difficult for the sons and daughters of the "New South" to push for progress while keeping the lid on old poisonous habits.

This was the situation at the end of 1969 and this was the stage onto which Robert S. Strauss walked. There needed to be a triggering change of leadership of the Democratic National Committee. I am proud to say that I played a role in it.

Most of the reports I brought back to Washington from these southern leaders were negative. All stated that financial aid for the national party would not be forthcoming. And this was not only a southern position. After a trip to California, it was apparent that Lew Wasserman and Gene Wyman, both premiere party financiers, wanted nothing to do with Harris. This was not disloyalty, but rather the suspicion that they would be funding a Harris run for the presidency.

By the summer I knew something had to occur to dramatize the situation. A Minnesota attorney, Pat O'Connor, had become treasurer of the DNC. I convinced him to make a southern swing with me to hear firsthand how the governors and others felt about Harris. I made a number of calls and in late August or early September we visited North Carolina, South Carolina, Georgia, Tennessee, and finally Texas. All the governors were cordial, but all were firm in their belief that Harris was the wrong leader. By South Carolina, O'Connor needed a drink. The problem was that all liquor stores (there were no bars there) closed at sunset. We arrived at the one down the street from our hotel five minutes or so too late. I called Governor McNair's office, he answered the phone (something that would be unlikely today), and I told him the situation. He laughed and said something like, "Well, I didn't commit to help Pat financially, but I'll send over a bottle of whatever he wants." Scotch was the request. A bottle was there in twenty minutes.

Then we went to Texas, to see not the governor but Bob Strauss. Over dinner we explained the dire circumstances. Bob didn't dwell much on Harris's shortcomings. He knew them all too well. There were some ideas kicking around about a possible fundraiser in Miami. I think Humphrey had talked to Frank Sinatra and other entertainers about helping. Miami and Florida wanted to bid on the 1972 convention and were amenable to hosting the event. We decided that maybe we could put on a national event together. Strauss thought that if Humphrey would come to Texas for some private meetings, he could persuade enough Texans to fill a chartered plane. Strauss assured O'Connor that he would talk with President Johnson, John Connally, and others. And he did. Bob worked tirelessly to fill that plane. He also convinced Governor Preston Smith and Lieutenant Governor Ben Barnes to weigh in. I worked out of party headquarters in Austin for over a month. With Strauss in tow, we called the southern governors. Strauss had a brilliant message for them: "Look, we've told Harris that we won't raise money unless there are changes. Now let's raise some money and show 'em we can, but we want in on the action."

At some point at dinner that night Strauss came up to me and said, "Stick around. You and Valarie might not be going back to Texas yet!" I didn't know what was being planned, and I now know that some viewed what transpired as disloyalty to Harris and the Democratic Party. My loyalty to the party was unwavering, though, and Humphrey asked me to stay in Washington. I liked Fred Harris and thought his wife, LaDonna, was one of the most beautiful and courageous persons I've ever known, but by the summer of 1969 I knew two things: I wanted to go back home and Fred Harris was the problem, not the solution. In late summer, however, Strauss and O'Connor persuaded me to stay on, with the understanding that I could work out of Texas on the upcoming national gala.

After dinner a number of us met in Fred Harris's suite. Things had been predetermined. Senator Harris had to resign. Larry O'Brien (an early Kennedy operative) would become chairman, and Bob Strauss would become treasurer. I think Hubert broke the news. It was not a pleasant scene, but political divorces never are.

Because Bob and Helen Strauss had a longstanding commitment to go to Mexico with the Connallys, I was asked to hurry back to Washington to do two things: identify the size of the deficit and make calls, particularly in the South, to support the O'Brien-Strauss ticket that would be voted on at the DNC meeting in March 1970. Pat O'Connor had brought with him from Minnesota a wonderful attorney, Andy Shea, who was immensely helpful in getting to the bottom of the books.

Party finances for both parties were an unholy mess in those days. There was some accounting and reporting, but it was not transparent, even from within. Furthermore, the Democrats had assumed Bobby Kennedy's debt, which seemed to reach a higher number every day. I loved President Kennedy and admired much about Bobby, but I thought the debt assumption was wrong. It was not the party that ran up the bills, it was Kennedy operatives. Following the death of Senator Kennedy, all his teams working in various states left to go home or to Washington for the funeral service. They left hotel bills unpaid and hundreds of rental cars unreturned. Two years later we were still getting irate letters from car companies. From time to time a car would show up. State party leaders, governors, and elected officials were also bedeviled by our creditors.

It was not a picture to encourage the fainthearted. But Larry O'Brien and Bob Strauss were not in that class. Each was not only a loyal party professional, each was a consummate political mechanic in the best sense. But both had to be sold to the committeemen and committeewomen, as both carried some baggage. Larry O'Brien was originally deeply devoted to John Kennedy, yet he became President Johnson's postmaster general and he stayed with Humphrey in 1968 to the disappointment and outrage of some Kennedy loyalists. Bob Strauss was clearly tied to the conservative wing of the party. So there was grumbling from the states. There was threat of revolt. Calls went out and—oh, how I loved making those calls on behalf of Strauss. First I would tell them about Strauss's role in carrying Texas. Then I'd tell them how much he'd raised for the Miami event (when few of them had lifted a finger). Finally I'd hit them with the fact that we had a $9 million debt—and did they want the job? That shut them up.

In March of 1970, the DNC met and elected both men to lead the party. Larry O'Brien was a known. Bob Strauss was not, but he had one thing going for him. He had been preparing for this moment all his life.

Strauss was born in Lockhart, Texas, in 1918. His parents were Jewish merchants. Soon they had an opportunity to move to the small town of Stamford, in West Texas. As children in the only Jewish family there, Bob and his brother, Ted, could easily have been scarred. But with loving parents who were somewhat successful and stayed in business during the Depression, and possessed with equally devilish senses of humor, the Strauss boys came out of Stamford whole. Demonstrating their flexibility, Bob and Ted attended the local Baptist church because there was no temple or other Jewish place of worship in Stamford. Not only did they attend church, Bob and Ted were members of the Royal Ambassadors, a Baptist youth group. When he first told me the story of this, I didn't believe him, but he produced a photo as proof: there was very Jewish Bob and Ted surrounded by admiring gentiles. That one picture foretold his life ahead.

From Stamford he went to the University of Texas at Austin. There in the late 1930s he met and worked with John Connally and with Lyndon Johnson who ran for Congress as an avid FDR New Dealer. Bob and hundreds of other up-and-coming Depression-motivated young men and women became part of the Johnson team. For Strauss, the underlying motivation was FDR. That great leader would be his guiding political light throughout his life.

One thing the Depression did, though this was certainly not universal, was to bridge some gaps of race and religion, at least among leaders like Johnson, Connally, and Strauss. LBJ's teaching experience in Cotulla, Texas, showed him the miserable hardship of young Mexican American kids. John Connally saw the waste of Texas's young people dropping out of high school and college while working for Johnson and the Texas division of the National Youth Administration. Bob Strauss felt the sting of religious prejudice. All chose to do something about these problems when they gained stature and power. Many Depression-molded children, other future leaders, vowed to obtain power, and most achieving this chose to use it for the public good.

Upon finishing law school, Bob joined the FBI. He fought communists and Nazis alike in Davenport, Iowa, and Cincinnati, Ohio—hotbeds of subversion. He loved to tell stories about those days. These were mostly centered on having to phone J. Edgar Hoover frequently. Hoover apparently kept close tabs on his agents, who had to contact headquarters at least once a day.

Following his stint in Iowa, Bob was assigned to Cincinnati. He and his wife headed east. The deal was that as soon as they reached Cincinnati they were supposed to phone in to let J. Edgar know that they had arrived. Bob and Helen devised a scheme, though, and as they drew near Covington, Kentucky, they phoned to say they'd had a flat, were about two or three hours from Cincinnati and would call again early the next morning. Then they hooked a right across the Ohio River. Bob and Helen Strauss both loved to gamble—a lifetime love affair—and Covington was one of the hot spots of illegal American gambling. They hit the first joint available and began to shoot dice. Suddenly, out of the darkened corner of the room, a thuggish character appeared and said, "The boss wants to see you." Over in the corner was a table of mafia-styled thugs. "We see you are packing a piece [FBI service revolver], Mr. Strauss. What gives?" In a flash, his life passed before him. Who did he fear most, J. Edgar or the mob? He blurted out, "Boys, I am with the FBI, but I won't tell if you won't tell Hoover I was here." He then hurriedly explained the circumstance. Everybody laughed. Bob and Helen even had their dinner paid for, and later laughed about it every time he told the tale. With Strauss, it always got better. Audacity softened by humor worked that evening in Covington and thereafter for Robert S. Strauss.

Strauss used his sense of humor in his first week after taking office as DNC treasurer. A great many of the national press had a jaundiced eye about this wealthy Texan, who had made money in the law, banking, and radio, who was now in charge of Democratic Party funds. Bob didn't duck their criticism. A female reporter said to him, "Mr. Strauss, I know you have a swimming pool in your backyard. Do you swim in it when you're in Dallas?" Bob was quick to respond: "Honey, I don't think I've ever swam in it. I go home in the evening, kiss Helen, call my kids, fix a double martini, then prop my feet up and look out the window at that pool and say, 'Bob, you are one rich son-of-a-bitch!'" The press howled. Then Bob went into some issue that was on his mind. The press coverage turned more favorable.

There were problems in the DNC as far as the eye could see, but we had to get on top of the debt first and deal with the monthly operating deficit that was running around $100,000.

We called in each department head and line-itemed each expenditure. We canceled cars, credit cards, and most per diems. To fortify his position (because we caught a lot of heat), Bob told them that he was going to have the press over for drinks once a month to point out progress and failures. Some pissed and moaned and took their cases to O'Brien or one of the national committee members, but Bob was brilliant. He told O'Brien and the entire national committee, "OK, then we will take out a $10 million insurance policy with the DNC as beneficiary. Once a month you will draw straws. Whoever gets the short one jumps." Then he produced a letter from some friend of his in Dallas who purported to be able to broker such a deal. Again Bob used a joke to point out how serious things were. For the most part, every department complied. Even so, we had to make cuts in personnel. Throughout my life, layoffs have been the most difficult task. Yes, there are incompetents and fools who deserve to go, but for the most part those having to lay people off are bearers of bad news for hardworking people with families and obligations. It is damned tough to call them in. I think that is why human resource and personnel departments were invented. Top management did not have the guts to fire people.

But the DNC had to lay people off. Quickly we worked our way through the entire DNC until I got to an ancient telephone operator, Mommie Walker. I called her in and told her the situation. She looked at me, as cool as a riverboat gambler and said, "You can't fire me!"

"Says who?"

"Says FDR and Jim Farley," she replied.

"Mommie, FDR's been dead for twenty-four years and Mr. Farley may have passed too."

"He's alive, but it doesn't matter. They promised me a lifetime job."

Well, that one got way above my pay scale in a hurry. I had a directive from Strauss, but I did not want to go up against FDR. Fortunately Strauss was in the office. I told him the story and he roared with laughter. "God almighty, Bristol, you let an eighty-year-old woman and a dead president bring us to a halt?"

He called his secretary and told her to get Jim Farley, former national party chairman and postmaster general under President Roosevelt. Bob knew that he was still alive and was chairman of the board of Coca-Cola International.

Farley got on the phone and Bob put him on the speaker. "Mr. Chairman, this is Bob Strauss and a very bumfuzzled George Bristol. Do you know Mommie Walker?"

"Hell, yes, I know Mommie. She was the White House chief telephone operator under the boss. She knew everybody and everything."

"She says she has a lifetime job."

"She does and I send a check every month to cover her expense to the DNC. Bob, what she really needs is a pension. She would go to the poorhouse without one. She has to work."

"What if we set her up a little pension plan and gave her a nice retirement party?"

Those two great men verbally set it up, worked out the details, and then a few days later we called Mommie Walker into Bob's office. Farley was on the phone to reassure her. She started to cry—with joy. "Oh, Mr. Strauss, I know I am getting too old, but I had to work. God bless you and Chairman Farley."

We threw her a party. Everybody hugged. Jim Farley came down from New York with a photo of FDR. An era had passed, but every few months Bob would call Mommie to see how she was getting along.

At the other end of the spectrum, we had to deal with creditors, and we had some big ones, like AT&T. As I remember it, we owed them over a million dollars. After carefully reviewing the situation, Strauss wrote a letter to all the creditors saying that he understood their situation, but we did not have the money. We were $9.3 million in debt. He assured them he would work around the clock to secure the debt and pay it off. I think he offered them ten or fifteen cents on the dollar as an immediate settlement, or a workout—which could take a long time. Some settled, but AT&T, among others, balked. There was a serious legal question of debt forgiveness to a political party. They demanded a meeting. We set one up at the DNC's Watergate office. A team of pinstriped lawyers and accountants came down from New York, led by AT&T's legal counsel and accompanied by Jim Rowe from Montana, a well-connected Washington insider. Solemnly they went through the numbers. Sorrowfully they said that the bottom line grew larger each month. Dutifully they pointed out that they had legal and fiduciary responsibilities. Sadly they saw no other alternative but to cut off the service and stop the bleeding.

Strauss interrupted. "Boys, you are right. We have a bum record, an indefensible record. Here's what I want you to do. Next Tuesday at 11:00 a.m., hold a press conference and announce your decision, but don't do it a moment before 11:00 a.m. because I'm going to hold a press conference at 10:00 a.m. and tell the world that the largest monopoly in the world is about to turn off the phones of the world's oldest political party. Bristol and I have been looking for a way to raise money and nobody likes a monopoly like AT&T." He let that sink in and then added, "Then I am going to tell them that you've been carrying the RNC Barry Goldwater debt since 1964." My jaw dropped. How in God's name did he know that?

There was dead silence. "Now don't flake on me," Strausss said. "I know you'll take heat, but you will have given us the issue to raise funds."

They asked if they could huddle. "Sure, use Bristol's office." Which was about five feet by ten feet, right off Strauss's office. They crowded in and shut the door.

"How did you know about Goldwater?," I asked. "Because, Bristol, I have been trained to know those things. That's why I am one fine lawyer," he winked.

A while later, the AT&T representatives filed in. "Bob, let's try to work something out." Bob already had a plan. If I remember it correctly, it ran something like this: The DNC would pay each monthly bill as incurred. It would also pay a percentage of funds available after meeting monthly operating expenses and another percentage if we had a major fundraiser—with the hope being that we could retire the debt in a few years. We honored that commitment each and every month. Because we did so, we were able to call upon that goodwill in early 1972 for a project that would go far to retire not only the AT&T debt, but also much of the total debt. While all of this was going, we started the long, hard process of raising money.

Once we got into the fundraising side of the equation, we were shocked at the lack of recordkeeping and lack of small donors. There were reasons for this. First, there were few laws then that made political organizations keep records of donations, small or large. Second, traditionally and over a long period of time, party fundraising itself had been funded by large donors—and that went for both parties. Finally, much of the mechanics of running presidential (and state elections) were handled at the state and local levels. Many states and cities had political machines with county and precinct leaders who would turn out the votes. These were very efficient and successful. Those organizations or "bosses" elected FDR, Harry Truman, John Kennedy, and Lyndon Johnson. They nearly elected Hubert Humphrey in 1968. Were they sometimes less than ethical? Yes. But for the most part they were in the election business. They did it at the local levels and they raised and spent their own funds. So a great deal of funds raised never reached the national political party's coffers.

For most of the late nineteenth century and into much of the twentieth century national parties were charged with holding conventions and funding presidential campaigns. But it must be remembered that presidential candidates for a long time rarely left their hometowns—this was the era of the front-porch candidate. Party leaders and elected officials traveled to see them, took measured of the men, and then returned home to fire up their troops. Thus there was no need to fund a huge campaign war chest. The Democrats for years had their headquarters in New York because that is where the preponderance of funding sources was. Television would change all of that. It was far simpler to reach more people by ads, so campaigns had grown more expensive by the 1960s. If radio made FDR, television made Jack Kennedy. Yet even then, large donors were responsible for the lion's share of funding. As there were party political regulars, there were also party financial regulars who covered a large percentage of a presidential campaign's expenses by contributing to the Democratic National Committee. Republican financiers made similar large contributions to the Republican National Committee.

The national parties, in turn, paid for their presidential candidate's travel and campaign media. At the national level the campaign was run out of the DNC. That's not to say that the candidate didn't have his people in place within the committee, but it was a given that the national party was the controlling body for funding and expenditures. On reflection, the amounts raised and spent pale in comparison to today's wasteful and shameful multi-hundred-million-dollar extravagances. So it was easier to raise those funds from a relatively few donors rather than going to the time and expense of building a small-donor base.

That strategy worked only up to the point that the candidate was acceptable to donors and expected to win. That was not the case in 1948 when Truman appeared to have no chance. The situation became so dire that from time to time Truman's presidential campaign train had to stop until funds could be raised to continue. But that only heightened Truman's appeal as little guy fighting for the common folks against the rich and entrenched barons of privilege and industry.

In 1968 Humphrey was written off early. Pocketbooks and checkbooks remained shut. The DNC went deeper and deeper in debt. Only in the last weeks as Humphrey began to close the gap did contributions begin to flow, but they amounted to too little, too late. Another part of Humphrey's problem was his campaign; the party was short of funds going into the campaign. Some, including me, began to think that there had to be a better way to wage a campaign for the most powerful office in the world. It was the beginning germ of campaign finance reform.

Strauss instinctively knew that it was unhealthy to rely solely on big donors, but he also knew it would take time to build a large small-donor base. He searched around and found a woman, Bobbie Gechas, who had done fundraising for one of the United Nations programs. She had a number of innovative ideas, but each required up-front money to test. Strauss liked her and committed himself to finding the money she needed to get the small-donor programs up and running.

One of our most brilliant ideas helped us keep going and begin to rebuild. Knowing that we had to regain the confidence of all types of party supporters—donors, elected officials, and other leaders—we proposed to send a letter asking them to measure our success in restoring the party by contributing $72 a month. We would report to them regularly and if donors didn't think we were measuring up, they could drop out. It was a pay-as-you-go policy to meet monthly obligations.

The problem again was finding the names and addresses of potential donors. We thought we needed at least two hundred contributors. We scratched and scrambled, and as I remember it we came up with about a thousand names. We all knew that we would have to do more than send a letter in order to convince two hundred out of one thousand. At some point I suggested a phone bank so we could personally call as many of the potential donors as possible. While the staff sought names, I began to assemble the mechanics. Matt Reese, a Democratic get-out-the-vote guru, offered a phone room at a small charge. There was a larger pool of Capitol Hill staffers, young lobbyists, and lawyers I recruited to work the phones. Then we got very lucky. Working in the phone room was a woman named Vera Murray. Somehow she let me know that she thought she could set up our system and run it. What an understatement! Vera Murray is one of those perfect diamonds in the rough. Her work on the solicitation program was so great that I told Strauss we needed her in the treasurer's office. I never knew of a task she could not perform with charm, grace, and high intelligence. She stayed with Bob through it all: DNC chair, US trade ambassador, private law practice, and ambassador to Russia.

At some point we launched. Things went pretty well, but not great. Most contributors did not know Strauss, save for Texans, a few elected officials, and DNC members. They wanted to hear from Bob personally. That was impossible for two reasons. First,

Bob was working his Texas friends, elected officials, and DNC members. Second, we were trying to set up fundraising trips all over the country. There weren't enough hours in the day.

After about a week I asked to see him after work. We had a drink and reviewed the situation. I told him that folks wanted to visit with him, but knew that wasn't feasible. Then and there I launched what may have been my best idea. "Bob, these folks, outside of those you are calling in Texas, have no idea who you are or what your voice sounds like. I want to make calls saying that I'm you, or phone those who insist on talking with you."

"Good Lord, Bristol, have you lost your mind?"

"Think about it. I know this will hurt your ego but you are truly unknown. I know your spiel and mannerisms. If I run into a problem I will hang up and you can call back."

"Well, it might work, but be careful."

So the next night I placed my first call as Bob to a man named Jimmy Muslow of Louisiana. I reached him, though I quickly wished I hadn't when I heard him ask, "Bob, are you and Helen going to meet us next week as we've discussed?"

Horror flowed through me, but we were broke, so what the hell. "Jimmy," I mumbled, "I've got a cold and unless you and your friends can start sending me $72 a month, count me out. I'll call you back in a little while." I called Strauss.

"Bob, who is Jimmy Muslow?"

"Oh, Bristol, he's only my college roommate and one of our best friends. George, what have you done?"

Time passed slowly. A while later the phone rang.

"George, Jimmy Muslow bought it and committed to get ten people to come in on the program. Then I told him it was you calling. We both laughed our asses off. But Muslow told me to tell you to keep calling." And so I did, and in a short while we hit our target.

Once the direct mail, the $72-per-month effort, and some big contributors began to kick in, Strauss and I fanned out all over the country, gathering in new and old supporters alike. In West Virginia it was a young secretary of state, Jay Rockefeller. In Kentucky it was Lieutenant Governor Wendell Ford (soon to be governor), former governor Ned Breathitt, and a young entrepreneur, John Y. Brown. Fortunately Kentucky was one of my key 1968 states and I had made a great many friends in and out of government, so we had good crowds and support.

Arkansas was the home of great Democrats. We relied heavily on Charles Ward, the national committeeman who was devoted to Strauss. He delivered and introduced us to Dale Bumpers, who would beat former governor Orval Faubus (of Little Rock High School infamy) and go on to oust sitting Republican governor Winthrop Rockefeller in 1970. It was my privilege to introduce Strauss to Congressman David Pryor. We had worked together for Humphrey. Both Bumpers and Pryor went on to be governors and senators from Arkansas. Both were wonderful friends and supporters, bringing Arkansas fully back into the Democratic camp and setting the stage for future governor Bill Clinton.

A digression is in order here. With all our financial problems, O'Brien and Strauss were determined to raise some funds to support key races, if for no other reason than to show the campaign flag. At a planning meeting I spoke up, saying that I had worked hard raising money and thought I might throw a couple of names in the pot. I mentioned Dale Bumpers of Arkansas and Lawton Chiles of Florida who was running for a US Senate seat. At the time of this meeting both were long shots. O'Brien and Strauss thought little of their chances, but to their credit they recognized my accomplishments and let me have $25,000 or so to dole out. I think I sent $10,000 to Bumpers and $15,000 to Chiles. Both won and I had fun with that for a long time. Neither man forgot my faith in them. Both went on to serve America with distinction and honor. It was the best investment I ever made.

All in all, 1970 was productive. We were not only putting the Democratic Party on a sound financial footing, we were rebuilding a party that temporarily had lost its way with the split over civil rights, Vietnam, and the 1968 defeat. I could feel it change. Phone calls were pleasant and productive. Meetings were harmonious. The proof was in the pudding. Richard Nixon's 1970 southern strategy—attempting to help the Republican Party win elections by exploiting southern racism—failed. Democrats held on to the Senate and the House.

Throughout 1971 we continued to build. In the spring we felt confident enough to hold a national fundraising dinner. We set a goal of $1 million and made it. Again governors made up our base, but senators and House members came too. The DNC was back in business. It showed in the smiles on the faces in the crowd, and the camaraderie was genuine.

But from time to time, there were small warning bells that something was amiss. A contributor here, a candidate there, or a concerned national committee member, for example, began to tell me and others that the FBI or the IRS had been around. As it later turned out, Richard Nixon was assembling his enemy list and we found out the extent of his intimidating tactics, but in 1970–1971 occasional mentions by Democrats of the FBI's appearance seemed only a coincidence. We were so busy that I don't think we had time to sit down and analyze the situation. Every workday was about ten hours long.

In July of 1971 I took a few days off. Our daughter Jennifer Bristol was born on July 3. The next day I took our son, now two and a half, to a Fourth of July party with fireworks. On the way we stopped at the hospital and he got to see his baby sister. On July 5 or July 6, Bob Strauss sent his driver, Nat, to pick up mother and child. We went to our home in Cleveland Park. From then on until we left Washington in December 1972, we had wonderful family time, with incredibly great friends and neighbors, such as Jim and Elizabeth Shiver, Ethna and Jack Hopper, and J. D. and Carol Williams.

At some point in the early spring of that year we had added another layer of responsibility to our fundraising chores. In 1972 the Democratic Party would hold a convention and nominate our candidate to oppose Nixon. The frontrunner was Senator Edmund Muskie of Maine. He had been Humphrey's running mate in 1968 and had come off the experience with high marks. However, it looked to be a heated primary season, as Humphrey, Scoop Jackson, and George McGovern were casting about for delegate support, as well as others. Muskie wouldn't last long.

Our job at the DNC was to remain neutral and give the candidate, whomever that might be, a good pay-as-you-go convention and a party that was not saddled with debt. We had made some progress, but we were still about $9 million in the hole. The convention would add a couple of million more. So at some point I split left day-to-day operations sustaining fundraising and concentrated on convention financing.

After a series of visits by party officials to various cities, we settled on Miami Beach. There were a number of reasons for that choice. The convention had not been held in the South since 1928 in Houston. Miami Beach and Florida presented a nice package of financing support. Governor Reuben Askew was enthusiastic and was a man to be trusted. Conventions need an honest, honorable, respected broker with muscle. A national convention has a great many moving parts and it is imperative to have that center of support. Hotels, union and non-union workers, network television demands, delegate demands, security—inside and outside the hall—all having to be coordinated and synchronized in a year. And there was money to be raised. Nothing like the outrageous $25–40 million spent today, but a great deal in 1972 for a party out of power. So Reuben Askew fit our needs perfectly. Of the thousands of political people I've met over nearly fifty years, Askew would be in the top twenty as a civil servant, political leader, and human being.

The math ran something like this. Out of the $2 million to be raised, the State of Florida, Miami Beach, and Dade County probably promised a total of $750,000 or so, in cash and in kind. Various licensing fees and complimentary hotel rooms and cars came to $250,000. That meant that there was still a million-dollar shortfall staring us in the face, not to mention the debt left over from 1968. But by now we had a finance council and a convention ad campaign.

Over 1969 and 1970, Strauss did a masterful job of nursing party financiers back to the fold while at the same time engaging a great many new players, most of whom were outside Washington. While Strauss was the ultimate insider, he fully understood that Washington was a fickle town, full of folks who could, and often did, turn on a dime with their support. Furthermore, senators and members of Congress had their own money to raise. Some helped, but not many. But there were a great many governors, lieutenant governors, mayors, and young business and professional leaders who gave or agreed to raise money. They became our base. Maybe they were good for $300,000 or so—peanuts now, but not back then.

Traditionally the two parties had sold ads in their convention programs. There was some controversy because Democrats and Republicans had both hit up defense contractors. This was bad in two ways: these were companies doing substantial business with the government, and such advertisements had little commercial value since they were not selling products to the general public. However, for others who bought ads, there would be value received if enough programs were printed and properly distributed. So we brought in a couple of advertising executives to make sure we were on the square when it came to the ratio between ad costs and copy distribution. Once we got as close as we could, we set the price and went out to drum up support. Eventually we sold some eighty ads at $10,000 per page, but we were still short and there were still the monthly operating and debt expenses to be met.

At that point John Y. Brown of Kentucky——and Kentucky Fried Chicken—stepped in. He was in the process of selling his company in late 1971 or 1972, and he had time and money. He wanted to help the party while at the same time make a name for himself. He brought us an idea that was bold and unique: a twenty-four-hour Democratic Party fundraising telethon. Strauss and I immediately cottoned to the idea, but there were many questions and potential problems. First, it would cost a great deal of money to produce and air. Second, could we find a network that would sell us the time, and could we get the right mix of celebrities and entertainers to fill that much time? We kept coming back to our agreement that it was one hell of an idea. We could reach out to millions of Americans in a short period of time. Even if we broke even, we would be ahead by thousands upon thousands of names of small donors—maybe, we hoped, a hundred thousand donors at an average of $50 per donor. We were still in the hoping business. John Y. would put up a great deal as a loan or guarantee, but not all of it. We turned to the finance committee members that Strauss and I had worked so hard to assemble. If I remember, we asked each to sign a guarantee of at least $50,000. I think we needed fifty, and we oversubscribed thanks to the leadership of great friends like Lee Kling, Arthur Krim, Lew Wasserman, and others. I really began to believe that we could pull it off: pay for the convention and erase a great deal of the debt.

But we needed more help and a break or two. For inside help we gained Gordon Wynne and George Dillman. Gordon was an attorney from Wills Point, Texas, who in an earlier life had managed star performers and produced shows. Judy Garland was one of his principal clients. He would manage all the telethon production for Strauss. George Dillman took over the day-to-day production and distribution of the convention programs. Both brought their projects in on time and on budget. They became essential to our success—and became lifelong friends.

Now we needed to make a deal with AT&T—telethons run on telephones, we needed performers and celebrities, and we needed a network to carry the show. Finally, we wanted every state to participate, but we particularly needed the largest states.

John Y. recruited the celebrities and stars. He had star power and great presence himself, and, as Strauss said, "could talk a dog off a meat wagon." He had great help from Milton Berle and Ruth Berle, as well as others in the entertainment world.

Kitty Halpin (now Mrs. Birch Bayh) of our staff was designated to coordinate all the moving parts. She did a splendid job and would go on to coordinate future telethons.

Meanwhile Bob and I went to see AT&T. We went with some strength, as we had been making our payments each and every month. In fact, on some months when we got ahead we had been sending a little extra. We had also promised to pay for the convention phone system up front, so the executives were pleased to see us. But they knew nothing of our new request. They were up against Strauss again.

"We need to set up a nationwide phone bank and we want you to front the money. We've got guarantees, but no cash," said Strauss. There was no response, but we could hear the air suck in.

"You've got to understand, fellows," Strauss continued. "We can continue paying a little bit a month, and you might get your money in ten years if I'm around. But I'm not going to be. So you better dance with the devil you know, because if we're successful, we'll pay you off—every damn dollar!"

They now knew they were up against the master again, and they asked if they could think it over. We went to lunch. During or near the lunch hour Bob and Helen got the call that her dad was in the hospital near death. Bob told me to go back over to AT&T, and they rushed to the airport.

After about two hours, the lead negotiator came out and motioned me into his office. "George, subject to a lot of ifs and legal work on both parties' part, we will do the deal." I could have kissed him. He was good for his word and as events would prove, so were we.

From that moment on it seemed like I lived on an airplane. Not only did we have to wrap up convention ad sales, which often required in-person calls on corporate leaders and ad executives, but also we had to set up phone-bank organizations all over the country. This required several appointments with party leaders to spell out the split arrangement (we determined earlier on that if we gave the sponsoring local party a piece of the action—often expenses—they would be more inclined to play ball), with key financial supporters to get them to underwrite the AT&T local phone bank, and with the local AT&T officials to give them our requirements and written assurance that they would get the system in as specified and on time. A telethon without telephones is a thon. Every town was different. Some were difficult. Some didn't play along at all. Few were easy, except for Chicago.

Through Strauss from Mayor Richard Daley, I was given a name of an official who I believe was Chicago's commissioner of public works. We met first with local party officials who would run the phone bank, and with representatives of the hall where it would be held. I explained things and passed out all the forms and information sheets. There were no questions. It was clear that the mayor wanted this done and it would be done. Then we met with the AT&T representative who stated how busy they were that summer—they were really behind schedule and just didn't see how they could fit it in. I tried to butt in by showing him a copy of the letter of agreement from AT&T national headquarters.

"George, put your letter away," said the commissioner. Then I got a lesson in democracy—Daley style. The commissioner slowly and carefully went over the AT&T permits pending in his department, and then said that it would be a cold day in hell before they were granted unless the Democratic telethon phones were up and running in July. I didn't hear heels click or see a salute, but I heard an obedient "yes, sir," and that was that. Chicago went off my worry list, at least for the moment. Later Mayor Daley would pull Chicago's support, because his delegation was challenged at the convention and he was furious.

At some point ABC agreed to carry the show. It was going to happen.

Then I received a call, early one evening—I'm guessing that it February or March of 1972. The caller asked if Bob Strauss was in. I told him that Bob was out of town, and asked if I could help him. The caller chuckled and said, "Well, I don't know. My name is Dick Herman of Omaha, Nebraska. I'm manager of the Republican National Committee and we need a place to hold a convention, because we have just been thrown out of San Diego because of the ITT bribery scandal."

I may have hesitated for a moment, but I told him that I was aware of that and frankly gleeful to see Nixon once again rejected by his own state, adding that I thought this had been an embarrassing blow to the Republicans.

It turned out that Herman wanted to talk with Strauss about bringing the Republican Convention to Miami Beach. I knew I'd better try to run a little interference, because no one in the party trusted anything related to Nixon, so I asked if we might meet. Herman said he was downstairs at the Watergate Bar. I was about to meet one of the most honorable and engaging humans I've ever encountered.

Dick Herman had no choice but to turn to us, it seemed. Putting national conventions together is time-consuming and costly. There are miles of telephone and media wiring, lighting, platforms, and press boxes to be strung and built. There are hotel contracts to be negotiated and honored. There are security and credentialing to worry about, and the list goes on, right up to the moment the opening gavel cracks. Then there is the four-day convention itself, which runs twenty-four hours a day. So convention planners and cities need all the lead time they can get. Since the Democrats already had a hall nearly arranged and blueprints approved, we were in the catbird's seat, as Herman saw it, but since he knew we were still short of cash he was interested in making a deal with us.

I liked Herman right off. He told his story and was highly critical of "those damn fools" who had allowed the ITT fiasco to occur. He had nothing to do with the Committee to Re-elect the President (CREEP—aptly named, it turned out), since Nixon and his team did not even trust the RNC—which was reasonable, given CREEP's illegal antics. Herman was obviously a partisan Republican, but more obviously a sincere and honest midwesterner. We talked over drinks and then dinner, and we agreed that if we could establish a sense of complete trust, then having both conventions in the same city and in the same hall could make sense.

I promised Herman that I would call Strauss the next day, and I did. Bob made a couple of calls to check out Herman, and then called me back. "Bristol, if this works it could be a godsend, but we have a lot of hoops to get through. Not the least are Reuben Askew and Miami Beach." Bob told me that he would be back in Washington the next week, and he gave me the date of his return. "Get us a plane and set up a meeting with Reuben. Tell Herman we're going to see Reuben. I'll call Larry O'Brien to alert him."

There comes a time for an honest broker like Reuben Askew, and now his time was coming. He would have two wise and honest co-negotiators—Bob Strauss and Dick

Herman—to work with. As I recall, Bob and I flew down to see Governor Askew and Mayor Chuck Hall of Miami Beach. We went through the pros and cons, and Strauss made a strong pitch to seal the joint deal. There were few practical downsides. Except for Dick Herman and a couple of convention-planning types, there would be little, if any, Republican presence in the planning. Convention plans are convention plans. It may not have been exactly the ideal platform configuration for the Republicans, but there would be a month between our convention and theirs, and they could make changes.

The Republicans brought money to the table and we needed it. First there was a direct cash payment for work on the hall we had already done, and there was a promise to help sell convention program ads, which was an incremental plus to us, as we had already sold most of our ads. That was a bigger help to Herman and the Republicans, as they were running behind on everything.

The Floridians agreed to the deal that day, and Bob called Herman to tell him the decision. There was much gratitude—on both ends of the line.

On all matters of agreement Dick Herman kept his word. He and I talked practically every day, making changes to this and that. He was a trusted partner, unlike his counterparts at CREEP who were not only set to screw the Democrats, but who would screw Herman. After giving his word to us that both parties would sell the same number of ads and that there were to be no defense industry ads, Herman was commanded by CREEP to accept all ads, including defense industry ads. The day he was told to do this by CREEP, he called us to apologize. I told him to forget it. It wasn't his fault. When Herman told me this, we were in full convention-planning mode, and we were pretty sure we had the convention paid for. Then some damn fools broke into the party headquarters. Real-life Gang That Couldn't Shoot Straight operators actually broke in twice—on June 1 and June 17. So we had our own distractions, as both break-ins centered on the treasurer's office and its safe.

On June 1 a bunch of us were in Strauss's office, finalizing the convention program. We heard something and yelled out that we were in the back. There was no reply. We thought nothing about it, because by that time people were working around the clock. Only the next morning did we find out that there had been an attempt to open the safe. We laughed about this, because we had nothing in the safe and rarely did. We were an in-and-out, pay-as-you-go organization and still deeply in debt. Neither then nor later that month did we have any inkling of a White House–directed operation. That would have been crazy.

The biggest political and presidential scandal in US history, with the possible exception of when Warren Harding's pals set out to steal everything, went almost unnoticed by the immediate victims: the officers and employees of the Democratic National Committee. But several things have to be recalled. It truly looked like a bunch of lightweight amateurs had attempted the break-ins, and we were less than a month out from our convention. Furthermore, without our knowledge or anyone else's, the president of the United States and his cronies throughout the government were orchestrating a web of cover-up, so there were not many revelations at first. Things really went back to normal for us after the shock of the first few days surrounding each break-in, the police presence in our office and media coverage. With a telethon and a convention looming ever closer, normal meant sixteen hours of work each day.

Later I learned that I had earlier that summer met the planner of the break-ins. At some point, an odd-mannered man had showed up in Miami Beach, pedaling a fundraising scheme and wearing a weird, bright-red toupee. Whatever it was that he was pushing didn't work out. I never saw him again until he showed up on national television during the Watergate hearings. It was Howard Hunt. At some point it was mentioned that Hunt, among his many hare-brained assignments, had tried to induce the Democrats to buy into an illegal activity. In his testimony he confirmed having been in Miami Beach on a mission to embarrass the Democrats, and having worn a red wig and other CIA disguises to throw us off the trail. I am a believer in the CIA and its mission, but I have had a lingering doubt about their recruitment standards since that moment.

I also learned in the testimony at the Watergate hearing that one of the reasons for the break-in was to steal floor plans for the Democratic convention so they could tap the floor phones. That seemed dumb—Herman had our floor plans and I had theirs—but when I thought longer about it, knowing by then how Herman and other Republicans felt about those gumshoes, I realized that he might not have given them the plans. No one was more hurt and angry about the stupidity of the president and his midnight minions than Dick Herman. The distraction of the Watergate break-ins aside, there seemed to be a million loose ends for us with the July convention only weeks away.

There are hundreds of books, some very good, about the politics and antics of conventions, but few about the inner workings of making a political convention happen. In some respects the process resembles that for organizing industry conventions, large religious gatherings, and the like: there are hotels, meeting halls, media facilities, and sponsored parties to be planned for and coordinated. But national political party nominating conventions are unique, each an incredible story within a broad history. The 1972 Democratic National Convention was a case in point, with a twenty-hour national telethon added onto the weekend before the opening of the proceedings, something that had never been attempted before, and that has not been done since, regrettably.

In our weeks of planning, a typical day started for us at about 5:30 a.m. or so. Dick Herman and I, sometimes Strauss and Andy Shea, would confer about last-minute changes and added costs—rarely savings. (As major events draw closer, vendor and contractor heels dig in and costs go up.) I would put out a phone bank fire or two. At some point John Y. Brown or his representatives would call in with a request. Some nearly forgotten star wanted to be on the show, but demanded to bring along a supporting entourage. The best one: "She'll come for free, but her dress will run $20,000 plus." The lesser the light, the more glitter needed. But for all of these requests and offers we had a simple answer. If one wanted to participate, one had to play at the going rate—period. We thought we could make it financially, but it was tight, and everyone knew it was tight, so we would dance a bit but then tell the fading star to forget it.

On balance there was great teamwork. Dick Herman was incredibly effective and honorable. The entertainers John Y. recruited were first-rate and accommodating. The historic footage that would be used for the telethon and the convention was dramatic. Strauss was driving in the last big money. It was going to work out, and come in on budget.

A month before the convention Strauss's team had moved to Miami Beach for the duration. Larry O'Brien's convention planners had been there for months. For the next three weeks sleep was a distant lover—often missed, rarely touched. The pace intensified. Meetings upon meetings with representatives of this group, that television network, those bent-out-of-shape delegation representatives who thought their hotel was too far from the hall or too shabby. There were cars and drivers to be assigned, and there were those who were slighted (who would not get a car) or envious (of those who would—but didn't deserve one). At nine or ten each evening, just when it was all seeming to come together, another wheel would come off.

At some point in the last two weeks, one of the hotels, the Deauville, revealed that there was a looming labor problem they had not disclosed when the Miami Beach package was being negotiated. This was of major concern, as the Deauville was where we would originate the telethon. Were there a strike, neither political or entertainment personalities could cross the picket line. It would wreck the telethon and dash our hopes of making a substantial dent in the debt. Strauss was furious at the hotel. We couldn't move to another venue because, as I remember it, the entire telethon facility had already been completed. Calls were put out to Washington labor leaders. Heated meetings were held with the hotel management. No progress was made. On Wednesday or Thursday before the show, I did one of those unplanned actions that surprisingly changes events. On a hot morning I walked over to the labor demonstrators who were gathered on the picket line. I asked to see the local union leader. We shook hands and I told him who I was and what the problem was. We sat down on the curb. He told me his problems with the hotel. They were justified. I told him we were unhappy with management, but that the telethon was an absolute necessity if the Democratic Party had a chance to make a comeback.

He asked me to hang around. A while later he returned and said that there was a method to honor the picket, a way that would allow telecast participants to enter the hotel through a different entrance. There was a term he used that I can't recall. But he said that he had a problem: it would look like he and the union had capitulated to the hotel. On the spur of the moment I said that we could put him on the air at the beginning of the show to explain his position. "You mean national television?," he asked. "Yes, sir." "I don't know. I've never been on television." "Well," I said, "whichever way you go on this deal, you will be on television." He about died laughing. "You've got a deal." We shook hands, and I told him that I would go clear it with Strauss. I did—Bob loved it. We went out to the line and shook hands again, all around. Then Strauss told the hotel management. They were horrified and demanded equal time. Bob told them a few unprinted things and we left. On telethon night that fine labor man explained his union's position with dignity and humility to a nationwide audience. Then he made an eloquent pitch to support the telethon.

Another problem arose, however, that was more vexing, saddening, and mysterious. Larry O'Brien and his convention team turned on Strauss for no apparent reason. The ultimate team player, Bob had done much to rehabilitate the Democratic Party. We had stanched the financial bleeding within the first year. We had held the first million-dollar dinner in DC, which boosted the morale of all. We had settled some debts and negotiated acceptable payment schedules. We had sold almost a million dollars in ads, and we were just about to produce the first national Democratic telethon, which would inspire 350,000 callers to pledge $3.6 million, netting the party $2 million that would be used to settle debt. And all the time we were recruiting new supporters. Aside from the money, it is my opinion that the telethons (there were eventually four) did much to cement relationships between the national, state, and local party organizations. They were fun, they were inspiring, and yes, they were profitable for all concerned. Later telethons would split the proceeds with participating states. Most important, the telethons represented healthy democracy: for the first time, a mechanism was in place to allow all citizens a chance to easily contribute, and most were small contributions, under $10. Once signed on, however, small donors continued to give. I thought then and now that both parties should have been given twenty hours by the networks, on a rotating basis, to communicate their message, describe their history, and promote their champions.

Bob Strauss and his staff had done all that was expected and much more. I suspect that was the problem with O'Brien: jealousy. Not only did we accomplish a great deal, but Bob Strauss was a master of the media. With his intellect, his bravado, and his sharp wit, he was a natural and the press loved him. Did he take credit? You bet, but he also gave credit to O'Brien and others. He knew he had to build credibility for himself. He said to me one time that he had taken it to heart after I'd told him that no one knew who he was. He knew he had to build a reputation and had to do so in a hurry, with demonstrable results.

What happened was weird, uncalled for, time-consuming, and petty on the part of whoever orchestrated it. A few examples:

- Strauss's convention speech was cut from television coverage without notice.
- Even though we had all-area credentials, Strauss and I were asked to leave the podium, on orders of O'Brien. We literally were prepared to throw his lackey off the stage, but the lackey would have landed in the press corps.
- Arriving at the security gate on the second night of the convention, Strauss was told that his clearance had been revoked. This may have been the dumbest move. It embarrassed Bob in front of Helen, an absolute no-no, and they were trying to oust the person who was paying them. We had checkbooks for all convention accounts in the trunk of our car, which prompted me to go get the one that had the security account while Strauss was trying to reach the head of security by phone. Here's the gist of what Strauss said: "You tell that SOB O'Brien that if he expects anybody to get paid, and that includes paying you, he better get this taken care of now." While this was going on, I was telling the gate guards that they wouldn't get paid either. I think they let us in before they could reach O'Brien. I took their names and told them that they would be paid, regardless of who else didn't get paid. I'm not sure what happened next. I think Strauss went to find O'Brien and I went off to tell the top staff that all checks for their pay would not be issued. That flew around the hall in a hurry. Then I went to a hideaway we had established in the convention hall, and turned off my phone.

At some point, Bob said that things had been squared away with Larry, but did I know anything about some convention watches that O'Brien had ordered? I said that I didn't, but would check. Sure enough, in the accounts payable was a bill for some watches that had not been authorized. Something on the billing led me to believe that these were commemorative watches for O'Brien's top people. They weren't Mickey Mouse watches. There were ten or twelve of them and the bill was $3,200, as I recall. Then it dawned on me. Someone had tried to slip the bill by the treasurer's office because there were no watches for Bob Strauss, George Bristol, or Andy Shea. Within a matter of hours the situation would reach the pinnacle of high humor and incredible stupidity. Over the course of the afternoon I had a million things more important to deal with than an unauthorized bill for watches and whether I was or wasn't getting one.

That evening (I believe it was Wednesday), a meeting was held in either Senator Scoop Jackson's or Hubert Humphrey's convention trailer to discuss possible alternatives to what was surely going to be a McGovern election disaster. Labor leaders, some members of Congress, and others were there. Bob and I attended. The truth is that there wasn't much anyone could do. Everyone there just wanted to vent, although I'm sure we talked about setting up a committee to help fund House and Senate candidates that fall, as there was serious concern that the Democratic Congress might be in trouble. Mainly there was anger. The McGovern people had totally lost control of the convention, if they ever had control. The first two sessions ran into the morning hours and acceptance speech evening would turn into a disaster. McGovern would not speak until 3:00 a.m. EST. He would miss prime time in all of America except Hawaii, and sadly so because he gave a fine speech.

Sometime that night of our meeting in the trailer, the phone rang. It was O'Brien's top assistant. The Dade County sheriff was at the podium with a warrant for O'Brien for nonpayment for the watches. Strauss could hardly contain himself. I was listening over his shoulder and thought we ought to let O'Brien go to jail. By then I was fed up with his treatment of Strauss. But that wouldn't do, not on national television, so I whispered to Bob that I would go raise the money and have the check ready by Friday before we left Miami—if, and we were sure there would be, three watches for Bob, Andy, and me. Oh, yes, that was the case all along, we were told. I think Bob talked with the vendor and assured him we would pay.

Then I left the meeting, went out on the convention floor, and raised $3,200. How silly and unnecessary. The convention came to a close, and we never saw the watches, the merchant, or the sheriff.

The McGovern people didn't want us around any longer, which was in their right. A new chairman was elected—O'Brien was out. We left Eric Jaffe and other staff members to clean up the bills. Valarie and I headed to Montana with the children to rest and renew.

I think Bob and Helen went to Del Mar, California, to rest and watch the horses run, but a week later he called me. The call was the culmination of the concerns of the Democratic leadership of the House and Senate at the convention: that the McGovern defeat would be so great in November that it could take down the Democratic Congress. Bob wanted me to return to Washington as soon as possible. We were going to quickly set up and fund the Committee to Re-elect a Democratic Congress.

Those in the know might ask why a separate campaign committee was needed: there were already committees for the House and Senate. The problem was that both of these committees were at the time inbred and stagnant, with funding going to incumbents who often didn't even have opponents. This was so obvious that even the leadership knew there had to be change. They also knew that Bob Strauss had the reputation and the muscle to pull it off. Our Rolodexes were much larger than those of the committees, and represented a wide range of potential givers. We had been unceremoniously thrown out of the DNC by the McGovernites, but we had the lists of donors—and we had recruited, romanced and retained most of them ourselves.

I didn't drop everything and head straight back to Washington. I'd been away from my family for too long. I was in my beloved Glacier National Park and I had a few hikes and outings to honor before returning. I needed to recharge as I was completely drained after a three-year whirlwind fundraising high. While Mark and Jennifer were too young to appreciate the full beauty of the experience, Jim, by then eight, took to all of it like a natural-born outdoorsman. We hiked and fished and played outside with my brother David's family. It was glorious and restful. I have found over the years that regardless of the situation, I can immerse myself in the healing presence of Glacier Park and come out whole and renewed within a day or two.

CHAPTER 12

With Strauss and On My Own

I would need every bit of recharging because August 1972 through the election in November was a blinding blur of activity. Even with the best lists and Rolodexes it took time to organize this national campaign, because we had to plan and execute trips involving multiple senators and representatives. The good news was that the Democratic Congressional leadership cracked the whip. Most members knew the majority Senate could be at risk, so for the most part they did what they were asked to do, as did governors and others.

It wasn't that all or some of them were against McGovern. He was a fine man, a World War II hero and a patriot. But his team was amateurish and suspicious. At the convention he delivered his acceptance speech to practically no one, given the late hour. He selected Senator Tom Eagleton (whom I admired a great deal) as the vice presidential candidate, only to ask him to resign when it was discovered that Eagleton had had electroshock therapy for depression. McGovern was tagged as the candidate of "amnesty, abortion, and acid." It was quickly going straight downhill.

Sometime during those weeks the Dade County sheriff showed up in DC to serve O'Brien again. In all of the post-convention blur I had forgotten about the damn watches. I hadn't seen the things but I still had the money I had raised to pay for them. I had a briefcase full of unfinished business, including bills that had arrived after the convention. We went over to McGovern headquarters and paid for the watches, taking three that were not inscribed.

During this period we also began to hear more about the Watergate scandal, and the sense of its utter stupidity grew. Nixon would have beaten McGovern in almost any scenario, except one in which he was pegged as being the small-minded and vengeful head of a gang that couldn't shoot straight. The president and his minions managed to keep the lid on their secrets until after the election.

At some point, at the bar at the Madison Hotel, Bob and I talked long into the night about his running for chair of the Democratic National Committee. The pluses far outnumbered the minuses except for one thing. Bob was from Texas. Bob's close friend, John Connally, was backing Richard Nixon. We decided that we had to back McGovern and raise some money for him. So in the middle of everything else, I got on the phone and raised $10,000 or so, and Bob looked for an audience for a pro-McGovern speech.

Before long he told me that he secured a forum at Southern Methodist University in Dallas. I knew that Bob was from Dallas, and I knew that he had power and finesse, but why did he pick SMU, which was conservative and not particularly credible as a national forum? I was quietly skeptical.

A week went by, then late one night he called. "Bristol, Bob the genius calling." I could tell he was pleased with himself.

"What happened?," I asked.

"I thought SMU would have a small, conservative crowd, but when I got there the place was packed with hippies and antiwar young people, and they more or less sat on their hands when I was introduced. I knew my little patriotic speech was not going to fly, so I threw it away.

'Ladies and gentleman,' I said. 'I want to tell you why I'm for George McGovern. In World War II this brave patriot was a B-24 bomber pilot. He flew over Germany and bomb-bomb-bombed those bastards. They shot him down. He escaped. He got in another plane and he bomb-bomb-bombed 'em again.' Bristol, there was dead silence. Then the biggest, hairiest sumbitch you've ever seen stood up, started clapping, and yelled, 'We've been had by the master!' Then they all start clapping and yelling, and I got in the swing of things and start clapping back. Pure genius, George."

I had to agree. Only Strauss could have pulled that one off. Later in life he and George McGovern would become good friends.

From then until Election Day we scrambled. As I remember we arrived at the conclusion that we needed to concentrate on twenty-five to thirty candidates—incumbents who were in trouble or non-incumbents who had a chance to win. At one point we flew all the leaders and ten or so committee chairs to a huge West Coast fundraiser at the home of Gene and Roz Wyman. Wyman was a major Hollywood lawyer. Their cohosts were Lew and Edie Wasserman. Lew was the powerful head of MCA/Universal. The evening was a who's who of Hollywood—and all California. One of the speakers was

Congressman Hale Boggs, Majority Leader of the House. As did others, he talked about the overwhelming need of maintaining a Democratic Congress and mentioned Congressman Nick Begich of Alaska who was with us that evening. Hale said that the Alaska race was close and needed all the support we could muster. The race was so important that he was going to Alaska with Begich to lend support by barnstorming the state.

We never saw either one of them again. Sometime over the next day or so, somewhere over Alaska's wild terrain, their plane disappeared, never to be found. Back in Washington I immediately went to the home of Tommy Boggs, Hale and Lindy Boggs's son. The situation was all the more difficult due to the uncertainty.

The good news within that framework of horror was that after Boggs was officially declared dead in January 1973, his wife Lindy was elected to take his seat. She served admirably for years. She was a lovely woman and became a strong congresswoman and a leader in her own right.

On Election Day 1972 Nixon routed McGovern, but the Democrats held on to both houses. There were many reasons why that was important, but none more so than what was beginning to unfold—the true nature of Watergate. The entire story hadn't come to light, but enough to lead us to suspect that higher-ups in the White House were involved. Had the Republicans captured one or both houses, I am convinced Watergate would have been swept under the rug. Lord knows they tried, even with a Democratic Congress. Except for the stupid decision by Nixon to hang onto the tapes, they might have been successful.

As that unfolded, Strauss announced his candidacy for chair of the Democratic National Committee. We had a great deal of support, mainly from labor and the more conservative wing of the party, but there were exceptions. Here and there liberals, who had come to see the manner in which Strauss had conducted himself as treasurer, including how he had addressed the debt and helped rebuild a base of small donors, signed on. It was going to be close. George Mitchell of Maine and Chuck Manatt of California mounted major campaigns and had solid pockets of support. At some point Larry O'Brien entered the picture for reasons I never understood. We met to assess where we were and what damage, if any, Larry might cause. We went around the room. Bob listened and then spoke. "Everything you have said is true, if Larry were to get in the race. But he won't. He'll choke and I won't." Sure enough, within a few days O'Brien bowed out.

Years later Bob would say that he thought that Larry O'Brien was a decent fellow, but he really didn't know how to play hardball politics. "The best thing about O'Brien was he never got in my way."

The election had one mean incident. Somewhere in the closing weeks, when things were very close, a letter from Larry Lawrence of California surfaced. It claimed that on a visit to Strauss's summer home in Del Mar, Lawrence had heard Strauss make racially charged remarks. This was not true for two reasons. First, Strauss was not a racist. His law firm in the late forties handled civil right cases when few would. Strauss was colorblind. He looked for people who would work and could deliver. Azie Morton, a leader in the civil rights movement, was his special assistant and dear friend thereafter. He would later hire Vernon Jordan as a partner in his firm. Second, Larry Lawrence never went to the Strauss's summer home.

We put out calls to black leaders. Azie Morton worked every angle. They spread the word that Lawrence was a liar. But for the Strausses, Helen had the last laugh. The next summer, in 1973, they were having dinner at the race track in Del Mar. Larry Lawrence gushed up with his new female best friend. Bob shut him down immediately by saying that he deeply resented Lawrence's letter, particularly since Lawrence had never been invited to the Strauss home. Lawrence tried to recover by denying it, but Helen Strauss stopped him short. "Larry, I have the letter you sent. I've kept it, hoping I'd see you." She produced the letter and Lawrence fled the scene. An elderly woman stood up and said to all gathered, "Mr. Strauss, I'm a lifelong Republican and I've known Larry all my life. He's always been sorry. You and Mrs. Strauss have gladdened my heart and I'm sending a contribution to you for the DNC." The dinner crowd clapped in response. Again I got one of Strauss's phone calls, this time not pleased with himself but with Helen.

So in December 1972, Robert S. Strauss of Stamford, Texas, became chairman of the world's oldest political party by the closest of margins. I was prejudiced to the core, but I thought—and still think—that this was a perfect match at a crucial time. Bob is one of the most principled men I know, but he also is a nuanced political mechanic. He knew how to organize and he knew how to lead. It would take all of this, plus his high sense of humor, to put the party back in the game by 1976. He would make it work with more than a little help from Nixon and his gang that couldn't shoot straight.

There was another reason for Strauss's success as DNC treasurer and chair. He would sometimes state this, but it was often overlooked. During his time at the DNC in the early 1970s, Strauss did not have to answer to a president or White House staff. There are many advantages to having a president of your party in power, but also encumbrances and problems. Bob was able to operate without having to await clearance from on high, and he did not have to bear the expenses that flow from the political activities of a sitting president. Even with a frugal president, such as Jimmy Carter would be, those expenses are enormous. The use of Air Force One alone for a political trip is an incredible cost.

With the luxury of a party out of presidential power, Strauss could rebuild and refinance the Democratic Party so that it was ready to do battle in 1976. He would do it without me, though. Sometime in 1972, Bob and I sat at the Madison Hotel bar with one of his close friends and clients, Chuck Kuhn. Somehow the talk came around to my future. I told them that I had never planned to come to Washington permanently. Now with two children, Valarie and I began to talk seriously about going back to Texas. It was not that we didn't like Washington. We loved it. We loved its history, its dynamic, its parks, and its location near mountains, beaches, historical battlefields and monuments. We loved our friends, people who would still be friends forty years later. But there was the pull of Texas, specifically Austin and the Hill Country. Additionally, my son Jimmy lived in Austin, as did Valarie's parents.

Both Bob and Chuck agreed to begin to help us plan our future. In doing so, Bob always reaffirmed that I had a place with him and near his heart. Furthermore, he said that I could always come back with him in whatever role he was playing. His position was strengthened by my growing respect and friendship with Chuck. So, even with all that had to be done over the course of 1972, I felt grounded in the knowledge that all I had to do was keep plowing ahead, doing what I had to do, and the future would be secure.

In December, after the election and after settling a few outstanding convention and Committee to Re-elect accounts, we headed to Texas, and went to Dallas shortly before Christmas. I had accepted a position with Chuck Kuhn's corporation, Weil-McLain, a multifaceted conglomerate. We bought a house and settled in for what we thought would be a long and profitable career in the private sector, with the promise of plenty of political activity with Strauss at the national level and within Texas.

At some point shortly after my return to Texas, Strauss and Dick Herman asked me to serve on a bipartisan committee to critique convention financing and explore the possibility of public financing. Over the course of 1971–1972, some of us had become concerned that the methods of financing conventions were open to possible corrupting influences, such as the ITT Republican convention scandal and the solicitation of unwarranted (and unneeded) defense contractor ads. Bob, Dick, others, and I strongly believed there was a better way to conduct the official meetings of the nomination process of the two major parties. It was unacceptable and criminal that the Republicans had felt so much pressure to raise money that they had accepted a major corporate gift in exchange for a favorable Justice Department ruling for the ITT Corporation.

During our deliberations I think we even got into the question of limits on personal and corporate campaign contributions. At the time I was completely committed to limits, but I was—and am to this day—more in favor of automatic, immediate, and complete disclosure of all contributions and expenditures. Limitations do favor the incumbents, but disclosure doesn't. If you want to play in the political arena with a contribution, fine, but you must be subject to immediate scrutiny, with no exceptions. You want to give your best friend or brother $100,000? Fine. But it has to be reported upon receipt.

I've watched all the efforts at reform over the years. I think we need strong and well-run public financing of at least the presidential campaign for those candidates who want to use it. I have grown disillusioned about limitations, but never disclosure. I came by this the hard way. On one of our trips, Strauss met with some executives of Ashland Oil in Kentucky. They gave him $30,000 in cash (such cash contributions were not unusual). In New Orleans Bob told me of the contribution, saying that it was cash and asking me to take it to Washington because he was going to Texas. All the way back to Washington I worried that everyone on board the flight was a robber. Upon arrival I hurried to the DNC offices at Watergate and counted out the $30,000 in the presence of the DNC comptroller. "Twenty-seven, twenty-eight, twenty-nine, thirty, thirty-one." Then we counted again but once more came up with $31,000. Bob had said it was $30,000. We brought another person in to recount. It was still $31,000, so I called Strauss. "Bob, it's $31,000. We've counted and counted!" "Bristol, I put an extra thousand dollars in there to see what you would do. I have always trusted you but just wanted to test you." Then he started to laugh. I was dumbfounded but then started to laugh too. We hung up. I asked for a receipt and stuck it in my billfold. That was the best single unplanned action I ever did, as later events would prove.

From 1973–1975, the Watergate investigation was in full swing. Federal prosecutors were looking into all aspects of the growing scandal, including illegal campaign contributions by corporations, including those from Ashland Oil Company. The company's $30,000 to the DNC was pretty easy to find, because it had been reported, I am not sure in what detail—probably not much—but reported under the inadequate method of the time. I got a subpoena from a federal prosecutor in 1975. Bob had told me it was coming. He said that Edward Bennett Williams would represent me. I was horrified, but said that I would come to Washington and tell my story.

Under no circumstance is an appearance before a grand jury a pleasant thing. I was scared, but I went. Toward the end, the US Attorney bore down on how and why I was so sure it was $30,000. I told him the story of our counting out the money. Then I pulled out the receipt, that worn, thin receipt from Eric Jaffe, that receipt that I had stuck in my wallet and forgotten about, a glorious scrap of paper. There was silence in the room. Then I handed the receipt to the prosecutor and shortly thereafter was dismissed. I never heard from them again.

I would never have had to go before the grand jury had there been all-encompassing disclosure and reporting laws in place, as well as ones precluding cash contributions of sizeable amounts. In 1974 Congress began to address the need for campaign reform, limitations on contributions and convention financing. I was pleased. Today I think the whole thing has been thwarted by changes, court decisions, and rank partisanship among the members of the Federal Elections Commission. Now even disclosure has been ground asunder by a Supreme Court that struck down most of the campaign finance laws.

When it came to trying to reach personal donors, the party had to take the message to the people to insure a lively and broad base of financial support. Today, thanks to the likes of the Internet and Twitter, there are all sorts and inexpensive ways to tap into millions of donors. But in the early 1970s, television was the only broad-based answer. Telethons should have been institutionalized by both parties, with the support of the networks.

In the summer of 1973 I had run the Texas portion of the second Democratic national telethon. By then we knew the numbers and how much all those hundreds of thousands of donors meant, in both the short and long term. Many givers tend to repeat, especially if fortified with a big annual event like a telethon. With Senator Lloyd Bentsen's permission I did the same thing in 1974. We had a formula worked out with the states on cost and revenue sharing percentage. It was a successful and worthwhile endeavor. Not only did we have big political and entertainment celebrities, we also had cutaways where Texas politicians and celebrities could make their pitches to support the Democratic Party. Equally important, we had perfected great and moving presentations on Democratic presidents and their policies. In my opinion those telethons simultaneously produced two very positive results: raising funds from thousands rather than the few and reminding folks of the greatness of Democratic presidents. Propaganda, sure, but propaganda with a positive purpose. It is one thing for network news or cable talking heads to filter a party's accomplishments and failures down to ten seconds, or to filter all politics through thirty-second negative ads. Why not, on the other hand, allow and sponsor passionate, creative geniuses to produce good historical pieces that might not only inspire the faithful but also perhaps convince doubters? I was very disappointed when the telethons failed to continue.

In the next several years, Strauss's efforts would position the Democratic Party to not only take advantage of the windfall of the Watergate break-ins and the ensuing cover-up scandal, but also shield it during the Reagan years. Yes, we would lose control of the Senate in 1980, as well as the presidency, but the foundation had been laid to weather even that storm.

Bob and I would go on to work on a number of projects throughout the '70s and into the '80s, and several especially bear mentioning. With the election of Jimmy Carter in 1976, Bob became US trade representative and special envoy to the Middle East. Governor Ken Curtis of Maine became chairman of the Democratic National Committee for a short time, followed by our mutual great friend, John C. White of Texas. John was one of those rock-solid, national Democrats from Texas who always supported the presidential ticket. While he had his own people, he also relied on Strauss and his team for support. He would need all that and more as President Carter and his close advisors never really understood national politics, particularly at the congressional level. They were always in hot water.

Because Bob had such strong ties on Capitol Hill and among the governors, he was able to vouch for John White. On a number of occasions we were called upon to come in to help push legislation or other policy. Fortunately, Carter did have a wonderful aide, Anne Wexler, who thoroughly and professionally understood the need for political outreach, so we did have support at crucial times, such as during the ratification of the Panama Canal treaty. US possession of the canal had long been a sore spot in US–Latin American relations. Throughout the 1960s and early 1970s, presidents Johnson and Nixon had both tried to resolve the issue. Nixon made good progress, but Watergate and a much-weakened Gerald Ford presidency slowed the progress. Then in 1975, Ronald Reagan, in one of his demagogue days, denounced the treaty. "We bought it, we paid for it, it is sovereign US territory, and we should keep it," became the cry. Thus it fell to President Carter to restart the process. It seemed like it would take forever to be successful, if at all. But Carter, with support from Congress as well as from Strauss and others, pulled out all the stops. That included calling in our good friend Dick Herman, a Nebraskan, to find and talk with Nebraska's newly elected senator, Edward Zorinsky. A former Republican, Zorinsky had turned Democrat and won a seat in 1976, replacing longtime Republican senator Roman Hruska. Zorinsky knew the treaty vote was anathema in Nebraska, but Dick promised Republican business support and delivered. And so did Zorinsky. The final vote was 68–32. Measured by today's standards where partisanship reigns, it was a good, meaningful margin and a truly bipartisan effort.

In 1978 President Carter, with Bob Strauss and John White at his side, called to ask me to chair a five-state fundraiser for the Democratic National Committee. I wouldn't turn the president of the United States down and I couldn't say no to Bob and John. I got them to lower their expectations, though, as Carter was not all that popular in those five states—Texas, Louisiana, Arkansas, Oklahoma and New Mexico. The president had carried three in 1976, but not by much, and that support had been eroding ever since.

After we hung up I called Lowell Lebermann who was my dear friend, an active Democratic fundraiser, and asked him to meet me that night. He said that he had something else planned. I said that this was straight from the president of the United States and of national import. "Wonderful," said he. Then he shouted to an aide to cancel his previous engagement. We had dinner, and I asked Lowell to be a cochair. He readily accepted and then we talked for hours about how best to put it together. The political mood in Texas and the surrounding states was not conducive to fundraising but we thought that with a great deal of pushing, and with support, we could pull it off.

Every state met the goal we set for it. Strauss and White lent invaluable support, as did Senator Bentsen and Governor Briscoe. I called in practically every chit I had, from Dale Bumpers and David Pryor in Arkansas, as well as a fellow named Clinton there, to Governor Ed Edwards of Louisiana.

One of the most vexing constituencies was the oil and gas industry. On balance I've never met a more conservative bunch. They were for no government except government that protected them or gave them incentives: the oil depletion allowance, tax deductions for intangible drilling, and deregulation. It seemed they were never happy. With Lowell's help and that of a few good industry friends, we stitched an energy group together. Then Lowell and I decided to take the group to Washington—representatives from every tough-talking state—where they would be briefed by the president, Robert Strauss, and James Schlesinger, secretary of energy.

By design it was to be a no-holds-barred meeting. Lowell and I met the various delegates at the Mayflower Hotel the night before. The talk was tough, with puffed cheeks, inflated chests, and a lot of "by God, here's what I'm telling the president." Fortunately Ann Richards, a county commissioner at the time, came with us. I think it was Lowell's idea. He knew a number of the independents and rightly perceived that humor would be needed. And Ann Richards had that in spades.

The next morning off we went. We were shown into the Roosevelt Room. Strauss led off and lightened the proceedings a bit. Many knew and trusted him. Then in came the president. He made a few remarks, although nothing specific, as I recall. A question-and-answer period arrived, and I stated the ground rules. Within the bounds of civility they could ask whatever was on their minds. There followed at least thirty seconds of silence, then the head of the Louisiana delegation rose.

"Mr. President, Louisiana's independents stand behind you 100 percent!" I nudged Lowell. I thought he was going to split in two. He wanted to laugh out loud as others fell into courteous chorus of agreement. As we trooped out of the White House, Ann Richards broke it down. "Well," she said in that recognizable twang of hers, "I have never seen so many towers of Jello!" We had to help Lowell onto the bus.

After our meetings we went home to Austin on Chuck Kuhn's brand-new jet. Not only was it new, the jet had been decorated by his latest wife, Pat. There were four passengers: Lowell, Lowell's aide David Jaderlund, me, and Lucky, Lowell's beloved guide dog. At about thirty-five thousand feet, David asked why we thought Lucky might be scratching at the door. "Oh, my God!," yelled Lowell. "She is going to be sick." Fortunately we had three or four newspapers. (One of the great pleasures I had with Lowell was reading papers and discussing issues.) We went into action. I've never seen anyone, much less a blind person, spread that much paper so quickly and thoroughly. As I recall we were only about 90 percent successful, so we stopped in Memphis and cleaned out the plane. The pilots were white with fear, anticipating Chuck's reaction, but eventually deemed our efforts adequate, and we went on to Dallas. Sometime later we told Chuck about this. Kuhn could be a frightful bear, but laughed long and hard. I don't think anyone ever told Pat what had happened.

Shortly thereafter we went to Houston and had a rousing fundraiser dinner. The president was pleased and the party was richer by more than $1 million. That event brought in about $1,000 per person, unlike the overpriced rituals held today.

At Christmastime in 1978, I was on vacation with my family in Montana. We were about as isolated as one could be at the time: the Izaak Walton Inn near Glacier Park without the benefit of cell phones or laptops. I learned, though, that White House switchboard operators can find a person anywhere. The innkeeper came to me, saying that Ambassador Robert Strauss and a John White had called on White House business, asking me to return the call immediately. He said I could his private office phone. The inn staff was practically standing at attention. No one from Washington had ever called there, much less from the White House.

John White said, "Bob and I have been looking all over for you. The Chinese leaders are coming to the United States and we need you to come to Washington to help us set up the Houston leg of the trip. Apparently, Bill Clements [Republican governor of Texas] is already grousing publicly that he is not going to meet any communists and will not greet them in Houston."

I told John that I would be there as soon as possible, but he would have to get the White House to get my family and me back to Austin, as it was the Christmas season and my staff was gone for the holidays and could not make arrangements. He said not to worry and that it would be taken care of. By the time I got to Columbia Falls, where my brother, Dave, and his family lived, the White House had called with all the travel plans. Thus began one of the most interesting and memorable experiences anyone could wish to have.

In Austin I repacked, as the initial briefings would take several days, went to the airport, and flew off to Washington. A car and driver were there to meet me. It was then that I knew this was a very big deal. President Jimmy Carter had cut all things he deemed unnecessary, including meeting guests with White House cars. It was this sort of micromanagement that got this most decent human in trouble on a great many fronts, but not for this event. I went immediately to the White House, bags and all.

Anne Wexler, a bright spot in the otherwise less-than-stellar Carter staff, was in charge. A lesser light might have blown the whole affair, not being able to cut through the red tape and negotiate the turf battles that were to come.

My first meeting was with strictly White House and Strauss staff and others like me who had been called in to handle the details of the Chinese leaders' visit. As I remember, after DC there were to be two stops by the visitors: Houston and Seattle. My friend Gerald Grinstein was the Seattle point man. He had been Senator Warren Magnuson's chief of staff in the US Senate and was a top mover and shaker in Washington State. The key part of the Seattle visit was Boeing, a company whose leaders hoped to have a major stake in future China trade, but I will focus here on Houston.

Anne gave us a thorough briefing. The visit dates for Houston were January 31–February 2, 1979. The visitors wanted to see the huge Texas Medical Center, which is a credit to Houston, the United States, and the wise men and women of Houston who raised the money to make it happen. A number of Houstonians would be of immense help to me, including dealing with our irascible governor and other "commie" fighters who had rarely, if ever, met or seen a "commie." The visitors also wanted to see the NASA Space Center and an oil exploration company. I would have to decide what oil company would get the honors—and the opportunity (China was a country of one billion people and virtually no oil business).

I raised the question of a barbeque and rodeo, a Texas tradition. Some State Department officials were immediately and forever hostile to that suggestion, but it went on the agenda to discuss with the Chinese advance team we were to meet with the next day. That night I stayed with John and Nellie White and read the briefing book. I was fascinated with China, going back to some of my earliest reading—the Red Randall war stories I bought or borrowed as a child and at least one book about the Doolittle raid. I had come to like those people who had saved our boys from the Japanese.

The next day we met with the Chinese team, and they were delightful, intelligent representatives of their government, particularly the young man who was to be my counterpart and interpreter. The meeting went smoothly until the rodeo came up. To this day I don't know why some of our folks had their dander up, but they did. Not me and not the Chinese. At one point my counterpart leaned over and said, "Keep the rodeo, please." By the look in his eyes, I knew there was something extra special that was most important. So, regardless of who might try to thwart it, I was prepared to override them, which I had the power to do under my agreement with the White House, and that agreement was reinforced with my meeting with the president. I was to be his personal representative and had final authority, or at least the authority to take it to the president. But there was resistance brewing in the red, white, and blue Lone Star State.

I went back to Texas to regroup and plan my strategy. One inspiration I had on the trip back was to contact Beth Hardesty, who was the daughter of Bob and Mary Hardesty, long-time friends. Beth had studied China and spoke Chinese. I quickly made arrangements for her to join me in Houston. I let Senator Lloyd Bentsen know what I was doing, and he offered any help he could give which was going to be important in view of the governor's position, which would grow to be a major concern until it was resolved to my personal satisfaction shortly before the visitors' arrival.

I don't remember how Mrs. Oveta Culp Hobby came into the picture, but that remarkable woman—she owned the *Houston Post,* had been head of the Women's Army Corps in World War II, and had served as Eisenhower's secretary of health, education and welfare—weighed in with her sound advice and influence. It was she who suggested that the two leading local newspapers—the *Post* and the *Chronicle*—host a Houston business leadership luncheon for the Chinese visitors. Ben Love, of Texas Commerce Bank, and others signed on to help. That changed the potentially hostile atmosphere to one of reluctant but interested acceptance, except for Governor Clements who was getting to be a real pain in the ass.

Encamped at the Hyatt Hotel, with Beth Hardesty down the hall in one room and the my Chinese counterpart down at the other end of the hall, we began to make it all come together into a two-day happening that would be a credit to the United States, China, and Texas.

Without my letter of authority from the president, I am all but certain that we could not have pulled the visit off, particularly in the time we had for planning. The number of people and organizations that had to be coordinated was immense, and someone had to have the final say. We had to deal with the White House, the Chinese embassy, the State Department, the air force, the City of Houston, the town of Simonton, the Houston business community, a hostile Taiwan-American community, and operators of hotels, buses, and helicopters, along with a governor who could not keep his mouth shut. The list seemed to grow every day.

The first order of business was to contact the Texas Medical Center, NASA, and an oil exploration company, to make sure they could accommodate the party, which had grown to nearly 400, including over 160 Chinese visitors. Through the intervention of Mrs. Hobby and Ben Love, for the oil company we quickly settled on Baker-Hughes, the merged corporate entity founded on Howard Hughes's fortune.

What became apparent quickly through my counterpart was that the Chinese delegation, from Deng Xiaoping down, did not have much grasp of modern technology. They were eager to learn and to absorb what they could into Deng's plans for a communism based on limited capitalism. I would learn later that this concept had been formalized in a 1921 compact by Mao and the founders of the Chinese Communist Party. The compact's objective was to spur the creation of wealth so that it could, in good Marxist-Leninist style, be redistributed to the poor—who were 90 percent of the Chinese people in 1921 and 1979. But in 1949, after Mao came to power, he wanted a pure communist state more than a hybrid, and he tore the compact up. Deng had other ideas, but he knew that he had to have the tools of capitalism to make a true "great leap forward." He had a great deal of ground to make up, as China was far behind the times technologically.

Our planned tours in Houston had to take into account that we could only show highlights to our visitors to demonstrate twentieth-century advancements in medicine, energy exploration, and space travel, with the hope that these eager and intelligent people would come back some day for more. For now they were a people and a country that had been cut off from much of the world since 1949. And that is exactly why the rodeo was so important to them. Before they had shut themselves off (with our misguided help) in 1949, the Chinese loved Americans and much about the United States, including our cowboy movies. I was told that some reels of Roy Rogers, Gene Autry, and others had been secretly shown around China until they had worn out. Once I understood this, the rodeo was on, regardless of what some at State might think. Through a series of calls, we selected an indoor arena in Simonton, Texas. The town is a few miles east of Houston but that remoteness was important for security, as well as for its parking lots could accommodate not only guests but also hundreds of news media buses and vans and law enforcement vehicles. By the end of our first week of talking, we had the makings of a full and educational schedule, capped off by a rodeo, which deeply pleased my Chinese counterpart. Once the rodeo was nailed down, he became a devoted fan of mine, and that made the next weeks of planning rewarding and exciting.

In the several moves I have made since 1979, I somehow lost my China files, including one that contained that dear man's name. I hope someone reading these words now will identify him and say to him, "Didn't you work on that trip to Houston in 1979?" He was a worthy guide, partner, and friend.

We had settled on six main events: visits to the medical complex, NASA, and Baker-Hughes Energy Company, plus a press conference, a business luncheon, and the rodeo. Now we had to make it all work. Never was the cliché "the devil is in the details" more aptly applied. We had to arrange to move three hundred to four hundred people around in vans, limos, and buses, through traffic in the fourth largest city in the United States. Everything from arrival to departure from Ellington Air Force Base had to be timed. Rooms at the Hyatt Regency had to be reserved and secured. A week or so out, the Secret Service and Houston police would begin sweeps. Security clearance passes had to be issued to not only the traveling party, but also to the press, Houstonites, and all manner of personnel. Routes had to be test-run and swept clean. Then there was the logistical nightmare of getting the entire party from downtown Houston during rush hour out to Simonton, which was a good thirty miles from the hotel.

Joint meetings were held. All possibilities were discussed. Someone mentioned helicopters, and offshore energy companies were contacted regarding the availability of craft. There weren't enough for all to travel by air, but enough to ferry the principals, and this appealed to the Chinese. They could send many of their party on ahead, which would give Deng and the other top dignitaries more time to relax a bit. Deng and his top leadership were getting on in years.

There were two Chinese premiers of equal status—on paper, but not in reality. Deng Xiaoping was the leader and strong man in fact. The other leader was probably Hua Guofeng, although there are no accounts of him that I could find, but we had to prepare two places of honor at every stop—and secure two honorary Texas Stetson hats.

As for the helicopters, State Department officials nixed them. (This would turn out to be a good move—as it would pour rain during the Chinese visit.)

Once the events were scheduled, I figured that the best thing I could do was let professionals work out the details, review them, settle disputes, and add value to the visit. Beth and I did decide on our own that we would have the rodeo program printed in Chinese and English. My counterpart thought this a marvelous idea. We obtained the services of a Chinese-language scholar at Rice University to interpret and write the translations. The self-important State Department official who didn't like the rodeo demanded that the program be sent to him in advance, so that it could be checked for accuracy and so that it could be verified that none of the Chinese language on the program was "commie" propaganda meant to embarrass America. I sent him something by regular mail, and we kept working. I never heard from him again, probably because Beth, the Rice scholar, and my Chinese friend got it right, though a well-timed call to Anne Wexler at the White House may also have helped.

I also had to meet with dissident individuals and groups who threatened one thing or another. For decades US citizens had received a steady drumbeat of anticommunist propaganda, but this was especially true for those who had come to the United States from Taiwan. Not only did they hear the constant US propaganda, they also received well-orchestrated propaganda from Chiang Kai-shek. The Chinese who followed Chiang had been our staunch allies in World War II but they had been driven from the mainland of China by a communist, peasant uprising led by Mao.

Revolutions don't occur in a vacuum. The conditions of poor people in China—the vast majority—were pitiful, and they were ripe for revolution. The question was which dictatorial revolutionary would win out. The communists won and Chiang fled to Taiwan. What followed was thirty years of finger-pointing propaganda and faultfinding. There was blame enough to go around, but Americans, including Taiwanese Americans, had only one side of the story, even though Mao was not a knight in shining armor.

There were, if I remember correctly, forty thousand Taiwanese Americans residing in the Houston area at the time, and no one was pleased that the leader of the People's Republic of China was coming. The good news for us was that there were civil and reasonable leaders among them who demanded a protest but did not want to disrupt the visit, and that's what would happen. Protesters were assigned several blocks downtown across from the Hyatt, and they would be boisterous and evident, but not threatening. It would be interesting to see how little attention the Chinese visitors paid them.

Now everything was falling into place. Everyone was working together effectively at a fevered pitch. But Governor Clements continued to rumble. About four or five days in advance of the visit, a solution gelled in my mind, and I made my move. I placed a call to a mutual friend in Dallas. "You know I'm not a China expert by any stretch of the imagination," I said to Clements's friend, "but I've come to know them enough to tell you that they think in terms of centuries, not minutes and hours, and if you think for the next thousand years or so they will forget the slight our governor has visited upon them, then you tell him to try to obtain a drilling permit within a thousand miles of China for SEDCO. He better show up with a big smile and ceremonial Stetson hats in hand. If he doesn't, I will personally tell the Chinese leaders that he wanted nothing to do with them."

I hung up after delivering this rant. Late that evening there was a knock at my door. Standing in the hall was my counterpart. "May I come in?," he politely asked. Once inside he came right to the point: "Would it be possible to get me a cowboy hat?"

"Of course," I said, "I should have thought of that myself. You have been invaluable. But don't tell anyone."

"Most assuredly," he intoned. And off he went, all smiles.

Within minutes I heard another knock. There stood two of our Chinese coworkers, all smiles. They too inquired about the possibility of hats. I yelled down the hall, and out of his room popped my sheepish friend and ally. "What in God's name did I just tell you?," I hollered at him.

With much embarrassment he came running toward my room. "Oh, I was so honored and happy that it slipped out. I am terribly sorry. What shall I do?"

"I tell you what we are going to do. We are going to get hats for everyone. They won't be as fine as the ceremonial Stetson, but everyone in the party will have a genuine Texas cowboy hat!"

I thought he was going to cry.

Then I had to figure out how to pull this off. The solution came from two opposites: a Chinese communist and a devout anticommunist. The first, my Chinese counterpart, came up with the solution of how to quickly obtain hat sizes for all. By using a piece of string they overnight furnished me with 160 sizes. A thing about heads is that they basically come in four or five hat sizes if you aren't looking for a perfect, Hollywood fit.

The second problem was a bit tougher.

For years I'd been buying hats of all sorts from Manny Gammage, the owner of Texas Hatters of Austin. He had statewide fame for the best special-made hats. He was a red-hot conservative, but had a sense of humor and purpose. I reached him late at night and said something like this: "Manny, I am calling you to duty for your country."

"What do you mean, George?"

"I need two special Stetsons and 160 other western hats in a variety of sizes. Color and material don't matter."

"Who's it for?"

"The leaders of the People's Republic of China and their entourage. They're coming to America and Houston."

There was silence for a few seconds. Then Manny said, "Screw 'em!"

"I'm paying cash up front," I said.

There was silence. Then: "When do you need 'em?"

"Day after tomorrow."

"Screw 'em."

"I'll send a truck."

Silence again. Then Manny agreed: "You got a deal, but no publicity."

And so it was that upon our visitors' arrival we had genuine western cowboy hat for all. Never was headgear worn with such pride and pleasure.

Which leads, as Paul Harvey might have said, to the rest of the story. Upon the Chinese party's arrival there were all those western hats on Chinese heads, and Governor Bill Clements, forced smile and all, who dutifully and patriotically presented the two principals with their hats. Then he departed. Years later Clements would claim credit for the hats and their presentation, but he had nothing to do with any part of the visit, including the hats.

Clements's initial reaction and subsequent, begrudging action was a mirror image, ironically, of what made the trip a major success. By the week of the visit it had dawned on a great many business leaders in Houston and elsewhere in the United States that while the leaders of a communist country were coming, these people were the leaders of a country of one billion people who needed everything. Two or three days before the visit one would have thought that the Pope was on the way. Business leaders flocked to Houston to get in on the action and have a chance to meet Deng and his companions—many of them important decision makers in their own right. Because the medical center, NASA, and Baker-Hughes were tightly reserved for our guests and hosts, the rodeo became the hottest ticket in town, particularly the pre-rodeo barbeque reception. Had I been shameless or crooked, I could have scalped slots to that event for prices that would embarrass Super Bowl hawkers.

Grown men and women of every business and political stripe beseeched me and others at every occasion, somehow finding my hotel room number and knocking on my door. For the most part I let the Houston Host Committee filter them out. The White House made a couple of requests that were honored. As far as I know, the only persons granted a private meeting with Deng Xiaoping were George and Barbara Bush. Bush had been US special envoy to China and had gotten along well with Deng.

Shameless capitalism aside, all the planning and cooperation by business and civic leaders paid off. The entire trip was a success and well received. Deng aided his cause a great deal. Within reason he was open and quite humorous. He was a media hit and nowhere more so than at the rodeo. He had a grand time at the barbeque reception. He was gracious to the guests and to me. Bob Strauss, through our interpreter, told him that I had dropped everything to put on the Houston events. He stood up, put his hand on my shoulder, and thanked me.

After the reception we walked to the rodeo arena. The crowd went wild. Deng mounted a small stagecoach for an agreed-upon, one-time circle of the arena. Instead he circled for twenty minutes or more. He loved it, we loved it, and all those Chinese officials in their cherished cowboy hats beamed from ear to ear.

During the rodeo a local cattleman presented the Chinese leader with a highly prized young bull. If my memory serves well, it was of a type suitable for a climate common in China. At some point Deng had commented on how much that breed was admired in China, but said that they had few. When the stagecoach stopped, the presentation was made, to the very apparent pleasure of the leader and his comrades, not to mention all those anticommunist Texans who suddenly envisioned a new cattle market.

As we went back to the parking area beneath the stands, I saw a set of spotlights and a young bull being presented. I thought it was the same critter I'd seen earlier, but didn't think twice about it. Then we climbed into buses and headed to Houston. Early the next morning my Chinese counterpart knocked at my door. It seems there had been two bulls given to the Chinese, and now he was at a loss regarding how to get them to China. I looked him in the eye and said, "Now that you have a cowboy hat, start acting like a cowboy. Figure it out." He was horrified. Then I winked and said I'd work it out.

He broke into a big smile and threw his arms around me. We both knew that the hug meant more than gratitude, it was good-bye. He was off to Seattle, then back home to China and the rest of his life.

If ever there was evidence that our rodeo was the highlight of the 1979 Chinese visit to the United States, it came after Deng died in 1997. Both *Newsweek* and *Time* used photographs of him, in broad smile, at the rodeo.

The positive energy of the Chinese visit to the United States was immediately erased by the worsening inflation and the Iran hostage crisis. To top it off, Ted Kennedy challenged the president in the 1980 primary. Carter eventually bested Kennedy, but at a terrible political price. An already weakened president needed all the support possible, and a lot of breaks. As it turned out, no breaks were to be had. To make matters worse, Jimmy Carter chose not to campaign in 1980 due to the Iran crisis. This called for a great many people to act as surrogate campaigners on his behalf.

By then my family and I had temporarily located to Montana to recharge as a family and to explore investment opportunities around Glacier Park. Eventually we would build a ski lodge on land that I owned, and—later, with other partners—a resort hotel in Whitefish: Grouse Mountain Lodge.

I was already working on a major side project, something near to my heart: a national salute to Bob Strauss, with funds raised going to the Strauss Chair at the Lyndon B. Johnson School of Public Affairs at the University of Texas in Austin. I called every person on my Rolodex. I called on every corporation I could think of, starting with our friends from AT&T. We put a first-class committee together. But I also had another Strauss-related duty to fulfill. I became one of the Carter campaign surrogates.

I traveled from Montana to most of the western states, as well as going to talk with some of my southern friends. Mainly I was putting events together for Bob who would usually travel with another Carter cabinet member or a high elected official. Some events were great fun, such as going to Johnny and June Carter Cash's home near Nashville. Many country-and-western greats were there, and I was in hog heaven. Among them was Tom T. Hall who was a great singer and an even a better songwriter.

In 1972 at the Democratic convention, I'd had to arrange entertainment. I love all parts of a convention, but there have to be program breaks featuring entertainers. Nowadays the networks choose who goes on the air and who doesn't—the parties don't decide. But Tom T. Hall went on in 1972 and later wrote a song about it while he was in Miami: "Old Dogs, Children and Watermelon Wine." Since then he has always dedicated that song to me, whenever I am in his audience. I love the poetry of the piece. Later in our lives, President Carter, Tom T. Hall, and I would all become published poets, and we have shared each other's books.

So even in those bleak campaign days of 1980 there were gratifying moments, if not many. Every time President Carter got a bump ahead, it would be negated by news from Iran. The most devastating of that bad-news flood was the failed hostage rescue attempt in Iran. The image of the charred ruins of those men and helicopters drove nails into the coffin of Carter's presidency.

Even when the president tried to do the right thing, like visiting seriously wounded troops at the burn unit of Brooke Army Medical Center in San Antonio, much of the press tried to turn it into a calculated, political ploy on Carter's part. One only has to understand the role of our commander in chief and the compassion of Jimmy Carter, who carried with him at all times his deep Christian faith, to know that Carter had no choice but to go to San Antonio to visit the men he'd sent to near death. Some of the media chose to ignore facts and played instead on the falsehood of political purpose. I revere the freedom of the press but it is not a license to lie. Bob Strauss saw it that way and made a stand in Houston.

Strauss, Secretary of Energy Charles Duncan Jr., and I were on a surrogate swing through the South, winding up in Houston. We had no more gotten off the plane, when we were confronted by the press. A young man aggressively stepped forward and shoved a mike in Bob's face, saying, "Mr. Strauss, don't you think that President Carter's trip to Brooke Army Medical Center was nothing more than an ill-concealed political stunt?"

Strauss paused, allowing silence, staring the reporter in the face. "You know, son, I told Duncan and Bristol earlier that before the end of the day some dumb son of a bitch would try to belittle President Carter's duty as commander in chief and as a human being. Through Nashville, Little Rock, and Shreveport, I knew we'd meet that dumb son of a bitch. Then I began to have doubts. But here we are and here you are. Shame on you!"

With that we got in the car. Some of the members of the press were clapping for Bob, and the reporter, destroyed, was running along the side of the car yelling, "Mr. Strauss, I didn't mean it that way. I didn't and I'm sorry." Our car drove off.

And so it went wherever we traveled. There were no good winds to clear away the deep fog of failure that seemed to loom above Carter at every turn. Domestic and foreign demons were everywhere, and Carter was not out there in person, defending his record and his vision for the country. Even the fact that he finally bested Ted Kennedy for the nomination left the party split. He lost to Ronald Reagan by a wide margin. That defeat was unfortunate, because President Carter had a number of good policies and initiatives. A problem was that he could not articulate them clearly and strongly.

Energy policy is a case in point. Carter had a fine policy based on three concepts: conservation, deregulation of oil and gas production, and alternative sources. He also had Charles Duncan as secretary of energy, who, if given time, had the business sense and political acumen to pull together and implement a plan and then sell it to Congress. Carter also had the respect of all sides in the Middle East,(although that is certainly not the case today) and he stuck with it until a peace accord was laid on the table for signature.

But it didn't matter. Iran and inflation would have been enough to fell even a giant. President Carter was a good man but no giant. Fortunately he would become one of our best ex-presidents.

With the 1980 election over, there was no rest. There was still the Strauss event, which would take place in Washington in December. Through a great deal of effort on the part of a nationwide cast of players, it was going to be meaningful and profitable. We had a mixed slate of notables lined up to attend, including President Carter and the newly elected vice president, George H. W. Bush. Congress and governors would be well represented. Bob Strauss's friends and followers would be arriving from all parts of the country, indeed the whole world.

I left Montana and flew to Washington well before Thanksgiving. I hated to leave my family, but a major fundraising dinner, any major dinner, has a thousand moving parts toward the end. Even with all contingencies envisioned, if something can go wrong it will, and someone at the top has to be there to plug holes, smooth ruffled feathers, and deal with last-minute cost hijackers. I was used to this role and never really needed stress management. I have found that if you stay on top of the parts, the whole will look reasonably well executed. But I wasn't ready for a new wrinkle.

All of the LBJ School and Foundation matters were run through its wonderful dean, Elspeth Rostow, and Frank Erwin, former chairman of the Board of Regents at the university, a power unto himself. They, in concert with the LBJ Foundation, had approved several funding events and I had been contracted to run them.

In October, though, Frank died. While saddened, I thought his death would have little impact, if any, on the dinner. We were too far along in our planning, I thought. His death, however, allowed cowards to come out of the woodwork, people who had been afraid to take him head-on who now criticized this and pointed fingers at that. None was more vitriolic than Dan Williams of Dallas, a member of the Board of Regents. An insurance executive, it turned out that Williams hated Frank and despised Jews. In short order following Frank's death I learned something that Strauss then called me to tell me that *he* had learned. Williams was calling all over Texas, asking outright what the University of Texas was doing honoring a Jew, and what the university was doing paying "the kike's boy, George Bristol," a big fee without full University of Texas approval. Bob and I talked. I was more furious about the anti-Semitism than the allegation about my pay. The latter been carefully negotiated and would be paid by the LBJ Foundation, not by the University of Texas.

I have never understood anti-Semitism. There were no Jews I knew of in the small Texas towns I where grew up, and in Austin they were friends and classmates. I'm not even sure where I first heard a real expression of anti-Semitism, although I knew of the deep and monstrous prejudices of Nazi Germany, of course. But anti-Semitism struck home because of my friendship with Bob Strauss. One night we were sitting in the bar of the Madison Hotel in Washington. I guess it was in the summer of 1971. Bob asked what I thought about the possibility of his running for the US Senate in 1972, and I went into a long response—all of it positive. The prospect of going home to Texas was always attractive, but I am sure I was enthusiastic about Bob running. I loved Strauss and liked living in Washington,

Bob thought for a few moments and then said, "All that may be true, but there's one drawback. I'm Jewish." I was dumbfounded. I said that I didn't think that would be an issue. After ten minutes or so, however, he convinced me that it *was* a serious issue. And the subject of his running for Senate never came up again. After that, anti-Semitism didn't rear its head in my world until Dan Williams started shooting his mouth off in late 1980. There was really nothing I could do then but complete the Strauss Chair fundraiser as successfully as possible.

On the afternoon of the dinner, Lew and Edie Wasserman dropped by the organizers' suite to pick up their tickets. Wasserman was a devoted friend of Strauss and also on the board of directors of the LBJ Foundation. While their tickets and passes were being packaged, we went into the back bedroom for a visit, and Lew asked how things were going. Without thinking, I poured out the whole Williams story: his horrific slurs about Bob and his threat to block my contract.

Lew was a debonair man with large glasses. Behind those glasses were kind eyes that could turn steely. In a quiet voice he said that he and Edie would pay my fee and that I should remember that they too were "kikes." "Don't worry about anything. Just go put on a great show for Bob and Helen." I breathed a sigh of relief and did just that.

It was a memorable evening. President Carter did attend, as did the vice president–elect, George H. W. Bush. We roasted and toasted Bob. Members of both parties participated. Regrettably, that sort of bipartisan event of goodwill and cheer has gone by the wayside, for the most part. It is too bad for the country.

After the event I went back to Montana to complete the planning for our new ski lodge and to begin to plan for Senator Bentsen's reelection bid in 1982. Then Christmas, New Year's Day, and a new ski season set in, and I all but forgot about Dan Williams. A couple of months later, the phone rang and it was Bob Strauss, who said, "Bristol, what did you tell Lew Wasserman, again?" I told him that I had explained the situation to Lew and Edie and that he had told me not to worry about it—that he was a kike too. Strauss died laughing. "Well, you ain't going to believe it, but Dan Williams came to my office in Dallas today and tearfully apologized. Wanted me to know there'd been a big misunderstanding. I told him that I knew better. Too many friends had heard it from him firsthand."

Throughout the 1980s and 1990s, Bob and Helen kept in touch with me, but we never again had the close association we'd had in the '70s. Bob went on to serve on many important corporate boards and commissions. He helped President Reagan, through Mrs. Reagan, formulate a new policy regarding the Soviet Union, and along the way he gained the confidence of Mikhail Gorbachev. President Bush appointed him ambassador to the Soviet Union, and he witnessed the fall of the empire and Gorbachev. It is important to note this, because here is a man who is a Democrat to the core, yet who served a Republican president with honor and distinction. In doing so, he served his country without regard to politics. That is as it should be. I hope we as a nation regain that sense of civility and civic duty some day.

As the 1990s passed, Bob slowed with age and Helen developed dementia. It was a rough time. When she passed away, it was difficult on Bob. They had been partners and best friends for over sixty years. She was his sounding board and grounding. She could bring him back to reality. Often, with glee, Bob would tell the story of his self-imagined rise to the presidency. "I got up this morning and looked in the mirror and said, 'Bob, you'd make one hell of a president. Then in the car I tell Nat the same thing. Maybe during the day a couple of staff would nod in agreement, but that night over a martini, I said to Helen that there were very few qualified to be president." She'd smile and say, "Yes, dear and I'd imagine there's one less than you're imagining." He would chuckle at her wisdom. She was his anchor.

Still he found the resilience to bounce back from the loss of Helen. At ninety-three he is still active, alert and wise. In 2010 my wife, Gretchen, and I had lunch with him in Washington. We talked of old times and great moments, but he kept coming back to Helen and the fact he is at peace. He has much to be at peace about.

CHAPTER 13
Lloyd Bentsen

August 13th (1944)

Dear Dad -

Today, Sunday, August the thirteenth, I attended church services 20,000 feet above the blue Mediterranean. We were tuned in to the Overseas Broadcasting Service during their morning ceremony. I visited St. Peters in The Eternal City and thought it the most magnificent church I had ever seen, but this morning St. Peters became just another work of man in comparison to our place of worship. Even Michelangelo would have bowed to the beauty that was ours. A deep blue sky arched above us, the sun spilling through the clouds below us covering the earth with ever changing shadow mosaics. A line of towering cumulus clouds ahead to remind us of the white robed choir in the church at home. Our pew was in the first row, a B-24. The congregation - ten silent, thoughtful men on a mission to bomb targets in Occupied France.

The minister finished his sermon and then over the ether waves we heard "Onward Christian Soldiers", never could a song have been more appropriate or more closely listened to. Every word was weighed, searching for that assurance that what we were about to do was just and that we are on God's side. The pastor then gave a prayer for the success of the

Allied cause. I am certain the others must have silently joined in the prayer and then added with me a request for Christ's blessing. By then we had to change to other frequencies as we were nearing enemy territory.

Thoughts on this combat mission, well I suppose mine are the usual ones - my wife, Mom and Dad, our baby in October, the kids, home. Then the target draws nearer and thoughts of survival seem to blanket out all others. That bail out procedure, r.p.m. and manifold pressure OK, then a voice over the interphone, "Waist gunner to bombardier, fighters at 3 o'clock high". You tighten the formation until the wings interlace a few seconds later, "Those beautiful P-51s".

Approaching the bomb run, our flak suits and helmets receive a last minute check. Here it comes - you pull your neck down into the flak suit until you resemble a turtle who has just retired into his shell. Hands a bit moist, although its 15° below outside, buttocks tight, and now flak, nothing to do but sweat it out. Will that bombardier ever say bombs away so we can get the hell out this place.

"Bombs away", now its heel over and make a run for it. The interphone barks, "B-24 just exploded over target, 5 o'clock low" just that, nothing more. A hasty check of the formation, no not one of our group.

Finally out of their fighter range, lets lose some altitude and get these oxygen masks off. Believe we can slip between those clouds and the mountains. Lets have some music on that radio, tilt the seats back, how about some hot coffee. The fellows begin to loosen up and joke over the interphone, another milk run. A BBC announcer cuts in, "Today Allied aircraft attacked targets in Southern France. 28 planes are missing from the days operation. You wonder at the speed of news dissemination.

There's the field, I got by another mission.

There it is, a few tense jam packed minutes, then to the other extreme. No glamour, no heroics, just a job.

Dad, I haven't told Beryl Ann, and Mom about my flying combat because with Don and me both in it, I'm afraid it would be too much. Beryl Ann has too much to worry about now with the baby expected in October. Just in case anything should ever happen to me, I want you to know how things stood and make them understand. Dad, nothing will happen, it just couldn't to a fellow who has the finest family in the world waiting for him. This morning, another day nearer to my return home.

Your eldest,

B

The insightful letter reproduced above was written in 1944 by a young US Army Air Corps officer and pilot, Lloyd M. Bentsen Jr. Writing about a bombing run over the Mediterranean, he mentions the things most important to him, then and throughout his life: God, family, country, and duty, and he does so with clarity and simplicity that is almost poetic. Later in life, during his years as a congressman, business leader, US senator, and secretary of the treasury, many would sometimes miss this side of Bentsen. What they saw was a public figure of great depth, exceptional ability, and courage, but one who could be guarded, reserved, and patrician.

Lloyd Bentsen was all that and more. He was among the most qualified and gifted public servants and he should have been president of the United States. It was not to be, due to the times, his moderate political philosophy, and his state of origin, Texas. Coming to the Senate and national prominence in 1970, so soon after Lyndon Johnson's tumultuous reign, punctuated by the Vietnam War and shortly before John Connally's switch to the Republican Party in 1972, being a Texan carried too much baggage. That was particularly true for a party that was anti-Nixon, left of center, and antiwar. Furthermore, he'd not been in the Senate long enough to develop a national following or to allow his gifts of leadership to become more apparent.

I would not come to know Bentsen until after his 1970 election to the Senate, but I knew of him because of his primary and general election campaigns. I had grown to like him from what I had read and heard. I quietly toured the old Tenth District in the early spring of 1970 for Bob Strauss and others in Washington, to gauge the race between Bentsen and Senator Yarborough there. Due to family politics and personal friendships I was for Yarborough, but I kept that to myself so as to get an accurate read. What I found was that Yarborough was in deep trouble.

Yarborough had over the years ignored some and angered many. He no longer had the protective umbrella of Lyndon Johnson that he'd had in 1964. I reported that Lloyd Bentsen would carry or break even in most of the counties outside of Austin. That was big news because the Tenth was for the most part still New Deal populist, but Yarborough had for too long taken support there for granted. Bentsen redoubled his efforts and did carry a large portion of the district, and won the primary. Then he went on to beat George H. W. Bush in November. This was a shock for the Republicans, who quickly tried to recover, claiming through a misguided Vice President Spiro Agnew that Bentsen would be part of the "Silent Majority" supporting Nixon. They were wrong. Bentsen's first vote set them and Washington straight. Lloyd Bentsen never liked to be painted into a box by others or taken for granted. Yes, he would and often did work on both sides of the aisle, but it was on equal standing, without rancor or ballyhoo. He would compromise, but he would also draw the line.

In the fall of 1973 Senator Bentsen asked me to organize a statewide fundraising dinner for him in Houston. I still didn't know the senator well, but I was indebted to him. In 1972 my brother-in-law got into a trumped-up jam in the military. I talked with Strauss about it and he called Bentsen. Then I went to see Bentsen to explain the situation. Without hesitating, the senator picked up the phone and called a World War II pilot friend who by then was high up in the Pentagon. All Bentsen asked was that the matter be looked into. From then on, Senator Bentsen had my support and that of my entire family.

So the decision to organize the dinner was an easy one. And everything went very well: we raised a great deal of money. Shortly before the event, Bentsen and his wife, B.A., invited me to dinner. He made a pitch that I come to work for him, running his statewide offices but also preparing for his reelection run for the Senate in 1976, and, by the way, for a run for the Democratic nomination for president at the same time.

I told Bentsen that I owed a great deal to Chuck Kuhn and would have to clear it with him. Bentsen smiled and said, "George I have already cleared it and Chuck is totally supportive." We shook hands. Not only was it an opportunity of a lifetime, a chance for me to learn the whole of Texas, it was an opportunity to work for two people for whom I had the highest regard politically, people I would come to love.

That night I talked for a long time with Bob. While he had no qualms about the deal, we both understood that there was no way we could remain as close, nor would I be able work on a number of projects we had discussed. At the end of 1973 my family and I moved back to Austin, but not out of Bob and Helen Strauss's lives, as it turned out.

When I realized that we would be moving back to Austin, I was so joyously grateful that I forgot to talk about salary with Bentsen. But Chuck Kuhn paid for our move and gave me a generous severance. I didn't have to think about such mundane things as salary.

We found a house in Austin and filled out the loan papers. At closing we went to the office of the chairman of the board of a savings and loan. "George," intoned Gene Fondren, "we are pleased to have your business, but we don't have an income amount on the form." In shock and embarrassment I called the senator in Washington. He came on the line immediately, and when I asked him my salary he responded, "One dollar!" After a moment of silence, he and Fondren laughed. "I will pay you what Chuck Kuhn was paying you, and more if you need it." That was a deal for me: working for Lloyd Bentsen, living in Austin, for a very good salary. I practically danced down the stairs after closing.

Lloyd M. Bentsen Jr. was the eldest son of remarkable parents, "Mr. Lloyd" and his beloved Dolly. Danish in ancestry, Mr. Lloyd had come from South Dakota to San Antonio for World War I Air Corps training. He laughingly said one time that anything south of South Dakota was a godsend, but the Valley of Texas was paradise. At the urging of Ray Landry (father of Tom Landry, the highly successful Dallas Cowboys coach) who was in the Air Corps, Lieutenant Bentsen went to the Valley—Mission, to be exact. Not only was the landscape and climate paradise to him, there was a young Red Cross captain walking on the other side of the street whose apparition struck Bentsen momentarily dumb. Then he turned to Landry and said, "I'm going to marry that girl." Landry replied, "Well, Lloyd, you're going to have to go to church." He did—and shortly thereafter Lloyd and Dolly Bentsen became loving life mates.

If there was anything to rival it, it was his son Lloyd Bentsen's devotion to *his* wife, B. A.—Bentsen's Best Asset. Time after time B. A. would prove to be invaluable. Born Beryl Ann Longino in Lufkin, Texas, her parents died when she was very young, and she was reared by a grandmother. She grew to be one of the most beautiful women I have known, inwardly and outwardly. She was the perfect match for her man from the Valley, in politics, business, and family. I deeply and profoundly respected Lloyd Bentsen, but I adore B. A. to this day, mainly because I saw her bring so much joy and rock-solid support to him, their children, staff, and friends.

Much has been written of the senator's bravery as a bomber pilot. But he did not go into air combat only out of a deep sense of patriotism. He had been in the service for a time and somehow wound up in Brazil on some sort of coastal duty with a friend, Joe Kilgore, who was also from the Valley. One night Lloyd rushed up to Joe and asked how he could get out of there. According to Bentsen and Kilgore, Joe told him that hazardous bomber piloting was the only way that he knew. Bentsen joined right up, but not to get to Europe or the Pacific. He had to get to New York City, it seems, to head off a rival suitor. B. A. was a model for Harry Conover, one of the leading modeling agencies of the day. No combat peril was too great to thwart a determined Bentsen—a trait that stood him in good stead the rest of his life. He made it to New York just in time, hazardous duty be damned, and the two then married and went from base to base for his training. When Bentsen went overseas, B. A. went to Mission where she was welcomed and loved by the parents she'd never had. Thereafter they were "Mom and Dad" to her, and she was their other beautiful daughter, along with Betty Bentsen, who is every bit as gorgeous and gracious as B. A.

Details are unclear, and will probably remain a mystery because Bentsen did not discuss the war in great length, but on one mission Bentsen and his crew were shot down over northern Greece or Yugoslavia. After securing his men from the wreckage, Bentsen and his crew found themselves deep in enemy territory, surrounded by partisans, including women with pitchforks. They were led to a camp. As they approached the light of the campfire, a young man stepped forward. "Lloyd Bentsen, I know you. I sacked groceries for your mother in McAllen!" Bentsen often said that luck was a big part of his success. That event pretty well confirms his belief. And so the wounded airmen were cared for and would later be hidden by Marshal Tito's anti-Nazi partisans until an escape route became available and safe. Senator Bentsen and Marshal Tito kept in contact over the years. I haven't been able to find out what happened to the young man.

After rejoining American forces, Bentsen again flew combat missions until the war ended. Then he flew home to B. A. and their new baby boy, Lloyd III, his mother and dad, and his brothers and sister. He was much decorated and mustered out as a lieutenant colonel at the age of twenty-four. He started practicing law (he had graduated from law school at the age of twenty-one), but Lloyd Bentsen was a public servant at heart. In 1946 he ran for county judge of Hidalgo County and won. Then in 1948 he ran for Congress. Things were a little different then, not just in Texas, but in many states and cities. Local bosses ruled. Young Judge Bentsen went to one such county *jefe*.

"Oh, Lloyd, I was afraid you'd come around. I have so much respect for your family and your military career, but I've already committed to your opponent. I can't go back on my word."Bentsen said that he fully understood that and would not ask him to do so. "Just don't hurt me too much," he asked.

"Now there's an idea worth considering. I promised him I'd carry the county for him, but I didn't say by how much. How many votes do you need?"

Bentsen threw out a figure and that is what he got—enough to be elected to Congress.

Much has been written and said about the old-line boss system. Some bosses were corrupt, some were dictatorial, and some manufactured votes, but many were high-minded, savvy politicians, professionally political. I wish we had a bit of that back. Today we pay hundreds of millions to get-out-the-vote consultants who can't get out the vote, and hundreds of millions more to inform the public with slick, negative ads that drive down the very voter turnout the other "experts" are being paid to rally.

The boss system in the last century produced Woodrow Wilson, Franklin Roosevelt, Harry Truman, Adlai Stevenson, John Kennedy, and Lyndon Johnson. Not a bad track record, and that's just on the Democratic side. On the Republican side we have Teddy Roosevelt and Dwight Eisenhower, although Roosevelt was chosen to be McKinley's vice president to get him out of New York's governorship.

There were also great failures, such as Warren G. Harding, whose early-twentieth-century boss cronies and their friends were every bit as bad if not worse than twenty-first-century scoundrels like Majority Leader Tom DeLay, lobbyist Frank Abramoff, and some of Vice President Dick Cheney's pals. Bosses made mistakes, but because they were in the business of elections and electability, they were more often than not the best judges of candidates. They not only looked for the best, they filtered out the losers.

In 1944, with a very ill, dying Roosevelt at the head of the ticket, Democratic bosses, led by Ed Flynn of the Bronx, successfully moved mountains to stop the vice-presidential nomination of Henry Wallace, former secretary of agriculture and Roosevelt's third-term vice president. Wallace was brilliant in many ways, but a mystic and a far-left-leaning political figure—a very lapsed Republican. Flynn thought that Wallace would ruin the country and the party if he became president, which surely he would do, it seemed, given Roosevelt's health. "I felt he would never survive his term." Flynn later said.

Bosses, because they were in the business of winning and perpetuation, had to look down the road and anticipate as many future moves as possible in the chess game of politics. I think that is exactly what that South Texas county boss did in Bentsen's case. He'd given his word, which was sacrosanct and binding, but he saw in the young Lloyd

Bentsen Jr. more than just a candidate. He was looking to the future at a new generation of leaders.

In Congress Bentsen was an anticommunist cold warrior, but surprisingly liberal on such matters as the abolition of the poll tax—a time-honored way in the South to line up the vote or thwart it. He was a favorite of Sam Rayburn's and became a friend of the new senator from Texas, Lyndon Johnson. He was not, as some would later claim, "Lyndon's boy." As an elected official and as a businessman, Bentsen was his own man. Loyal, yes, but never a rubber stamp.

Throughout his career Bentsen was a Democrat to the core, partly because it was the party of his roots in South Texas. As he began his rise in politics in 1948, the Democratic Party became the party for equality, and the Bentsens believed in equality. They were some of the first whites, particularly landed-gentry whites, to extend their hands and financial support to Mexican American businessmen and candidates in the Valley. If there is such a thing, I think they had a Danish sense of democracy and fair play. And this fairness paid off: Lloyd Bentsen carried South Texas by huge numbers every election. It didn't hurt that he spoke fluent Spanish.

I know little about his business years in Houston. He and B. A. often talked about their personal lives there, their children and friends. A great deal of what I learned came from those friends and acquaintances in Houston and around the country. With very few exceptions they deeply admired Bentsen for his business acumen and fairness. In every race, Democrats and Republicans supported him with "money, marbles, and chalk"—a political phrase often used in Texas to describe support across the board.

Ed Cox, a Dallas businessman, is a case in point. I never asked Ed his party affiliation, but I suspect that he's a Republican, though a moderate one—one of a dying breed. Ed and his wife were friends and tennis buddies of the Bentsens. He told me when I first met him that he would do anything for Lloyd Bentsen. He thought Bentsen was the most qualified person in either party, and I am sure he supported Bentsen for Senate in every election. In 1974 or 1975 he wanted to do so in a big way to aid Bentsen's goal of the presidency. The only problem was that new campaign finance laws were going into effect and he was limited to $1,000, which came as a shock to him and many others.

Based in Washington during Bentsen's 1970 campaign for Senate against incumbent Ralph Yarborough, I heard bits and pieces about the politics and financing of the primary and general election, but would learn more later on, during my tenure with the senator. What I would find out was that while Johnson and Connally had been helpful, many of their supporters were split in the race against Yarborough. In fact, Bentsen told me that President Johnson warned him that he didn't stand much of a chance. Yarborough was too well-established. Furthermore, many of their long-time supporters were getting old and tired of the game and a number were turning Republican.

The Yarborough claim that Bentsen spent "millions and millions" was a great distortion. As best as I can ferret out (there were no real campaign finance laws in place in 1970 and little reporting), Bentsen's campaign spent about $2 million on the primary and general election together. That is not completely accurate, because many county organizations and individuals raised and spent their own funds locally, often without the candidate's knowledge.

One of the side issues in the 1970 November election may have meant the difference, something that often is the case. A statewide "liquor by the drink" initiative was on the ballot, and this was highly controversial, especially in East Texas, a region that was heavily Baptist and dry. The Baptists and the bootleggers joined forces to defeat "demon rum"—and for the most part the Baptists and the bootleggers were Democrats. They poured out on Election Day to defeat booze and elect Lloyd Bentsen. He won, but the bootleggers lost—the "liquor-by-the-drink" initiative passed.

Somewhere between 1970 and 1974 Senator Bentsen decided to run for president. (Actually, he may have decided that when he was twelve.) He told few right away, but made some initial soundings. In one of our introductory briefing meetings after I was hired, we discussed the idea and he asked what I thought of it. By then I was a Bentsen man through and through, but I told him that it would be rough. I thought that we first needed to protect and finance his upcoming Senate reelection in 1976. There was some opportunity for presidential support, particularly in the South, but the South was dominated by George Wallace. Other moderates and conservatives would surely be for Senator Scoop Jackson of Washington, another cold warrior with liberal credentials and a huge Jewish following. Jimmy Carter of Georgia was not even considered by us or others at that stage.

We talked some about the old "Johnson Law" in Texas, which allowed a person to run for two offices, president and Senate in the same year. We had a strong financial base in Texas, and Bentsen had friends and associates across the country. He had a great number of colleagues in the House, former congressional colleagues back in the private sector, and many friends in the Senate, particularly from the South, senators who liked him and despised Wallace. All were rooting for him to one degree or another.

It was going to be a political tightrope act. Bentsen took his Senate duties very seriously, and Texans (no matter how proud they were about the prospect of another president) expected him to tend to those duties. Even though we discussed everything in great detail, I still can't comprehend how he and B. A. arrived at the decision to pursue both offices at once. I drew up a financial game plan that factored in a substantial sum we had raised in Houston in 1973 for the Senate run. If my memory serves well, I thought we would need $2 million for the Senate race and about $10 million for a successful outcome in the presidential race. I also said that I thought we needed a quick $1 million for the presidential coffers to establish that Bentsen was a serious candidate.

All of this was going to be complicated by the pending campaign finance reform legislation. While it had not been finalized, we had a good idea that individual and PAC contributions would be greatly restricted. Above all, we needed to nail down our support in Texas, politically and financially. It was essential to have that base secured before we struck out to capture others. We would use 1974 to secure this support.

Too often, candidates and campaigns run, win or lose, then shut their doors and do nothing until the next round. That certainly was the case before computers. But that was not the case with Lloyd Bentsen. Among his many attributes, he and his staff were the most organized I've seen, before or since. Thus there was constantly a great deal of fine tuning, including updates on financial supporters.

At first I was on the senator's state staff as executive assistant. That was legitimate because I had to learn the ropes and the issues. However, it soon became apparent that Joe O'Neill, a talented Bostonian and LBJ School graduate, could handle the state office with one hand tied behind him. We were both aided by the superb Washington staff headed by Loyd Hackler, a former Texas newspaper man with a brilliant political head on his shoulders.

We added other staffers, none better than a very young Jack Martin, who claims that I rescued him from a life in West Texas. I seriously doubt that. Jack is one of those people who would have risen to the top anywhere, any time. We hit it off and have remained friends to this day. I don't even remember his first job, but he became the senator's travel aide. He took to it like the professional he would become. He was good for the senator, B. A., and me. He always reported in, sharing important matters and pointing out flaws.

We were becoming a well-run operation, although sometimes we would mess up in scheduling an airplane or where one was supposed to land. Then hell would break loose. Jack and I hated those calls from Bentsen: "George, why are B. A. and I here and neither the plane nor Jack is?" The silence that followed could only be considered life-threatening. We would fix the problem right away and try never to repeat our sin.

There were other small problems. Early one morning a call came and the familiar voice was on the line: "George, do you know why B. A. and I were scheduled into a Michigan hotel with no heat, and short sheets and blankets, by the Washington staff?"

Fortunately I did not know why, and said so. Then Bentsen started laughing. "I know you didn't, but I got your attention. We have already talked to Kathryn Higgins who did. You know she's getting married next month, when it will be even colder, and we've promised her and her husband an all-expense-paid honeymoon to this very hotel." It was a laughing matter, but no staff member of Lloyd Bentsen ever tried to save money by booking cheap rooms in unknown hotels after that.

Sometimes the machine broke down. George Tagg and Richard Hardy had gone ahead to prepare for an upcoming visit in East Texas. Separately and collectively they were wonderful organizers and fundraisers, but as a team they often lived on the edge— of epic comedic proportions. The scene was a small-town hotel, probably having seen better days, likely on its last legs. Tagg and Hardy finalized plans, then enjoyed a beer or two and went to bed. When the senator and B. A. arrived after midnight, their traveling aide discovered that the elevator seemed stuck on Tagg and Hardy's floor, and gave their room a call. Up they shot—and then, without thinking, ran into the hallway in their underwear, and began to pry at the elevator doors.

Meanwhile the senator and B. A. had grown impatient and hiked up the stairs. Reaching their floor, they witnessed the two grunting and groaning, struggling to open the elevator doors, by this time in full sweat. Walking past them, the senator tapped Hardy on the shoulder and asked, "What time is breakfast?" Hardy, in red blush and red underwear, answered without looking back, and the two just kept working to get the door open. Bentsen could not wait to tell the tale.

For the most part we were efficiently organized, although we did not find effective top-to-bottom party organization in every county we visited. Many needed a makeover. Some counties, like Loving (population 164), wouldn't make a difference even if we got every vote.

We discussed each county, deciding that there were about sixty that needed complete overhauls, or at least more-effective cochairs. Lloyd Bentsen couldn't always bring himself to cast off old friends or party loyalists, but some of them were hopeless. There was a fellow in Wichita Falls who was an old UT classmate, and Bentsen knew he was not fully committed to campaign work. When we went to Wichita Falls, the fellow picked us up and got us lost. We were looking for the home of one of the city's prominent citizens, but we kept getting lost and were running behind. Finally Bentsen said to stop the car. He got out, walked up to a house, knocked on its door, and a surprised occupant came out and gave directions. The senator wrote them down, then came back to the car and read them to the horror-stricken coordinator.

At a reception in Wichita Falls, Bentsen asked me if I knew Ray Clymer. I said that

I knew him casually. Bentsen retorted that he was our man—if we could get him. He was, and Clymer would serve Bentsen well for from then on. He would also serve the state in a number of appointive positions.

Another fellow the senator had put a great deal of faith in for his Senate and presidential campaigns called asking to meet the senator in Dallas. As they were riding through downtown, the colleague explained that Governor Dolph Briscoe wanted him to be for Jimmy Carter for president and so he had no choice. With quiet fury, Bentsen said, "Stop the car. Get out." I'm not sure that the two ever spoke again.

For the overhaul effort we put together a team of Bentsen organizers. We would use the upcoming state convention to back slates favorable to the senator and Briscoe, although Briscoe was on our list of those to watch very closely. With the rise of Jimmy Carter, it was a question of fellow governors and fellow Baptists. I also thought that there always was a little jealousy between South Texans and their egos. For both Bentsen and Briscoe this alliance was a matter of political convenience, and it held. Our stake was not as high as Briscoe's. He had to control the state party for all sorts of reasons, political and personal. We wanted to flex our political muscle, but we also were testing our system for the run-up to 1976. We wanted to know who could produce and who couldn't.

We won the state convention, but not without a fight, and it left some bruised feelings among some liberals. This would set the stage for the legislative session in 1975 and a bill to resurrect or renew the "Johnson Law," which would become known as the "Bentsen Bill." We knew we were going to have a fight. The liberals didn't like it and the Republicans didn't like it, but after a good deal of checking and assurances from our House floor manager, Tom Schieffer, of Fort Worth, the bill was moved onto the House floor. We got our clock cleaned. Momentary pandemonium reigned. Then cooler heads came to the fore: Jim "Snake" Nugent and Lynn Nabers took over. There was a procedure to bring the bill back up. We twisted arms, counted the votes, and then met. This time we knew, but didn't let on, that we had the votes.

Late in the evening I got a call from a staffer with Representative Sarah Weddington, Ann Richards. They wanted to talk about capitulation—ours. I went and listened, and then said that we wanted no compromise. The vote would take place as it stood. I'm not sure they understood who was now in control. I think they even thought that it was some sort of death wish on our part. But the next day we won with room to spare.

When the bill went to the state senate, Lieutenant Governor Bill Hobby controlled the gavel and the calendar. He thought it a good idea to bring Senator Bentsen to Austin to firm up support and put a little spine in some of the "crawfishers." He did, and nearly scared one wavering state senator to death when he walked up behind him and whispered, "It is only I, your United States senator and admirer. Help me retain both." The flabbergasted senator stammered, "Count me in, Lloyd!" We did and won the senate vote in the next day or so. We had control of the party and the ability to run for both president and the Senate in 1976. We also had a pretty good handle on the Senate and presidential campaign funding.

Before the end of 1974, when the new federal campaign finance law went into effect, we held a series of meetings at the Bentsen family ranch—Arrowhead. We had invited groups from all of the state's major cities, plus others, to fly in for three days of morning, noon, and afternoon get-togethers, with the hope of raising $3,000–$5,000 from each for the presidential race. Some people, like Ed Cox, were asked to come for supper. Close to $1 million was raised during those three days. On the final evening, only the senator, B. A., family members, and two top staff members remained: Loyd Hackler and I, who shared a guest house. Loyd told me he had decided to resign as the senator's chief of staff, having been offered a terrific job with a major trade association, the American Retail Federation. He told me that he would be available whenever necessary, but I had a stiff drink. We were losing a steady, day-to-day ally.

Then Loyd and I decided to get ready for dinner. I said that I would shower first and went into the bathroom. Opening the shower door, I saw that there was a huge rattlesnake, fully coiled, about to strike. I slammed the door and ran into the other room, buck naked. Loyd was in his underwear. I loudly explained the situation. There we were, two of America's leading political strategists, discussing how best to kill a snake in a shower. I finally said that I thought I should boost Loyd over the top of the shower door, so he could turn on the hot water and scald the snake to death. In we went and up went Loyd. At the apex, peals of laughter rang through the window. There were Mr. Bentsen, Don Bentsen, the senator's brother, and the senator, all watching. And there we were, with nothing to hide the blush of our embarrassment. This became a Bentsen story for years. At every appropriate opportunity Lloyd Bentsen would tell it to audiences large and small. Much later I would tell it on myself.

During his first term, Senator Bentsen established himself as a reliable, hardworking, focused senator's senator. His staff organization was a marvel to his colleagues, especially other incoming senators, and to a man who'd been in the Senate, Hubert Humphrey. One thing Humphrey had learned over the years was that he wasn't very well organized. For all their differences, the taciturn patrician and the talkative Happy Warrior had much in common: agricultural support, concern about health care (particularly for the elderly and the young), and a desire for fair treatment for all. And Hubert wanted a well-run office. They were an odd couple, but held great affection for one another to the day Hubert died. Bentsen would help Senator Bob Dole have the new Health and Human Services building renamed for Humphrey.

In his early years in the Senate, Lloyd Bentsen made significant contributions. Even as he was learning as a freshman, he joined the fray and helped pass the Employee Retirement Income Security Act (ERISA) in 1974, which protected retirees and their pension vesting rights. As with many such endeavors, he had discovered the problem in Texas among his constituency: people who had worked hard all their lives and were counting on their pensions were terminated, often wrongfully, before vesting. Bentsen, with the support of Senator Russell Long, recognized the problem and went about curing it. Even as a freshman he was able to do so because he was focused, knowledgeable, and marshaled his problem-solving intellect.

All in all we were proud of our efforts in 1974 and 1975. By the end of 1975 we had raised more money than every candidate except Wallace and Jackson, but we were close. Texas was in good shape—polls confirmed it. Bentsen was beginning to get some national coverage and notice, and some other states showed promise.

Organizations that run completely smoothly have no tales to tell. It's the flaws and the failures that make for stories. We had a big one in our presidential campaign manager, Ben Palombo. I knew it, Loyd knew it, and so did some others. Palombo was in Washington and had the senator's ear, but over time his status would erode and collapse. In the summer of 1975, as I recall, Palombo called me. "Have we got an opportunity in Missouri? Political support, media coverage and money! George, lots of money!"

"What's the catch?"

"We need Roy Clark."

Clark was very popular then, having been a cohost of *Hee Haw,* a nationally televised comedy and country music show. He must have been particularly appealing to the proposed host in Missouri.

I said that I could get Clark if he were available, but that he would cost several thousand dollars—and that was $25,000, as it turned out. Palombo's plan was to organize a high-dollar reception at a private home and an event for thousands at the rodeo area in Sikeston, and he made every assurance that both events would be well attended. I assigned a couple of staff to go to Missouri and make sure things were falling into place. This was to be Palombo's event, perhaps to show me up, but I never lost a wink of sleep over that possibility.

Time passed, and then I called and was informed that tickets weren't exactly flying off the shelf. So we faced a dilemma since we had a no-cut contract with Clark. I pulled four or five of our best fundraisers and organizers, and we went to Missouri to take a look and try to fix things. In order to pull it off we ran two strategies at once. Some of the team kept selling tickets at various prices, as best they could. And I called a former governor, Warren Hearnes, who gave me a couple of good hands from his part of the state. I made some big-contribution calls personally and then went on the radio, television, and newspaper circuit with every promotional scheme we could think of that wasn't illegal. "Buy one get fifty free" was not out of the realm of possibility. We pulled out all the stops. And Ben was called back to Washington for consultation.

We began to feel comfortable if not satisfied. Hearnes helped raise a few thousand, I pulled in some chips, and the twin barrage of low-price tickets and freebies was building a tolerable crowd—two or three thousand for a rodeo arena that held ten thousand. Even so, everyone was on edge. Driving back from a radio show, George Tagg, one of my favorite aides, suddenly said, "It's going to rain." I nearly ran the car off the road. How in the hell did he know that, I asked. "Cows are lying down. Sure sign!" Rain on our rodeo—that was all we needed.

Funding for the $25,000 for Clark hung in the air. Then, right in the middle of a staff meeting that had grown to twenty to thirty people, the phone rang. I took it in my room. Roy Clark, it seemed, was deathly ill in Baltimore. I feigned shock and gnashing of teeth, bemoaning our loss. The act must have been good because Clark's manager said that he would put a show together featuring Minnie Pearl and a few other Grand Ole Opry stars for $5,000. I nearly wept. Instead I soberly accepted, went into the bathroom, and turned on the shower to cover the sound of my hysterical laughter. We had just made $20,000. I put on my best sad face, went back into the staff meeting and solemnly announced that Roy would not be with us. Men and women actually cried.

So we pulled it off. We had a sizeable crowd, it didn't rain, and we actually made money. That night I told the senator that I didn't want to work with Palombo anymore, inadvertently saving Jack Martin's bacon. I didn't know it then, but there had been a major snafu in St. Louis prior to the event in Sikeston. A Bentsen visit to a Young Democrats convention (all of one hundred people expected in attendance) had been scheduled by Palombo or his team, and Palombo—without consulting with the senator, me or anyone else—was adamant about keeping that on the calendar, even when a major media event presented itself. Jack was in St. Louis at the time and took the blame for sticking to the schedule. I cleared that up and laid it at Ben's deserving feet.

Even though the money was flowing in at a pretty steady rate, during the rest of 1975 and on into 1976 we suffered steady erosion. Whatever strategy Ben had never took hold. And slowly but steadily another son of the South, Jimmy Carter, began to take root. We had hoped to be the voice of moderation that would appeal to southerners, but Texas was not viewed as a truly southern state. Wallace faded, Carter rose rapidly, and after the disastrous presidential primary in Oklahoma (where Bentsen was originally thought to be the favorite), we folded the campaign.

On reflection (which I have done more than once), I have come to the conclusion that the underlying factor in Lloyd Bentsen's 1976 presidential campaign failure was not of his making. Between the pall cast by President Johnson's Vietnam War policies and the cynical disregard for all things constitutional uncovered by the Nixon Watergate revelations and aftermath, the country was truly fed up with Washington. Only Jimmy Carter fit the image of an honest outsider who would change the course of politics and government. He was the right person at the right time to reignite the American sense of an honorable government working toward honorable goals. There was nothing Lloyd Bentsen or any other candidate could do to turn that tide.

At the time we had no respite to reflect, because an unknown Texas A&M professor, financed by loud-mouthed Fort Worth oilman Eddie Chiles and some of his pals, was challenging Bentsen in the Democratic primary for the Senate race.

I always found it slightly amusing and totally hypocritical when oil and gas executives used their political mouthpieces, like Phil Gramm, to criticize Lloyd Bentsen for failure to support their positions. Ironically, Bentsen was often and wrongly referred to as "Loophole Lloyd" because he did foster a number of bills to benefit the independent oil and gas industry. He thought it was essential to get them back in the game at the time of the OPEC price increases and declining production. Such incentives were the order of the day and widely supported by both parties.

It was particularly laughable when editorial writers bloviated about the need for such subsidies. The oil and gas industry has been one of the most subsidized and protected industries in US history, with the possible exception of railroads, water, utilities, and Wall Street. Yet today many who support the industry rail against alternative energy industry subsidies.

Oil and gas executives were never satisfied. There was never enough. Bentsen often shook his head and said that they were hard water to carry. That was not true of all. Many, like Jack Warren, Perry Bass, Lucien Flournoy, and others, were trying desperately to find new sources, and enhance older, depleted ones, and were not opposed to new ideas. But Chiles and his pal Gramm would not let up. Bentsen never thought much about Phil Gramm, one way or the other. We knew we were going to beat him like a tin drum. When someone in our campaign found that Gramm apparently had had photos airbrushed to exclude his Asian American wife, Wendy, Bentsen scotched the idea of going public. Why bother? Why hurt someone, especially when the outcome of the Texas primary—a 2 to 1 victory—seemed so assured.

At some point during that time, at a luncheon in Fort Worth sponsored by Perry Bass and other industry leaders, Eddie Chiles jumped up and berated Bentsen unfairly and ignorantly. I watched the senator's eyes grow their most steely gray. Then he said something like this: "Eddie, I get up every morning trying to do right by America, Texas, and our citizens. Whenever possible, and if justified, I do my damndest to help the vital industry of oil and gas. We need the products and we need the jobs. Given the response of this crowd and others across the state, I'd say that they agree. It is only damn fools who can never get enough from the very government they cuss that make this job so difficult. I resent your remarks and I will remember them." There was dead silence and then applause. I gathered that many were tired of Eddie Chiles. I was never prouder of Bentsen.

After the primary season was over, we settled all our accounts—for both the presidential and senate campaigns. Now we had to turn to the fall campaign. At some point I was changed back to being the Senate campaign manager. In effect, I was both campaign manager and finance chair. We had all the machinery set up. We didn't have to raise much more money, as we had never considered Gramm a real challenger and so had spent sparingly.

After school was out in early June, my family went down to Lake Jackson where the Bentsens had a secluded second home. The senator and I worked several matters out over two days. In the evening we dined together. And at dusk B. A. took the children—Mark was seven and Jennifer not yet five—down to the end of a dock to watch various birds return to nest and perhaps see their favorite deer, a huge, antlered buck. The senator, Valarie, and I watched that idyllic scene from a deck near the house. In her gentle way, B. A. pointed out things to Mark and Jennifer. At that moment, as in as many others, she was the First Lady. Suddenly, as if shot from a gun, the children levitated and started running as fast as their small legs could carry them. B. A. trailed behind, laughing all the way. It seems a large alligator had forcefully slapped its tail on the swamp water. Mark and Jennifer ran right past us and might have kept on running had we not corralled them and fed them supper.

Those two days were peaceful and rewarding. But Bentsen was not at peace. I think he was deeply hurt that he had not done better in the presidential primaries. He didn't dwell upon it. It was simply present in his eyes and sometimes he would mention it in passing. The truth is that we never stood a chance once Jimmy Carter, a true son of the Deep South, entered the race. Lloyd Bentsen, with his background and intellect, could have been the middle-of-the-road moderate alternative to Wallace and the more liberal candidate. But Carter would fill that middle ground in the South and elsewhere.

In July we took a break and went to New York City for the Democratic National Convention. I wanted to go to see old committee friends, thank those who had helped Bentsen (and there were many), see Strauss in action, and—to the degree possible— measure Carter and his people. We knew that we would have to help in the fall campaign, if for no other reason than self-preservation.

The senator and B. A. came to New York for some of the same reasons, plus they had long-time friends in New York City. The Bentsens, Valarie, and I stayed at the apartment of a former Bentsen business associate, Bill Grant of Kansas City. Bill was one of those people I have mentioned: probably Republican but a Bentsen supporter to the core, based not on philosophy but trust in the man and his integrity.

I had arranged through another campaign friend, Bob Nederlander of Michigan, to reserve some seats at one of his theaters for a large group of the senator's Texas friends. Bob was one of the Nederlander brothers who owned a chain of theaters and other entertainment venues. I had also invited the friends to come to a local watering hole to raise a glass to the Bentsens. I think it brightened our time there considerably. Except for the honor of it, though, the Bentsens didn't want to be there. The results of the past two years still weighed heavily. Lloyd and B. A. really didn't like crowds. They preferred smaller gatherings, although they could work crowds masterfully. Part of the problem was the fact that he had lost some hearing in one ear due to wartime flying and later hunting. The ear damage distorted sound, and he couldn't hear conversations in crowds, which was difficult since Lloyd Bentsen liked to listen.

Like practically everything political, we ran late all day and through the reception—New York City is hard to maneuver in, even in the best of times. So we showed up only a few minutes before curtain at Bob Nederlander's prized production—a Shirley MacLaine one-woman show. Nederlander tells it best: "There I was standing out front to greet my heroes, Lloyd and B. A. Bentsen. Cars flashed up, doors flung open, and the whole crowd roared past into the hall. I finally shook hands with one of the drivers." In high good humor and with much ribbing by him, we took Nederlander to dinner after the show. To this day he is one of my favorite people.

We took in another play and went to hear fellow Texan Barbara Jordan give the speech that propelled her to national prominence while eclipsing John Glenn's speech (fine, but not earth-moving) and his chance to be on the ticket. That would fall to Walter Mondale of Minnesota.

After that evening the Bentsens left for Texas. For the first time I was deeply saddened. We had invested a great deal of time together on the presidential campaign trail. It was a shame, I thought, that more people wouldn't have a chance to measure Bentsen's qualities. It would be twelve years before he would capture the imagination of the American people and draw attention and praise.

Sometime in August I went to Houston. The senator and I evaluated the November election. We had a recent poll that showed—again—a solid victory in the Senate race. We were well funded. We came to the conclusion that if we did nothing, we would win. However, there was a potential fly in the ointment—the Carter campaign. Carter's staff in Atlanta and Texas was running amok. They had already ticked off Governor and Janey Briscoe. They had gone to the wrong people in key counties, particularly San Antonio, where Congressman Henry B. Gonzalez was fuming, although Henry B. was usually in a dither about something. Then Carter went and lusted in his heart in *Playboy*, and then indirectly slighted Lady Bird Johnson.

The phones lit up. It was decided to have a "come to Jesus" meeting in Dallas. Bob Strauss, our strong ally John White (then Texas agriculture commissioner), Governor Briscoe, and I represented the senator. We agreed that with a little luck we might carry the state if we could shut the collective mouths of the Carter campaign, and if they would withdraw all their staff from Texas except for Chuck Parrish. We needed a liaison and Parrish had his head screwed on straight.

We all gathered around a phone in a hotel room. We called Hamilton Jordan, the national campaign director, at the appointed time. "I am sorry but Mr. Jordan is not in. May I say who is calling?" Before anyone else could chime in, Strauss spoke. "It's the governor of Texas, Senator Bentsen, Bob Strauss, and Jimmy Carter's Texas chairman, John White. We were told to be on this goddamned phone at this goddamned hour. So you go roust him out and get him on this call in five minutes or we'll call a press conference and let the world and Carter know that you all don't need Texas!" He slammed the phone down and in a few minutes it rang.

It was probably best that Jordan was on the defensive: he heard us out. John White would chair. We would collectively help. Jordan would pull all the staff and workers. I reported to the senator. He agreed that we should help Carter but not get too close. Carter had already demonstrated the ability to unravel a tightly rolled ball of string.

But as November drew nearer, we did become more involved. Our polls were holding strong. The rest of the statewide ticket was in good shape and Carter was competitive, but there was something else at play. John Connally was active for President Gerald Ford around the country but particularly in Texas. He was bragging that Ford would carry Texas. Things had cooled between Senator Bentsen and Connally since the Connally milk producers scandal and trial. While secretary of the treasury under Nixon, Connally had been accused of and indicted for taking a sum of cash from the milk industry in 1972. Connally went to trial for this. A number of Connally friends and associates, including Barbara Jordan, were called as character witnesses, but not Lloyd Bentsen. Here stories verge. The senator said that he sent word that he would be a character witness if called. Connally and his friends said that Bentsen had ducked. And so the old friendship dissolved. By 1976 I sensed that there was a bit of ego pushing and shoving.

The Bentsen team, particularly in the Valley, helped set up a get-out-the-vote effort that would help the entire ticket. We also planned and organized the last statewide fly-around. John Connally kept saying, "Just wait until West Texas comes in."

Early on Election Day I found out to my shock how wrong Connally had been. The phone rang. I was at home, around two in the afternoon. It was Bill Heatley, cantankerous member of the state House and chairman of its Appropriations Committee. "George, Bill Heatley. Do you want my county results—good West Texas counties?" It was only two in the afternoon and the polls closed at seven. I politely took down the numbers and thanked the chairman. Then I sat staring at the numbers. What in the hell? Was I part of some voting scandal? Who could I tell? I called John White, my dear friend and someone close to Heatley. I told him the story and my dilemma. "Oh, George, those aren't exact numbers. Bill Heatley is a recovering alcoholic. He compensates for drinking by calling people in his district night and day. He's got as good a feel for those counties as anyone running a poll weekly. They are not accurate, but they are close enough and we will carry Texas."

That night before the numbers started coming in, with Connally on the screen saying again to wait for West Texas, I told the senator of Heatley's call. He smiled, winked, and shook my hand. The Democratic Party carried the entire ticket from the courthouse to the White House.

Not long after the election I was asked to chair the inauguration activities for Texans wishing to attend the festivities in Washington. It was to be a massive undertaking because Jimmy Carter was going to be a healing balm after the shady turmoil of the Nixon years. Texans of all stripes and political persuasion wanted to go and be a part of what promised to be a new beginning. Two airplane loads of them wanted to go, not to mention many others who went by private planes, trains, and automobiles. Some three to four hundred signed up. This would be a challenge, a logistical nightmare. There were the Braniff airplanes to charter, hotel rooms (at a premium) to be reserved, buses to be rented, and inauguration tickets of every sort to be secured. And therein lay a problem.

Jimmy Carter had appointed an inaugural committee that didn't seem to have a clue and seemed to think it owed nothing to all those folks (with the exception of Georgians) who had worked tirelessly to elect Carter. Texas was the only state west of the Mississippi that he had carried, and without Texas all those who didn't have a clue would have been without jobs (or at least overblown titles).

Thanksgiving went by and we heard nothing. Around the first of December I took matters into my own hands. I wrote a telegram that appeared as if it would go to Jimmy Carter and Charlie Kirbo, Carter's most trusted Georgia friend and confidant, but that really was sent only to Kirbo. A scathing attack on the inauguration team from top to bottom, it ended with the promise that without immediate action I would hold a press conference to explain to the world that the Carter people could care less about the contribution Texas had made to Carter's victory. Within hours Charlie Kirbo called. In his most dignified Georgia accent he exclaimed that he sure wished I hadn't sent that telegram to Carter, not to mention Senator Bentsen, Governor Briscoe, Bob Strauss, and a host of others. I laughed and told him I hadn't, but wanted his undivided attention. He said that he would fix it straight away—and he did. Within the hour a person of rank called to say that he would meet me on December 23 in Washington. I told him that was impossible—it was Christmastime and I had plans. I said that I would come right after the first of the year. We then discussed ticket needs, but he said that tickets were impossible. I said, "Fine. Call Kirbo." He replied that he would try. I said that he'd better try hard.

By Christmas all arrangements were in place, except for the tickets. After New Year's Day I flew to Washington, and was met at the airport by a ramrod army officer who held up a sign for "George Briscoe." I went over to him. He saluted and said, "Welcome to Washington, Governor." Somehow that crack inauguration team had confused me with the governor of Texas, Dolph Briscoe. I rode that mistake throughout the day. At every ticket station I received carefully numbered packages along with the prayerful and respectful question, "Is everything in order, Governor?" In my most gubernatorial voice I would praise them for their efficiency and many kindnesses.

I caught a plane home, but not before I called Bob Strauss, who hooted in satisfaction that protégé had become master. On the plane to Austin I found that every package of tickets had personal notes of thanks for the Texas role in Jimmy Carter's success—and a few extra tickets. Arrangements were set and we came. No matter that it was bitter cold, with ice covering the streets, we came. What was most amazing was that we got every Texan who wanted to come a hotel room, a bus, a seat at the inaugural ceremony, and a ticket to one of the balls that night. And we did this without computers and cell phones. The entire Texas group was entered on accounting balance sheets, with handwritten notes. Every name, every event, and every ticket request. As people picked up their ticket packages, they paid for the trip, and a "paid-in-full" entry was noted. We didn't lose a single Texan. They all paid and then we returned to Texas to take up where we left off—our jobs, our families, churches, and friends—having witnessed once again, but this time in person, the peaceful transfer of power in the world's oldest democracy.

After the 1976 elections I set up a small public relations and fundraising firm. I needed to make money while at the same time allow myself flexibility to aid Senator Bentsen, Bob Strauss, and others when called upon—which was often. I was very selective about my clients, as any bad turn would reflect through me onto the senator. I was happy, rich in family and friends, lucky for Glacier Park visits and Christmas skiing in Whitefish.

In 1977 I cochaired the successful fundraising salute to Hubert Humphrey, and Senator Bentsen and B. A. sat at my table. From time to time Bentsen would call on me to raise money for certain Senate candidates. And he and Strauss asked me to serve on a blue-ribbon committee to advocate for the Panama Canal treaty. The United States had promised at the outset to give the canal back to Panama after ninety years. With US naval might centered on huge nuclear-powered aircraft carriers and huge transport tankers, the canal had grown obsolete for many critical needs. As a military man and businessman, Lloyd Bentsen looked past the rhetoric to the practical, and many of his Latin American friends quietly told him it would be a huge mistake to renege. At some point he traveled to Panama at his own expense to talk with our military people and Panamanians. He came away convinced that the time had come and that it was the right thing to do. But contrary to Gerald Ford, who had endorsed returning the canal, Ronald Reagan began to say, essentially, "We paid for it. We built it and we're not giving it back." This Reagan posturing nearly brought Ford down in the Republican primaries of 1976, and, as is the case with many highly charged issues, lasting negative residue remained during Carter's presidency.

Some of those who learned Lloyd Bentsen's position on the Panama Canal called his patriotism into question. This came out of sheer ignorance, blind following, and, in some quarters, an easy way to raise money. The senator addressed this criticism head on, with press conferences and editorial board meetings. Sentiment was beginning to turn, and then John Wayne came out for the treaty—that shut up Reagan and his naysayers, and signaled the end. I'm sure that Richard Vigurie and his fundraising artists must have rushed to the post office to try to retrieve and save money that was about to go down the drain. After a long, contentious battle, two Panama Canal treaties were ratified by the US Senate by 68–32 margins.

Throughout the remainder of the '70s, the senator and I worked on a number of projects, specifically fundraisers for Senate colleagues as well as a midterm statewide event to replenish his coffers. Bentsen always insisted that we keep the mechanics of fundraising and political support up to date, looking forward to the next election.

In 1978 we held the fundraising event for President Carter in Houston. The Bentsens came and the senator introduced the president. Carter was down in the polls and Bentsen thought it important to show support, even though he had serious disagreements with the president on many issues and style of governance.

As 1978 flowed into 1979, the Carter style and lack of ability to articulate his vision for America was creating havoc throughout the country. As one of a number of informal advisors who met to bring forthright observations and opinion to the president, I was becoming extremely frustrated. The reports from Texas were of anger, frustration, and political disaster. One of the things that concerned me was the spate of seemingly endless mixed messages of cabinet members. Cabinet members often came off as disloyal and self-serving. Some seemed to have their own agendas, separate from the president's. In July 1979 a meeting was called by Anne Wexler, a member of the White House staff who really knew what she was doing. We mainly discussed the content and play of the president's Camp David retreat, where it was hoped he would successfully sort out his vision, message, and governance. At some point the question of cabinet loyalty and policy confusion came up. There was much discussion. Finally I said something in effect that Carter ought to fire someone. I didn't care who, but I said that Carter had to demonstrate toughness and a take-charge stance. Malaise may surely have been part of the problem, but confusion reigned and that led to questioning of his leadership and backbone to lead.

The meeting broke up and I headed to Montana. On July 15 or July 16 I received a call from Loyd Hackler and Washington lawyer (and native Texan) Harry McPherson. "Bristol, you're the most powerful man in America. President Carter has just fired four cabinet officers and apparently a great many other underlings." I was horrified as the news played out. Carter's actions only added to the crisis of confidence in the president. It was so heavy-handed and amateurish that it had a reverse effect, even though there were among those who resigned some I had in mind for firing. What I'd had in mind and had explained to the best of my ability was a single firing—a forceful firing—not the wholesale dismantling of a cabinet.

There were far greater consequences. Only days before, the president had made a forceful speech on a national energy policy. It was inspiring and specific. It was well-received and his poll numbers went up by double digits. Then this was all erased by the debacle that followed.

The crisis left no time for constructive work during what should have been the apex of the Carter presidency, with positive results for years to come. Carter had a great energy policy that substantially drove down foreign imports, spurred domestic oil and gas production, and injected massive funds into alternative fuel resource and production. This policy worked in the short term, and if its results had been highlighted and reinforced on a timely basis, citizens would have demanded continued action and improvement. But whatever chance that this might still have occurred after the flash and passion of the Cabinet massacre had subsided was negated by the Iran crisis.

On November 4, 1979, the US embassy in Tehran was stormed and captured by hostile Iranians, followers of the emerging Ayatollah Khomeini after the overthrow of the shah. This event and what transpired afterward would not only hurt the nation, but overshadow Carter and his accomplishments, not the least of which were the Camp David Accords that Carter had worked tirelessly to engineer between Israel and Egypt. Carter's image as peacemaker dimmed with every new image from Iran that filled television screens night after night. The crisis was so pervasive and intense that it spawned its own nightly news show—*Nightline with Ted Koppel.* It was unceasing and ruinous, although the world continued to notice Carter's peacemaker role, which continued after his presidency, and he went on to receive the Nobel Peace Prize in 2002.

To top it off, Ted Kennedy began to sound like a challenger in 1980. By the early fall of 1979, I began to seriously think about a change of scene and lifestyle, if only temporarily. I wanted to spend a year in Montana, near Glacier Park. I wanted quality time with Valarie and the children. Between Bentsen, business, and national political commitments, I had reached the pinnacle. I just didn't know of what.

My family and I talked it over. At first they were incredulous, but then the thought of skiing and hiking on a regular basis captured their imagination. There was also the thought that all too soon I'd have to gear up to help Senator Bentsen again. We talked it over at the Bentsen home in Washington. The Bentsens had grown to love our family and were supportive. There was even a bit of wishful envy. Then I talked with Strauss. While supportive, he extracted a promise that I would help on the 1980 campaign. I assured him that I would, but I wanted no title or timeline. I would make calls and travel with him for the president.

Right after Christmas we left for Montana. The further north we drove, the colder and snowier the landscape became. The children were excited, Valarie was skeptical, and our two dogs were of differing minds. Rusty, our sheltie, was in love with the weather. Snow was to be run through and rolled in. Tanti, our small poodle, thought we had lost our minds, and disdained all things snowy white. To venture into snow was to risk life.

But we made it to Whitefish without incident and settled into our new home after the movers unpacked. Hailing like us from Texas, the movers had to struggle over snow and ice as they went back and forth, to and from the house. "Mister," asked one, "why in the hell did you move from Texas, and, more to the point, why'd you move in January?" He shook his head and did not wait for an answer.

We enrolled the kids in school and ski classes, and on the first weekend we bought ski outfits for all. Our time on the mountain was truly a once-in-a-lifetime experience. It was not that I had left the world. I was usually on the phone and sometimes in the air— flying off somewhere. But I was there when the children came home from school on most evenings, although the children now say that I was there for a week at the beginning and a week at the end of the year-and-a-half sojourn. Their exaggeration of their abandonment grows with each passing year. I am certain with my passing that I will never have been there at all. The truth is that we did enjoy too-often-denied quality time.

By the spring of 1980 it was decided by the LBJ Foundation to have a fundraising salute to Bob Strauss, sponsored by the LBJ School of Public Affairs and the LBJ Foundation. With no computers and cell phones, I worked in Montana to put together a major event in DC. I set up a small office with a phone device called a telex that cranked out flimsy paper copy. Lists were gathered and new ones created. Meetings were held and preparations were made. I would use the week of the Democratic convention in New York City to buttonhole Strauss's friends and colleagues and nail down commitments.

And despite what my children may say, I enjoyed outings with my family in the great Montana outdoors. As soon as the snow melted, following an April Little League opener in which Mark starred, we packed hot dogs and buns and struck out in the late afternoon for a campout, no matter that it was near freezing or that it was raining on our arrival. Winter was over. Glacier campsites were open and plentiful. We were again happy to be part of the great American national park tradition, even in the rain. I think we only got one tent up before the skies opened up. Even Rusty, who loved the cold and wet, would have none of it. Valarie, Jennifer, and the dogs slept in the car. Mark joined me as the rain pounded our tent. At some point in the night he called out that he was drowning. I said something like "Oh, Mark, get to sleep." In the early morning light I saw that Mark had scooted up next to me from his end of the tent, which was filled with water. It seems Dad, in his hurry to make camp, had erected the tent over a small dry rivulet. We broke camp and went back to Whitefish to ski.

May 18, 1980, on the other hand, was mild, sunny, and inviting. Early that Sunday we headed off with my brother David's family for a day hike in the Great Bear Wilderness across the highway from Glacier. David, who had returned to northwestern Montana with his wife and three children, had set up a veterinary practice in Columbia Falls. We drove down US 2 to the Stanton Lake trail, one suitable for children. One of the things I love most about the Glacier area is that even as patches of snow remain, flowers began to peek through. Growing season is short and they have much to accomplish before winter returns. Up we hiked, cresting a rise, and there below was the lake, surrounded by mountains, postcard perfect, with an outflow creek at one end and a beaver dam downstream. The children went wild, wading and skipping rocks. We had a picnic and were going to go further up the trail when we noticed grave, black clouds to the west, closing fast. So down we hurried. By the time we reached the cars it was practically pitch dark, strange for the time of day. Then it began rain not water but dust, dust like I'd seen blow in West Texas in the 1940s and '50s—but there were no dust storms in this part of Montana. Without radio, we hurried home, ran inside, turned on the television, and learned that Washington's Mount St. Helens had exploded at 8:30 a.m. Volcanic debris rose to heights challenging airliners, hurdled the Cascade Mountains, and settled on Whitefish, most of the Flathead Valley, and much of Montana. Everything ground to a halt. And "ground" can be taken literally here: the dust was actually a fine glass, like pumice, that permeated automobile and locomotive engines, damaging some beyond repair. At home we placed towels and newspapers in every windowsill and doorway.

For the next week, on the rare occasion that we left home, we wore filtration masks. The governor called a state of emergency and shut down all commerce. By Thursday he had to open grocery stores and banks so citizens could cash checks and purchase essentials. Everyone had to wear masks. Down the road from Whitefish, in Kalispell, employees of the Conrad National Bank, all in masks, were taken by surprise when a lone stranger without a mask entered and robbed the bank, then disappeared into the volcanic fog, never to be seen again.

After a week or so, life returned to some semblance of normal. The children finished school. Our Dallas friends Buzz and Carolyn Crutcher and their children joined us in late June. By then I'd purchased a property on the ski mountain with hopes of putting a partnership together to build a fine lodge. Buzz and Carolyn had agreed to participate and came for a bit of due diligence and vacation. Buzz said that they would only be passive investors, rarely if ever returning to Montana. One day we rode horses and hiked together to Sperry Chalet, an arduous climb on the Gunsight Pass Trail—over thirteen miles. That was thirty years ago, and Buzz and Carolyn now live part of the year on the road to the ski mountain above Whitefish. They are the dearest friends, and I look forward to seeing them whenever I return to Whitefish, which is not often enough.

On July 10 or July 11, 1980, I flew to Omaha for a board meeting of Herman Brothers Trucking. Dick Herman had asked me to serve on the board a year or so before. Several of us on the board were also involved in purchasing a Budweiser distributorship franchise in Los Angeles. The Hermans owned a small Budweiser franchise in Lincoln, Nebraska, but the Los Angeles one was huge, and the brothers did not have the financial strength to go it alone. We had formed a partnership and were preparing to close the deal.

At the meeting Dick Herman mentioned that George Bush, having been decimated by Reagan in the Republican presidential primaries, was a private citizen again, and asked if I, the token Democrat, would make a motion to bring Bush in as a member of the board and as a partner in the beer deal. I happily agreed. Jim Baker seconded each motion. That made me perhaps the only man to nominate George Herbert Walker Bush for office and partnership on the same day.

The next morning I was invited to the dedication of Gerald Ford's boyhood home. The former president was most gracious. We talked about Jake Pickle and Bob Strauss. He thanked me for coming. Ford, Herman, and Baker then flew off to Detroit to the Republican convention and I flew back to Montana.

The Republican presidential nomination during the week of July 14–17 would clearly go to Reagan, but the vice presidential selection was up in the air. For two days the pundits and many pros, including Walter Cronkite, went on and on that Gerald Ford would be Reagan's choice. Nothing was heard from the Reagan camp about the matter.

Late on the night before the selection had to be made, my phone rang. "George, it's Jimmy Baker. What are you doing?" I said that I was reading a book, but keeping an eye on convention coverage at the same time.

"Well, stay tuned!"

"What do you mean?"

"I can't say." There was silence and then a light went on for me. I continued: "It's Bush. Good ol' 'Voodoo Economics' Bush."

"Voodoo economics" was a phrase Bush had used to deride Reagan's economic policy. Baker said that he couldn't say more. I did stay tuned, and sure enough, early the next morning Reagan announced Bush as his running mate.

I had a chance later to relate this story to Bush when he was vice president. He laughed for a long time. Bush never would serve on the board of Herman Brothers Trucking or own part of a Budweiser beer distributorship.

In August Valarie and I went to New York City for the 1980 Democratic convention. It was to begin on August 11, my fortieth birthday. She, the Strausses, and the

Bentsens threw a splendid party off the convention floor. Many of my longtime political buddies came. I buttonholed them for the Strauss fundraiser. It was a joyous occasion, but the convention was not. There was a hangover from Iran, inflation, and the ill-conceived, damaging Ted Kennedy challenge. President Carter was distracted. Valarie and I muddled through. Our best times were spent with the Bentsens. We made the rounds of receptions. They treated us to a birthday dinner and an evening at the theater—*Evita*. I learned that the senator had been on a congressional mission to Argentina and had come to know the Perons, gaining an unfavorable opinion of them.

After the play we had a drink and spoke a bit about 1982. We all agreed that at the right time we would regroup and once more wage political battle. For the most part we enjoyed each other's company.

The convention closed on a very sour note. Ted Kennedy was barely civil to Carter and made a point, during the closing ceremonies, of refusing to shake the president's hand. I thought it was third-class, rude and selfish. Ted Kennedy had only himself to blame for his failure. He ran against an opponent who was in disfavor among Democrats, behind in the polls. He ran against a president who had not campaigned, due to the Iran crisis, and still Kennedy lost. The reason was simple. Ted Kennedy thought that the Democratic nomination was his by divine right. He was totally ill-prepared and it showed.

As much as I had criticized of Carter, he deserved better than Kennedy's slap in the face as he went up against Ronald Reagan. It was a Gene McCarthy moment all over again, including the November results.

Valarie and I went back to Montana, filled with the certainty that we would do well to enjoy sunsets and autumn colors, and prepare for the Strauss event in December. I did make a few obligatory campaign trips with Strauss to Tennessee, Louisiana, and Texas, which I thoroughly enjoyed, but there was a foreboding sense of futility. Carter lost, overwhelmingly.

The Strauss fundraiser was a success. It also brought old friends on both sides of the aisle back together. President and Mrs. Carter came, but were obviously still in shock over the election loss. Bipartisanship reigned, thanks to Strauss, Lloyd Bentsen, Bob Dole, George H. W. Bush, Jim Baker, Ronald Reagan, and Tip O'Neill, but there was a growing edginess.

The election also cast the Democrats in the minority in the Senate, a role they had not played in decades. It was a setback, but also an opportunity for Lloyd Bentsen if he could win reelection in 1982. On my way back to Montana, I stopped in Austin for a long visit. Bentsen asked me to head campaign financing for him and told me he was planning to select Jack Martin to run the political side of the campaign. I could have leaped for joy. I trusted Jack completely and had every reason to believe that he would do a good job. I had been uncomfortable in 1976 handling both the political and financial aspects of the Senate campaign. I returned to Montana feeling renewed and ready to take up the Bentsen cause again.

After a great deal of discussion we decided that Valarie and the children would stay in Montana until school was out in the spring. The children loved Montana, had many friends there, and ski season was in full swing. We also wanted time to sell our house in Austin and get a bigger one, as Mark and Jennifer were fast approaching the teen years—the separated and unequal years.

Meanwhile my friend Lowell Lebermann said that I could have the upper floor of his home. An evening with Lebermann could carry me for several weeks. Imagine what a visit of five months could do for me.

From the outset the senator was in good shape politically and financially, but we were going to leave nothing to chance. Reagan had carried Texas by a sizeable margin and Bill Clements, a Republican, was governor. Time and time again Bentsen would exclaim that it didn't matter if he had a 90 percent approval rating, come Labor Day the political juices would begin to flow and Republicans would revert to form. And there were more Republicans in the state than at any time in the past.

Bentsen's stature as a senator was growing. In the late 1970s he'd moved to the Senate Finance Committee and chaired the Joint Economic Committee. While much of the committee work was technical in detail, Bentsen dealt with it with the clarity of a former businessman. He sought and passed amendments to mold depreciation to better boost manufacturing and the economy. Though often unrecognized and unappreciated, Lloyd Bentsen knew by training, experience, and sound thinking that a robust business climate, particularly for small business, is "the strong horse that pulls the whole cart," as Churchill said.

He also thought that this thinking applied to research and development. He paid close attention to agricultural news and formulated policy and law to promote and expand agricultural research and development. If healthy businesses were the strong horse of the economy, agricultural breakthroughs in production yield would feed the horse and the world.

All this put him in good stead with business and agricultural leaders in Texas, so much so that they trusted and respected him when it came to controversial votes or more "liberal" votes on social issues. When we lost that balance of pro-business, fiscal conservatism (real fiscal conservatism, entailing balanced budgets and debt reduction) coupled with a deep and abiding concern for workers and their well-being, we lost the moderate middle of the Democratic Party in Texas and elsewhere. In Texas we never recovered and it is now a solid Republican state.

We had to mobilize our vote and keep it focused on November. That was going to be expensive—$4 million to $6 million, depending on other Democratic candidates' participation. Lieutenant Governor Hobby signed up immediately, even though he had no opponent in the primary. Most of the other statewide offices had serious primary battles, so it would be some months before we would know their level of contribution.

We instinctively knew not to count on much. Candidates with primary fights usually come out in debt, even with a win. Fortunately Bentsen drew only a token primary opponent, thus we had the spring and summer to prepare. While Jack was setting up what was to be a magnificent get-out-the-vote organization, I concentrated on the money.

We now knew that our November opponent would be Congressman Jim Collins of Dallas, who most knowledgeable people thought a lightweight. Therefore the brunt of our fundraising task was to convince supporters not to underestimate Collins, because the state appeared to be leaning Republican and we might be swept up in a stampede.

We quickly organized the usual suspects: Houston, Dallas, San Antonio, the Valley and a number of smaller communities. We spent a good deal of time working political action committees, but they were limited to $5,000 for the general election, and our campaign had set a rule that no more than 20 percent of all donations we received would come from PACs.

Meanwhile we also put in play a number of events hosted by the senator's friends from the presidential race, events held in New York City, Los Angeles, St. Louis, Chicago, Tulsa and elsewhere. We were working every angle, because $4 million (at a minimum) was an unheard of amount to be raised and spent. By midsummer we were nearly there. Because of the $1,000 limit on personal contributions, we'd had to cast the net far and wide, which created a healthy influx of smaller contributions and a much larger base. As we suspected, the other Democratic candidates had limited funds available, so the heavy lifting fell to Bentsen and Hobby. Right around Labor Day I went to Houston to meet the senator. Based on what we had raised, what had been pledged, and what we hoped to bring in during several late events, we were confident about meeting our goals, even envisioning a possible surplus. What we didn't know was where Governor Clements would come down and how much he would spend. In 1978, when he bested John Hill for the governor's seat, Clements had spent vast sums of his own for direct mail and phone banks. If he got his back up he could spend whatever was needed, as he was a wealthy oilman.

Well, Clements did get his back up, but not about his own race. He became furious at Jim Collins. At some point in late September or early October, Collins, out of desperation and stupidity, attacked Mr. Bentsen, the senator's father, a man of great integrity and patriotism. Clements knew right away that he'd made a fatal mistake. The senator would not let that attack go unchallenged, and we countered. The senator asked how much money was still available, as we had paid for practically all aspects of the campaign. He commanded us to shove it all in. We discussed Collins's most glaring flaw. At some time in the 1970s, before and during the Nixon-Ford years, Collins, a wealthy man, had demanded kickbacks from his employees, and one of the offended employees ratted him out. There was huge press coverage and an investigation by Nixon's Justice Department. The affair had been swept under the carpet, but the essential facts were made public. While claiming not to have done it, Collins paid the money back. Although this saved him a possible trial and conviction, this hung over him, and we remembered. We had already run a number of damning ads, including an award-winning one on Collins's vote against Social Security, but now we prepared one focusing on the kickback scandal. With piles of cash being tossed on a congressional desk, it ended with the question, "If you didn't take the money, Congressman, why did you pay it back?" It was one of the toughest ads I've ever seen, and it was based in truth.

But the ad didn't run. For many reasons, including the fact that Clements and other Republicans were shunning Collins and openly denouncing him, it was decided to withhold it. The polls were still showing that we were going to win big and probably sweep the rest of the ticket to victory. So why bother? Well, it bothered Senator Lloyd Bentsen. His father was his idol and confidant. He deeply loved and respected "Mr. Lloyd" and could not understand why Collins had attacked him. It was neither civil nor decent, even by Texas standards.

Valarie and I had planned a getaway trip to London and Switzerland after Election Day, before heading to the eastern shore of Maryland for Thanksgiving with our friends J. D. and Carol Williams and their children. The Bentsens, who were to be in London for an Inter-Parliamentary Council meeting, knew of our plans and invited us to witness Parliament and to have lunch with them. Roaming the halls where Winston Churchill stood and defied Hitler and the Nazis was the highlight of our trip. Lunch was then a pleasant time filled with laughter about family and campaign stories. Other members of Congress dropped by to say hello and congratulate the senator on his smashing victory. Out of the blue the senator turned to me and asked, "George, is it official that we won? Has the secretary of state certified the results?" I answered yes to both questions.

"Do we have any money left?"

"Yes, sir, due to some late events and checks I think there's about $30,000 on hand."

"Good. I want to run that ad one time before Christmas in Dallas."

"Which ad?," I asked.

"The kickback ad," was his reply.

There was silence at the table. Then B. A. firmly but gently said, "Oh, Lloyd, let it go. He was thoroughly beaten and embarrassed by Bill Clements and the other Republicans. Why don't you and George go up the street to Purdy's [an internationally famous gun shop] and Valarie and I will look in on some of the shops and meet you in an hour or so."

We did as she suggested, and once in the shop the senator's attention turned to the beauty of the craftwork. Lloyd Bentsen was one of the most accomplished marksmen I've ever witnessed.

Thus the 1982 campaign was officially ended. Or so I thought. Years later, in 2004 or 2005, when Jack Martin and I were traveling to Houston to visit the senator (by then felled by a serious stroke) and B. A., we were telling stories to pass the time and to prepare some to tell the Senator during our visit. Somehow we got to the London restaurant episode. I ended it with a laugh. Jack laughed too, but then added, "George, I ran the ad!" Totally nonplussed, I must have appeared slack-jawed.

"Yeah, I'm guessing after they got back and were probably down in the Valley with his dad and the family at Thanksgiving, it all came back. He called me and you were right. We did have a small surplus, so around Christmas I bought a one-time ad and shot it across Mr. Collins's bow."

We agreed not to tell that tale during that visit day, as we didn't know if B. A. knew that the ad had run after all.

Following the 1982 elections I went back to my businesses, which now included a partnership in a major resort hotel in Whitefish, some real estate in Austin, and a failing oil partnership. Sometime in late 1981 or early 1982 a friend of Chuck Kuhn's and mine brought us a partnership deal with potential and a substantial tax write-off. If I remember correctly, that tax provision was about to expire. Chuck had been in the energy business. We did due diligence on the partner company in Houston. The bank for the company was joyously making loans to one and all, if needed, and only requiring partners' interest as collateral. Chuck was supposed to be the general partner and me only an investor.

Far along in the deal-making process Chuck became deathly ill. I thought we would lose him. When he finally had recovered enough, we talked at the hospital. He said that I should be general partner. Most of the investors were my friends and they would trust me. I reluctantly agreed, partly because of Chuck and partly because of the continuous importuning of the bank and the energy company. Additionally the company had a clean bill of health from their auditor—Coopers & Lybrand. Shortly thereafter the deal started south and kept going. As general partner I faced substantial liability. Fortunately several of my partners were lawyers and collectively we smelled a rat, in the company, the bank, and perhaps the accounting firm. At some point we filed a lawsuit.

For seven long years we pressed the case. The bank and the energy company went into bankruptcy. Even to our lawyers and partners it was a surprise to learn that under federal law, a national bank in bankruptcy could not be held liable for its actions, no matter how grievous. There were times when I was at wit's end. Senator Bentsen was supportive, telling me to report regularly and in some detail, no matter the news. "They will appreciate it, even if begrudgingly, because it will show them you've nothing to hide." Good and caring friends, like Bob Strauss and J. D. Williams, urged me to take bankruptcy. I wouldn't, and then in 1988 we got a break. The lawyer for Coopers was taking my deposition in Houston. At the end of the day one afternoon he asked me a series of questions that rang a bell. I'd read a book, *Funny Money*, about the financial scandals of the Penn Square Bank of Oklahoma. When the bank went under it took down partnerships, other banks—nearly including Continental Illinois—all of which had jumped on the participation bandwagon with little or no due diligence as to the credit worthiness of their oil and gas loans. What rang the bell was that Coopers & Lybrand had issued the bank a clean bill of health (an unqualified opinion letter) two weeks before Penn Square. I had my secretary in Austin get on a plane and bring my copy of the book to Houston.

The next morning, as the lawyers and court reporter were setting up, I slid the book with the page opened to the damning passages to my attorney. He read it, smiled, and slid it across the desk to the Coopers attorney. Most lawyers make good poker players, expressing no emotion. But this one changed expression several times. He looked up and said, "We'll be in touch." They were, and we settled, and most of my partners were brought whole. I avoided bankruptcy but I paid a terrible price.

And I wasn't alone. Those years were filled with oil and gas deals and other tax gimmicks based on nothing but the appeal of a tax write-off. Going on at the same time was the criminal activity of savings-and-loan Ponzi artists. This all collapsed. Much of it was due to lack of supervision by the IRS, bank examiners, and the FDIC. Loans were made to investors that had to put little or no collateral down or who had little knowledge of the deal, or both. Sound familiar?

Deregulation in many areas is appropriate and beneficial, but not where OPM— other people's money—is at risk. It doesn't matter if it's a fivefold land flip or a toxic derivative. Most of those legal crooks used everything but their own money. They went out and got appraisers, accountants, and rating agencies to back their play and look the other way. And, sadly, we never seem to learn: witness Enron and Wall Street in the twenty-first century. It was—and remains—all smoke and mirrors, greed and fraud, use of other people's money with little to no supervision.

Had I not had my personal financial problems or read a single news story on the oil and gas, banking, and savings-and-loan crisis, I would have known of it shortly. Calling around to set up fundraisers or solicit individual contributions in 1988, I began to hear one horror story after another. There was financial blood running down every Main Street in Texas.

One friend who'd in the past had position and wealth had lost everything and moved to a small town in West Texas where he worked in a record store. Another had simply disappeared. By the end of the '88 campaign cycle there were few major banks left in Texas that were locally owned. The bank that had so recklessly loaned money to me and others became part of the North Carolina National Bank. A once productive saving-and-loan industry that encouraged savings and then in turn lent money for home loans (usually with a 20 percent down payment provision) lay in ashes, never to rise again.

Although much of the economic disaster in Texas in the 1980s was out of the Senator Bentsen's control, he did call for a reasonable approach to forced bankruptcy and foreclosures. He knew that the economy, given time, would right itself. He worried a great deal about the fact that the banking and financial system was falling into out-of-state hands. Local control meant local participation by home-based businesses and entrepreneurs, and they were becoming a dying breed.

That aside, the years right before 1988 were the most productive ones of Lloyd Bentsen's career. Even as a member of the minority in the Senate, he was able to pass measures of import and thwart moves by the Reagan administration which he deemed counterproductive or simply wrong. Early in the '80s he began to pay attention to health-care matters, particularly those affecting children, women, and the elderly. As a member of the Finance Committee the entire span of Social Security, disability, Medicare, Medicaid, and welfare flowed across his desk. But I've long held the thought that matters of a more personal nature also intervened. In the late 1970s the senator lost his mother. In the early 1980s he and B. A. lost a beloved granddaughter to cancer. Consciously or subconsciously the senator began to take on matters concerning the elderly and the young because he not only felt the heartache of loss, but also knew the expense of health care. Though he and his family were well positioned to cover such cost with the best of treatment, he knew that did not apply to many Americans.

Through the Joint Economic Committee and then the Finance Committee Bentsen began to champion the concept that these issues should not be addressed simply in terms of health and compassion, but also in terms of the real economic impact to the patient and the nation. Over the decade, working with Democrats and Republicans, Bentsen helped close the Medicare deductible gap that was becoming unaffordable for retirees. He opposed Reagan's attempts to end Social Security's minimum benefits to the elderly as well as burial benefits and maternal and child health benefits.

Under Medicaid, benefits to children and women were tied at the state level to welfare. State legislators, particularly in the South, loathed welfare and kept that payment at a minimum, which in turn reduced Medicaid benefits for women and children to paltry levels. Bentsen, working with southern senators and governors, decoupled those benefits from welfare, which vastly improved the opportunity for good health care for children and women, particularly pregnant women. He also caused the coverage to be expanded under Medicaid by expanding the years children could qualify.

Directly related to the experience of his own grandchild, he tackled the scope of benefit problems. Again these benefits were tied to state policy and politics. Working both sides of the aisle, Bentsen expanded the scope of benefits to cover every child so long as the service was medically necessary—with no exceptions.

While Lloyd Bentsen would go on to fashion monumental economic policies as senator and secretary of treasury, covering everything from debt reduction to free trade, it was his work to expand and correct health-care benefits the elderly, the young, and women that should be looked upon as his crowning achievement. They directly affected real people with real needs.

By pulling out all the stops, and given the fact that Bentsen was chairman of the Senate Finance Committee, we began to cobble together a sizeable war chest in 1987 and 1988. Because it was a truly national effort, I was focused on Texas and other states when Bentsen's DC fundraiser was fired over the "Breakfast with the Chairman" brouhaha: an announced series of $10,000 lobby breakfasts with Bentsen. The contributions would have been perfectly legal, as was meeting with the senator or any senator. It was the perception that caused a problem. Rather than let it fester, Bentsen held a press conference and shut it down the series, saying that that he always tried his best to avoid mistakes, but that this one had been a doozy. The matter soon blew over. Fundraising was also aided by Bentsen's having chaired the Democratic Senate Campaign Committee in the years leading up to 1986. His efforts in that position helped to recruit the right candidates and then finance their campaigns sufficiently to win back the majority for the Democrats in 1986. Many of those senators weighed in to help the man who had helped them. By the summer of 1988 we were ready for any eventuality but one.

On July 13, less than a week before the Democratic convention, Governor Michael Dukakis of Massachusetts selected Senator Bentsen as his running mate. I was on my way to Dallas when I received a call from the senator upon landing. He told me about the situation, and because I'd had much experience arranging conventions, he asked me to go to Atlanta, the convention site, immediately.

First I flew back to Austin. The Bentsen staff held a hurried meeting to sort things out, and then I packed and headed back to the airport. There and on the plane I talked with friends on the convention staff, many of whom Strauss and I had hired and worked with in the 1970s. We had no rooms, cars, mobile phones, or tickets, and we needed a great number of each. We decided that the best thing to do was to meet that night for a late dinner and figure out exactly what we would need in every category.

Upon arrival I was met by a self-important young Dukakis aide who assured me that he would be as helpful as possible, while saying that things were tight in all categories—especially convention tickets. He also made it condescendingly clear that all things should be cleared through him. After we arrived at the hotel I never saw the aide again.

National political conventions are many things: colorful and crazy, electrifying and boring. They are as diverse as the constituencies they represent. But they are also a business and that business deals with hotels, cars, phones, and tickets. Representatives of each of those areas of responsibility were at dinner, as was an Atlanta businessman, Chuck Parrish, who'd been the Carter man all had trusted and asked to stay in Texas in 1976. I had called Chuck from the plane, as I knew that we would need a local with clout, someone who could expedite matters. By evening's end I was thinking that we would be in pretty good shape on all fronts. Knowing that the Atlanta convention hall was small, I had tried to be conservative regarding ticket requests. I had a must-have list, plus fifty more names of people who I had assured I would keep posted each day as our actual allotment became known. That good-faith effort plus my friendship with the staff earned me special status. Every morning before the ticket offices opened, Paul Wageman and I would go to the convention center, dressed casually and carrying a brown paper bag. Once there we would go in a back door and secure our tickets before the throngs arrived.

For the next three days we set up suites and assignments, made calls to family and friends to see who was coming, installed a phone system in the senator's room and a few others, reviewed the hall and podium, and generally made ready. By the time the Senator and B. A. arrived we were nearly prepared on all fronts. For an hour or so

I briefed them and key staff on the activities set for the days ahead. Once a day I met with the Dukakis arrangements committee, and we ironed out problems and exchanged information. Given the shortage of time to make ready, I was pleased. For the most part it went smoothly. Most gratifying was the treatment afforded Mr. Bentsen, the senator's father. I had arranged an all-areas pass for him. Even though he was now in his nineties, he wanted to go everywhere, particularly with his son, of whom he was obviously proud. Even in those rushed last moments convention staff members were gracious, pointing out how this and that would work. And Mr. Lloyd was interested in how everything worked.

But a problem arose. On the evening that Senator Bentsen was to make his acceptance speech, the hall was packed. We had arranged for his family to sit together— probably twenty or so, not counting the senator, B. A., Mr. Lloyd, and the children, who would sit behind the podium, ready to go onstage. Minutes before the speech, a young Dukakis flunky informed me that the Bentsen family would have to move. "On whose orders?," I asked. "The governor's," he replied. I laughed in his face and told him to get the governor on the phone. Well, he couldn't do that, but he was insistent by then, arrogantly and loudly so. I went down the aisle and told Don Bentsen, the senator's brother, about the situation. He graciously said they would move so long as they could watch the senator on television. I walked back to the young man and said, "The Bentsens have class and, so as not to create a scene, will move. I will take them down to our holding room. Then later I will tell the senator of your ignorant and arrogant behavior, and I have every reason to believe you will be hearing from the governor."

After Bentsen's speech we were all heading to a party where the senator would introduce Dukakis to his Texas friends and family. Before I jumped in my car, the senator approached. Obviously one of his family members had told him of the slight. He asked me to explain. I gave it to him, warts and all. I was still hot about it. As I remember it, he then went to find Dukakis. I watched them in conversation, with Dukakis shaking his head and motioning to an aide. The motorcade was lined up. Suddenly, as the cars started moving, out of the crowd sprang the young fool who had caused the stir. He ran alongside my car, profusely apologizing. Since there were women present, I thought of the most charitable thing I could say to him—and then told him to drop dead. The motorcade shot off. I never saw him again.

At the reception, Governor Dukakis came up to me and apologized, stating that he would not have given such a stupid order. I told him that I knew that and warmly accepted his apology. A decent man walked away. He would reaffirm his decency to me on two future occasions.

After the convention we closed up shop and headed back to Texas. Upon arriving, we had to totally separate the vice presidential and Senate campaigns. There could be no commingling of funds, staff, or advertising. This was reasonably easy, as we had finished most Senate fundraising and those events remaining were set and could easily be handed off.

I immediately went to Houston to meet with Charles Duncan, the former head of Coca-Cola and secretary of energy under Jimmy Carter, having known the president while at Coke and living in Atlanta. We planned an event for Houston on September 19: a million-dollar fundraiser. We blanched when we pronounced this figure, but we stuck to it. It would be a challenge, as we had just finished Senate fundraising and George Bush was from Houston. Obviously there would be mixed emotions and loyalties.

Then I went to Dallas to meet with Jess Hay. Jess was one of the most effective Bentsen fundraising operatives and a friend through thick and thin. Together we announced a million-dollar goal for Dallas and North Texas.

Before people had a chance to catch their breath we assembled blue-ribbon committees and went to work. In early August, Charles and I reported our accomplishments to the senator. I don't think there were tears in his eyes, but there was silence and then he said one word: "amazing." On several occasions Bentsen voiced that sentiment. He was growing increasingly embarrassed by having to tap his friends time after time for money.

One thing that was surely surprising was the number of energy executives and independents who signed on. Yes, Bentsen was their supporter, and yes, Charles Duncan had helped institute a fine energy policy under President Carter, but there was also the fact that many felt betrayed by one of their own, George H. W. Bush. During the Reagan years there were several controversial energy policies that Bush seemed to ignore or at least failed to support. So going into the campaign, Dukakis with Lloyd Bentsen as his running mate, had a chance to gain their support, which would have financial and psychological benefits throughout Texas.

Then August hit and the campaign ground to a halt. Dukakis had a longstanding rule of holding town hall meetings in Massachusetts. A fine idea, but in a presidential race when he would have carried Massachusetts regardless? As we began to cast the fundraising net across Texas, we began to pick up all sorts of alarming signals: Dukakis's positions on many issues were not sitting well with our constituents, and he was not there to explain or defend himself. Some of his positions were in conflict with the senator's own.

As Labor Day approached, I voiced my concerns to Duncan. He agreed. We decided that I should write a memo to the senator spelling out those concerns, and he would personally deliver it over the Labor Day week, as the Bentsens planned to stop off at the Duncan ranch in Wyoming for a day or two of rest and relaxation.

I drafted the memo and then called Jack Martin. We set a time and I drove to Austin. Jack thoroughly agreed on its wording, but we decided to have me sign it alone, to continue to abide by the campaign law. I did, and Charles took it to Wyoming. He gave it to Bentsen, who immediately called me to ask questions. Jack and I agreed that we ought to hold a council among the senator's closest advisors, off the radar. Try to pull that off during a presidential campaign with the press always at the door and a schedule that would choke a horse. Late at night we met in Waco, and we went over the options. It was decided that the senator was going to have to come into Texas as a Senate candidate more often, and that all were going to have to recheck every base to make sure we were holding the numbers on the Senate side. That did not mean Bentsen would abandon Dukakis. It simply meant that we had to face the reality that the presidential campaign in Texas was probably heading south, and we had to protect the Senate seat.

No more timely meeting was ever held. The events in Houston and Dallas went off well enough, and we did reach our goals, with about $25,000 to spare, in spite of an approaching hurricane that threatened to slam into Houston. Buildings were ordered to be battened down and evacuated. Duncan's office windows were cross-taped and equipment moved to the lobby. The sky began to take on that pre-hurricane hue to the south. At one point I finally said, "Charles, I believe it's time to get out of here." He allowed that we would stay with the ship and finalize the details. I thought he had lost his mind, but what the hell. The storm petered out, and the dinner was held, with an enthusiastic crowd. But after that the presidential campaign went downhill, from Dukakis donning a helmet and riding in a tank, to potshots at the governor's prison furlough program (the Willie Horton controversy), to his poor answer, during a nationally televised debate, to an inappropriate question about his wife Kitty's hypothetical rape and murder.

There was a bright moment. On October 5, 1988, a vice presidential debate was to be held in Omaha. Texas supporters of Senator Bentsen chartered a plane and flew to Nebraska. Tickets were equally distributed between candidates, and I happened to draw a great seat. Throughout the debate Quayle was called upon to answer the pressing question of his youth and lack of experience, and consistently compared himself to young Senator John F. Kennedy. Finally Senator Bentsen couldn't let this pass, saying, "Senator, I served with Jack Kennedy. I knew Jack Kennedy. Jack Kennedy was a friend of mine, and Senator, you're no Jack Kennedy."

For an instant Quayle looked as if he'd been electrocuted. Then he recovered and, grim-faced, said, "Senator, that was uncalled for." Lloyd Bentsen reminded Quayle that he had continuously brought the matter up. It is to this day one of people's most remembered political retorts. But it was far from enough. The Dukakis-Bentsen team would lose the race, and it failed to carry Texas. However, Bentsen won his Senate reelection bid by a historical margin, plus we picked up seats in the Congress and statehouse. Finally Lloyd Bentsen had received the national attention and stature he so richly deserved.

Not long after the campaign, tragedy struck the Bentsen family. Lloyd Bentsen Sr. was killed in an automobile wreck in January of 1989. Many friends and sympathizers went to the Valley for the funeral, including Governor Michael Dukakis, who upon hearing of the tragic crash left his office without entourage or state police, boarded a commercial flight alone, flew to McAllen, and came to pay his respects. Then he turned around and flew back to Massachusetts. Seventeen years later he and Mrs. Dukakis would make the same generous trek, flying to Houston when the senator passed away in 2006.

Before the 1988 election I knew that Lloyd Bentsen would not run for another term. He probably would not have run that year save for the fact that the Democrats had recaptured the Senate in 1986 and the fact that he had become Finance Committee chair, a position he relished and served with great honor and wisdom. Perhaps his greatest contribution during his term starting in 1989 was his handling of the growing deficits that Reagan and Bush had created. For all their rhetoric and demagoguery to the contrary, the last three Republican presidents have contributed more to the national debt than all other presidents combined and they did so while Republicans controlled Congress for the most part. By 1990 the debt was rocketing out of control. After much jawboning, a deal was struck—$300 billion in new taxes. Without fail, the Republican right went crazy, accusing Bush of everything but treason. But he had laid himself open with his famously stupid words at the 1988 Republican convention: "Read my lips. No new taxes." I have never figured out this one-way-street philosophy: cutting taxes, which can create crushing deficits that will tax our children and grandchildren, then standing pat, with proudly puffed chests, proclaiming that taxes will not be raised.

That insanity weighed heavily on Senator Bentsen. He wasn't against tax cuts per se, if they were targeted and aimed at something positive. But he was not for tax cuts that came at the expense of future taxpayers and at the expense of a healthy fiscal policy and worldwide credit worthiness as a country.

I think that the fact Bentsen was growing tired of the increasingly negative aspect of campaigns made it easier for him to leave the Senate. I recall one conversation we had, sitting on the front porch of Grouse Mountain Lodge in Whitefish in 1989. We had gone there in the hopes of recharging his batteries after the campaign, and to repair both from the death of Mr. Bentsen and a lingering case of the shingles. The senator dwelled on a talk he'd had with Senator Russell Long, his friend, confidant, and an earlier chair of the Senate Finance Committee. In late 1985 or early 1986, Long confided to Bentsen that he was not going to stand for reelection because politics were becoming too personal and dirty. That was the mid-1980s and came from a Long of Louisiana, where politics is always a contact sport.

Our time together in the 1990s was not as frequent as in the past. There would be no more campaigns, even though many urged Bentsen to run in 1992 for president. After 1988 he was head and shoulders above all of the candidates mentioned. Because of the intense spotlight of the vice-presidential campaign, Bentsen had come out the real winner. People across the country had come to appreciate his cool, analytical mind, his ability to articulate complicated fiscal policy, and the unwavering commitment he had to God, family, country, and duty. And, yes, they remembered and got a kick out of the zinger at Quayle's expense.

One who took special note of Bentsen's 1988 vice-presidential campaign conduct was Ross Perot of Dallas. Perot had always supported the senator, but no more so than others. In the summer of 1991 he called me and asked me to come to his office. A patriot unparalleled, time after time Perot has at his own expense supported programs to honor US war veterans and to find those missing in action in Vietnam. He wanted to honor the returning men and women of Desert Storm—the repulsion of Saddam Hussein's outlaw invasion of Kuwait in 1990—and he was willing to pay for the returning veterans' parades and honoring days, but wanted to make sure that his generosity was well managed, particularly in Texas. He asked me to oversee the Texas activities. That part of the conversation took about an hour. Then he launched into a seething criticism of Vice President Bush and told me he wanted me to go and talk to the senator about running. And if Lloyd Bentsen wouldn't agree to run, then I was to go see Senator David Boren of Oklahoma, who was a moderate-conservative in the Bentsen mold with equal intellect and principle.

I told Perot I could save him the cost of flying to Washington to see Bentsen and that I didn't know Boren well enough to approach him. However, I was interested in finding out why he thought either man could beat Bush, who had about an approval rate of about 80 percent at the time. Perot was insightful and prophetic. He explained that the Gulf War had no real heroes, that it was all smart bombs and computers, that Bush's popularity would fade, and then a worsening economic situation would drive the campaign debate. He concluded that Bush's economic policy was deeply flawed. As soon as possible I called Senator Bentsen and told him of the conversation. I asked him why Perot was so angry with Bush. Bentsen replied that he didn't know the root cause, but he knew of the ongoing Perot anger. Then I told him that it was my conviction, based on my conversation with Perot, that if Perot didn't find an acceptable Democrat to take on Bush, he would run himself. Bentsen thought that unlikely, but wondered aloud if I thought Perot would run as a Democrat. I said that I had no idea.

As borne out by time, Perot did not find a candidate, and he announced that he would run in 1992 as an independent. In the spring of 1992 he hammered Bush's policies on the deficit and the North American Free Trade Agreement. Perot began to rise in the polls, so much so that at one point he led Bush and Clinton. Not only was he aided by the perception of conservatives that Bush had caved in on the major tax increases, but also the revelations of a possible extramarital affair between Bill Clinton and an Arkansas woman. By the end of April, Bush was being hammered by Pat Buchanan and other conservatives, and Clinton was dodging the bullets from all directions regarding infidelity, draft dodging, and pot smoking.

But then by the end of May, the people seemed to have shrugged their collective shoulders and accepted Clinton. He began to right his campaign and sprang back in the lead as the Democratic convention neared in July. By convention time he had a fairly substantial lead over Bush, although Perot still had strength in places. Then Perot created one of the strangest incidents in American politics. He withdrew from the race, citing grave concerns that Republican operatives were going to sabotage his daughter's wedding. Rumors and commentaries were rampant, all trying to fathom Perot's real reason from dropping out, with none accepting the wedding story.

The Clinton-Gore ticket was nominated in July. They climbed in the polls for a while, but following the Republican convention, Bush began to rise in the polls and the race tightened. Then Perot doubled down and created the very strangest incident in politics. He got back in the race, stayed in until the end, and received 19 percent of the vote. This was not enough to carry a single state, but it was enough to insure Bush's demise. Clinton won by a plurality of the popular vote but carried a huge majority of the electoral vote, including a number of states, like Montana and Georgia, which he could not have won without Perot's name on the ballot.

Although every story under the sun was written about what happened and why, with every permutation of speculation, no one will know for certain until and unless Ross Perot himself publicly states his reasons for withdrawing from the 1992 presidential race and then getting back in. Based on my conversation with him in 1991, I have my theory, which was later fortified by his actions in 1994. That year, at the end of the Ann Richards–George W. Bush gubernatorial campaign, Ross Perot, contrary to his past history of not endorsing candidates, endorsed Richards. The endorsement was too late and too little, but it surprised most people. I can only surmise, but I am convinced that Perot was driven by deep, lingering anger about George H. W. Bush.

The Bentsens and I had lunch in New York at the 1992 convention, but we didn't discuss Perot then or thereafter. I often wonder if the senator ever had second thoughts about running that year, in view of Perot's attempted overture that Bush was vulnerable and that Bentsen could beat him. Bentsen would become President Clinton's secretary of the treasury, and in this position he would leave a lasting legacy, advocating for the North American Free Trade Agreement and Clinton's tax policy of 1993. Both were the product of a man who understood finance and fiscal soundness and the need to have both to compete in a global economy, with the further recognition that an expanding economy was the only real way to make sure that all citizens of the United States were given a chance to share in its bounty. He would graciously and continually sponsor my appointment to the National Park Foundation. He would call on me to help orchestrate the opening of the US Mint facility in Fort Worth. And would chew me out when I called him about President Clinton's intemperate remark in 1996 about raising taxes and about his fiscal package of 1993. Bentsen had worked hard to make that happen. He had worked Congress tirelessly and caught a great deal of grief.

I had received several calls from various Clinton folks who wanted to feel the senator out and see if he'd make a statement. I reported back that they would not like the statement he would make. Results would prove that Bentsen was right: the economy improved, the deficit went down, there were budget surpluses to pay down the deficit, interest rates declined, and faith in the US economy was restored abroad. In his mind there was nothing to apologize or equivocate about. Clinton would come to appreciate that.

I would see the senator only one more time after 1996 before his stroke in 1999. Thereafter Jack Martin, John Mobley, and I would make regular trips from Austin to visit the Bentsens. It was tough but something we felt obligated to do. Lloyd and B. A. Bentsen had enriched our lives. We hoped the visits and the retelling of old stories would be repayment in some small measure. When he passed away in May of 2006, I went once again to Houston to head up a group of long-time staffers to make the arrangements. Great and ordinary people gathered to say goodbye to one of the best of the "greatest generation." Many there were Republicans, but all listened attentively as Bill Clinton eloquently spelled out just what it was that made Lloyd Bentsen stand apart. There was no argument from any quarter.

There was something more that Senator Bentsen contributed that is too often ignored in the definition of greatness: civility. Senator John McCain put it as well as any, saying that the word "patrician" came to his mind in the most positive way. "He brought class and style to the US Senate. He always conducted himself with dignity."

That Lloyd Bentsen was a Democrat was beyond question. Yet he worked with Bob Dole, John Danforth, and others on both sides of the aisle to make sound and acceptable policy. He did so because he respected them and because they were his peers. He tried to meet them halfway, because they too were public servants, elected in their own right.

After the funeral on May 30, I waited for friends to come out of Houston's First Presbyterian Church. A late spring rain steamed off the pavement. Police motorcycles began to come alive in anticipation. Inside and out of the church old friends and retainers stopped to chat, possibly for the last time, before going back to their separate lives. Former Speaker of the House Jim Wright, bent with age, talked with former Texas governor Dolph Briscoe, who was supported by a walker for a broken hip. Former secretary of state James Baker came by, put a hand on my shoulder, smiled and walked away. Bill Clinton met off to one side with B. A. Bentsen.

With Lloyd Bentsen's death, a great deal of my life in politics—and even the reasons I got into politics to begin with—had passed. Unless our system of governance and politics reacquaints itself with the civility and bipartisan spirit that were the hallmark traits of Lloyd Bentsen, we will never see his likes or those of all the other patriots shaped by the politics of the Depression and World War II. The politics of giants have been hijacked by pygmies and pirates.

CHAPTER 14
Lowell Lebermann—In Praise of Friendship

Lowell Lebermann and I should have met in late 1976 or 1977, dis-cussed the fact that both of us were considering running for state treasurer of Texas, then walked away. But there was chemistry between us that immediately transcended our differences. We decided without conversation that we wanted to be friends. Somehow the treasurer's race would take care of itself.

It was not actually the first time that Lowell and I had met. We had known each other casually at the University of Texas. We had certainly visited during his tenure on the Austin city council and at political events. As Democrats, Lowell and I ran in the same circles. But it was that meeting about the treasurer's race that sealed the deal. As I remember it, we struck a Faustian bargain. Once we decided who would run, assuming both of us did not decide to run, the other would serve as campaign chair or finance chair, or both.

Shortly after this conversation Lowell called and asked if I would go to Victoria, Texas, with him to see Mr. Tom O'Connor. Lowell had been married to his daughter Louise, but the two had recently divorced. Lowell seemed to think that the O'Connors, who are some of the wealthiest people in Texas, would still be supportive of his politics. So off we flew.

We should have stayed home. Mr. Tom was gracious in telling Lowell that while he was beloved and that all were thankful for his role in helping to raise Louise's three sons by a prior marriage, there would be no support. Jesse James was state treasurer (ain't that a great name for someone minding state funds?), and, although ancient, was showing every indication of running again, and because Lowell wasn't technically in the family anymore—well, it was just business, and part of the O'Connor family's business was banks, and Jesse James held sway over banks.

We didn't go straight home to Austin. We went south to Rockport to a favorite hangout of Lowell's and had a few drinks and bewailed the closing of the O'Connor bank vault. I felt sorry for Lowell. I'm sure he was disappointed, but the wine and the sunset seemed to brighten him up. When Lowell was brightened and in good humor, he was without question the best companion and conversation partner one could have.

Even though Lowell Henry Lebermann had come from a family of some wealth, married into the O'Connor fortune, and become a very successful automobile dealer and beer distributor (Miller Beer), it was his high intellect and humor in the face of his disability—blindness—that set him apart and above. It was that resolution in adversity that impressed me that evening in Rockport.

I decided not to run for state treasurer because I had a family and needed to make some money. I had loved every minute of my Bentsen years, but I hadn't saved up any bankroll to fund a political race. With that impediment out of the way, Lowell and I settled in to being the best of friends. I can't remember a time thereafter, through the late '70s into the '90s, that we didn't talk or visit at least once a week, except when he was away on his fabulous trips. I will leave it to Lowell's aides who traveled with him during those days to tell of those adventures, but, if asked, I can relate many of those tales. Lowell would, to my amazement, give vivid descriptions of places he had visited, descriptions every bit as colorful of those that might be given by sighted persons.

I really loved it when he'd been to a new European museum, and when one or two in his enraptured audience were new to his storytelling. First they would listen in amazed silence, then their jaws would begin to slacken, and after it was over they always whispered, "How in God's name did he know the nuance of those colors?" It cracked me up every time. But it also made me realize how much Lowell put into every aspect of his life. I am sure this was partly due to Lowell's curiosity: he was one of the most inquisitive persons I ever met. He joyously loved new adventures, whether rafting on the Snake River or studying a Monet, but he also kept extremely busy to keep mental darkness at bay.

Not long after we became friends, I was driving in Austin with my son Mark, who was seven or eight at the time. The radio program was explaining the suicide of a young blind man who had given up hope. Deep depression had set in and cast him over the edge. "Dad, that man needed to know Mr. Lebermann," Mark said.

Some weeks later, Lowell and I were visiting late in the evening. His aide had left the room. I told Lowell about what Mark had said. After a long pause, he said, "George, it is damned hard being up and brave all the time." On the way home, I cried. From that time until today I have argued with myself about whether Lowell's blindness was what made him extra special or whether he would have been as good, as caring, as feeling with sight. Damned if I know. I do know that his blindness made him work harder to make a difference.

Regardless, Lowell Henry Lebermann loved politics and I did too. It was politics that brought us together and politics that bonded us thereafter. It wasn't that we didn't enjoy other things, but we loved the action and the people who made the action happen, in part because we were action makers ourselves. We didn't much seem to care whether it was national, state, or local.

The morning after the big Houston 1978 fundraising dinner, Lowell demonstrated his generous kindness. Sometime during all the preparations, President Carter called to thank me for putting the dinner together. He asked if there was anything he could do for me. I said yes, that my nine-year-old son, Mark, loved airplanes, all things military, and President Carter. Would it be possible to clear Mark into Fort Hood where the president would be going to review the troops? "Of course," said Carter, "that will not be a problem." In passing, I mentioned it to Lowell, who said that he would love to fly us up to Fort Hood. Lowell had a private plane and pilot at the time. That was a godsend, since I hadn't known how I would get from Houston to Austin to the base in time. Lowell understood that and offered to help without hesitation. So on a beautiful spring morning we flew to Austin and picked up Mark, then went on to Fort Hood.

But just because a president says yes doesn't mean that underlings will know of or abide by the president's wishes. Two days before the dinner I met with the presidential advance crew who were led by a self-important representative of the president. I mentioned that I needed to talk with someone about our trip to Fort Hood. "Oh," said he. "It will not be possible to let a nine-year-old boy onto the base."

"Oh," said I. "Well, then I am going to do two things: call the president and then tell the press in the morning that a staffer is defying the wishes of the president of the United States!"

Shortly a very hostile and curt reply came back: Mark and George Bristol would be cleared.

"Well, that's not all," I said. "I'll need clearance for Lowell Lebermann, David Jaderlund, and Lowell's plane."

"Okay, but that's it."

So the day arrived for the fly-in to Fort Hood. We landed and taxied to the designated area. Lowell and I had to help Jaderlund off the plane. He had celebrated our success until about ten minutes before we left Houston.

There on the tarmac was an officer and a car. The officer informed us that the car was for Master Mark Bristol and no one else. I suppose the advance person thought he had pulled one on us, but Lowell and I roared, Jaderlund blanched, and Mark Bristol, age nine, rode off to the reception area. A few minutes later another car pulled up and we went to join the official party. Shortly thereafter the awe-inspiring Air Force One appeared. Photographs would show Lowell and me with a little, beaming, blond-haired boy, shaking hands with our country's leader. (I think Jaderlund stayed in the air-conditioned reception area.) It was a lovely time and no one enjoyed it more than Lowell and Mark. Then we flew home. To this day Mark speaks of that moment with reverence, not only for the president, but also his friend Lowell.

On the way home Mark studied his presidential paraphernalia, Jaderlund slept, and Lowell and I patted ourselves on the back. We decided to celebrate our self-awarded kudos at the Headliners Club on the following Friday. The club is one of the leading press clubs of America, as well as a popular watering and eating spot for Austin and Texas leaders. Lowell loved the Headliners and sponsored me for membership. We often met at Lowell's reserved corner table for lunch, and after lunch we would repair to the members' grill.

On Friday, Lowell and I were in full celebration swing at the Headliners. Roy, the bartender, was singing with the blender on. Jaderlund was there, and at some point he stepped to the table and announced that the president of the United States was on the phone. We thought it was a joke being pulled by Lowell's first aide, Cappy McGarr, who was a great mimic, and in chorus we exclaimed, "Tell Cappy to take a hike!"—or words to that effect. Jaderlund went back to the phone. I watched him turn white. "Mr. Lebermann, Mr. Bristol, it is the president." Well, we yelled for Roy to stop singing and turn off the blender. We composed ourselves, and then I led off with something inane. "Mr. President, Lowell and I are sitting here discussing the grand evening, prayerful that you are the leader of the free world." Lowell got something just as fluffy out, then we got off the phone as quick as possible.

We talked ourselves into believing that we had handled that very well, thank you very much. Then we went home to sleep it off. The next morning at dawn Bob Strauss rang. "Bristol, did you and Lowell really think you could fool a teetotaling, Southern Baptist, born-again-Christian president?"

"Well, we thought we did."

"Well, you didn't!"

"Well, hell," thought I. Then Strauss laughed and I joined in. Afterward I immediately called Lowell and we laughed about it—for years. We often saw President Carter, but he never said a word about this.

Throughout the rest of 1978, 1979, and 1980 we were involved in a number of things: Mark White's campaign for attorney general; a major fundraiser for the LBJ School, honoring Barbara Jordan, whom we truly worshiped; and the even bigger one honoring Bob Strauss in the fall of 1980. I did a great deal of work on the latter from Montana. I'd grown tired of the day-to-day grind. I knew Senator Bentsen would run again in 1982. When my family moved to Whitefish after Christmas of 1979, we rented out our home in Austin. As time passed in 1981, when I needed to spend time in Austin I started staying at Lowell's house on 35th Street. He had a room and a bath on the top floor, next to his "school for boy" where one of his sons, who was less than a scholar, took private lessons.

Lowell included me in everything that was appropriate, and most was. My lodging arrangement was set until my family came home in the summer. On Memorial Day of 1981, Austin had a horrific flood. It turned everything upside down, including the habits of wildlife. One morning, a day or two after the flood, I went jogging. Soon I noticed I was being followed by a wild turkey. I turned around and headed for the house, followed by my new running buddy. I opened the front door and yelled that I had a wild turkey on my trail. Down came Lowell and his aide. No turkey was to be seen. Lowell said that maybe Wild Turkey was what I was drinking. I was perplexed to say the least. So in they went and off I started again. Out of the bushes came the bird. I yelled from the curb and out they came again. Well, we hooted and hollered to scare it off, to no avail. So we called the city and someone came and took it off. Lowell told everyone that George Bristol had enamored a wild turkey.

The remainder of 1981 and 1982 was mainly filled with Lloyd Bentsen's reelection campaign, but Lowell and I kept up with each other almost daily. He was deciding about remarrying. He had been dating two women, Diane Daniels and Pat Patterson. I liked them both, but knew Diane and leaned toward her. Lowell and I—and Lowell and others, I am sure—talked it through. I didn't push hard, but voiced my opinion that Diane was more suited for politics. I already knew that Lowell was considering running for mayor in 1983. In the end he chose Pat and we all rallied around. They had a splendid wedding in Dallas in February of 1982 and a better reception. A who's who of Austin and Texas came. It was a beautiful weekend.

Before the wedding we threw a bachelor's party in Austin in the Jim Hogg Suite at the Driskill Hotel. I had asked Diane Daniels to be the surprise guest of honor. I secreted her into the side bedroom, and a friend guarded the door. No one else knew. We went through all the long machinations of a bachelor party. Lowell sat on a makeshift throne with appropriate crown and cape, as we roasted him and toasted him. He loved it. Then, at the appointed moment, I announced, "And now the highlight of the evening! Our gift to you: not exactly a showgirl in a cake—better!" With that, Diane walked out of the bedroom door. There was dead silence, shocked silence in some cases. Lowell yelled out, "Oh, my God!" He smelled Diane's perfume across the room and knew he'd been had. He laughingly smacked his fist and palm together, in a familiar Lebermann gesture, and asked with a twinkle in his eye, "Okay, who did this?" He knew who had done it, and we later laughed about that evening often.

Within weeks after the wedding we began to talk about the mayoral race in earnest. We decided that after Christmas I would turn all my attention to Lowell's campaign. First I had to close Senator Bentsen's campaign, balance the books, go to London, and visit the eastern shore of Maryland at Thanksgiving time to hunt geese. (Lowell was intrigued about the latter.) We rented space on 15th Street. We called in every chit. We raised and borrowed money. The reception was favorable—but Austin truly is weird. Lowell was a candidate who not only was head and shoulders above the others, he truly was a "green panther" who should have been readily acceptable to environmentalists. But Lowell belonged to the Headliners Club and there was an underlying suspicion that "those types" were not to be trusted, especially after Lowell was quoted as having said that all real decisions concerning Austin were made at the Headliners. Roy Spence, who should have known better, used that to the advantage of Lowell's opponent, Ron Mullen. Spence was still bragging about his coup at Lowell's funeral. Lowell lost the election and Austin lost the chance for its greatest mayor ever.

I know that Lowell was terribly disappointed—he loved Austin and wanted to give back—but we kept busy on a number of fronts and in outward appearance he was back to his old self. That was one thing about his blindness that was a nuanced positive. Lowell simply could not afford to be down for long.

Somewhere during 1983–1984, I remember, he went off with his aide, then David Biegel, to lose weight. He always fought that demon. I was at the Headliners and got a call, then I went to find a quiet spot, because I had promised Lowell I would do something for him. When I got on the phone, I could barely hear him. Trucks and traffic were in the background. His voice was muffled.

"Where are you and what are you doing? I thought you'd gone to a fat farm."

"I escaped. I am at a 7-Eleven on the highway and I'm eating a Baby Ruth!"

Several days later I went to a Democratic event in Phoenix. There in the crowd was Lowell Lebermann. His aide whispered to him that I was there and he broke out laughing.

At some point in late 1984, Lowell and I met with Governor Mark White and his wife and Linda to discuss a project for the upcoming sesquicentennial of Texas in 1986. Former governor Clements had settled on a plan focusing on community diversity. I couldn't disagree with that (although it would turn out that the paid staff Clements had appointed had created a mess), but we felt we needed something the entire state could rally around. We reviewed several options, including restoration of the San Jacinto Monument and the USS *Texas*, but we decided on the restoration of the state capitol in Austin, for several reasons. First, the capitol is the most visited of our state icons. Second, it had nearly burned to the ground in 1983. The fire had exposed multiple dangerous and wasteful components, and what remained was shabby at best. Once we had decided on the capitol restoration, we also decided to concentrate on a few major, high-visibility renovation projects: the statue atop the dome, the governor's reception area, the House chamber, and selected art and furnishings. Focusing on these, we thought, would high-light the multitude of the building's other needs. When I say "we," I include the State Preservation Board, as constituted at the time. The board had recently hired an architect who had many innovative ideas but no money.

We formed a nonprofit, and Lowell and I cosigned a note for $100,000. We thought we could raise the $3 million budgeted but had no guarantees. Raise we did. We raised the statue off the dome with the help of a Mississippi National Guard helicopter (Texas did not have the right equipment). Then we restored the statue—the ugliest goddess one could imagine—with financial support from several corporations and the in-kind donation of an aluminum alloy from Alcoa. The governor's reception room and House chamber were restored to near-original design, and new furnishings based on period photographs were installed. When possible, we tried to match projects to an appropriate lead corporate donor, as with Alcoa. Brinkman Carpeting Company helped with funding and giving discounts on carpeting for the House chamber. Maryland Club Coffee wanted to restore the original flower beds and shrubbery.

We were making progress, with a great deal of attendant publicity including wide-spread press coverage, and then in the fall of 1985 we got really lucky. A group approached me about doing a television special on Texas, with profits from the sale of ads and tickets to the filming of the show dedicated to the capitol restoration. Then Prince Charles sent word that he wished to come to Texas during 1986 and to Austin, in particular, to honor the Scottish stonemasons who had built the capitol. The prince's representatives agreed to a benefit dinner and performance.

From September 1985 through April 1986 we worked around the clock, because the show (by then a two-hour ABC special), and the prince's visit were to be less than two months apart. We pulled both off, and Lowell and Prince Charles had a smashing time at dinner.

Somewhere in all the activity of 1986, Lowell's generous spirit manifested itself again, and again was directed toward my son Mark. In the early 1980s Lowell and I helped support and finance two of screenplay writer Horton Foote's Texas movie classics—*1918* and *Valentine's Day*. Mark had worked on both as an intern and had the movie fever in his blood. Lowell had joined the board of Robert Redford's Sundance Institute, and he knew Mark loved art and moviemaking. He was going to attend a board meeting or film festival in Utah and asked Mark to go along. I've never seen a person—child or adult—more pleased. It would have been enough to go to a few shows and walk around, but Lowell made sure that Mark was included in everything, specifically the closing-night dinner where he got Mark seated at Robert Redford's table. During the course of the dinner one of the participants said something, and Redford responded and then turned and asked Mark his opinion. According to Lowell, who called me later that night with the pride of a father, Mark, age fifteen, disagreed with Redford and gave a reasoned analysis of their difference.

Throughout the 1990s I continued to see Lowell but not as regularly as in the past. I spent a great deal of time in El Paso and on national park and client business in Washington. But we did go to a number of political events together, including national party conventions and White House affairs. And without fail we had our private Christmas lunch at the Headliners or at his house.

In early 2001 I went to see Lowell about my conservation and parkland plan. He was interested and supportive, but changes were occurring in his appearance and health. There were calls to me about intervention for his alcoholism, but I never got involved in this. First, there were plenty of other good and caring friends, but second, and most important, I always harkened back to that night in the 1970s when he had told me about how damned hard it was being up and brave all the time.

The interventions didn't work. Lowell and I got together from time to time, and he continued to contribute annually to my conservation efforts, even as his health continued to deteriorate. I became sorrowful and didn't want to see him waste away. That may have been selfish on my part, but we had been so close that I felt I was losing a brother, that this brother no longer had the will to live. Lowell had done a great deal with himself, his family, and his beloved University of Texas and its thousands of students, as well as Austin and Texas. I wanted him to go out on his own terms.

The day I heard that Lowell had died I thought of what my son Mark had said about how the young blind man who had committed suicide should have known him. Fortunately thousands did know him and are better for it. Lowell Lebermann was beyond a role model. He was the epitome of truly caring citizen. I loved him and miss him. I am glad he was part of my life. To paraphrase my son, "I am thankful that I knew Mr. Lebermann."

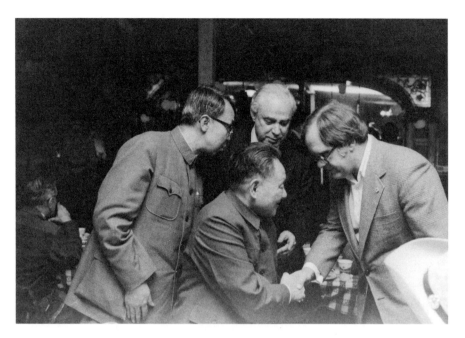

US Trade Representative Robert Strauss introduces me to Chinese leader Deng Xiaoping, Houston, 1979.

My son Mark goes to greet President Jimmy Carter at Fort Hood, 1978.

I inform Robert Strauss in 1971 that we have topped the fundraising goal of $1 million for the 1972 Democratic National Convention.

Recuperating at Granite Park Chalet, Glacier National Park, after the 1972 Democratic National Convention. From left: eldest son Jimmy, me, Valarie, sister-in-law Bey, and Mother.

Young Mark Bristol (infant in my arms) goes home to Texas for the first time to meet his Granny Bristol, Uncle David Bristol (left), and my cousin Judd Holt, Christmas 1969.

Shelby Bryan (left) and I (right) confer with President Bill Clinton concerning a national park matter at a campaign reception in Houston, 1996.

Daughter Jennifer, son Mark, and I greet President Bill Clinton at Houston fundraiser, 1993.

Me listening to one of Ann Richards's highly strategic jokes, 1990.

Left to right: Senator Lloyd Bentsen, our San Antonio friend Lowry Mays, me, and B. A. Bentsen enjoy beautiful Glacier National Park, 1989.

Me (second from left) with my heroes (left to right in hats) Monty Hale, Gene Autry, and Michael Martin Murphey, at the ABC television special on Texas sesquicentennial celebration, 1986.

I escort visiting Prince Charles to meet Lowell Lebermann and Pat Patterson, Austin, Texas, 1986.

Left to right: An unknown couple, my great friend and mentor Speaker Jim Wright, and I, 1987.

Me with former First Lady Rosalynn Carter and former president Jimmy Carter at an event in Austin, mid 1980s.

I present one of the entertainers (unknown) at Lady Bird Johnson's seventy-fifth birthday celebration, 1987.

PART V

America's
Best Ideas

CHAPTER 15

The National Park Foundation

On the occasion of the presentation of the 2009 Pugsley Medal for my years of conservation and park advocacy, I had to prepare an acceptance speech to a prestigious national audience, many of whom were past recipients of the award. The principal guideline for my speech was the long list of my life's work to appear in the evening program. The list was complete, but it did not answer the question that often haunts my own deliberations. Why? How did I come from Democratic Party activist and businessman to conservationist?

As is often the case, the answer entails sheer happenstance. Sometime in the 1990s I happened to come upon an old issue of *Life* magazine, one dated August 5, 1940, six days before my birth. I flipped through it, and found among the slightly yellowing pages an article on American vacation venues. Prominently featured there were two photographs in color—unusual for the magazine at that time—scenes of Glacier National Park. I was immediately struck, and I wrote a poem about what might have occurred in those days leading up to my birth, something that might have set the stage for my journey to Glacier, and thus for my future work to save a few more "last best places."

In All Likelihood My Mother Read the August 5, 1940, *Life* Magazine

How else on steaming evenings with me
only a week away could she catch
Corporal Hitler and the cancerous mole Mussolini,
as they moved from Compiègne across Libya?
All was far removed, nothing undone yet,
yet, she, and perhaps I, sensed the tension
as her fan, an Emerson oscillator,

rustled the pages of photos of dictators who,
like the Kelvinator, were poised to change our lives.
The upright radio reached out,
gathering scratchings from blackened skies,
Auden's "unmentionable odor" lingering
on the rim of raised Gilbey's gin
and the lips of Lucky Strike smokers.
The world was brewing anew—men, material, entire countries
soon wrapped in winter blankets,
suffering jungle rot, inhaling the inhuman stench
of gasoline leaking from reeking meadows.

My small world would know none of this
even as a cry went up down the block
and neighborhood women hurried
their own children inside
before they ran to comfort those
who had lost theirs.

Yet fifty-five years later, all of that
trails behind the beginning of my own history, spotted
with later conflicts, as I thumb
the near-yellowed pages, when color photographs
of Glacier National Park's emerald peaks
confirm that somehow
my mother began to steer me
toward those safe mountains even as the dread
of war ran through the darkness of her womb.

I was preordained, I think, to take up the cause of conservation and parkland enhancement. All of my life before that was preparation, a foundation upon which to build.

Each of my career steps, though satisfying at the time, to one degree or another meant walking and working in the shadows of those for whom I labored. I say this with no sense of unhappiness, simply as fact. I suspect this is true for many. As we learn, we ideally store up experiences so that at some point we can blossom into our own identifiable selves. The sad thing is that all too often people become weighed down with obligations, failures, and distractions, and when conditions are finally right—if such a time comes—they are unwilling or unable to take the leap. I am one of the fortunate ones: when my time came I was not only prepared but also able to make the jump.

My years with Senator Bentsen had been invaluable. Working on new endeavors that require statewide action and organization, particularly if these require legislation, can be daunting anywhere, but in Texas such challenges can appear overwhelming, bordering on impossible. Working as a statewide organizer in Texas gave me knowledge of the players, temperament, and diversity of the state, so much so that I had long gotten over the sense of impossibility. Yes, Texas is huge. Two hundred fifty-four counties spread from East Texas with its Deep South roots to the high plains and deserts of Deep West Texas, and from the area bordering Mexico in the south, with its rich cultural diversity, to the megacities of Houston, Dallas/Fort Worth, and San Antonio. Throughout are all manner of communities with some statewide ties but governed by local interests and customs.

Within each community are leaders: elected officials, merchants, members of the media, representatives of organizations, and others. Among these are typically one or two key players who might help get things moving in their community, particularly if a good relationship has been formed during the past. At the very least such a player might put me on to another person with shared interests, who might then make other wheels turn. My time with Jake Pickle, Bob Strauss, and Lloyd Bentsen gave me ample opportunity to get to know those movers and shakers.

From Bentsen and Strauss I took to the art of fundraising. It is a very simple art, really. You have to ask. In order to ask, you have to believe—and you have to explain your cause with conviction. You have to go where the money is. I have for a long time been guided by the Willie Sutton philosophy. Sutton was an accomplished bank robber, and when he was finally captured some reporter asked him why he robbed banks. Willie, with an expression of utter disbelief apparently said, "Because that's where the money is!"

A fundraiser must also be organized and focused. From my mentors and my own work I learned that causes, even good ones, take time to perfect. Furthermore, even the best of causes more than likely will be met with roadblocks, disappointment, or temporary failure. So add patience and perseverance to the mix.

I came to appreciate the absolute need for knowledge of the subject at hand. Not just knowledge of the subject at hand, but knowledge of all the players and competing causes that might affect the outcome. This requires listening to all points of view and, to the degree possible, appreciating other points of view. This does not mean caving in when others have perfectly reasonable counterpoints. What it does mean is trying to listen for commonality—no matter how seemingly insignificant. It might be enough to tie a knot.

From mentors and from the many organizations I served as either an officer or director, I honed the ability to work within organizations to move them toward goals, or, when necessary, toward my point of view.

Because of my longstanding love of Glacier Park, I had over the years begun to read about and visit other parks. The concept of a nation setting aside its most meaningful natural, historic, and cultural treasures for the benefit and enjoyment of all encompassed all the best parts of our democracy, I thought. I was also moved by the time and treasure that individuals and organizations had given so that some of those parks might be established, even in the face of competing forces, often driven by greed. What we now as a nation appreciate and revere about our park system often came at great cost and conflict: practically open warfare at the formation of Grand Teton National Park and criminal connivance over who would control the Grand Canyon. By the mid-1970s I had a sense that I someday wanted to repay my country for my own national park experience. I discovered an organization called the National Park Foundation (NPF) whose members were appointed by the secretary of the interior with the blessing of the White House. When late in his presidency Jimmy Carter asked me if there was anything he could do for me—he was hoping to repay me for the work I'd done on his behalf—I told him that I would like to serve on the NPF board. He wrote this down and said that he would see what he could do, but nothing ever came of it because there were no vacancies and some months later he lost to Ronald Reagan.

Twelve years would pass before the opportunity came again. In the interim I served as chairman of the Texas Conservation Foundation, a tiny, underfunded state agency. Its budget was so small that after my first meeting I wondered aloud why the foundation had been created and how it stayed in existence. My work with the foundation did give me insight into the agencies that played significant roles in Texas public lands and conservation—the Texas Parks & Wildlife Department and the General Land Office. I also met a number of wonderful people involved in conservation, including Ed Cox Jr., Terry Hershey, and Andy Sansom—these three all would join me in later endeavors. The foundation secured two large tracts of land adjoining the San Jacinto Battleground State Historic Site—gifts outright from Phillips Petroleum and Diamond Shamrock. This doubled the size of that hallowed site. Otherwise, without significant and sustainable funding and political support, we could do little more than pick around the edges.

In 1987 I had another one of those moments that kept me on my predestined course. Lady Bird Johnson was to celebrate her seventy-fifth birthday and there were plans afoot to recognize her vast contributions to the nation in the areas of conservation, parklands development, and appreciation and protection of natural beauty. The inner circle of her friends honored me by asking me to help raise substantial funds for her beloved Wildflower Center in Austin. Celebratory events spanned the country, with major ones planned for Washington DC and Texas.

Up until then I had been a conservationist, I suppose, if one without real conviction. But my work with Lady Bird Johnson moved me. Through news coverage and film footage I came to see how a shy young woman who had grown up amid the pines and bayous of East Texas had become a powerful adult, someone who could have chosen any cause and made a success of it. And I saw that when time and circumstance allowed her to put her talent and experiences to use after all those years devoted to business, politics, and family, she had looked back to her formative years as a child out of doors. There she had seen a way to move a nation to rededicate itself to conservation and respect for the land. Lady Bird Johnson helped me to recognize those traits in myself. I knew my call would come, and I sensed it would be a call to help buttress the conservation ethic.

I learned something else that applied with equal force. Success in any major field gives significant credence to entrance in another. As Mrs. Johnson had a wealth of experience in business and politics, she was already recognized as a competent leader when her time of calling came. And so my experiences put me in good stead, even though I was a novice in organized conservation efforts.

In 1992 I worked tirelessly for Bill Clinton before and after his nomination. Following his November victory I received calls from Little Rock, asking if I wanted to serve in Washington. I said that I had no interest in a full-time position but would like to serve as a member of the National Park Foundation. Assurances were made that I would be given every consideration. In order to make that happen I called Lloyd Bentsen, soon to be secretary of the treasury. He told me to be patient, and he said that he would put in a good and forceful word. I also let other key Clinton supporters know of my interest. A year passed, however, with no word. Finally, in late 1993 or early 1994, a smiling Bruce Babbitt, secretary of the interior, came up to me at a White House reception. "George, you are going to get that position." he said. "Lloyd Bentsen brings it up at every cabinet meeting! I think it will come through in the spring." And so it did. I was appointed for a six-year term beginning in the fall of 1994. My new assignment would become the best nonpaying job I've ever had. It would beat many of my paid jobs. What other board holds all its meetings in national parks? Wherever the site, NPF board members awaken ready to do inspired work.

In the late fall of 1994 I reported in, and I found that the vice-chair of the board was Mort Meyerson of Dallas (the secretary of the interior, by law, is the chair). I knew Mort casually, and we arranged to meet for lunch. I was in for a big surprise. During the 1980s, neither our national parks nor the National Park Foundation had been a priority of Ronald Reagan. His secretary of the interior, James Watt was barely supportive of the parks at best, and from time to time openly hostile. So the foundation and its board were given little to do, often ignored. Mort summed it up: "We meet several times a year, do a little good-ol'-boy fly-fishing, give a little money, pee on a tree, and call it a day."

Mort said that changes would have to be made from the top down. The current NPF president had fallen into a "go along to get along" mode. Members of the board had lost interest, and some never came to meetings. There was no driving vision for the future. I said that I wanted none of that and to count me in as an ally for change. Mort also stated that because there were no purposeful programs, there was no real fundraising. I wanted to help move that in a more proactive direction. Importantly, we hit it off.

In early 1995 I wrote a letter to friends and contacts around the country who I thought might support "America's Best Idea" if given the chance. I had to use my own stationery because there was no National Park Foundation letterhead for board use, and I had to write in general terms because there were no programs in place or yet being organized. We got a few small gifts in response, but then my phone rang. It was Mark Weiss, a friend who had worked with me in the 1980s to acquire a large corporate gift for the Texas sesquicentennial and a significant gift from Canon for the Lady Bird Johnson Wildflower Center on the occasion of her seventy-fifth birthday. Weiss still represented Canon, it turned out, and called to inquire about a partnership with the NPF. I squared with him, saying that the foundation had grand potential but was in the doldrums. On the other hand, there was little competition for sponsorship among other corporations, and none in the area of photography and copying products. That was a tremendous plus, but Weiss said there was a competing organization applying for the funding Canon had in mind. Canon wanted to make a statement in the conservation arena, he said, and I told him that the NPF needed to make a statement too, and that together we could capture wide attention. I asked him to give me a few weeks, telling him that I thought we would cobble together something meaningful. Then I called Mort and asked him to back my play. I was going to have to push the NPF president and staff. Mort assured me that he would do so.

Within the time frame agreed upon, we put a very good proposal together, thanks in large part to Jill Nicoll, the director of development for the foundation, who had been eagerly waiting to develop something. Over the spring of 1995 we worked in secret (this was a stipulation of Canon which wanted to evaluate our proposal and another one without lobbying or interference). None of the board, with the exception of Mort and a few of the staff, knew what we were up to. I'm not sure we told the president. And we moved forward without even knowing the amount that might be forthcoming from Canon.

At some point I told Weiss that it would be most helpful if we could announce the funding and the plan at my first board meeting, for two reasons. First, I wanted to establish my own credibility, and, second, we needed a major corporate show of support if we were going to expand our fundraising sights. We were assured that the National Park Foundation had been selected, and it looked like $1 million would be the initial grant, but there was still fine-tuning to be done.

Jill worked right up to and during the opening of the meeting. At a moment I will never forget, she stuck her head in the door, asking to see me. I went to the phone, and Canon's principal US officer confirmed the news and said that I could tell the board but asked that it go no further until an official press release could be perfected.

Since Mort was in the know, I walked back in and winked at him. He immediately stood and said that I had something to announce. Giving due credit to our small secretive band, I announced that the gift was indeed $1 million. There was genuine surprise and then applause. After things quieted down, Don Rumsfeld, the board member sitting to my right, leaned over and said with a big grin, "You have certainly raised the bar, and some of the folks are not going to appreciate it right off the bat, but count me in. It's time we make something of this."

Regardless of what would transpire later during his controversial time as secretary of defense during the Iraq War, Don was one of the finest board members during my tenure with the NPF. He and his wife, Joyce, loved the parks. Her father had been a dedicated park ranger and that commitment carried over. I still consider Don a friend and friend of the parks.

And he was right. That evening during dinner one board member came over to my table, leaned down, and with a frown on his face said, "Why did you do that? Are you trying to show us up?" I smiled and turned away. He would not get used to me for a long time but eventually came around. Naysayers are a dime a dozen. Doers are sometimes hard to find. Fortunately, between most of members from the first Bush administration and the new Clinton appointees, we had a talented group of doers. Mort reorganized the board, we fired the president and hired a new one, and we invigorated and empowered the staff.

As we went about reorganizing, I began to think and read more deeply about national parks, the wondrous and uniquely American concept we were charged with supporting. Each reading, each conversation, and every period of meditation instilled in me a deepening sense of renewed national purpose and pride. Our national parks are truly the country's best idea. At a time in US history when it appeared that overwhelming forces were hell-bent on sawing the country down, mining it raw, and coal-dusting it over, men and women, great and unknown, began to awaken to the realization that natural resources were exhaustible. They did so at a time when areas of the country were still being discovered, places of such immense and awesome beauty that they could not be ignored or sacrificed at the hands of those who found beauty only at the bottom of ledgers. The wisdom and fortitude of those who fostered the awakening conservation ethic in nineteenth-century America led to sane land and wildlife policies, policies required to keep us from being a barren people in a wasteland.

Books and films tell the story of the rise of this national concern and the men and women who took it upon themselves to fulfill the promise of conservation. Those curious should delve into the works of John Muir, Teddy Roosevelt, Ken Burns, Dayton Duncan, and Douglas Brinkley. John Muir gave spiritual poetry to the grandeur of the country's natural blessings. Teddy Roosevelt used his prestige and the bully pulpit to hammer a conservation ethic into the national conscience, as well as into lasting legislation. Families like the Rockefellers and Mellons used their vast wealth to secure tracts holding our most precious treasures until enabling legislation could bring national protection, often in the face of the forces of exploitation and corrupt elected officials. Paintings of awesome places by artists such as Alfred Bierstadt and Thomas Moran were shipped to Washington for display in the halls of Congress. And national parks were even legitimized in the business world by railroad owners, who surely hoped to make a buck off tourism but were also struck by the stunning landscapes that bordered their lines running to the West from the populated East. In years to come all of these developments were reinforced by the work of men and women who stood against overwhelming odds to save other treasures, such as Acadia, the Everglades, and Biscayne Bay. George Dorr, Marjory Stoneman Douglas, and Lancelot Jones are but a few among thousands who gave of their time and treasure to secure their places of the heart. This was truly a national effort of rich and poor, powerful and courageous ordinary people, all set on securing the extraordinary. I began to appreciate the honor of being a part of something so grand, such a righteous challenge.

The core of the charge of the National Park Foundation, set forth in 1967 legislation championed by Lady Bird Johnson and Laurance Rockefeller, is to seek private funding for our parks over and above that appropriated by Congress. Some perceive a fundamental problem with this, since it is the responsibility of the federal government to fund national parks. If private citizens and corporations are compelled or called upon to give, doesn't it follow that the Congress at some point might reduce the federal obligation? This question was raised among our board members, particularly since we were about to launch programs that we hoped would have great appeal to corporations, foundations, and individuals.

After a great deal of thought, then and since, I have come to the conclusion that there is no set answer, even among appropriation items that are not usually acceptable for funding by the private sector. Infrastructure is a good example. Roads, bridges, and water and sewage systems are thought to be the responsibility of the government. Yet during my term on the National Park Foundation board, circumstances of grave magnitude trumped that historical recognition. In the late 1990s the Potomac River flooded, destroying great segments of the C&O Canal National Historic Park. For a number of reasons it was deemed appropriate to solicit private funds on an emergency basis until Congress could act. Millions of dollars were quickly raised to repair essential locks, trails, embankments, and other infrastructure projects.

During the same period, great structural damages were discovered in the Washington Monument, one of our most revered and visited historic icons. Again Congress had failed to appropriate funds needed for repairs. Simultaneously Target Stores was looking for a major project to announce their entry into the Washington DC market. Not only did they fund the restoration of the monument, they did so accompanied by an all-out advertising blitz. The height of the company's achievement was draping the monument in a blue and white cocoon while the restoration was done. This garnered worldwide attention, greater visitation, and media comment on the lack of government support. In this case Congress moved and appropriated funding not only for the Washington Monument but also for other presidential monuments in the Washington DC National Mall complex. Sometimes private support causes public embarrassment and action.

Sometimes it even takes the threat of withdrawal of private support to motivate federal action. In the 1920s John D. Rockefeller Jr., his wife, Abby, and others formed the Snake River Land Company to purchase 35,000 acres of Wyoming valley lands incognito and hold them until the National Park Service (NPS) could take possession. The government would take no steps to accept the land for years. Discouraged by the stalemate, Rockefeller wrote to President Franklin Roosevelt that unless resolution was forthcoming, he would sell it to the highest bidder. Soon after, Roosevelt declared the Jackson Hole Monument, using a method devised by his distant cousin Teddy Roosevelt through the Antiquities Act, which permitted presidents to set aside national monuments—short of establishing a national park—without congressional approval. While it would take years to iron out a plan acceptable to Congress, the National Park Service, and Wyoming, it took the extraordinary generosity and then the steely determination of John Rockefeller Jr. to make present-day Grand Teton National Park a reality. This is an extreme example of private funding outside the realm of normal gifting. However, there have been many instances where private donors have bought and held land for later public purpose, for a time when Congress (or state legislatures) could catch up with their generosity.

More practically, the amount of private funds raised would have to be impossibly huge to cause Congress to shirk its duty in funding national parks. That is not to say that Congress always funds at adequate levels. It does not. But there are many other factors governing their funding decisions—sometimes valid, sometimes stupid and short-sighted. Some in Congress give lip service to national parks while privately (and sometimes not so privately) doing their best to injure parks or block the creation of new ones. Fortunately they are most often thwarted by the same sort of concerned citizens who made parks happen in the first place.

Balance is necessary, and this lies at the root of the national park concept and commitment to it. Since their inception, the parks have been supported by the personal treasure of citizens. That was and is appropriate. They are our parks—gifts to ourselves, which deserve private as well as public support. Most in Congress welcome and support public-private partnerships at the national and local levels, while remaining committed to congressional funding. However, there is a greater imperative. Even if Congress fully funds national parks, including the present $5–7 billion in deferred maintenance, there has to be—and will be—allowance for private support, for acts of generosity from those such as the Rockefellers to one-dollar deposits at park collection boxes. In part these private contribution fund things deemed outside the scope of congressional responsibility or so unique to a single park as to demand local support.

So our task with the NPF was to fashion programs and funding opportunities that would complement the appropriation process. Some funds we raised could be used without restriction, while others were highly restricted, aimed for specific projects. Three projects that took place during my term required particular imagination and coordination. The first started late in 1995 or early in 1996, when my friend Reed Hawn called. Reed was from Austin, an avid coin collector, and a recent appointee to the US Mint's Citizens Commemorative Coin Advisory Committee by Secretary Bentsen. Did I know that there was a Yellowstone National Park coin proposal and would NPF be getting any of the proceeds? I didn't know but said that I would check. I called the NPF office and the office of the secretary of the interior. No one had a clue. So I went back to Reed. He thought that it was unfair that this national coin should fund Yellowstone to the exclusion of all others.

Since no one seemed to be very interested, perhaps no one would interfere if we got the bill changed, which we did, directing half the proceeds to Yellowstone and half for the benefit of the other parks via the National Park Foundation. I cleared this with Lloyd Bentsen, no longer in public office, who called the director of the US Mint on our behalf and advised me who to see in Congress. After a quick vote in the House, we had to wait a while for the Senate to act. The bill finally passed in October 1996.

Although a coinage measure may pass, that does not mean instant minting. Such coins, and justly so, are queued in an orderly procedure so that too many don't flood the market in any given year. The Yellowstone coin was struck in early 1999 and went on sale in July that year. I announced it to the full NPF board in September at Olympic National Park. The coin had a projected revenue of over $1.5 million, all for no expenditure or effort save for my time and that of a couple of staff members, and the entire amount was unrestricted funding.

Some things are better accomplished without benefit of committee or debate. Others require full and open discussion. Such was the case in NPF efforts to establish an encompassing "Proud Partner" program. After the Canon gift, which eventually rose to $7 million in cash, products, and advertisements, we knew we wanted to raise our goals substantially for corporate giving. The proposed program would not only raise money but, through the use of corporate advertising, raise national awareness of our parks. While there had been many voices in support of the parks in recent decades, and many achievements—such as President Carter's Alaskan Lands Act, there had not been a clear and continuing support since the Roosevelts, Teddy and Franklin. Advertising would not fill the void, but it would reach out to millions to tweak the national conscience. First there were hoops to jump through, policies to be refashioned, and resistance among some organizations and individuals. The National Park Service and the foundation were both governed by a hodgepodge of bureaucratic restrictions, practically guaranteeing that nothing big would happen. What we were looking for was a sweeping, intelligent modification of these restrictions so that the NPS, NPF, corporations, foundations, and individuals would have a clear understanding of what was and was not acceptable.

It was not, as some misinformed naysayer might have the public believe, a wholesale invitation to throw up McDonald's arches around Arches National Park—and every other park. I'm not sure that James Watt and his minions would have dared go that far. And McDonald's on its worst day would not have gone near that deal. Corporate logo display in and around the parks was off the table from the outset, save in the most tasteful and low-key settings, such as a donor board in a visitor center.

Because it was new and far-reaching, our proposal did stir controversy, particularly in the corporate support area. Basically our plan was to create ten to twenty corporate categories and then put out what amounted to a strictly controlled and defined call for bid proposals. Airlines would bid against airlines, photographic companies against others in the industry, et cetera. The package was a multiyear commitment in cash and in kind. The latter, mainly advertising, was nearly as important as the cash, as we needed to correct a serious flaw: NPF was the best-kept secret on the planet.

Eventually, in 1998, after a three-year effort of educating and answering rumors and outright lies, National Park Director Bob Stanton proudly signed Director's Order 21. While not giving absolute exclusivity to each single corporation that made a deal with us, it did protect each from unfair undercutting on the part of competition. It led to meaningful corporate participation for a number of years.

Of all the NPF projects I worked on, none gave me more joy than helping to originate, fund, and implement the Park Partners program. When I came to the foundation, a number of parks, such as Yellowstone, Yosemite, Great Smoky Mountains, and Acadia, had wonderful and powerful organizations of "friends," but many had none. Such an organization can help fund programs and projects critical to a single park that has failed to receive adequate congressional appropriations. I thought it imperative to find ways to help expand this local support for national parks for two reasons. First, such groups could raise support and dollars from those entities surrounding their park that would not otherwise give to a national organization, and certainly not to other parks. They could also, once organized, be a constructive force to be reckoned with by their elected officials, who in turn could reach out for additional support from colleagues—you scratch my back and I'll scratch yours, a necessary ingredient in a successful democracy, so long as public benefit comes first.

At the urging of President Jim Maddy of the National Park Foundation, who was becoming a forceful advocate for change and innovation, a task force was set up, led by David Rockefeller Jr. and me. David thought the idea might appeal to Laurance Rockefeller. And it turned out that we had an upcoming board meeting in the Tetons that coincided with our need to visit with David's financier uncle.

In addition to David Rockefeller and me, Jim Maddy and Vice-Chair Ken West traveled to the Rockefeller Teton retreat (one of the most beautiful sites imaginable), and there was much discussion about who would say what. This was necessitated, I suppose, because neither Maddy nor West knew Laurence Rockefeller. Upon arrival we gathered on the front porch of what I would call a family meeting lodge. Soon a man driving a golf cart and wearing gardening clothes came down the hill. The others paid no attention as they did not recognize the driver, but I did and went out to meet the great man.

"Mr. Rockefeller, before we get started I wanted to say we share at least one thing in common—an undying love and appreciation for Lady Bird Johnson." He threw his arms around me and said, "That is certainly true. She is the greatest woman on the planet."

I was told later that Ken West turned to Jim Maddy and asked, "Why is George Bristol hugging the gardener?" Imagine his and the others' surprise when that gracious gardener ushered us in, heard us out, and then said that he was very interested in the Parks Partner concept. We then went up the hill to a reception where it seemed that most of the huge Rockefeller family was present to greet us. I have never met a Rockefeller I didn't like. Maybe unlikeable ones are out there, but they have eluded me.

It is difficult today to envision that the members of that remarkable family are all descendents of the richest, most despised man in America, John D. Rockefeller, and yet because he deeply believed in tithing and private philanthropy, he instilled a great sense of social responsibility to all his children and theirs. There we stood at the edge of the Grand Tetons on that September day in 1998, where a park had been willed into being by the visionary generosity of John D. Rockefeller Jr. and his wife, Abby. I considered it a great privilege to have the opportunity to discuss an important program with the Rockefeller grandson who most took to heart the love of nature and did the most to continue the tradition of conservationist philanthropy. I was inspired again to go forward and honor their legacy.

The Rockefeller enclave in the Tetons is now a part of Grand Teton National Park. Upon Laurance Rockefeller's death, the land and its buildings were willed to the park his father and mother, his wife, Mary, and he had first breathed to life and then nurtured. All of his children and heirs respected his decision, though they were saddened to lose the special family place, a place of the heart. I can only hope that other great families will step into the breach to continue to perpetuate our best idea.

In 1998 Laurence Rockefeller was neither dead nor dying, and in typical Rockefeller fashion he quickly answered our request with a challenge: $1 million to be matched by $1.5 million from other sources. With David and me as cochairs of the effort, we dove into the project with enthusiasm. Calls went out. Letters were sent. Visits were made. I spent two or three weeks in Washington in the spring of 1999 putting the parts together. David was magnificent in his support, and sometime in the summer of 1999 we reached the goal, aided by a generous gift from Lady Bird Johnson in honor of her dear friend Laurance—gardener to gardener, in the tradition of caring for the lands of America.

Somewhere in the midst of this effort I stated that I would like to see some of our initial funding go toward setting up a friends organization at Glacier National Park. David Rockefeller and Jim Maddy smiled and agreed: it would be appropriate as there weren't many such groups in the Northwest. Jay Vestal, a Texan living in Utah, was hired to organize the effort among the candidate parks. He and I went to Montana and at the home of Dave Mihalic, superintendent of Glacier, hammered out the original plan for what would become the Glacier National Park Fund. Mihalic enlisted the support of the governor of Montana, Mark Racicot, who agreed to host a dinner at his home for prospective board members. At that event we received enthusiastic pledges of support and membership. In the fall, an initial meeting was held and the Glacier Fund was launched with a generous supporting gift from the Park Partners of the National Park Foundation. For ten years I sat on the board with many equally dedicated members who first met at that dinner, as well as others who would join later. The Glacier Fund (now the Glacier National Park Fund) was not only a success story, it also inspired others to form similar organizations around the country.

By 2000 my term was running out (although I would serve until a replacement member could be recruited in 2001). At Mesa Verde National Park I was presented the standard awards of membership, but David Rockefeller gave me a cherished surprise— a framed print commemorating my work on behalf of the Park Partner funding effort, with each donor enumerated. It hangs in a place of honor among all my national park memorabilia and awards.

After the ceremony Don Rumsfeld came up to me and said, "George, you will never know how great you have been to the growing success of this organization. Joyce and I have cherished our time with you." That night, with tears in my eyes, I read through the citation and the donor list.

Along with the inspiring presence of Laurance Rockefeller, David Rockefeller, and Lady Bird Johnson, there were other men and women who walked with me through my remarkable journey as a member of the National Park Foundation. Many I may never see again. Others, such as Dayton Duncan, who wrote and coproduced the PBS series *The National Parks: America's Best Idea*, have remained close friends. Duncan and Ken Burns honored me in 2006 by asking me to serve as an advisor for the series. All of these people lingered in memory and inspired, and I would need their inspiration to bolster my continuing journey.

Another inspiration for me had been poetry. I had read and studied poetry, and hesitantly wrote some in the 1980s, starting in Montana, but had essentially neglected it since my college days. In the early 1990s, though, around the time Valarie and I were separated, I published a book of poetry and photography, *Visual Voices: Between Mountains and Me,* and was then encouraged by the poet Leslie Ullman who had attended my book signing party in El Paso. I instinctively knew I needed help, and Leslie and I became fast friends and saw each other throughout the '90s. In 1994 I went to visit her in Vermont—she taught at Vermont College in a low-residency course—was fascinated, and confirmed that I needed to broaden and enhance my poetic horizon. Thanks to Leslie I enrolled at the college in 1995 to work toward a master's degree in poetry, starting on the roller coaster ride of my life. It is difficult enough to plow through a course of study in a continuous flow of semesters. It is quite another to pick it up again after thirty years, based on what was limited exposure in undergraduate years. The low-residency agenda was perfect for me: three weeks in the heat of summer and three weeks in the depth of winter at the college, with correspondence and conversation in between, all the while keeping my day job. I had wonderful, patient, understanding advisors: Syd Lea, Cynthia Huntington, Rick Jackson, Jack Meyers, and Mary Ruffle, as well as fellow students who often helped their older and strangest of colleagues over the hurdles. I was strange because I came from the world of politics and business. The backstop to all of them was Leslie, who was a strict but loving critic. Nonetheless, it was like drinking from a fire hose. I had to read and write twice as much just to stay even with the others—or not far behind. Yet somehow, through perseverance and dedication, I received a master of fine arts degree in 1997 at the age of fifty-six. It was a moment of singular achievement. Many of my longtime friends were astonished but pleased, as were my children. Not only did I learn to write acceptable poetry that has frequently been published, I also learned to put my thoughts down in concise manner, something that would serve me well during my upcoming park advocacy years in Texas.

CHAPTER 16

Parks in a Changing Texas

I rotated off the National Park Foundation with deep regret but fired up with knowledge gained during my time on the board. In the summer of 2000 I sought out my friend Andy Sansom, who was executive director of the Texas Parks & Wildlife Department (TPWD), serving with great distinction and vision. I explained that I wanted to put my national park enthusiasm and experience to use in Texas. After an hour or so of conversation and exchange of ideas, Andy wrote something on a piece of paper, folded it up, and handed it to me. On it was one word: "Money!"

"George," he said, "the department is underfunded, particularly the park system, but we also need increased appropriations for fish hatcheries, wildlife areas, and a number of other conservation venues." I told Andy while I knew the legislative process, I had not worked on conservation and parkland issues and did not know the legislative or conservation players across the state. However, I thought I could raise enough money from friends and associates to give me breathing room to learn, while at the same time begin to build an organization diverse and strong enough to succeed. Andy suggested several people I ought to meet and in December of 2000 introduced me to the constituency groups he had assembled over the years to explain the upcoming legislative budget and issues situation. That was of immense help to me, as I met people who signed on with my next project early and who to this day I count as supporters and friends. This was the genesis of what would become the Texas Coalition for Conservation (TCC).

To form an organization takes time and planning. One of the early breaks I got was that the Trust for Public Land, headed by my ex-wife Valarie, had recently completed a poll and an in-depth but anonymous interview study of Texans' perceptions of parks, conservation, and TPWD. I spent a month or so pouring over those documents.

What was most apparent was how diverse and disconnected the various conservation and environmental groups were, and in many instances how suspicious they were of one another. Even for an amateur it was easy to figure out some of the organizations and individuals by the manner in which they stated their case or criticized their opponents, real or imagined. A TPWD commissioner said that dealing with the various constituencies was like herding cats through a fish market. Another keen observer pronounced, "It's like dealing with Afghan warlords."

I visited with friends and the people Andy had suggested. Most were receptive, but David Gochman of Academy Outdoor Sports and Mort Meyerson, my National Park Foundation partner and friend, were generously supportive. David agreed to chair the Coalition. I could not have begun without them.

Early in the formative months I decided that I did not want to have the Coalition board totally comprised of professional conservationists and environmentalists. Rather, I thought it essential to have a board that could help in key areas of accounting, law, organization, and public relations. That's not to say that an accountant who disliked conservation would be asked. All had to have at least a working knowledge of, and appreciation for, the natural areas of the state.

I had sat on and witnessed too many boards—for-profit and nonprofit—that were torn asunder by conflicts of interests and turf wars. I had no time for, or interest in, a debating society. However, I did choose two members to represent the environmental and the hunting and fishing (the "hook and bullet") conservation arenas, respectively. For the most part they have served with active and supportive participation. We also put together an advisory council, which was broad and representative of many of the fine organizations and individuals who were devoting themselves to leaving the landscapes, parks, wildlife, and habitat of Texas better than they found it. Over the years, many from the advisory council helped guide TCC through the constantly changing labyrinth of people and issues.

By experience and through instinct I knew that I did not want a big staff or operation. Obviously a large operation is costly to maintain, and money is always tight for a fledgling organization. More important, I knew that this start-up was going to take at least four years to complete and that we would need flexibility to meet changing situations and challenges. I could hire specialists to meet specific needs without getting bogged down in time-consuming overhead, staffing decisions, and grievances. The day-to-day work of TCC was done by me and by my assistant, Linda McElrath. Everything else has been farmed out, depending on circumstance and need.

It was also apparent early on that we would need a rallying cry—a hook—to focus our efforts and those of elected officials, volunteers, and donors. But first I had to immerse myself in the politics, personalities, and processes of the world of the Texas conservationism in the twenty-first century. I would never know as much as those with a single mission, but I needed to know enough to communicate with each on some level of intelligence and sophistication.

The year 2001 looked to be a good year to begin, partly because there were no huge issues that required immediate mobilization, even though the state senate situation was in a rare state of flux. After Governor George W. Bush was elected president, his seat was vacated. Lieutenant Governor Rick Perry became governor, vacating *his* seat. The senate then, for the first time in history, would elect a new lieutenant governor from among their own, and the senate had a Republican majority. In late December 2000, Senator Bill Ratliff, with the unanimous support of Democrats, was elected. As he was a moderate Republican, many breathed a sigh of relief. Ratliff had shown throughout his career that he could work with both sides, especially in his role as chairman of the senate's Education and Finance Committees. He would more than honor that expectation, although it would later cost him dearly when he stood for election in his own right the following year. The conservative Republican special-interest contributors forced him out of the race. While lieutenant governor in 2001, out of commitment and gratitude, Ratliff appointed Senator Rodney Ellis chair of the senate Finance Committee, which bode well for me because he was a friend from the Bentsen and Hobby years. The lieutenant governor of Texas wields more real power than the governor, in great part because he or she appoints chairs of the various committees. In turn the chairs become the lieutenant governor's lieutenants on the floor and in committee—for the most part. The lieutenant governor also controls the agenda and legislative floor action. Thus bills only move when and if the lieutenant governor allows them to move. The legislature of Texas is set up to kill bills, it seems.

The House was still controlled by the Democrats. Speaker Pete Laney and the chairman of the Appropriation Committee, Rob Junell, were both friends of mine. The committee chair with jurisdiction over park matters was Edmund Kuempel, an old high school mate and a strong advocate for parks. At least I had friends I could talk with and learn from.

We were also armed with two excellent reports. The first was by a blue-ribbon committee that had been appointed by Governor George Bush. *Taking Care of Texas* addressed private lands, public lands, and water. Each section explored present and future needs in each category. Without going into great detail, they reported to Governor Bush on October 28, 2000, the following recommendations.

- Create a statewide Purchase of Development Rights (PDR) program for retention of private lands to thwart agriculture and habitat fragmentation.
- Reform tax laws to support conservation.
- Develop a comprehensive system to assess outdoor recreation needs.
- Fund the repair, development, and maintenance of existing public properties to meet the needs of a growing and urban population.
- Acquire assets of statewide significance to meet those needs.
- Divest properties that [are] underutilized.
- Ensure adequate quantity and quality of water to protect Texas's land and water ecosystem.
- Include the requirements of fish and wildlife in current water resource management.
- Promote agriculture water uses that also benefit wildlife.
- Protect Texas's springs.

Each of these recommendations was unanimously adopted by men and women who were for the most part Republicans, with not a radical "tree-hugger" in their midst. Each recommendation was arrived at based on public testimony, existing studies, and the work being completed by what was to be known as "the Texas Tech study"—*Texas Parks and Wildlife for the 21st Century*—published in 2001.

To a degree, the recommendations were complementary. Private lands, new parklands, and water were all tied to meaningful ecosystems. Private landowners were encouraged to open up their lands to ecotourism. Water conservation was tied directly to fish and wildlife well-being, which in turn runs a significant economic engine through hunting and fishing. The estimated economic benefits of the recommendations totaled over $36 billion annually in 2000.

The Bush committee left it to the legislature to arrive at methods of finance and amounts to be appropriated. And I would soon learn that reason, common sense, and unanimity carried little or no weight among some elected officials. Both the committee report and the Texas Tech study were more or less buried by those who cared little for the land and its people or who were simply peeved at someone or the system. I had to obtain bootlegged copies of both reports in order to read the deliberations and recommendations, which were noncontroversial in content, language, and purpose. The documents called for planning and implementing policies and programs that were essential to meet the needs of a population that would double by 2050. There was little time to waste.

As the 2001 session opened, I went to see my old friends and sought out new ones, particularly people who controlled the purse strings and legislative process. I went to every appropriations hearing, committee meeting, and legislative session related to conservation or parklands. Some, particularly appropriations meetings, went on into the wee hours. It didn't matter. I was taking notes, learning, and asking questions. I was blessed to have State Representative Myra Crownover from my hometown of Denton to explain the process and personalities. She also sat on the Cultural, Recreation, and Tourism Committee and had a passion for parks. On two or three occasions we went hiking at Lake Ray Roberts State Park near Denton and shared thoughts, which helped me focus on the daunting task of increasing funding for parks.

Sometime during the session Andy called on me for advice. He needed an introduction to the chairman of the senate Finance Committee, Rodney Ellis. There was an opportunity for a major bond package, and Texas Parks & Wildlife had a chance to benefit by $100 million if it passed the legislature and a vote of the people. Because Rodney had not served on committees of jurisdiction that affected TPWD in the past, he and Andy had had no opportunity to get to know each other well.

Rodney is a man of tremendous depth and scope. Though most of his pursuits lay in issues important to urban areas—education, jobs, clean air, and the like—he and I went way back and genuinely liked one another. He and Andy hit it off, too, and there was the added bonus that Rodney is a passionate bicyclist who loves to ride through city, state, and national parks. He said that he'd sign on, and then proceeded to be good to his word. That became important because Rob Junell, chairman of the House Appropriations Committee, had no love for Andy, TPWD, or parks. It was essential to have the counterbalancing support of the senate, particularly when the appropriation bills of the House and senate got to conference.

Conference committees are where proposed bills are agreed upon, stripped, or modified. It is essential to have allies who will stand pat, or, if necessary, cut the best deal possible. At the right moment (late in the session), Rodney Ellis cut such a deal. It was unexpected but the right thing to do. In their earlier discussions Andy had told Rodney of the rich treasure trove of the Levi Jordan Plantation. Andy had tried for years to draw attention to its possibilities. With Rodney's blessing, he sought and received $2 million from the state to restore the plantation, which is near Houston and had long been rotting away. The artifacts there are some of the richest sources of slave history, art, and lifestyle in Texas. Among items found have been old buttons with African carvings on the backs (presumably carved on button backs so that slave owners would not see them).

In my naiveté I took it upon myself to go see Rob Junell. For five or ten minutes he vented, loud and clear, about his issues with Andy and TPWD. I listened and then told him that I was not there representing Andy or the department. I was his friend who happened to have a deep commitment to parks for the people, and Texas's parks were in a shameful state of disrepair. I also said that parks were very popular, and in most cases when they were contained within a bond issue, parks carried the initiative to victory. He cooled down and said that he would give it some thought. Perhaps I had some small gift of persuasion. That is all it could have been, because I still had much to learn—I knew only enough to be passionate, not knowledgeable. The parks and wildlife part of the bond authorization survived and was included in what was to be known as Proposition Eight—and voters passed it by a sizeable margin in November of 2001.

Bond financing in Texas is an authorization for the legislature to appropriate funds within a measure. It is not a blanket approval to spend all the monies designated. This remains in the purview of the legislature, which can and does approve or withhold as it sees fit. Regardless, passing of a bond issue is a signal from citizens that they give their blessing to the bonds and the taxes to pay for them.

For the most part I am a "pay as you go" advocate, particularly if funds are presently available to accomplish a task. However, there are a number of instances where the "buy now, pay later" approach make sense. If a project can be carried out with today's dollars less expensively, even with the cost of interest, and can be realized from payments out of present and future revenues, then a good case for bonds can be made. The acquisition of parklands and historical sites is such a case. There is only so much land, and so the price of land will rise, particularly land near urban areas. In Texas's case in the late twentieth century and early twenty-first, that is where most of us live and will live continue to live in greater numbers, so the parks of the future must be located nearby. Except in recessions, those lands often skyrocket in value. The time best time to acquire is at today's prices. Then bond financing is perfectly acceptable. That is equally true of most capital repairs, where future deferred maintenance is often at a much higher cost than would have been addressing the problem immediately.

At the session's end I thought I had learned a great deal and contributed modestly to the cause. The issue of the bond authorization allowed me to educate myself and others on the need for increased funding for parks and conservation measures, such as the important concept of Purchase of Development Rights, which would allow farmers and ranchers to retain their lands under favorable tax and payment provisions and forestall further fragmentation of vital habitat and ecosystem holdings.

But in the process and in my naiveté I didn't pick up warning signals that Andy Sansom's position as executive director of TPWD was in jeopardy. I did know that he was under serious consideration to become the next director of the National Park Service.

He was among the most qualified state park advocates and administrators, and we was a personal friend of Karl Rove, who would certainly have weight to make that recommendation to President Bush. However, I didn't learn of this opportunity from Andy. During the spring of 2001 I received a call from David Rockefeller Jr., who wanted to know about Andy. He thought that Andy and Bernadette Castro of New York were the finalists. While I made a passionate pitch for Andy, we agreed that both candidates would be outstanding and we agreed to support Bush's choice. In early June, to everyone's surprise, the president appointed Fran Mainella of Florida. The best anyone could figure was that Jeb Bush, the president's brother and Florida governor, had weighed in. But why Fran Mainella? She hadn't registered on anyone's radar.

Andy's missed opportunity was not solely due to the intercession of Jeb Bush. There was trouble and bad blood in Texas. For one thing, there was the friction between Andy and Rob Junnell. What I didn't know then was that this extended to Speaker Pete Laney, who was a close ally of Junnell. Both had endorsed George W. Bush for president. Perhaps both had weighed in against Andy, as did others.

Most important, there was the new governor, Rick Perry. Andy had served honorably and well for eleven years, but with new administrations come new appointees, and it was time to make a change. Such changes can be accomplished with grace, but this was not the case with Andy. Perry began the process of change at TPWD by appointing Katharine Armstrong, daughter of Tobin and Anne Armstrong of Armstrong Ranch fame, as chair of the Texas Parks & Wildlife Commission. I knew the Armstrongs casually through the South Texas Bentsen connection. Though strong Republicans, they were never anti-Bentsen and often contributed to his campaign. My only meeting with Katharine, prior to her appointment, had been at a luncheon where we talked about the Bentsens and she inquired of the senator's health.

Therefore I had a favorable impression of her when she called in late June and asked to see me. We met at her home in San Antonio. We discussed issues and the need for a concerted effort to advocate passage of Proposition Eight. She specifically asked me what I thought her role should be as chair. Because I firmly believe in the concept of noblesse oblige, as demonstrated by the Rockefellers, Mellons, and others who had given their time and treasure to the national parks, I thought she had a golden opportunity to continue that tradition in Texas, coming from one of the great landed families. Without in any way abandoning property rights or the crucial and productive conservation efforts of private landowners, she could become a champion for the future enhancement of public lands. I went away pleased that she had been attentive and gracious with her time, and nothing over the summer led me to think differently.

At Andy's urging we called a luncheon meeting of all the agencies that would benefit by the passage of Proposition Eight. House member Talmadge Heflin, who had shepherded the portion of the appropriations bill dealing with the bond issue, attended. With his assurances that the leadership would support passage, we urged all attending to contact their various constituency groups at the local level. If all actively participated, most importantly the larger beneficiaries, we thought there was a good chance of success in November.

In August I set up an election PAC, began to solicit commitments, and laid out an inexpensive but adequate campaign. At the same time, TCC continued to grow, holding meetings in Houston, Dallas, and elsewhere. I didn't see much of Andy in July and August—there was no need for me to see him. I had an organization to build and I only had to share thoughts on the bond campaign every so often, as it seemed to be falling into place. Furthermore, no staff of an agency can actively participate in the operations of a political action committee. To a degree, that also applied to nonprofit organizations. While TCC had not received formal notification from the IRS, we were already operating within the ground rules dictated by the IRS and the Texas Ethics Commission.

My new friend, David Gochman, again rose to the occasion. Academy Outdoor Sports agreed to a shared advertising campaign, as well as shopping bag stuffers and window signs reminding people to vote in November and vote for Proposition Eight. At the end of the campaign he told me that several hundred thousand pieces had been distributed statewide and "vote for Prop 8" ads had run several times in all the communities where Academy had stores. Furthermore, because of his leadership, others in the industry participated.

In August, though, Andy told me that things had gotten ugly and untenable, and that he would announce his resignation the next day at the TPWD Commission meeting, but that he had made a deal to resign effective December 31, 2001, to allow a smooth transition, while being available to help to the degree allowed on the bond issue. I was heartsick. I knew that I was losing a valuable ally and would have little to no support from TPWD for the foreseeable future.

Regardless of the circumstances we had to press on. There was the bond issue, as well as a TCC-sponsored conference planned for September 14, 2001. "Seeking Common Ground: The Future of Texas Land-Water-Wildlife and Parks" was to be TCC's first attempt to bring representatives of as many as possible diverse groups in one room to work together on conservation. But it was not to be. September 11, 2001, put all thoughts of proceeding out of mind. Fundraising also came to a halt or slowed down during those dark days when America and the world held its breath.

Things did not come to a complete standstill. I was in Atlantic City at a board meeting on September 11, and with all air traffic grounded, four of us rented a car and headed west, hoping to catch the first plane available along the way. By September 13, Americans in Pennsylvania, Ohio, Indiana, and Illinois were clearly at work: farmers were in the fields, merchants were behind their counters, and school buses rolled, US flags adorning them all, it seemed. Finally in St. Louis a TWA flight to Texas had an available seat for me.

I'd been home only a day or two when Armstrong called. She wanted me to turn over the reins of the PAC to someone of her choosing. I told her that was not possible because the proper papers had been filed with the secretary of state, after consultation with the Ethics Commission, and no one directly connected with any agency could be part of the PAC or give it direction, including commissioners. I further said that all I could do was terminate the PAC and transfer the funds. I had the clear impression that this was part of the purge of all things relating to Andy Sansom, real or perceived.

It seems that while Governor Perry wanted Andy terminated, he left the details to Armstrong. For whatever reason, she took it upon herself to purge all Andy's friends and vestiges of his time with the agency. Her purge extended beyond the agency to other organizations, such as members of the staff and the board of the Texas Parks & Wildlife Foundation. At some point even photos of Andy, formal and informal, disappeared from the walls and halls of TPWD. This was totally unnecessary. A simple visit between the governor and Andy would have sealed the deal. Armstrong's petty and ham-handed action would split the Commission and the staff. Carol Dinkins, one of the most respected commissioners, resigned in protest. Others grumbled and complained but remained.

In retrospect it was a blessing to be relieved of the formal duties of the PAC. It allowed me time to figure out the direction of TCC, while in no way ending our involvement in advocating that Proposition Eight was necessary to the well-being of parks. As suspected, the prospect of additional park funding carried the $800-million proposition. News media had editorialized about parks. Support for parks had appeared in stuffers and on window signs. Organizations had pushed parks. On November 6, the proposition passed, 62 percent to 38 percent.

After the election I had a chance to regroup. Shortly before September 11 TCC had received IRS notification of our nonprofit status. Therefore, we could formally proceed. I concentrated on grant writing and reviving the "Seeking Common Ground" forum. The postponement allowed me time to enhance the program as well as better focus the message and mission in grant requests.

It was becoming most clear that for any chance of success in funding parks (or any new conservation venture), the focus had to be on economic benefits to local communities and the state. It may have been more rewarding to praise the spiritual, physical, and other intrinsic values of our shared natural and cultural treasures, but this would never have had the appeal of the almighty dollar. For me the epiphany came in a small insert that I had nearly overlooked in a 1998 study by Texas A&M. Dr. John Crompton, professor in the Department of Recreation, Park and Tourism Sciences, had surveyed four or five state parks and come forth with a revelation: parks, if properly maintained and financed, could give economic benefits to local communities, businesses, and merchants far in excess of the amount appropriated to the parks by the state.

Several nights after reading this, I would sit at a table with John Crompton and State Parks Director Walt Dabney. I told them that I thought a more substantial study was called for, and in the next day or so I went to see Walt. He was enthusiastic about the possibility of a major, park-by-park study. We called Crompton, and the delightful UK native said that, yes, such a study was possible and in his opinion long overdue, but that its validity rested on an accurate visitation count. I told Walt that I thought I could raise the funds to commission a study, but that it would be was incumbent on his department to verify the counts. I then drove to College Station to meet Crompton. After spending some time with him, I had a clear understanding of his method and what it would cost to commission a sample survey to calculate visitors' expenditures and economic impact, not with perfect accuracy but close enough to make workable assumptions and a valid case. We agreed in principle, subject to funding.

I was adamant about the visitor count because the matter had become an issue with the national parks during my term on the National Park Foundation. A number had been publicized, and then revised downward after a similar study, even though with the adjustment the number remained huge, more than enough to make the case that national parks continued to be one of the most enduring attractions for both US citizens and foreign visitors. I had every confidence this would be the case in Texas. That count was necessary to lend credence to the economic impact survey that TCC would commission and fund. After some negotiation and discussion of the parks to be selected, we struck a deal. Over the summer and fall of 2002, thirty-seven parks (a good cross-section of existing parks and historical sites) would be surveyed.

With that in progress, I turned my attention to the rescheduled "Seeking Common Ground" forum. We wound up with better speakers, including David Schmidly, who spoke convincingly about the scope of his Texas Tech study (ignored by those apparently uninterested in the collapse of one of Texas's richest assets—its landscape), and John Crompton, who not only is an educator but a motivator, and who made a complete case for the benefits derived from well-maintained parks. I came away satisfied that we had established an underlying foundation for our efforts.

The other thing we did right was to mix the forum's characters and content so that the diverse groups could share their missions and experiences with counterparts. A number of participants told me before the meeting that they thought Ducks Unlimited was a hunting club; that they had no idea it was a major rehabilitator of wetlands. Progress ever so small, but progress. In 2002 we would continue to listen and educate ourselves on the priorities and purposes of others.

By that summer I had substantially defined the problem. The solution would take time, more organization, refinement of mission, and eventually luck, a break, or both. It was becoming apparent that private landowners, water specialists, and hunters and fishers had well-financed and well-organized advocates—usually on both sides of any position. Parks had little voice and no clout—within or outside TPWD. While my natural inclination was toward parks, I did not think they were the only meaningful aspect of conservation, but I was coming to the opinion that they were ignored to the point of disrepair and might soon be irrelevant to citizens of Texas as well as out-of-state visitors. That was confirmed in TPWD's 2002 *Land and Water Resources Conservation and Recreation Plan*, which stated:

> The window of opportunity for conservation of natural resources and providing adequate access for outdoor recreation in Texas is closing. The state's population is expanding rapidly, land fragmentation is increasing and water resources are already stretched in many areas. Failure to ensure adequate water for wildlife now will impose a great cost on the citizens of Texas in the future. The loss or decline of these resources will have a greater impact on the economy than is readily apparent: it will negatively impact local economic development from the loss of hunting, fishing and other recreational tourism; it will increase state and federal regulations; it will increase costs to businesses and industries; and it will impact public services including municipal water supply and treatment. Furthermore, the cost of acquiring land to serve the public's recreational needs will also increase over time.

While I thought the Texas Tech study was an excellent blueprint for the future, its recommendations far exceeded any realistic consideration by a legislature (Democrat or Republican) prone to do little more than begrudgingly fund the status quo. That certainly applied to parks and even more so to appropriating funds for new land acquisitions crucial to meet the needs of an ever-increasing urban population. But if on that issue of parkland acquisition the Texas Tech study was too ambitious, *Land and Water Resources Conservation and Recreation Plan* was the opposite, giving only lip service to acquiring new park assets: a minimum of four new parks of five thousand acres (a valid calculation to meet ecosystem considerations as well as recreation ones), all to be located within an hour and a half driving time from major metropolitan areas—another valid criterion. What was distressing was that this minimalist recommendation was intentionally minimal, and had been added begrudgingly. Subsequently no parks of this magnitude have been added to the system, even though strongly supported in public opinion and even though funds have been available to do so from revenues from the "Sporting Goods Tax."

The so-called Sporting Goods Tax is not a separate tax but part of the state's sales tax revenues derived from sales of designated sporting equipment. It was made law in 1993 to replace the old tax on cigarettes, which by then was a diminishing source of revenue to fund state and local parks. The sponsors of the legislation saw the Sporting Goods Tax as a better source of revenue and one that would increase over time, due in large measure to an increasing growth in population in hikers, bikers, joggers, and their families.

Policy advancement on any issue, including setting aside more parklands for recreation, requires commitment not only from the public, but also from within appropriate government agencies. In our case this would not be forthcoming for several years. I knew that the efforts of TCC and its supporters would have to be mounted without any tangible support from its eventual beneficiary—TPWD, which even into the twenty-first century was dominated by a good ol' white boy mentality that weighed heavily on the side of private land and hunting and fishing. With this in mind we took our show on the road, with public forums, testimony, and visits with outdoor columnists.

Because I am an avid hunter and fisherman, I regularly read the outdoors column in the *Austin American-Statesman*. Mike Leggett is a superb outdoors columnist, but I saw that he rarely mentioned parks. And this was true of other such columnists around the state. To me that showed that park advocacy needed improvement to demonstrate the economic benefits of parks and their growing state of disrepair due to totally inadequate funding.

As 2002 progressed I became more convinced that the park-by-park analysis might hold the key to our ability to give substance and effective voice to our cause. Because the parks are localized, they would have relevancy to community leaders, elected officials, and local media. They would become more relevant than the distant and amorphous state park system. They would hit close to home.

In the fall TCC held a board retreat to sharpen our mission and focus. Through a facilitator we arrived at the conclusion that we would give weight to those areas of concern that called for funding, such as parks, water, and Purchase of Development Rights (PDR), while at the same time attempt to act as an "honest broker" among sympathetic but diverse groups. Each of these clearly fell within the purview of the Bush study, the Texas Tech study, and the TPWD study. All needed addressing with ample funding to achieve even modest goals. But the state, like the nation, was in a recession and faced a budget deficit going into the 2003 legislative session—a deficit of $10 billion as it turned out. That threw a damper on any sort of new or increased funding. However, I thought it would be a perfect time to highlight methods of financing in other states in the areas of park and, PDRs, and water.

Through the Texas Trust for Public Land, the Nature Conservancy, and others, we found measures that had recently been passed that addressed problems with more than platitudes. I also thought it important to invite to a symposium representatives of some states governed mainly by Republicans. Texas's statewide leaders were Republicans. Following the 2002 elections Representative Tom Craddick became Speaker of the House and Talmadge Heflin became chairman of the House Appropriations Committee. A wealth of measures had been passed in Republican states by Republican leaders such as Jeb Bush and Senate Majority Leader Jack Latvia in Florida, and former South Carolina legislator Chip Campson. The Florida Forever initiative was a multibillion-dollar program that covered the same needs as Texas's parks, PDRs, and water issues, financed by bonds and a documentary stamp tax. South Carolina's Conservation Incentive Act and Conservation Bank Act were financed by a deed transfer fee. Other methods of finance included state lottery funding, real estate transfer fees, license plates, and dedicated sales taxes. All in all it, this was a good mix that should have sparked great interest and thought-provoking dialogue. We even decided to hold the symposium in the capitol to facilitate attendance by legislators and staff. Unfortunately bad weather and bad timing would dampen attendance literally and figuratively.

On Monday, January 27, 2003 it rained. More significantly, the legislative session was just underway and it is a cardinal rule of legislative advocacy to never push new programs as the session is just beginning. We had a fair crowd, with some legislators and staff (particularly Speaker Craddick), but not all I had hoped for. The symposium speakers did give legitimacy to our contention that parkland and conservation measures were universal in appeal and that citizens were willing to pay for them. It also highlighted the completion of the 2002–2003 Texas A&M economic impact study, and again John Crompton's comments drew attention. Most importantly, we demonstrated that TCC could deliver diverse personalities, philosophies, and causes within a common framework and advance fresh ideas to the benefit of all who cared to listen and learn. TCC was now established as a major player in the conservation arena.

We did catch the attention of the new chair of the Cultural, Recreation and Tourism Committee, Harvey Hilderbran. At some point in February 2003 we talked, and we agreed that there was little chance of enhanced appropriations for anything. However, Hildebran asked me to give him my best thoughts, with the promise that these might be discussed in intcrim hearings after the session to amplify the plight of state parks, land fragmentation, and water problems, coupled with methods to finance measures addressing these. Given the budget deficit, that was all we could hope for. It was a start.

Then I had a brainstorm. What was lacking in all the reports was a dollar amount for appropriate funding. As I had said many times before and since, we could pass non-binding and non-funded resolutions of support, even authorizations, but without money, these are like kissing your cousin—pleasant, perhaps, but without meaningful results. So I wrote to Hilderbran in early March, asking him to file a "shell" bill to fund a $1-billion bond package for parks, PDRs and water. Why not? You might as well start high. You can always back off. To bring it back to reality, I suggested that the bill be taken to a public vote in November 2004, with bond funding not to kick in until 2005. After negotiation we agreed on $500 million.

A "shell" bill is a legislative method of filing before a deadline so that if something unforeseen occurs there will be a germane bill in play. Any expectations of final passage should never go beyond a faint hope. HB 2449 fit that category to a tee. Nonetheless it was on the table, with specific dollar amounts attached for each potential beneficiary: parks, PDRs and adequate water conservation programs.

Hilderbran then held a hearing. We expressed our thoughts for the record, and— lo and behold—he passed the bill out of committee, even without a word of support from commissioners or staff, though this was not surprising. That would be it for the session. It was all that could be hoped for, given the circumstances. But unbeknownst to me, favorable notice was taken.

As expected, we didn't have much to show for 2003, although a freshwater fish stamp was authorized to build new fish hatcheries and rehabilitate ones. Like many of the state's parks, most of Texas's hatcheries were products of the Depression, built with substantial financial help from the federal government's CCC and WPA. (Oh, those the ever-intrusive feds!) Additionally, a bill was passed to raise motorboat registration fees and motorboat manufacturers' and dealers' fees, and 85 percent of the increase would go to Fund 9 (hunting and fishing), but 15 percent would flow to Fund 64 (the state park account). This addition ($2.5 million, as I recall) was welcomed and necessary, as many of our state parks are located near lakes and rivers and were in need of boat ramps and other water-related improvements.

The other major accomplishment of the session was the passage of a major contingency rider (commonly referred to as the Entrepreneur Rider). Its passage meant that additional funds raised by various fee increases (estimated to be $31.5 million) would flow to Fund 9 and Fund 64, and be spent by TPWD during 2004–2005. Had it not passed, the department——and parks in particular—would have been thrown into chaos, though this would come soon enough anyway.

What remains a mystery to me is why the legislature doesn't take this particular rider off their all-too-crowded agenda. Every session it comes up again: the department and the legislature root around on this matter. It seems to me that if by valid and approved means the accounts generate revenue in excess of the comptroller's biennial revenue estimate, they should be allowed to be spent or saved. Most often and assuredly, as it applies to parks, the needs are so great and repairs and maintenance are so lagging that savings are unlikely. With declining numbers and revenues from hunters and anglers, I am sure that would hold true with Fund 9. This added revenue would allow some long-term business planning, which is far better than the hit-and-miss, beg-borrow-or-steal process that continues to engulf each session.

So 2003 was better than a poke in the eye, except for the local park grants program, also funded by the Sporting Goods Tax. At the outset I wondered why the state, given the apparent shortage of funds and the milking of the Sporting Goods Tax for other purposes, would be in the local parks business. But over time I came to support this local grant program enthusiastically. First, the state was nothing more than a seed-money venture capitalist. At relatively small cost this program could create significant leverage. Competing communities had to put up dollars or land or both, and successful bidders had to operate their programs with local funds and personnel. Furthermore, by way of the highly respected bidding matrix fashioned by TPWD and local communities, taxpayers were guaranteed of getting the best projects. It is only when outside influences enter the system that taxpayers are put at risk and conned.

Some legislators, often with no communication with their local park planners, and certainly without public hearings, cheat the system by inserting riders, often in the dead of night, that earmark funds for local grants in their districts. This is not only cheating but also hypocritical, because they go home and announce that they have accomplished this great thing at no increase in taxes. But this is not true, for two reasons. First, the local park officials have to scramble around for funds and lands. Second, it robs taxpayers in other locales from having their projects judged openly and fairly. It makes a mockery of process.

As part of a growing team that was capable of mounting an educational public awareness campaign and advocating effectively, I had now reached a position where I could articulate both message and process with some knowledge and nuance. It was gratifying to hear back from folks who not only had received our message but seemed to understand what we were talking about and who wanted to do more next time. And there would be a next time, because important people and institutions were now taking notice.

For all our efforts through 2003, we still lacked a coherent case for substantial increases in funding for parks and the need for a sustainable source of revenue. That was also true for purchase of development rights, but proponents of that crucial legislation were hesitant to place a price tag on the table. When asked about the validity of the $500-million bond package, my standard answer was, "Thank God it never got to a discussion of underlying numbers." The truth lay somewhere between the neglect by TPWD to develop a short-term and long-term case for funding to adequately finance operations, capital repairs, acquisition, and other essentials, and the fact that many among the commissioners and the staff really had no interest in enhancing the status of parks. By reputation the department was viewed by many as the pleasure ground for those who only cared about "hook and bullet" matters, private lands, and game warden issues. Parks for the use of the greater population were a by-product of former governor John Connally's consolidation and enhancement efforts of the 1960s. In 1967 he passed a major parkland acquisition package—$75 million in bonds. No equivalent effort to secure additional parks for people has been forthcoming to this day, over forty years later. Subsequent bond issues, like those of 2001 and 2007, were for repair and renovation.

It was becoming clear that funding needs and a reliable source of revenue had to be joined at the hip and sold together. To do that we had to make the case that economic benefits far outweighed the appropriated outlay. We had the tools—the first economic impact study of thirty-seven parks, with another forty-two parks commissioned to be surveyed, and the various aforementioned studies (most mandated by the legislature or the Sunset Advisory Commission)—and we had a growing base of supporters.

We were beginning to generate some press and community support. I had sent the initial Crompton survey to elected officials and chambers of commerce, as well as local media in communities with park sites. In the statehouse, committee chairman Harvey Hilderbran had the heart for the fight but clearly needed additional support. I was about to add another tool—a monthly series of four-color, two-page fliers on the economic and societal benefits of hunting, fishing, water, wildlife appreciation (especially birding), and parks. The pieces were intentionally short and easy to read. With design support from the firm Public Strategies, I crafted every page personally. Great support staff and designers can only take a project so far. By the spring and early summer I knew exactly what I wanted to convey with images and words, and I hoped to provoke thought and make a lasting impression.

We gathered into a master file all pertinent lists: donors, support organizations, media, chambers of commerce, and elected officials, state and local. Each month from June to October we sent out a slick position brief. Each month we got a few more responses and words of appreciation and encouragement. But it was the response that showed up at my office (generously donated by Public Strategies) in June of 2004 that was the most amazing and gratifying. There framed in the doorway was Ernest Angelo of Midland. Ernie had been a Bush appointee to the TPWD Commission, but was rotating off after completing his term. By any measure, Ernie fit the "hook and bullet" profile. He would move up or delay a medical procedure so as not to interfere with the opening of dove season. He financially supported TCC through our annual duck and goose hunt outings. He fished all summer in Colorado. He was as conservative as they come. As someone said, he was "the first full-time Republican in Texas." An oilman by profession, he was a public servant at heart, serving as mayor of Midland and on a number of federal and state boards and commissions.

"George," Ernie said, "I've followed your program with interest. I think you're on the right track and I'd like to help if I can." I could have kissed him, but that would have been awkward. We visited for a good while, and sometime during the conversation he allowed that he was about to leave for his summer home in Colorado. I must have asked where, because I was scheduled to visit Colorado with Jack and Patsy Martin in July. Ernie said that Beaver Creek, where I would go, wasn't far from his place, and he suggested that I stop by for a day or two of fishing and talking about parks.

Later that summer I took him up on this offer. After a much-delayed flight, I drove to the Angelo place, arriving around 3:00 a.m. Rather than disturb my hosts, I slept in the car. At dawn, Penny Angelo stuck her head out the door, then hurried away to tell Ernie that a strange car was in the driveway. Ernie came out, we had a good laugh about my late-night campout, and I was invited in for a good breakfast. For the rest of the day we fished in the Taylor River, one of the most beautiful flows in Colorado, and full of trout. Then, true to his word (an ongoing trait of Ernest Angelo), we sat down and visited about parks, their positive economic impact, and how they either directly or indirectly pay for themselves, with a substantial return on investment. He asked probing questions—and I had the answers.

By 2004 Texas ranked next to last among states in per capita expenditure on parks, and the case for additional funding could be made from simply the numbers alone. Calculations gathered from TPWD, the state's comptroller, and the Texas A&M economic impact report clearly proved the case. User fees and the Sporting Goods Tax paid for all but a small portion of the expense of parks. The Sporting Goods Tax revenues had increased and would continue to increase in sufficient amounts to cover even the most ambitious legislative appropriation. Finally, over and above these direct revenues, was the revelation that parks generate significant economic activity and sales within local communities.

What numbers do not enumerate is the spiritual, physical, and family well-being derived from well-maintained and attractive parks, especially for young people. Parks are inexpensive classrooms and fitness centers that provide recreation and renewal.

I asked Ernie Angelo why so unlikely a candidate as he would take such an interest. He said that he thought parks made good sense economically and were the last best places where young people and their families could connect or reconnect to natural and cultural treasures. In doing so he hoped that they would carry a conservation ethic with them throughout their lives.

Our time together was well spent. We mapped out a plan and drafted a letter I would send to Ernie that he would share, upon his return from Colorado, with Speaker Craddick. By late August he called and asked me to send a fuller letter of explanation to Speaker Craddick with as many back-up materials as I thought appropriate to make our case, and he asked me if I would make an appointment and visit with Craddick. I agreed and scheduled a meeting for right after Labor Day.

I was going to see an elected representative who had toiled as a Republican in the Democratic-controlled Texas House for thirty-four years. While remaining a partisan Republican Craddick had honed his legislative skills and abilities to work with members on both sides of the aisle to the degree that he had been appointed to several important committees by Democratic Speakers over the years. For years he was chairman of the all-important Ways and Means Committee. At one time he had been quite close to Speaker Laney, but they had recently had a falling out which I believe heightened Craddick's desire to obtain a Republican House. In 2003 his goal of a majority became a reality, and he became the Speaker. Smart, tough, and magnanimous in victory, he honored the tradition afforded him and appointed Democrats to a number of chairs. He also demoted and sometimes belittled Republican members who did not toe his line. Accommodating, yes, but demanding absolute loyalty.

I knew Craddick only by reputation, save for one chance meeting on an airplane. During the flight he asked where I had been. When I told him I'd been to a national park meeting, his eyes lit up, and he described at some length how he and his wife, Nadine, loved national and state parks. He recalled with great enthusiasm and joy how much his family looked forward to those outings. I had tucked that fact away. Even so, I didn't know what to expect.

He could not have been more gracious. He could not have been more attentive. My basic pitch was that there simply had to be a lifting of the cap on the Sporting Goods Tax, if not completely, then up to a number adequate to stop the bleeding and start re-habilitating the state park system. I think we discussed a new cap of $85 million. He kept listening and I kept talking, pointing out that this increase was not for a new tax but was part of the sales tax revenue flow that had long been diverted to other uses and programs. I said that I thought this increase would pay rich dividends and should be looked upon as an investment for the future, particularly in view of the A&M survey, which was being up-graded to seventy-nine parks as we spoke. Craddick kept listening. Then I raised a serious concern. Lifting the present $32-million annual cap, imposed in 1995, by any amount would create the need for additional appropriations, causing a negative fiscal note. A $53-million increase to $85 million in the Sporting Goods Tax might well be a deal-killer.

Craddick smiled and said, "Not if it is accompanied by a 'Dynamic Fiscal Note.'" My face must have conveyed confusion and ignorance. He explained that John Sharp (at the time the state comptroller) and he, as chairman of the Ways and Means Committee, had invented it. The crux of their "invention" was that there would be recognition on the part of the legislature and the comptroller that certain expenditures, while creating a temporary negative budget impact, should be looked upon as a long-term investment that would generate new and increased revenues.

We both smiled. Clearly all the work that had been done—and that was being done on the seventy-nine-park survey—would prove that parks are a wise investment. Craddick then told me that there was a problem that had nothing to do with our case or the validity of our calculations. He and the current comptroller, Carole Keeton Stray-horn, did not get along, so much so that the Speaker told me that we would have to seek out members of the legislature who could approach her. I told him that I would work on that and that perhaps I could informally broker the matter, as Carole and I were friends going back to Austin High. He said that would be fine at the right time but that we also needed a member, like Jim Keffer, current chairman of Ways and Means, to make a formal request. Keffer would be the most logical member to shepherd the tax part of the measure through the House. All tax matters under Texas law and legislative procedure must originate in the House of Representatives and go through that committee. We ended the meeting on a gratifying note.

Within hours after the meeting, staff members from TPWD were nervously calling to find out what was afoot. Because the meeting had been exploratory in nature, I saw no reason to tell anyone. It could have ended on a negative note, so why bother? Too many chefs in the kitchen, particularly at the outset, never complete a meal. They just argue. Much gets burned, nothing gets cooked. At some point I did brief them, giving my best analysis of what needed to happen to forge a complete package with an attendant but separate lobbying team, media and organization education, distribution of the forthcoming seventy-nine-park study, and a public opinion survey.

In 2001 and 2003 the lobbying efforts of TCC had been minimal and well within the guidelines of the IRS rules. But 2005 was going to be different and more intense. I got a thorough briefing on the law, just to be sure of what we and other supporters could do, and then I went to see David Gochman. Years before David had set up an organization, Texas Outdoor Recreation Alliance (TORA), which lobbied for the original Sporting Goods Tax legislation and other matters pertaining to the industry. The organization was still in play—on paper. David agreed to renew its activities and help finance the effort through its members and Academy Outdoor Sports. Paige Cooper, who had been the clerk of the Cultural, Recreation and Tourism Committee, and Corky Palmer, a veteran sports product distributor and former TPWD employee, were chosen to be the lobbying team for TORA. I also registered as a lobbyist with the Texas Ethics Commission.

That handled, I went to Brownwood to meet Jim Keffer. I did so through a first-class citizen and park enthusiast, Brad Locker, who was a TORA member and Republican county chairman of Brown County. Keffer was very receptive to lifting the cap and other aspects of our proposed legislative initiative to enhance the parks. He offered to be the primary cosponsor to what would be Hilderbran's bill. This all made good sense as Jim was chair of the Ways & Means Committee that would have to pass on the portion of the bill lifting the cap and would have to accept the Dynamic Fiscal Note. We still needed help with Strayhorn because Keffer had a problem with her.

With Speaker Craddick's assurance that he would talk to the Calendars Committee chair at the right time, the House had come to order, at least in theory. But we had to educate Carole Strayhorn on the validity of our fiscal case, we had to educate the press, and we had to gain the support of Lieutenant Governor David Dewhurst and the Senate. Nothing was set in concrete, although there was reason to be hopeful that parks were to be given a fair hearing, and the machinery was in motion to substantially increase funding by at least $53 million annually.

From mid-October until the end of the year we marshaled our forces and resources. We reached out to every contact and organization that might hold sway with legislators. We supplied informative ammunition. We prepared letters to editors and set up teams to visit with editorial boards. We prepared to issue the upcoming seventy-nine-park survey. We commissioned a public opinion survey that was conducted in early December. We now had a hook, and we could focus on a disciplined, well run, and adequately funded statewide campaign. For the first time, I felt a real sense of accomplishment, with prospects of success.

But the Texas Legislature is set up to kill bills and it can, in its manipulative ways, confound seasoned lobbyists, the press, and others not used to being confounded. We weren't even out of 2004, so we had to lead from strength early in 2005, and then apply and keep the pressure on. In February (when the session went into work mode), we released the A&M study, which again demonstrated our case that parks—good parks— have direct and indirect economic benefit that will generate a significant return on investment. On February 16 we released the poll data that showed that Texans strongly supported measures to protect natural resources and parks. The support was very strong in every region, political party, and ethnic group. Seven out of ten Texans were willing to pay $12–60 per year in additional taxes for new parks, as well as land, water management, and natural habitat. To accomplish that, 65 percent of Texans favored lifting the cap on the Sporting Goods Tax, and this included a healthy percentage of those who called themselves "fiscal conservatives."

Two other items of note were apparent. With the poll numbers practically a mirror reflection of earlier polls, David Hill, founder of Hill Research Consultants, offered an analysis: "The remarkable consistency of these attitudes across time suggests that we are measuring long-term values rather than floating opinions. The values are so well internalized that they are likely to influence public opinion far into the future."

Texans of all persuasions, by an equally large percentage, did not like, however, the fact that their state legislators could divert funds from their intended purpose for other programs. That would have been an even greater number if in a poll we could have explained how the revenues from the Sporting Goods Tax had increased from about $58 million in 1993 to around $100 million in 2006, but that hundreds of millions of dollars had been diverted from use for park operations and development over a twelve-year period.

The Sporting Goods Tax is a dedicated account to be used by state and local parks for the well-being of Texans. Between park visitor fees and this tax revenue a great portion of the budgeted expenses are generated. According to Comptroller Strayhorn's estimates for fiscal years 2006–2007, the dedicated sales tax revenues would total $205 million in the biennium, leaving some $141 million after deducting the capped amount of $32 million annually, so why was the legislature hesitant to honor the intent of the 1993 legislation? The overarching reason is the legislature's dislike of truly dedicated accounts. The Sporting Goods Tax account is dedicated in name only, and only for cosmetic purposes. To be binding, a measure to permanently dedicate such revenues would require a constitutional amendment and a vote by the people. Legislators and statewide elected officials know that such an amendment would pass—park-funding measures succeed in the polls—but that would take the matter out of their hands, and that is unacceptable. Some in the legislature, regardless of party, come to believe that the people's money becomes theirs. To the best of my knowledge, the chairs of the House and Senate committees of jurisdiction introduced bills every session of the remaining years of the twentieth century and early twenty-first century to allow such an amendment to be voted on by the people, but the arguments of Representative Edmund Kuempel and Senator Buster Brown arguments fell on deaf ears.

The other reason for the lack of consideration of any increase in the cap—or its outright abolition—was that there had never been a concerted chorus of concern about the plight of the parks and about the fact that taxpayers and parks had been short-changed for years. At least as far back as the 1970s, when the penny-a-pack cigarette tax dedicated to the acquisition and development of state parks and historic sites was passed, diversions by TPWD commissioners immediately took place. In a 1995 article entitled "The Strange Case of the Missing Parks," Griffin Smith in *Texas Monthly* wrote of the continuing saga. Of the $53 million collected under what was then Fund 31, less than $9 million went to acquisition. What was TPWD funding? A new headquarters building, salaries, and projects pushed by influential legislators and commissioners.

Even though to one degree or another we faced these same oppressive forces, HB 1292 was introduced by Harvey Hilderbran on February 17, 2005. It raised the cap to $85 million: $58.5 million to state parks, of which $18 million was to be used for acquisition and development, $25.5 million to the local parks grant account, and $2 million for bond debt service. It would not bring the state's parks back to world-class status, but it was a start in the right direction. Furthermore, as the bill moved, we would have an opportunity to amend it if necessary.

Hopes and expectations were high then. We had support up and down the line in the House. Senator Whitmire of Houston agreed to sponsor and handle the bill in the Senate and we had the blessing of the Speaker. But we didn't have the Dynamic Fiscal Note, and Harvey Hilderbran, who claimed he was close to Comptroller Strayhorn, would not move. The Ways and Means Committee stood ready and by then a majority of its members had signed on.

Weeks went by with no action in the statehouse. That did not mean inaction on our part. Throughout March into April we met with the editorial boards of major dailies. We sent out letters to the editors to all the rest. The response was favorable, with both editorial and column coverage. We had local organizations and individuals visit or call representatives. We hammered home the poll results at every opportunity.

Then the bottom dropped out. By mid to late April the Speaker and the lieutenant governor were in a fight over school financing—and I'm sure other matters. They never seemed to get along. Because of the uncertainty of the cost of school financing, the Speaker pulled down two hundred to three hundred bills with negative fiscal notes. Yes, HB 1292 had a negative note. Strayhorn had eventually issued her opinion, saying that while she had confidence that enhanced parks were a good investment, with every prospect of a substantial return on that investment, she had (without telling anyone, to my knowledge) decided not to issue such opinions, except for those measures that exceeded more than $100 million in fiscal impact. By May 1, HB 1292 was dead. We tried to perfect several legislative substitutes, but to no avail.

By session's end I was ready to throw in the towel—and almost did. But word came to me over the summer from Ernie Angelo who asked me to hang in and go another round. I said that I would think about it but would have to do a great deal of checking, especially with supporters and donors, specifically the large foundations: Houston Endowment, the Brown Foundation, and the Meadows Foundation. I had assured them that our work would be completed in 2005.

Over the summer my interest was again stirred because it was apparent that the park funding that finally was appropriated in 2005 would not be sufficient to cover rising utility costs, fuel costs, and other expenses. If $4 million was not made available through a process commonly known as "budget reconciliation," many parks would have to be partly closed, staff laid off, and programs curtailed. Some consideration was given, though not wholeheartedly, and then Hurricane Rita hit and any chance of supplemental funding went by the wayside.

Simultaneously TPWD was caught up in a controversy that caused a firestorm of protest. Through a proposal that was less than transparent, there was a pending sale of a portion of land of the Big Bend Ranch State Park to a private landowner. The question of its validity never rose to the fore. Regardless of the merits of the transaction (and there were some), what was significant was the perception that the department was dealing in secrecy. And there was truth in that. Organizations and newspapers raised hell. I had a different take, and said so to several newspapers. My position was that this was the byproduct of the long neglect of adequate funding and the desperate act of commissioners and staff who were looking for a dollar wherever possible. Because of the statewide flap, the commissioners backed down and canceled the contract. By December of 2005 and early 2006, parks were partially shut, employees were laid off, and programs were curtailed. The wheels had come off.

But the crisis led to a rallying cry—it seemed perverse that it took such a crisis to motivate protest—and action. All those surveys, polls, letters to the editors, and materials we'd generated suddenly were relevant and useful after all. The A&M survey pointed to the impact on local communities and it placed park closings and potential closings in a whole different light. This wasn't just a system-wide failure—it was one that could shut down your local park. That put it right at everyone's doorstep. Before we entered the 2007 legislative session, every major newspaper and most smaller dailies and weeklies ran editorials and columns about the parks crisis, some more than once, and some—like the *Fort Worth Star-Telegram* and *Houston Chronicle*—often.

With this opportunity at hand, another one arose. TPWD Chair Joseph Fitzsimons and I had had several conversations about renewing the Texas State Parks Advisory Committee. The committee hadn't done much in the last few years. I told Joe that it was a good idea as long as the members carried weight and covered the waterfront from conservation to tourism. Fitzsimons is a multigenerational South Texas ranch owner, who by heritage and circumstance should have stuck to policies regarding private lands, water, and property rights. But he is a decent man with a capacity to grow, and he embraced the need for a strong committee. We recruited several people and then I went to see a friend, former state senator John Montford, who had authored the original Sporting Goods Tax in 1993. John had served in the statehouse with distinction, receiving the "best of legislators" designation from *Texas Monthly* magazine on several occasions. Former lieutenant governor Bill Hobby told me that John Montford and Kent Caperton were the best state legislators during his long tenure. John went on to serve with great success as the chancellor of Texas Tech University and more recently as president of the western region of AT&T. Because of his background and his reputation for firm but nonconfrontational leadership, he was the perfect choice to chair the committee. He heard me out and agreed to do so—so long as I would handle the day-to-day lifting. In March of 2006 a well-rounded and influential committee met. Our charge was multifold, but focused on defining the method of financing that would best fit the needs of Texas's parks within a framework of legislative reality. Of tantamount importance was that the staff spell out those financial requirements on a category-by-category basis. In 2003 and 2005 we had flown by the seat of our pants because we had no true figures from TPWD on what was necessary to at least adequately meet requirements.

Over the next several months in formal meetings, subcommittees, and informal discussions, we pulled together a working document that eventually called for substantial increases for operations, major repairs, local park grants, and acquisition of at least four major new parks near urban centers. We also reaffirmed that the Sporting Goods Tax was the best and most reliable source of revenue. For 2008–2009, it was estimated that the "tax" would generate $110 million annually—more than enough to wholly support our recommendations, particularly if the major repair component ($25 million annually) and the land acquisition component ($15 million annually) were funded through a voter-approved bond issue. However, we also strongly urged that our recommendations be addressed on a pay-as-you-go basis.

Finally, we stressed the need for increased public-private partnerships, as enshrined at Government Canyon State Natural Area near San Antonio, and recommended that the department continue to explore transfers of existing units within the system to local governments, but only if those transfers resulted in significant savings and where appropriate requirements for future use were clearly enumerated.

This document was not a Cadillac but a good, solid Chevrolet—adequate and meaningful, but without frills. We released our findings in late August to much fanfare and good reception from almost all quarters. Our recommendations were presented to the TPWD commissioners a few days later and were unanimously accepted. From that acceptance came the request that was forwarded to the legislature as the 2008–2009 Legislative Appropriation Request. Euphoria reigned, but barely perceptible storm clouds were gathering.

Lieutenant Governor Dewhurst and at least one senator, Steve Ogden, were not happy with the critical press coverage. They thought that somehow it was directed at them. I reviewed all the articles I retained, and very few mentioned either one—or any other legislator—by name. This was a longstanding problem, going back to the years when Democrats controlled the statehouse, although Republicans had not done anything to improve the situation since they had gained power. John Montford and Commissioner Ned Holmes were deputized to visit with Dewhurst. I went to see Blaine Brunson, director of budget for the lieutenant governor, and Ogden, who then chaired the Senate Finance Committee. Blaine had been very helpful to me since my first years of Texas conservation work. The crux of my conversation with Blaine was that Dewhurst and Ogden had been caught by surprise, that TPWD had never presented a case to them. I told him that all sorts of materials had been sent by TCC over the years, spelling out the crumbling circumstances of our parks, including the studies mandated by various sessions of the legislature or the Sunset Advisory Commission, a legislatively controlled body. Blaine allowed that that was probably true, and said that it was unfair for me and others to have gone to so much trouble, only to be ignored by officials and staff who apparently have little time to read, much less study, even basic documents. We then discussed the unhappiness that prevailed. I told him none of our work was meant as a personal affront, and that the park problem went back for decades, particularly the last twelve years after the capping of the Sporting Goods Tax by Democratic leaders. Then I asked, "What would happen if we'd done nothing to highlight the plight of the parks?" "Probably nothing," was Blaine's reply. All in all it was a pleasant meeting, but he did impart his suspicions of TPWD and its habit of changing numbers. I could not comment on that, but did say that I would raise hell if it changed the calculations we had recommended. We parted with the understanding that we would stay in touch as the session drew near.

The other sign of storm was rumors that the Texas Historical Commission (THC) was going to make a run at stripping all or some of the historic sites from TPWD. Over the years John Nau, the chairman of the commission, had coveted some of the sites, even though historic sites had been a part of the park system since the outset, when the San Jacinto Monument was built in the 1920s. Like other state parks they had deteriorated over the years, not due to purposeful neglect on the part of TPWD but to lack of funding.

The word went out that Nau had the Speaker in his hip pocket. I thought that was a bit crass. John Nau was a big Republican contributor to many legislators, including the Speaker. In my opinion he was perfectly within his rights to seek support for his point of view. What was vexing, though, was that there seemed no clear reasoning behind his desires. There were no hearings, and there was certainly no thought given to looking at each property to ascertain whether it belonged under a particular state agency, something recommended by the State Parks Advisory Committee. That recommendation was fortified by the recent Historical Commission's Sunset Commission review and the Senate's Government Organization Committee. Both entities would not condone such transfers without adequate review, and certainly not unless such a reassignment would mean substantial net savings.

All this aside, it was clear that the battle was to be waged on a political, not a scientific or cost-saving basis. It would ultimately nearly wreck the chance to finally lift the cap entirely and provide substantial and sustainable funding for state and local parks—and historic sites. What followed would require an effort unmatched in the history of conservation legislation or politics in Texas.

TORA would again serve as the lobbying arm, with a budget of $100,000.00. All supporting organizations were put on notice that they would be called upon to mount e-mail campaigns and media efforts. *Texas Monthly* agreed to run a pro bono ad reiterating the plight of parks. A plan was reinstated regarding letters to editors and visits with editorial boards, and this time we asked local supporters to visit the smaller dailies and send letters. The local parks groups circulated a resolution among cities, towns, and chambers of commerce. Over two hundred local groups would sign on.

Testimony was prepared for the various committee hearings. I had asked A&M for a new update on the parks survey, so we would have reaffirmation from the latest data. Based on seventy-nine state parks, the total annual economic activity was calculated to be an estimated $859 million in sales and $484 million in residents' income, accounting for an estimated thirteen thousand jobs. Not a bad return on an investment of less than one-tenth of one percent of the budget, particularly given that Texas was second from last among all states in per capita expenditure on parks. Almost any increase would produce a greater return.

Specific tasks were assigned to John Montford, former House member Clyde Alexander, and TPWD commissioners, as well as major political donors who supported parks. The chairman, commissioners, and staff of TPWD weighed in within the limits of their legal boundaries, providing resource materials and support. By the opening gavel in January of 2007, I thought that we had done everything possible to bring outside influence to bear on an institution that bordered on indifference and complete inertia with regard to parks and conservation in general.

At the earliest opportunity, Representative Hilderbran filed HB 6—on January 8, 2007, and the governor included it on his list of "emergency items," which meant that it would be on a fast track if acted upon. A companion bill—SB 252—was filed in the Senate by Craig Estes. Then nothing happened, even though in short course we obtained 25 Senate sponsors (out of 31) and over 120 House sponsors (out of 150). Even with the historic sites brouhaha, the bill should have been moved forward to take advantage of momentum. We had finally positioned park enhancement and funding as a major legislative agenda item, but nothing happened.

Not until February 21 was a hearing in the House held. Then, to confuse matters, a substitute bill (HB 12) was filed on March 9, but did not pass on the House floor until May 3, very late in the process. Recall again that the Texas legislature meets only every other year.

One matter particularly caused heartburn. In early March a state auditor's report was released that was highly critical of TPWD and parks. It was a bombshell. Its timing was suspect and some of its recommendations were nonsensical. Its findings on park visitations were done hurriedly, with particular emphasis on the so-called "phantom loss of $16 million." This amount was arrived at because it had been the long-established policy of the parks (not to mention most other private and public recreation and entertainment venues) to allow scouts, seniors, children, and church groups to enjoy the parks at discounted rates or for free. TPWD policy makers could not have been too derelict in their duty, because from FY2002, when the A&M visitation study was commissioned, through FY 2006, park visitations had dropped from twenty million to ten million visitors, while annual revenues had increased from $22 million to $33 million.

But among the recommendations in the auditor's report there was that public hearings be held before any transfers, closures, or sales of parkland. This was reasonable, but it had been totally ignored by the Texas Historical Commission. Parks & Wildlife should have unilaterally called for such hearings and hung the site transfer issue out to dry. But they didn't—and nothing happened.

Or at least nothing on the surface seemed to be occurring. Backroom doors were opening and shutting frequently, however. Transparency was ignored. Tempers flared in some quarters. From time to time we would hear bits and pieces—the number of parks recommended to be transferred to the Historical Commission moved from thirty-four to zero to twenty-one and every number in between. The major problem was that the Speaker would not step in and slam the gavel down for a resolution. In the meantime, the House Appropriations Committee was left waiting to assign numbers to complement the various funding slots of HB 12, so they left big-ticket items pending, subject to HB 12 moving and passing the Senate. It was turning into a dangerously delayed mess. The key players were the Speaker, who kept hands off; John Nau, who coveted what wasn't his but didn't want transparency; and Harvey Hilderbran, who was trapped, not knowing which way to turn and not having a House support team with any firepower. The latter problem was clearly of Hilderbran's own making. Others and I had urged him to assemble such a team to help him through the process. But Harvey wanted the credit all to himself. As we would learn, he came within an inch of receiving all the blame for abject failure. But we were not to be counted out yet.

We redoubled our visitation and e-mail campaign effort, so much so that someone at one friendly office asked me to turn off the "bubble machines." We went back to news sources and editorial boards and explained that the entire effort was in jeopardy. The measure was stuck in the House because of the historic sites issue and in the Senate because Lieutenant Governor Dewhurst would not let either SB 252 or park appropriations move.

Finally, on May 17, two weeks before the session's end, the lieutenant governor called a meeting of all interested parties—TPWD commissioners, three citizen leaders (including me), senators, and staff of the Senate and TPWD who dealt with budgets and appropriations. He began by smiling at me and said, "We've gotten the message." It was time to hammer out a deal. We went through what we had asked for in the various categories, and what might realistically pass out of the Senate Finance Committee. There were holes, but the numbers was closing. Then Dewhurst said that he wanted $25 million for the USS *Texas*. This was not a surprise because the State Parks Advisory Committee had given that item back to the legislature. Since it had been given to Texas by the federal government (which was glad to get rid of it), the battleship had been planted in a saltwater marsh that had continuously eroded the great ship's outer hull and innards. Even with two or three major repairs, it had always fallen back into serious disrepair—rotting and rusting because enough funds were never forthcoming to permanently dry-dock the vessel. To do so would cost millions of dollars, and so we had concluded that the legislature needed to decide once and for all what to do. The lieutenant governor had decided on the figure of $25 million over the biennium without any supporting analysis. This would be part of a bond package to be announced, he said.

The second matter was a shock. Land Commissioner Jerry Patterson, it seems, with no public hearings or transparency of any sort, had wheedled a $25-million commitment out of Dewhurst and his former Senate colleagues for a beach erosion project of questionable benefit. Other such projects along the East coast—federal and state—had fallen into the pork-barrel boondoggle classification. And, oh, by the way, the project was to be funded out of the revenue from the Sporting Goods Tax, robbing Peter to pay Paul. This is an egregious example of "good ol' boy" backroom dealing. How could the legislature, the state auditor, the Legislative Budget Board, or any other governmental body demand transparency, accountability, and cost analysis after having handed out $25 million, attaching none of these? Then they cry crocodile tears when they are accused of wrongfully diverting funds for purposes other than intended.

Then there was the freshwater fish stamp fiasco. The stamp was passed in 2003, and its revenues were to go to pay for new and rehabilitated fish hatcheries. Income from sales of the stamps was to be deposited in Fund 9 for the sole use prescribed. But the stamp was producing revenue greater than expectations. In 2005 the legislature in effect diverted most of those funds by switching to bond debt service, which is less expensive in the initial years but accumulates great cost over time. It used the remainder to balance the budget. In 2007 the sportsmen and sportswomen of the state were still fuming and advocated full funding out of proceeds—and there were plenty of proceeds. What the lords taketh away, they usually do not give back, even if it is a bait-and-switch scam. But enough pressure was applied in this case and they gave in.

Finally someone with a magic Ouija board concluded that eighteen was the right number of historical sites to transfer and that THC would receive 6 percent of the Sporting Goods Tax appropriation to "run them better." Whether they are now "run better" remains to be seen to this day. But many individuals and organizations had toiled for years to achieve that money, with not a drop of sweat from any THC member or staff. With no effort and no transparency THC got more funding to do what TPWD had cobbled together with duct tape and baling wire over the years because of underfunding.

And so it was time to vote and declare victory for the time being. In spite of the flaws, machinations, and hypocrisy, a significant increase in funding in every category save acquisition would be enacted. It was a new beginning, with one more hurdle ahead.

Legislatures usually run true to form (except for the one in California). The odds for this increase if the Speaker has significant power, has appointed allies from the opposing party, has majority ownership of his own House, and a majority status in the Senate. Throw in a governor with little power and you have a winner. That is, unless in the course of a session that Speaker alienates the governor, the lieutenant governor, a majority of the Senate, and a new majority of his own House, consisting of mostly Texas Democrats and fifteen or so Republican members who are ready to risk life and limb in revolt.

The revolt started in 2004 and ramped up in 2006 when Speaker of the House Tom Craddick, with money supplied from right-wing conservative sources, demanded absolute loyalty. If someone did not toe the mark, opponents were recruited and financed. Most of the "disloyal," eight or so, won anyway. They had been ticked off to start with and they were furious in victory, as were most of the Democrats who had come only a few votes short of a majority. Add to this a group of Republicans who had become fed up with Craddick's all-powerful interference, and things finally boiled to a head on May 24, the Thursday night before session end in 2007.

Rumors began to float that there would be a move to vacate the Speaker's chair, a dethronement of monumental consequence. On Thursday night the explosion erupted. Heated criticism came from Republicans, with Democrats egging them on. Finally there was a call for a vote to end Craddick's reign. He ruled that the motion was out of order. His handpicked parliamentarian ruled against him. He fired her on the spot and replaced her with strong-willed allies with cast-iron stomachs. The battles and verbal abuses raged back and forth. Craddick held firm, but a new, previously unseen resolve ran through the House—and a coalition of Republicans and Democrats broke the quorum and shut down business two days before adjournment. It now looked like sayonara to HB 12.

At the time many of my friends in the House galleries were in agreement: "Throw the bum out!" But I was horrified and maddened because Tom Craddick held the fate of our bill in his hands.

While all this theater was afoot, HB 12 was having its own problems. Hilderbran had been urged to recruit wise and strong co-leaders, but, wanting all the credit himself, he had sent as his representative to the House-Senate Conference Committee his clerk, a person of little weight when matched against the senators and their staff. Todd Kercheval was outclassed to the point of jeopardizing acceptance of the bill by me, others and TPWD. Instead of a straightforward parks-funding bill with a resolution about the historical sites jurisdiction thrown in, it became a Christmas tree with every imaginable garish ball attached. It was so bad that Hilderbran called, wondering if he should pull the bill. I tried to calm him down and said I'd poll some of the most affected and get back to him. Sometime late on Saturday afternoon the staff of TPWD decided that on principle it should be pulled, but there was enough good to make it digestible—barely. I called Hilderbran back, only to discover the House revolt had exploded, and the quorum was broken. No business could be conducted. Finally I reached him and said that while we agreed that we had been poorly represented, there was enough good and necessary that we ought to live with the bad.

Overnight and into early Sunday morning John Montford, Clyde Alexander, and I, with the help of our team, called and begged our friends in the House to return to establish a quorum. Sometime later that day that occurred. But we were not home free yet. It seemed the Speaker had a major water bill that Lieutenant Governor Dewhurst wanted as his legacy, and Dewhurst held HB 12 in the Senate, awaiting passage of the water bill. But on the vote for this bill in the House, Harvey Hilderbran voted "present, not voting," and it lost by one vote. The word came to me from the Senate that unless the water bill was turned around, we could say goodbye to HB 12. I tried to reach Hilderbran. Then I called Kercheval who said, "We are ready to negotiate." I can't recall whether the pregnant silence came before or after my expletive in response, but I told him that there was no time left to negotiate and to tell Hilderbran to switch his vote or face grave consequences—from the press, his colleagues, from me, and every constituency group I could reach.

It is impossible for me to make sense of that mentality. All one can do is yell at it loud enough to make it react before it is distracted. The water bill was reconsidered and passed, as did HB 12—the last bill in the last hour of the 80th Session of the Texas Legislature. After nearly seventy-two hours of a nonstop ride and practically no sleep for many, the session ended.

The good news was that the bill did lift the cap on the Sporting Goods Tax. It did direct a preponderance of new funding to parks in every category, for every need save acquisition. Then it wandered off in all sorts of small favors and mischief-making riders.

On the surface they looked harmless enough, but most were penalizing make-work that no one would pay attention to, particularly in the legislature. There was even an insert saying that future funding was subject to appropriations, meaning the increases could be honored or not by future legislatures. The Senate sponsor publicly declared victory for the parks, but I wasn't so sure. There were significant increases, particularly when coupled with a new bond package, Proposition 4, which added more funding to capitol projects. It did raise the bar and aid a system so starved that crumbs might have seemed a gourmet meal. This was far more than crumbs, even more than the proverbial half a loaf. Was it worth all my effort, and the efforts of so many others? If so, what lessons were learned?

These questions can be answered on several levels, but for me personally it was a new experience. It was ultimately soul-rewarding to build an organization that through education, perseverance, patience, and gathering clout would create a loftier paradigm for parks and conservation. I now know that this work was meant to be my repayment of debt to the earth. To see our individualized park survey take on meaning not only across Texas but also among other states and federal agencies was welcomed proof of our judgment and methodology. Because we surveyed only park visitors who resided outside a park's host county, we had the most accurate picture of the economic impact of the parks on those counties and their businesses.

For all my criticism of some in the statehouse and the legislative process, I thoroughly enjoyed the opportunity to start with a nearly blank slate and to move park funding to a position of much higher priority among the many elected officials who do care— there are many who care, on both sides of the aisle. Above all, I was lucky to meet and be befriended by an extraordinarily diverse collection of Texans dedicated to the task of leaving our state better than they found it: Republicans and Democrats, urbanites and rural dwellers, liberals and conservatives regardless of race and gender, who generously gave time and money. And for all the ups and downs and heartburn, Harvey Hilderbran deserves a special note of appreciation. He came early and stayed late. He was there when others stood aside.

At the end of the 2007 session and again in 2009 we were successful in raising the bar and then keeping it from being lowered. We certainly raised awareness of a problem that demanded attention and action, but problems remain and some loom especially large. The Sporting Goods Tax, for one: to be or not to be? That is truly the question. Why must the entire machinery of funding for Texas parks grind to a halt every other year when, following the comptroller's estimate of revenue from taxes (every year since 1993 has shown an increase), there is a hue and cry that our state and local parks are again being shortchanged by millions of dollars? A better method of funding might have merit. But every time the possibility of switching to a real estate transfer fee, a documents fee, or a fund from lottery revenues is mentioned, it is shot down by the affected industry's lobbyists. Even when HB 12 called for a joint House and Senate study of the Sporting Goods Tax, it went nowhere because at least two methods appeared to raise more revenue than the existing formula. Now, because Texas Legislature is not about to add more to direct park funding, we are left with the Sporting Goods Tax. In my opinion it is by far the best source because it is derived from those who most enjoy and use parks and outdoor recreation. That has been the continuing recommendation of two Sunset Commissions, the State Parks Advisory Committee, and, by implication the inaction, of the House and Senate interim committee.

What is not widely recognized is the underlying thrust of the Advisory Committee's ten-year recommendation. In its entirety and within the categories of need, no consideration was given to appropriations exceeding the revenues generated by the Sporting Goods Tax. When the Advisory Committee arrived at the $105-million annual appropriation recommendation, we did so in recognition of basic ongoing needs—not bells and whistles—within the present bounds of the Sporting Goods Tax revenues. What we did highlight was that revenue stream had risen and would continue to rise, year in and year out. In 2009 Comptroller Susan Combs put the figure at about $125 million annually for the coming biennium and projected growth thereafter.

Further "borrowing" of these revenues not only invites additional criticism, it is a corruption of original intent. It seems that each session of the legislature has one or more culprits who want to "borrow" just a little from the Sporting Goods Tax revenues without hearings or justification, even before the basic needs of parks are met. That was certainly true in 2007 when the Texas Historical Commission and the General Land Office carved out, through backroom deals, large pieces of the Sporting Goods Tax revenue. Add to that the actions of a few legislators who earmarked noncompetitive appropriations from the local parks grant program. It is apparent that there are those who, while publicly acknowledging the plight of Texas's parks, continue to move funds out the back door.

To address these problems, a constitutional amendment might set a base amount of annual parks funding—say $110 million—arrived at after extensive hearings, and allow this to rise annually $3.5–4 million, cap it at $130 million or so, and then take another look before moving on.

What if the total annual revenues from the Sporting Goods Tax decline? Then the budget request and appropriation is diminished by that amount. And what if there is a major budget deficit crisis? The legislature could still require reductions based on the last biennium's appropriation but they could not make that reduction permanent and they could not divert or swap them to other programs. Funding would resume where it left off when the revenues began to increase again. Take the measure to the people for a vote and be done with it. Make it a constitutional dedicated fund. The beneficiaries would include not only the people and parks but the legislators themselves. Why would any elected official want the continuing grief of having to justify the unjustifiable? Diverting funds and abusing the public's trust—and people's wishes for their taxes are spent—is an unseemly and self-defeating business for legislators.

Throughout my journey in conservation politics and parkland enhancement, much of my time has been spent in fundraising and the call for more public-private partnerships, seeking pledges of land, cash, or both. The federal plan embodied in the National Park Foundation and the satellite friends groups have made great strides in shaping contribution guidelines that encourage private donations while protecting the public interest. To a degree, this strategy has been adopted in Texas, but there are holes. Eagle Mountain Lake State Park is a case in point.

The Eagle Mountain Lake parkland, four hundred acres, was acquired by the state some twenty or so years ago to preserve some natural space in the rapidly populating areas around the lake, which is just northwest of Fort Worth. Because of lack of funds for development, though, and lack of interest in general, the land was ignored. In 2005–2006 this ran afoul of the underutilized land provision of General Land Office rules and regulations that state, in lay terms, use it or lose it. This being the case, Commissioner Jerry Patterson of the Land Office had no choice but to put it on the market. Once the grave reality of the matter penetrated, TPWD's Joseph Fitzsimons, the *Fort Worth Star-Telegram*, and a number of concerned organizations called for an alternative solution. One was found thanks to Tarrant County Commissioner J. D. Johnson and the Texas Trust for Public Land. Through months of deliberation, negotiation, and fundraising, the land was purchased by Tarrant County using gifts from local governments and private donors—gifts totaling $9.3 million. There were no state funds applied toward the purchase. The land was converted to a fine county park and proceeds were to be set aside for a state park near Fort Worth that fit within guidelines: five thousand acres within an hour and a half of the city. Public pronouncements by Governor Perry and Fitzsimons pledged that this was how the funds would be used, and the transaction received praise from every camp. All interested parties had been brought to the table, and a win-win solution had been found. But then a legislative twist entered the picture. When those funds arrived at the state coffers through Parks & Wildlife, they became state money subject to appropriation. All good intentions and assurances can go by the wayside if those funds are diverted for another use, which was the initial recommendation by the Legislative Budget Board (LBB) staff in 2007. That recommendation was roundly and immediately discredited, but the money from the sales of the Eagle Mountain Lake still sat there for years, held in a non-interest-bearing general revenue account until a suitable new state parkland could be located and purchased. Fortunately present Speaker Joe Straus and Senator Steve Ogden pushed it through the LBB process.

If we are to foster meaningful public-private partnership through individual, corporation contributions, or from other government entities, contributor-friendly laws and guidelines that honor gifts must be in place. This issue is part and parcel of the final gaping hole in our present policy. There must be a concerted effort to ensure that a portion of dedicated funds and private gifts are directed to new parks to meet the demands of an ever-growing urban population. While our present system affords Texans and our visitors opportunities to go out into the countryside, which is important, far too many do not have the time or the wherewithal to travel great distances. We must begin to put new parks where people are.

We can certainly explore new methods to reach those goals, such as those employed at Government Canyon. A partnership there, which was nurtured by Tim and Karen Hixon of San Antonio, brought to the table every entity that had a potential stake in its creation: private landowners, the San Antonio Water System, the Edwards Aquifer Authority, the Trust for Public Land, the San Antonio school system, the National Park Service, and TPWD. Together they perfected the public-private partnership concept, and Government Canyon State Park has grown to twelve thousand acres within the city limits of San Antonio.

Another possibility is to go back to the concept fostered by Governor Pat Neff in the 1920s. Communities then were asked to, in effect, bid on park locations to benefit their communities. If the validity of the economic benefits of parks is taken into account, it would follow that parks near urban settings would pay for themselves in short order once they were fully operational.

No matter how meritorious, I see little chance of passing a constitutional dedicated fund for parks in the near future. There are simply too many legislative impediments at play given the current leadership (and prospective leadership) and political makeup of the Texas Legislature. However, there are a number of members, even of the Tea Party persuasion, who are embarrassed by the wholesale diversion of funds from the Sporting Goods Tax and other user fees. And well they should be. Over $4 billion in fees and taxes that were to have gone to many state programs, including those designated for parks, hunting, fishing, and other conservation measures, were diverted or left unspent by the

2011 legislature. Regardless of the obstacles, there must be a continuing effort to right these biennial bait-and-switch deals. These are scams on two levels: First user fees and taxes are diverted or held in suspension. Then members hurry home to proclaim that they balanced the budget with no new taxes. In a perverted sense they are correct. They partially balance the budget on old taxes and fees already paid by Texas citizens who thought they were contributing toward a specific program.

Short of a constitutional fix, it matters little what other reforms might be forthcoming to protect or enhance park appropriations or funding from private sources until and unless the budget-making process is truly reformed. One problem is that there is little to no communication between legislators, particularly appropriators, and TPWD staff and commissioners during the eighteen-month interim between sessions. The Texas Legislature is a part-time job for legislators, but it has a full-time, ongoing budget, and that budget gets more complex with each passing year, particularly when legerdemain is in play. How the budget of an agency such as TPWD is implemented is of little concern to most. That work is left to the staff of the Legislative Budget Board staff who for the most part have no expertise on matters of implementation and absolutely no real-life management experience. They would have difficulty arranging a one-car funeral procession. This incompetence has no place in good financial times and is a formula for egregious failure and mischief-making in bad times, when robbing from Peter to pay Paul becomes the norm.

With a budget deficit originally estimated to be $27 billion in 2011, the opening budget shell game was formulated by faceless bureaucrats with no sense of ownership, public responsibility, or transparency. And the game started well in advance of the session. In August preceding each new session, all state agencies must submit to the legislature (but for all practical purposes to the staff of the LBB) a Legislative Appropriation Request (LAR). The making of that document should have the joint and continuing attention of elected representatives, senators, their staffs, and staff of the agencies. That is not to say that they should become bosom buddies, but each should be an integrated part of the process, because each in their own way have to live with the results over time.

The session of 2011 was a case in point of how the present system has a serious disconnect between the budget-making process and implementation. Early in the 2011 process all agencies were directed by the governor, lieutenant governor, and Speaker to begin the appropriation requests with a 10 percent cut—that it, 10 percent below the bottom line of the LAR submission. Plainly put, these cuts were in anticipation of a major budget shortfall but were only guideposts to be used if actual deficit warranted them. This was onerous, in and of itself, but even back in August of 2010 there were ominous signs that this did not reflect the true deficit looming. Governor Perry and other elected officials were running on a platform that all was fine in job-producing Texas because the true nature of the shortfall was not known. No one would know with certainty until the comptroller, Susan Combs, made her budget certification public, and this would not occur until January 2011. That delayed sharing of knowledge, which is a longstanding practice, is part of the problem in our budget-making process. No real numbers, not even working estimates, are made public until the session begins. Then there are only 140 days to fix the entire budget, not to mention all other necessary (and unnecessary) state business.

Nonetheless, after months of work, the TPWD submitted its LAR in 2011 with the full knowledge and unanimous approval of the commissioners (all Perry appointees). After reading and attending a briefing on the document for members of the State Parks Advisory Committee, I thought it was a balanced method of facing up to the called-for cuts without ruinous consequences. At this juncture all parties should sit down together, so that all will have a clear understanding of the reasoning behind the initial submissions. This is such a crucial step in budget-making determinations that it should not be given over to the LBB staff to filter and manipulate. This imperative for elected representative participation must continue through every stage leading up to the session. If the leadership of the Texas Legislature, and indeed the whole of that body, will buy into and then enforce that continuing involvement, they will have the tools and the knowledge to fully understand all the consequences between budget-making decisions and implementation. Furthermore, they can do so in times more conducive to listening and learning, so that independent analysis can thoughtfully measure impact, and do so without relying on the LBB to be the sole and secretive arbitrator of the budget presented to the legislature the following January.

By the time the session opens in January, there is such a crush of activity that rational, logical thought goes by the wayside even among members who would prefer a more balanced approach. In that atmosphere the green-eyeshade-wearing numbers cruncher is queen or king. By January 2011 the recommended cuts were deeper than 10 percent. For state parks it was closer to double that. Within those January LBB staff recommendations were all sorts of staff-generated jewels that could wreak deeper havoc on parks and other programs—all generated without the knowledge of most, if not all, legislators.

I will note a few of the most scandalous ploys in order to make a case for change. You may recall my prior criticism of the biennial dance that occurs surrounding the Entrepreneur Rider (Rider 27). That dance is a waste of time but takes on added folly when the LBB staff becomes involved. Initially they recommended that the rider not be included at all in 2011. Through the leadership of Representative Drew Darby and others, the House Appropriations Committee countered with a clean version of the rider with no impediments. When the rider arrived in the Senate, it was retained, but the amount to be available was capped at $3 million per year for parks (Fund 64) and $3 million for Fund 9, which finances administration, wildlife, and fisheries. At that moment the LBB staff and some legislators had stopped fixing and gone to meddling. There are two flaws here, probably more. First, in the case of parks, the $3 million capped must be derived from increased park fees. Second, in order to raise and spend such revenues there must be a Rider 27 (Entrepreneur Rider), but those fees are replacing funds stripped out of the bill that were previously paid for by park users through the Sporting Goods Tax. That is a new tax and a hidden one at that. Given the way it was handled, it was hidden from most legislators. The rider was quietly shifted to Article IX, a perfecting article during the budget process that establishes budget policy that limits or expands expenditure authority. Again the LBB staff stepped in. Without consultation with TPWD or legislators, they stripped the funding from slated agency programs and gave them over to TPWD law enforcement. Why such a diversion? That's a good question. No one from TPWD appears to have asked a single legislator to do so. This lack of transparency alone is enough to warrant criticism, but again the greater issue is that it represents micromanagement of funds and policy by those who don't have a clue.

Unfortunately that was not the only issue that failed the test of transparency and accountability. In a move to further strip funds from the Sporting Goods Tax, the LBB staff created and then recommended a "method of finance swap." They took $1.6 million from the Sporting Goods Tax and substituted it with an unproven, highly problematic, new source of funding—a voluntary $5 contribution from Texans who register new motor vehicles or renew existing registrations. This was to be accomplished by an "opt-in" provision based on what had been done in Washington State. What the LBB didn't say was that the "opt-in" method had not worked in Washington: that state had switched after one year to an "opt-out" provision that produced $22 million in its first two years! To make matters worse, because of the way the LBB had stealthily manipulated the recommendation, the measure had to pass or the $1.6 million would have been an automatic additional cut to TPWD funding. To counter that twisted logic, a $1 "opt-out" provision was sought that, based on the Washington results, would have generated $7–8 million annually. That would have been a way, based on a voluntary fee, to cover some of the shortfall created by the mandated cuts. With the immediate and alarmed support of members of the Senate and the concurrence of the House chairman who had already passed the "opt-in" provision, the bill was amended with the "opt-out" provision. This was set to pass when Governor Rick Perry's staff, the Department of Motor Vehicle staff, and the Tax Assessors-Collectors Association of Texas weighed in with the flawed argument that one method was a contribution and the other (opt-out) was a new tax. Governor Perry was dead set against new taxes or even the appearance of a new tax, which this was not. So all that remained was to pass the "opt-in" provision, hold our noses, and hope that it would generate $1.6 million. Through it all, the LBB gave no hint to anyone as to how they had arrived at the figure of $1.6 million and whether the provision might come anywhere near their pie-in-the-sky projection. If it doesn't work, no LBB staffer will take responsibility for its creation or failure, I think.

Then there was the remaining desire by some to see parks shed more blood—meaning park closures. The legislature went into session, and the other shoe fell. Working through the waning weeks of 2010, the LBB staff had discovered a recommendation in a report that had been mandated by the legislature in 2007, that TPWD evaluate the feasibility of transferring seven specifically named parks to a nearby city, county, or nonprofit organization. To this proposed transfer of seven parks, Tina Beck of the LBB assigned a dollar amount for 2012 and 2013 of $2.7 million per year for the coming biennium. If no transfers took place, or only some, all or a portion of the $2.7 million would be an additional cut, causing curtailment or closure of other parks. This was wrongheaded under any scenario. To begin with, none of the House or Senate members in whose districts these parks were located were notified. If ever there was evidence of the lack of consultation between the LBB staff and legislators, this was it. When members of the TPWD staff contacted those affected legislators, there was shock and anger. And that was not the only flaw in this illogical scheme. Even in good times it is difficult to transfer or turn back park properties to local entities. In dire economic times, when cities and counties are facing their own budget crises, it becomes near impossible. That is not to say that transfers have not been made in the past or should not occur in the future. There are park properties that should never have been in the system or that no longer fit the state park mission. But such transfers usually take time to perfect. There is more to it than walking in and putting the keys on a local mayor's desk. These are state assets staffed by state employees. Therefore, there must be a binding contract to cover all sorts of present and future contingencies. Either the LBB crew did not know this, or it did know but didn't care. I suspect the latter was true.

Here again was an attempt at micromanaging by unaccountable persons with no business sense and little concern for realistic outcome. When coupled with a complete lack of responsibility for consequences, seen and unseen, and fueled by whatever grudges were held against parks, it took an inordinate amount of time to educate and explain those consequences to elected officials who had little time to listen and act.

Fortunately, setting aside all the technicalities and simpleminded errors that were written into the LBB's recommendations, the aforementioned examples of mischief-making were brought to the attention of those who did care, did listen, and did act—for the most part with positive results. So much so that with a great deal of readjustment and some curtailment of operations and maintenance our state parks probably can remain open to the public—the public that owns them in the first place. The real owners of the parks are the citizens who have supported them by huge majorities in every recent poll, in every demographic and political stratus, and who by practically the same majorities are willing to pay for them, even to the extent of modest fee or tax increases. But that support will last only so long as Texans believe their expenditures are used for the purposes specified. I am convinced that some lawmakers and LBB staffers want that faith by the citizenry eroded so they can starve parks to wreckage without the bother of public scrutiny or criticism. Presently there are enough good and concerned legislators who are willing—once and if they know about these budgetary slights of hand—to stand up to protect our natural and historic gifts to ourselves.

Even though most of the recommendations put forward in 2011 were thwarted or modified to avoid ruinous consequences, and even though it appears as of this writing that most, if not all, Texas parks will remain open, it is and will continue to be a shallow victory unless the power and scope of the LBB is curtailed. It is not acceptable to allow anonymous LBB staffers to set policy for and micromanage the TPWD, or any other agency for that matter, especially when those staffers are incapable of running any entity of any size. But even if they were capable, that is not their job. Their job should be to work through the LAR with the agency and then to inform legislators in a timely manner. To those who say that legislators are informed, I say hogwash! In 2011 the LBB recommendations to the Senate Finance Committee were passed out to the members only moments before the meeting that was held well after the session began in January. Senators, Republicans and Democrats, were surprised and in some cases angry at what they read. And the LBB staff, led by Beck, hurried through each recommendation with little or no disclosure of their methods or consequences. The Motor Vehicle Registration issue was a classic case in point. Robert Norris of the LBB spent only a minute or so going over the Washington State experience. He failed to mention that the "opt-in" method had been a failure and that the "opt-out" method had been substituted the following year with very positive results. No mention was made of the fact that on its own LBB had swapped $1.6 million of the known and revenue-producing Sporting Goods Tax for the highly dubious registration contribution—betting on an unknown outcome. That was confirmed later when House and Senate members agreed and moved to substitute the potentially more lucrative "opt-out" method. Does the difference between "opt-in" (being a contribution) and "opt-out" make the latter somehow a new tax? We only have to look at the Washington experience. Even when that state switched to the "opt-out" program, only 38 percent of the participants agreed to do so. Clearly a choice was presented to each citizen and 62 percent chose not to contribute. This was not an across-the-board, involuntary tax. Governor Perry got bum advice on that and one can imagine where it came from.

Nor was there any robust discussion at that Senate hearing about the fact that the $1.6 million was contingent on results. If $1.6 million is not reached, the shortfall will go to the parks' bottom line as an additional cut. Again, to my knowledge, no Senator or House member fully understood this. This staff-devised deception is example enough why it is imperative that elected officials get involved at the outset and then stay involved. It is also ample proof why public knowledge must come at a much earlier date. Otherwise the lion's share of the budget-making process will remain in the hands of staffers who have no practical experience, little oversight, and, in the case of some, an overblown and unchecked sense of power and prejudice.

The other essential reform goes hand and glove with the first, or at least it should. The TPWD commissioners and staff fully appreciated the financial predicament the state was in. By 2011 all the TPWD commissioners were Perry appointees, and while they have the best interest of the agency, including parks, at heart, they were not about to ignore the governor's directives or directives from the rest of the leaders in the statehouse. They made a good faith effort in 2011 to meet the order to cut the budget by 10 percent, and to my mind did so using a balanced approach. At that point, they could have also begun to explore contingency plans in case significant, additional shortfalls occurred. When all parties were satisfied and a final negotiated deal struck, that part of the budget that is finally appropriated should be turned over to the agency to administer without the baggage of LBB staff (or legislative) micromanaging via amendments and riders. Let agency professionals with expertise, guided by trusted political appointees, move to keep their departments running as well as possible under the circumstances.

If legislators and their staffs will become involved and stay involved; if the power and lack of transparency of the LBB is curtailed; and if the finally determined appropriation for TPWD is given over to the agency without hidden agendas or cuts, then our parks can survive in bad times. In better times they can be enhanced. In the best of times, perhaps, with a substantial and sustainable flow of funds voted on by the people of Texas, they can be allowed to become a park system of the first order. The ultimate beneficiary will be Texas citizens and out-of-state and foreign tourists. Local businesses and communities will flourish. A sense of state pride will be restored, enhanced, and perpetuated.

Of more importance than the economic benefits of parks is a greater benefit: to connect and reconnect people to the natural and cultural treasures of Texas. There is a primordial urge for humans to be of the land. To be awed. To be renewed. It does not matter what station in life one inhabits—rich or poor. Well-off people may have ranches or getaways, the vast majority of people need public parks, but whatever the place is called we need somewhere to connect with the land and renew. And from that renewal comes a consequence rarely articulated. In those settings, something remarkable happens.

The reason for conserving the last best places is to let all people be of the earth—as we originally were—and be moved in a wholesome setting. From that connection comes deep and lasting civility and patriotism: having a sense of place and a stake in it gives people pride of ownership and fosters responsible citizenship. The reason I have devoted so much of my time and energy to parkland conservation is that I am committed not only to conserving natural treasures, but also to preserving that crucial relationship of people to the land, so that they will appreciate the meaning of those treasures and pass it on from generation to generation.

As this book was going to press it occurred to me that the reader might want to know what has happened to the budget and the recommendations of the LBB. It is not a pretty picture.

When the final budget numbers for 2012–2013 were finalized, only $27 million per year were realized from the Sporting Goods Sales Tax, even though the Texas Comptroller certified $125 million per year in revenue. That is less than the original cap of $32 million per year estabished in 1995. Coupled with the questionable recommendations fashioned by the LBB staff dealing with increases in park fees and revenues and the motor vehicle registration donation on the "opt-in" basis, there was no room for error or negative circumstance.

Fire, drought, and the heat wave of 2011 destroyed parks and park visitation which seriously curtailed revenue. Even though visitation and revenues have increased substantially through April of 2012, the growth rate for the remainder of the fiscal year will have to be a stunning 15% just to break even. Not a dime toward the projected $3 million per year increase. As far as the $1.6 million projected for the vehicle registration donations, a paltry $254,000 has been raised since January. Projected to the end of the fiscal year, this scheme may produce $400,000—some $1.6 million short. These shortfalls of approximately $4.2 million will go on already seriously depleted state parks' bottom line. The end result will be that some parks will close and many programs will be lost or curtailed, particularly those benefitting families and children.

Taking in the beauty of it all on the Gunsight Pass Trail, Glacier National Park, 1980.

On my sixtieth birthday, hiking again along the Gunsight Pass Trail, sixteen of the most spectacular miles on earth, Glacier National Park, 2000.

Jointly celebrating our seventieth birthdays, Gretchen Denny and I (back row center) are joined by my children and grandchildren on a hike to Hidden Lake, Glacier Park, 2010.

A week later Gretchen (left), her son and sister (beside her), and her daughter, son-in-law, and grandchildren joined me on a hike to Avalanche Lake, Glacier National Park.

George Bristol and First Lady Laura Bush at Lake McDonald, Glacier National Park, 2004.

David Rockefeller (left) and I at National Park Foundation retirement ceremonies, Mesa Verde National Park, 2001.

Celebrating my sixtieth birthday with (left to right) my children Jim, Mark, and Jennifer at Sperry Chalet, Glacier National Park, 2000.

I introduce Laurence Rockefeller (center) to Jim Maddy and Ken West at the Rockefeller Lodge in Grand Teton National Park, 1998, as Rockefeller advisor Henry Diamond stands in back at right.

Me with Secretary of the Interior Bruce Babbitt (left) and National Park Director Robert Stanton (right), 1997.

Members and staff of the National Park Foundation gather at Logan Pass for a hike in Glacier National Park, 1997.

Commencement address at Vermont College, 1997.

Left to right: The five cousins—Don Holt, David Bristol, Carol Ann Garrison, me, and Judd Holt—laugh it up at a family reunion in Salado, Texas, 1994.

Me with my friends Ken Burns (left) and Dayton Duncan (right) on the production of the PBS documentary The National Parks: America's Best Idea, *2006.*

Bob Armstrong, Dick Bartlett, George Bristol, Andy Sansom, unknown guest, and Joey Park after a successful goose hunt at Bucksnag Lodge, Texas, 2005.

Buzz and Carolyn Crutcher, Jim Bristol, Jay Vestal, Don Holt, Gretchen Denny, and I gathered to celebrate the presentation to me of the Pugsley Medal, Salt Lake City, 2009.

I am instructed about an abandoned structure on newly acquired property at Bastrop State Park, Texas, by my daughter, park employee Jennifer Bristol, 2008.

EPILOGUE

The last decade of the twentieth century meant more than national parks and poetry to me. I would have been satisfied feasting on only the two, but I always had other agendas on my plate.

After a bruising primary, primary runoff, and general election, Ann Richards won the governorship of Texas by the narrowest of margins in 1990 over a Republican who took every opportunity to shoot himself in the foot. By the end of the campaign, Claytie Williams had bloody stubs sticking out of his boots yet lost to Ann by only two points. Throughout her term that ominous fact seemed to be overlooked by some in her inner circle. A two-point margin against a man who seemed to advise women in case of rape to lie back and enjoy it, and who appeared not to have paid taxes over a period of time, was not an overwhelming clarion call for progressive change. Ann won because a great majority of women, including huge blocks of Republican women, voted for her over a man who gave them no other choice.

While in office, Ann was exciting to watch in action—and fun. There is no question that she opened doors for women, minorities, and gays. I thought it was the right thing to do and courageous, but it rankled the good ol' boy coffee shops and would come back to haunt her reelection in 1994, when whispered untruths about Ann's own sexual preference were fanned by some of George W. Bush's closest confidants. Regardless of that drumbeat, her term was highlighted by a number of notable achievements. I will leave it to others to analyze the sum of her term, but I would like to acknowledge her unwavering support, by law and example, for conservation in Texas.

By upbringing and natural bent, Ann loved the outdoors. Much of that flowed from her father, who made sure that his only child was introduced to the male Texan's world of hunting, fishing, canoeing, and the like. Later through political friends, particularly Don Kennard and Malcolm McGregor, she took to outings on the Rio Grande as if she were born to run the river. Once in office, she did more than raft for pleasure.

Even before being sworn in as governor she moved to set the tone at the Texas Parks & Wildlife Department, as well as all other agencies. Early on she called Andy Sansom who had only recently been appointed executive director by Governor Bill

Clements. Andy was a Republican, albeit of the Teddy Roosevelt mold. Without hesitation Ann told him of her outdoors background and love of nature. This was, according to Sansom, so deeply held and apparent that he immediately took to her. Based on a conversation I had with Ann later, it was clear that Ann's appreciation of Andy was mutual. She went on to tell Andy that she would set broad policy, but that he and his staff would run the operation. She would appoint board members without influence from headquarters and in turn Andy would make the agency work. "You stay out of my business and I'll stay out of yours," she had said with a grin.

And she went out of her way to do just that. Two of her first three appointees were a woman, Terry Hershey, and a Hispanic, Nacho Garza. She also attended one of the first meetings of the new commission and laid out what she had told Andy about her love of nature and her enjoyment of hunting and fishing. It went over well with a commission that still had a majority of Republicans, had been all-male until Hershey's appointment, and had never had a governor visit them at all, much less in such a natural, heartfelt manner. Even among the Republicans on the commission she won converts, to form a working majority. She would need these Republicans to make sure that Nacho Garza became chair of the commission, and for other reasons thereafter.

By her second legislative session in 1993, Ann would need her appointees and the Republicans to back a budget initiative that she had called for—a small but not insignificant budget cut among all agencies. Part of the proposed cut would affect state parks. Through careful planning there would be no park closures but some curtailment of services. This and other proposals did not sit well with certain legislators. It was so unpopular among those legislators and Lieutenant Governor Bob Bullock that they threatened to take over the process. The issue boiled down to a crucial supporting vote by the nine-member commission.

To carry full weight the vote had to be unanimous. Before the meeting began the hall was packed with threatening lawmakers and other interested parties. There was much consternation. As the meeting began, Andy was called to his office for a call from the governor. "Andy, you go in there and tell those Republican commissioners that they've got no balls unless they support this budget!" Andy dutifully passed this pithy comment along, and the vote was nine to nothing in favor.

Throughout her term Ann Richards would use her bully pulpit to rally support for hunting, fishing, parks, and conservation. Former commissioner Tim Hixon of San Antonio, an avid Republican, makes no bones about it: as far as he is concerned, Ann was the best governor for parks and wildlife issues he has served with or since witnessed.

After Ann left office, during the time when I began to work on parkland and conservation issues, she would drop into my office to see how things were going, offering sound advice, and she became a regular and generous contributor to TCC. Because her office was right down the hall at Public Strategies, the communications firm to whom she was a senior advisor, she was always a presence. When she died she left a huge vacuum on the twelfth floor, throughout Texas, and in my life.

In 1992 Bill Clinton was elected president, much to the joy of Ann Richards. He and Hillary had been friends with Ann since 1972 when they had come to Texas to campaign for McGovern. With others, Ann Richards lobbied the president and Bruce Babbitt for my appointment to the National Park Foundation.

I rarely asked President Clinton or the White House staff for anything, even though I had ready access and was frequently invited to various functions. But from the moment of his election and inauguration in 1992–1993, it seemed that my mother was in daily contact about the possibility of a trip to Washington to meet her president. She was persistent, and I assured her that I would make it happen as soon as possible. I was aided by the fact that my grandniece Holly Holt, Don's daughter, worked at the White House Visitor Center and would be helpful with arrangements, such as a special tour and a White House Mess luncheon.

When it looked like there was a time approaching when I needed to be in Washington and I appeared to have an extra day or two open, I wrote to the president, requesting an Oval Office visit for Mother. An invitation was swiftly forthcoming. Holly and the national park staff went into action and two or three full days of activities were planned for Lottie Bristol of Austin, Texas. On the appointed day in October of 1995, we flew first-class on American Airlines. Mother took full advantage of the service, the meals, and the wine. The attendants loved her and she them. She had a splendid flight, but I noticed from time to time that she seemed to wince. I asked if she was all right. She quickly assured me that she was, so I wrote it off to old-age aches and pains (she was eighty-three then).

At the hotel, with a view of the Capitol, she settled in, read, and went to sleep early. Again I thought about her health but shrugged it off. She seemed to be having a grand time. The next morning I walked to her room early. She was up and ready. The National Park Service had a vehicle available and off she went for a full day of park and monument tours, but only after she was assured that the driver could and would get in touch with me. Later that evening I arrived back at the hotel and called her room. She said that she'd had a very interesting day, that the park personnel were wonderful, and that she was happy, but that she was going to have dinner in her room and go to bed early. The White House tour and visit was the next day.

Near noon the next day we arrived at Holly's office, and then walked over toward the Mess. On the way, President Clinton and his new chief of staff, Leon Panetta,
stepped out of a side door. Without missing a beat, the president lit up and said, "Hello,
George, this would be your mother." Mother shook his hand and held it, all the time
chattering. For an instant, in what can only be described as the Clinton moment, he gave
her his full attention. Then, with grace and sincerity, he told her that he had important
matters at hand but would see her later at his office. Lottie Bristol could have quite easily
and readily gone to heaven right there on the spot, wholly fulfilled. All the way to the
Mess she could not stop talking about how much time he had devoted to her, even on a
chance encounter.

The White House luncheon was anticlimactic. She did ask for and accepted one of
each small token gift that is part of the White House fare, but she really was ready to get
back to Austin to tell her bridge buddies about "her president." After lunch we returned
to the hotel for a rest and then taxied to the White House at 5:00 p.m. for the president's
radio address, a tour of the Oval Office, and a photograph. Although she said that she'd
had a good nap, she looked drawn and wan. I inquired again, but she assured me she
was fine.

It was early evening, toward dusk. The White House was aglow. We stopped at
the gate and peered in. Mother did so for the longest time, as if she was committing the
whole scene to a memory that would help her break the bonds of earth when her time
came. I was noticing that deep concentration frequently. Then Holly met us at the visitor's gate and we went to the room off the Oval Office where President Clinton would
give his address. Due to White House rules we had to arrive somewhat early to make sure
all were settled in before the president spoke. Some sixty or seventy people were there
around five-thirty, with a six o'clock airtime. Because I knew to do so, I asked Mother
whether she needed to go to the bathroom. With a good seat on the front row she wasn't
about to leave, though. The thirty minutes or so flew by. At five after six there was no
Clinton. At ten after, my mother exclaimed for all to hear, "Well, where is he? I need to
go to the bathroom." Several aides and Holly rushed over. Another went into the Oval
Office. Shortly a very amused Bill Clinton walked out into the room and went straight to
Mother. "Mrs. Bristol, this is going to take six minutes. Can you wait?"

"Yes," she replied.

"Okay then, when I'm finished you can go with one of my aides or Holly and they
will show you the bathroom."

"Well, what about our picture together?"

"Don't worry. When you get back we'll have a good visit and take that photo."

Clinton took six minutes. Then Mother went off, and upon returning she went into the office of the president of the United States. There for the next four or five minutes Bill Clinton escorted Lottie Bristol, citizen and admirer, around his office as if he had all the time in the world and she was the only other person in it. I stood off to the side and watched a natural work his magical gift. Then we said our thanks and goodbyes and went out into the autumn night.

On the flight home Mother confessed. She had fallen before the trip, bruising or breaking a rib or ribs. Fearing her doctor would not allow the trip, she had taped herself, gulped Aleve or some other over-the-counter pain reliever, and painfully made the trip. As she told me, I teared up. The phrase "real All-Americans play hurt" ran through my head.

When we arrived in Austin we went immediately to the doctor and verified what she'd told me. Within days I wrote to the president about this. He was touched and immediately wrote to her of his appreciation of her determination to visit him given her condition.

My timing could not have been better. Soon after, Mother began to have one malady after another, culminating in a series of small strokes. Finally a fairly extreme one laid her low. We had to seek help and a facility that could handle her in her rapidly declining state. It was apparent to all that she was not going to recuperate. It was also apparent that she knew this and didn't want to stick around in a vegetated, burdensome state. She'd had a rewarding life and was ready to see old friends and family—most of all, Daddy.

By early November of 2000 it was apparent that she was slipping away. David and I redoubled our visits, and began the final watch at the nursing home in Johnson City, Texas, where we had placed her two or three years before, after a series of debilitating strokes made home care impossible. We had selected the facility for several reasons. It was equal distance, roughly thirty miles, between Austin and David's home in Boerne, making it easy for one or both of us to see her several times a week. Further, I had been advised that more often than not, small-town homes provide better care than ones in cities, because many patients are longtime town folks, thus their families are known and present. The same applies to staff, who are for the most part local. This was essential, not only for Mother's well-being but also for our peace of mind. It is no light matter to entrust a loved one to others under any circumstances. The knowledge that management and staff were dedicated to providing surrogate family care eased the burden of guilt that was attendant. Maybe Lyndon Johnson put it best when he returned to the Texas Hill Country after his presidency. "I am going back home, where they know when you're sick and care when you die."

Johnson City is in the heart of the Hill Country. From there, country roads wind through some of the most serene beauty in Texas. On weekends and after work, we would load Mother into one of our cars and drive through the flowering scenes of spring, late evening animal sightings of summer, and crisp colors of autumn. In the dead of winter we simply drove for the sake of getting out. Often we'd stop at small roadside picnic areas for sandwiches, supplemented in the summer by Hill Country peaches and peach ice cream. Lottie Bristol never gave up her love of the Hill Country or anything peach. Her boys shared both, so there was a regular, frequent, and relished pattern to those outings, with no sense of burden.

By the weekend of November 11, 2000, we realized by observation and hospice counseling that only a matter of days if not hours remained. For the previous week or so I'd been staying in the guest house of wonderful friends, Claire and Jack Ratliff, who lived only a few miles from Johnson City. I went early every morning to be with Mother and stayed until she went to sleep at night. David was there too. Throughout the days we spelled each other to grab a nap or make arrangements for the final eventuality.

On Saturday David and I went to the home to see her for what would be the last time, but we did not go in a death-watch mood. Texas A&M was playing Oklahoma that day, and Mother had gone to TWU, the sister school of A&M. Daddy and most of his uncles and cousins had attended A&M. David was a veterinarian school graduate from there. Maroon and white ran deep in the family. Even in her much-diminished state Mother seemed to perk up at the prospect of watching the game on television, especially since we brought a little wine to sip.

By the third quarter A&M appeared to be hopelessly behind. Mother let us know she wanted to go back to her room. There she lay for a day, into the night of the next, and then passed away early on the morning of the November 13, well into her 88th year. There was sorrow, but also a sense of relief. She had prayed to leave to be with Dad, her mother and father, and all the other family and friends she had lived without for so long. David and I laughingly opined that she had simply given up rooting for the Aggies after another disappointing season. Several days later we buried her, according to her wishes, next to Dad in McKinney.

After 54 Years
November 2000
Even at the speed of God light,
it took time
for her death notice

to appear at Heaven's station,
sorted, then posted
into the ethereal mind waves
that deliver messages
pulsating toward a mirror
image of his last known address,
arriving just as bois d'arc apples
dropped against the sun-peeled porch
and a rooster roused itself
for its July duty.

The man in the coal-oil kitchen
sits drinking coffee, listening, watching
ghost images of two summer boys
bathing in the back-porch tin tub
while neck-wrung chickens fry,
when the whisper's heard.

Standing, he goes to the back bedroom,
lays out the dark suit he'd been lowered
in, then, before reflections
of all the faces she would know,
he chooses to add a shock
of black hair to complement
the re-forming Celtic chin, and
the mischievous eyes that
flash with the smile once
shared. Satisfied,
he disappears.
Back past the still chuckling
towheads, needle-clicking mother,
father mucking horse stalls,
out into layered waves
of history he never witnessed:
the haberdasher giving 'em hell,
the red stain again—Korea,

DiMaggio's limping single,
a young president smiling,

civil rights rectified,
the stain again—Vietnam,
a strange figure's lunar landing,
an angry rocket disintegrating,
television spewing millions of images into
the cosmic endlessness, along
pathways he now hurtles through,
stopping now and then,
checking the lay of his tie,
listening for the whisper
of reply among past faces that
pass by before entering their own
black holes of infinity, then,
there: Sinatra's "Witchcraft,"
Hank Williams's "I'm So Lonesome
I Could Die," the serene
"White Christmas," one star too far,
backtracking, until somewhere
unseen in a hush—appearing
through clouds of cosmic dust where
there's a wink of celestial recognition.
A light shines
through a kitchen window, framing
two figures talking, taking up
as if neither time nor hurt had occurred.

After the funeral and accounts were settled, David and I made a final trip to Johnson City to personally thank all who had tended to Mother. To each we gave small gifts. For one, in particular, we did more, because he had gone out of his way to make her waning days pleasant and peaceful.

In only whispers and half sentences she had let us know that there was a special attendant who spoke and sang to her in Spanish every night that he was on duty, that on his days off he would drop by to say hello. Because David speaks fluent Spanish, we learned much about that amazing Samaritan. He and his wife were highly educated and successful in their Central American home country, but had had to flee during a time of revolution. Both worked as orderlies and went out of their way to provide that extra touch of grace that only comes from shared experiences of hardship and resignation. Both openly wept when Mrs. Bristol died.

Through David's conversations we learned that the two were saving their meager funds to gain higher training in nursing and medical care. We decided we wanted to help make that happen. So on a cold winter day we went to their home. David explained that Mother had some funds left from her own savings, and that we wanted to share her inheritance with them. While pleased, they allowed that they didn't know whether it was proper. We assured them that it was, that we were glad to do it, and only asked that they let it remain between us, so as not to create any ill will at the home. They finally agreed. We wished them well and bid them a merry Christmas. We never saw them again, yet I cannot think of Mother's passing without recalling those two who had begun to give back from the moment they arrived in Texas.

There was another relief that soon swept over me. I realized that I had spent a great deal of the previous five years tending to Mother, never straying far, never fully committing to new endeavors. But by 2001 I needed to turn all my attention to Texas conservation work. Although it is speculation, I have come to imagine that because Mother had begun to define my conservation journey before my birth, perhaps she finally let go all those years later knowing that I had to get on with my journey and the task at hand with no bother on her part. Having known her for sixty years, I am positive she would have insisted on leaving at the appropriate moment. And I knew for certain she didn't want to be a burden. She had put that in writing, in no uncertain terms.

So 2001 dawned without any ties, but as I put together the puzzling pieces of a conservation coalition I began to focus on how much a certain smile continued to mean to me. From time to time since our 1998 high school class reunion, I had called Gretchen Denny when I was passing through Fort Worth or at times of great joy and sadness. She shared in both with kind grace and, I am certain, mystified questions. Who was this caller once every month or so—an old friend or a new suitor? Whatever her answer then, if any, she good-naturedly allowed me to move at my own pace, snail-like though it may have seemed. She would attend events important to me: a poetry reading, family weddings and gatherings. In 2000 she and her daughter, Andrea, visited me in Montana for my sixtieth birthday celebration (hers too) and to meet my old trail crew mates. Then, in an act of great caring, she attended Mother's funeral wake with the family in November.

But there was nothing hasty on my part, no whirlwind courtship. In my defense, I was wrapped up in the evolution of the coalition. My son Mark and Jennifer Clark were married in April of 2001, and at age sixty I had doubts about newfound romance and relationships. Still, I found myself having to go to Denton on a more regular excuse—my son Jim, who was by then an American Airlines pilot, lived in nearby Irving. And so a stop in Fort Worth for a visit, even on Christmas morning, became part of the pattern.

The trouble was that no one, including Gretchen, could discern any sort of pattern. Finally, in August of 2005, my cousin-in-law Vicki Holt, Don's wife, laid down an edict at a family gathering in Denton. Either I could make a decision about Gretchen (who all in the family genuinely liked) or I could not count on a place to stay at her house, nor could I count on her washing my clothes, which had become a regular part of the pattern. Serious words indeed, particularly the clothes-washing boycott, now part of a family inside joke.

On a Saturday in early September I called Gretchen and asked to see her the next day. After pleasantries I hemmed and hawed my way toward the purpose of my visit. After I'd made my case, she carefully stated hers. She was surprised—pleased, but surprised. Whatever inkling of a serious relationship she had sensed had been trumped by my long absences and a failure to communicate. I pled guilty. She smiled that smile of hers and said that she was going to Italy with friends shortly, and that this trip would give her time to think about this sudden circumstance. We agreed to meet as soon as she returned. I said that I had a photography show to produce that would keep my busy. On the way to Austin I called Vicki and told her of the conversation. She said that this was enough for me to regain bed and breakfast privileges, but the clothes-washing issue would remain open, subject to final resolution.

An intervening occurrence eased my transition toward a commitment to Gretchen. Mark and Jennifer had moved to Austin, bringing with them from California the only female who might have caused disruption: Evelyn, my first grandchild, who was the apple of my eye. All the rings were aligning.

Upon her return from Italy, Gretchen told me that in spite of all her misgivings about age and widowhood, she wanted to make a go of it. We did for over a year, and then decided to get married on July 7, 2007—fifty-five years after we first met in the seventh grade. All the family on both sides attended. Even before we took our vows, there was a mutual joining of our families. We liked one another. Her family became mine and mine became hers. In the exchange we each gained two grandchildren. It has seemingly been a natural acceptance on our part and theirs. With some luck and great fortune I have found new beginnings toward the end of the line.

My conservation journey began at the Whitefish, Montana, train station some fifty years ago, and has run, with all sorts of sidings, through the first decade of the twenty-first century. I do not intend to stand aside or disappear. But as I venture into my seventy-first year and beyond, I want to board other trains and planes, to travel to places I've never seen. I would like to experience other Glacier Parks, protected marvels of nature, parks and preserves the likes of which I have long championed. Particularly I would like to witness these in other countries—the exported legacy of our best idea.

While on these excursions I plan to take bags of books to read. That grounding foundation, reading, has stayed with me since my youth, but I've only scratched the surface of literature and there are so many pages left to turn. And I want to enjoy these new travels with Gretchen. With few exceptions we share desires to visit the same places, and we have made ambitious plans to do just that.

On occasion it would be rewarding to take "the grands" with us, so they can witness those landscapes and historical wonders. I would like them to see a mountain rising above morning mist, unsullied by dust drifting from countless belching stacks and fires destroying rain forests. I want to take them down a pristine river (whether they fish with their granddad and Uncle Jim or not), before it becomes clogged with the chemicals of progress. Yet I want to detour to some scenes of earth degradation so that they can come to know that the time to restore and repair is growing short.

If the generation of my grandchildren has no frame of reference to encourage a renewed conservation ethic, then it may very well be that their children will have no opportunity to experience anything more than reruns of nature films viewed in the confines of capsules rocketing away from the once blue and green planet, all because we failed to say "enough is enough!" I hope that I have contributed in some measure to justify betting against such a dark scenario.

For now I want time to reflect without competing tasks or deadlines. Some of these musings will have a purpose, such as the need to revisit campaign finance reform. While I have criticized past campaign reform, in general the new laws served a constructive purpose. They led to an expanded base of contributors, and transparency was added. But now the Supreme Court of the United States has done away with the level playing field and much of the transparency safeguards. We are back to the days of the Teapot Dome Scandal when cash and corporations bought politicians and policy without fear of incrimination. This is a shoddy landscape full of giant pygmies and small-minded pirates, roaming at will without fear of interference.

I will certainly continue to focus on parks and conservation. But at times I want to float free, letting mind and memory alight and then dwell on people and places who have affected me. I want to embrace the men and women who gave some small kindness. And

I want to give the back of my hand to those few scoundrels who violated my space, even disrupting the calming peace of Glacier National Park.

When age confines my hiking to short walks and shallow streams, I want to sit on the lakeside porch of the Many Glacier Hotel in the solitude of the park's sunset. I want to sit there in silence, without purpose or regretful nostalgia, and call up faces and voices of people who from the beginning of my time there helped create my bond with those beautiful peaks and valleys—I've never escaped those bonds, nor have I wanted to. I want to smile to myself in remembering satisfaction. Then, God willing, I want to go inside, enjoy dinner with Gretchen, then listen before sleep for the pine-breeze song that has sung to me for fifty years.

Many Glacier Valley

For fifty years I've appeared
upon this wind-worn knoll
to wrap myself in ice and wind,
to silently repair my soul.
At first it took a day or night
to still the black savage
that burned raw, open sores
and fired a thunderous rage.
Now, in the surprise of a breeze,
I begin to purge the grime
that clogs the psyche pores.

This is the anchor of my soul,
the mistress of my fantasy
who does not fade with time
but beckons stronger
than any siren's song.
And now the question becomes:
is heaven necessary?

Believing this to be perfection,
then to here my final rest.
What need for cosmic eternity?
Then heed my request:
I am earth-born and -bred.
I do not seek the stars.
Let sun heal the pain.
Let wind smooth the scars.
When a thousand years pass,
then here seek my soul.
Look to the rain-splashed sunlight
on the edge of the roving stream.
Somewhere in the crags and shadows
I will repose and call your name.

A proud grandfather teaches his first grandchild, Evelyn Bristol, a magic ball trick, Austin, 2005.

Gretchen Denny and I at the entrance to beloved Glacier National Park, 2010.

All of my grandchildren play in the autumn leaves on Thanksgiving Day in Fort Worth, 2009. Left to right: Henry, Evelyn, Sam, and Walter.

Gretchen and I on vacation in Italy, 2006.

Walter and Evelyn Bristol give full attention at the 2007 wedding of their grandfather and Gretchen Denny.

Gretchen and I (front left) run the Middle Fork of the Flathead River with others at trail crew reunion in 2000.

Gretchen and I celebrate a family wedding, 2006.

ACKNOWLEDGMENTS

When writing a book of one's life, particularly when that that life has been as varied and full as mine as been, it becomes impossible to fashion a complete acknowledgement of one's debts. While some have contributed more than others to my life, occasionally an offhand comment from someone has sparked a major act of discovery or rediscovery. Here I will acknowledge many who contributed to my life story, with the full knowledge that I am neglecting many.

Without my Scots-Irish-German parents and grandparents I might have missed the opportunity of literature and the base foundation of storytelling. My maternal granddaddy, W. S. Donoho, shared the classics with me and helped shaped my view of them. My dad, Lambert Bristol, left a poetic bent and a billfold filled with signposts of his short life, and these became the initial motivation for telling my story.

Lottie Donoho Bristol was the classroom door that was always open for my continuing education. Not only did she love books, she also loved to tell a good story. She did so in many ways, but especially through the copious photo albums of her travels, something she put together over seven decades. Paging through them I came across evidence of many people and events that molded my life. I hope my children will strive to keep those albums intact. They are a small history of the twentieth century. When linked to all her later work in family genealogy, these become a reference guide of the past and perhaps the inspiration for a future book.

Practically every other member of my family—including children, cousins, and aunts, as well as near relatives—helped verify my memories and frame events with their own recollections and photographs. But special thanks must be given to my daughter, Jennifer, who has become the unofficial keeper of the family history and memorabilia. What is more important, she has been able lay her hands on just the right information for me in almost no time at all.

Many former staff members, family, and friends of Jake Pickle, Bob Strauss, and Lloyd Bentsen helped me give dimension to these mentors and friends of mine. Jake and his daughter Peggy Pickle wrote a marvelous book of his life and times. Not only did it give me added insight into him, it also reminded me of events in which I played a part.

Vera Murray of Bob Strauss's staff clarified a number of dates and personalities who came and went throughout his career. Katherine McGarr, Bob's grandniece, was an invaluable source of fact checking. She was for a very special reason. After several attempts failed to find a suitable Strauss biographer, Katherine took it upon herself. She did find a publisher. The book, *The Whole Damn Deal*, is a great read and has been well received.

B. A. Bentsen and Senator Bentsen's sister, Betty, were always available, and if they didn't have an answer they suggested someone who might. Marina Weiss and Mike Pate, both of whom played major roles in aiding the senator in making law, related their experiences and insight, which was particularly invaluable since my role with Bentsen was not legislative. I had been part of his inner circle, and knew his accomplishments and failures and his impact on Texas and Texas politics, but not the day-to-day Washington maneuvering.

Jack Martin was not only an advisor on the Bentsen years, but a wonderful sounding board on a broad range of topics. It didn't hurt that he not only is a good storyteller but also a good listener to stories. We shared a great deal of both.

Although I have known and been influenced by many complex characters, and even known many of them well, I only knew them within the context of my time with them. Other eyes and ears were indispensible for me so that in painting more rounded portraits. My years of work in Texas on parkland and conservation matters are a case in point. I came to know a great deal about the pieces of that complex puzzle, but it was comforting to have Andy Sansom always at the ready to verify or challenge. Andy has been around in the thick of the conservation fray for many years and in many venues so that he has easily been able to fill in and flesh out details for me, doing so with patience and kindness. We regularly finalized confirmations and denials at the Magnolia Café on Lake Austin Boulevard at 7:00 a.m.

Linda McElrath of my office typed and collated chapter after chapter through so many drafts that she won't need a copy of this book. She knows it by heart.

Shannon Davies, Louise Lindsey Merrick Editor for the Natural Environment of Texas A&M University Press, is a gracious but tough taskmaster. I only disagreed with one or two of the hundreds of suggestions she made. She has been a patient adviser on structuring and time-lining the book.

Just because I wrote a book that was accepted for publication by Texas A&M University Press, doesn't mean I rushed it to the printer. There is much that goes on before press time. While I will probably not meet all the talented people would have taken part in readying my book for print, I must thank those with whom I have worked: Pat

Clabaugh, Gayla Christiansen, Holli Estridge, Caitlin Churchill, Kyle Littlefield, and David Neel.

Gretchen Denny's support allowed me to write, often for hours at the Fort Worth Public Library, and then for two months in Fort Davis to finish the rough draft.

The Fort Davis experience came about because a great Texas couple, Dick and Joanne Bartlett, gave their time, treasure, and property to provide an in-residency conservation and environmental writer program, complete with an apartment and a library. Dick Bartlett's library is so diverse in subject matter that it is no exaggeration to say that his interests were boundless. For two months I sat on a mountaintop and wrote, thought, and contemplated the life flow of the Chihuahaun Desert. The gift the Bartletts gave to me—and to others—is measureless. Although Dick passed away in May 2011, his and Joanne's good work will be a continuing legacy.

Finally, I thank all those who are not mentioned here, but who are nevertheless part of the fabric of my life and the telling of this story. Some contributed that significant offhand remark. Others provided safe harbor from the storms that occurred from time to time, allowing me to reflect and rest in peace until the tempest passed.

The telling of a tale comes down to one person, the teller, yet none can complete the story without the insight of many. I am fortunate to have had these people at every stage of my life.

INDEX